EVERYDAY
PROBLEM
SOLVING

EVERYDAY PROBLEM SOLVING

Theory and Applications

EDITED BY
JAN D. SINNOTT

New York
Westport, Connecticut
London

Library of Congress Cataloging-in-Publication Data

Everyday problem solving : theory and applications / edited by Jan D.
  Sinnott.
      p.   cm.
   Includes bibliographies and indexes.
   ISBN 0–275–92691–5 (alk. paper)
      1. Problem solving.   I.Sinnott, Jan D.
   BF449.E94 1989
   153.4'3—dc19   88–15537

Library of Congress Catalog Card Number: 88–15537
ISBN: 0–275–92691–5

First published in 1989

Praeger Publishers, One Madison Avenue, New York, NY 10010
A division of Greenwood Press, Inc.

Printed in the United States of America

The paper used in this book complies with the
Permanent Paper Standard issued by the National
Information Standards Organization (Z39.48–1984).

10 9 8 7 6 5 4 3 2 1

*For
James and Gwenn,
who will lead the next steps
in the dance*

Contents

Tables and Figures

TABLES

FIGURES

Acknowledgments

My working hypothesis as a scientist and as a human being is that we co-create social reality, our perceptions and the world "out there," in conjunction with other persons and events; and in doing so we, too, are created. The intricate, beautiful folk dances and medieval dances are wonderful metaphors for this process. While virtuosos do take part, the moving quality of that pageant comes from the presence of all the dancers, the movements of each complementing those of the others. So I cannot write or edit alone. Acknowledgment is a poor thanks, given the extent of involvement that others must, of necessity, have had in my life and thought.

I will pick a few people to thank, knowing that over my 46 years of life, over the centuries, and all around the globe are countless hearts and minds that have sought and cared and contributed. And, even more exciting, I look forward in time to those many persons who, if we do not die as a species by our own hands, will run like the wind with these thoughts and other thoughts to future ideas even better than our hopes could create. I know that all these share in the work and should be acknowledged. I honor all these brothers and sisters who are creating knowledge with me.

I owe a great debt to the persons and institutions that have supported and encouraged me in the exploration of this relatively unknown area of everyday problem solving and in the preparation of this book. Primary among these is Dr. David Arenberg, Chief of the Cognition Section, Laboratory of Personality and Cognition, Gerontology Research Center, National Institute on Aging, National Institutes of Health, who has stimulated excellence in many people, including me, and has been a friend, a colleague, and a cheering section when I needed that. Through the person of Dave Arenberg, and through the mechanisms of an earlier postdoctoral fellowship and my current guest scientist status, the National Institute on Aging has helped further this important "cutting edge" work. Other colleagues at the Gerontology Research Center who contributed significantly to the work include Donna Baumgartner, Diana Bobbie, Jennifer Cook, Cathy Dent and the participants in the Baltimore Longitudinal Study of Aging, Cecille Doherty, Dr. James Fozard, Dr. Leonard M. Giambra, Barbara Hiscock, Deanna Howard, Karen Kinnacome, Elizabeth Licht, Kelly Palicki, Lena Phillips, Judith Plotz, Susan Robinson, June Sacktor, Lisa Shanahan, Lynn Walbeck, Cornelia Ware, and all the other members of the Cognition Section.

Thank you to Towson State University for its support and acknowledgment, and for the faculty research grants, released time grants, sabbatical leave, and summer stipends it has contributed. Special thanks are due to Dr. Joan Rabin, whose ideas and spirit have inspired my work; to Janis Carlos, Jean Foley, Kathleen Henderson, and Dr. John Webster for their support; to the administration; and to all my colleagues in the Psychology Department. Thanks also to the students, clients, and interns (some named earlier) who provided stimulation. A thank you to those professors at Catholic University who first stimulated my thinking along these lines, including Dr. James Youniss, Dr. Hans Furth, and Dr. Bruce Ross.

Exchange of ideas is crucial to creativity, so I would like to recognize several groups who contribute in that way to my thinking. Those in physics who have focused on the paradigms inherent in the "new physics" of relativity theory, quantum theory, and general systems theory have led me to see the applications of these views of the world to psychological studies. A group of colleagues who sometimes call themselves the "missing links" (i.e., between the laboratory and life) has been very supportive and stimulating. The Philosophy of Science in Psychology/Systems Study Group, which will soon be publishing a book on change and transformation (Kramer and Bopp [Eds.], *Movement Through Form*, Springer), to which I'm happy to have contributed, is another stimulating group of clinicians and academicians. Individuals in the Institute for Noetic Sciences, in Washington Focus, and in the "family" that has explored ideas about consciousness and development and change, especially Rima Shaffer-Meyer, and Drs. Jean Houston and Gay Luce, are among those to be thanked. Participants in the Harvard Symposia on Postformal Operations and Positive Development in Adulthood have been strong sources of growth, and the reader is urged to explore the three volumes coming from this conference, published by Praeger, edited by Commons et al., in which I also share ideas.

Finally, thanks to Dr. George Zimmar, our very helpful Praeger editor, and to my parents, Dorothy and Edward Dynda, and all my family and friends, who came together with me to "be in this good place."

EVERYDAY
PROBLEM
SOLVING

Background: About This Book and the Field of Everyday Problem Solving

Jan D. Sinnott

This chapter discusses how this book came to be written, its audience, what the writers are trying to accomplish and are *not* trying to accomplish, and the interesting issues in everyday problem solving research. The various chapters that make up the body of the book are summarized at the end of this chapter.

HOW THE BOOK CAME TO BE WRITTEN

If we question adults who are not too overwhelmed with the business of their own lives to answer, or if we question ourselves, about what is the most interesting or important thing humans do with their thinking skills, the answer usually is "They solve problems." Problem solving is a skill we value in students, managers, parents, creators, and people undergoing personal changes. We fear those dead ends in life that come when we are unable to solve problems. We probably find problem solving interesting because it is not easy to do or to analyze; we are fascinated by a computer solving even a very simple problem, but think nothing of the fact that it remembers extremely well. This attitude, interest, and need for understanding of how individuals use complex mental processes to survive and adapt in a problematic world has spawned a large literature summarizing numerous studies of problem solving. In order to concretize their problem solving questions so that the questions can be addressed within experimental designs, researchers—very appropriately—usually have addressed the logical, creative, or concept formation aspects of problem solving. These efforts have been fruitful. They were immediately fruitful enough that developmental psychologists, growing in number in the more recent history of psychology, began to ask how children attain the ability to solve problems so that they finally get to the point, as college sophomores, where they manifest "normal" problem solving skills.

Let me digress for a moment to notice, along with philosophers of science, that once some "facts" are in circulation in the scientific community, we seem to forget that they represent simply one attempt to formulate and approach a question, not the only way things are. We concretize and make the process into, as learning theory predicts and describes, an end in its own right. For example, it was useful in the past to study logical problems; now problem solving *is* logical problem solving. It was useful in the past to test college sophomores; now college sophomores have become the standard-bearers for developing children and everyone else. These processes of acceptance make sense in letting us avoid overload in wrestling with amorphous knowledge bases, but may ultimately be maladaptive if they keep us from seeing more options and even more useful answers. But until old answers or theories seem almost overwhelmingly insufficient, we very adaptively make use of them.

This seems to have been the state of things when developmental psychologists began testing mature and old adults, and when organizational psychologists began watching customers and managers solve problems. These groups were tested against the young adult/logical standard and were found wanting. What's worse, some of these mature respondents didn't seem to care about doing well on the problems. This made problem solving researchers think. Many of the researchers had once been college sophomores. They found it difficult to accept that they were less skilled problem solvers as adult professionals than they had been in college. But the data said so, and the data seemed reliable. How could this discrepancy be resolved?

This discomfort was eventually the impetus for a reexamination of the premises upon which the studies of problem solving rested, and the field of everyday problem solving was off and running. How do mature adults adaptively solve problems? What kinds of problems do they typically encounter? What special forms might their logical thought take? How do younger persons compensate for the lack of experience that the mature person has in abundance? Asking these kinds of questions broadened the parameters of what could be studied or conceived of as problem solving processes. Under the general rubric of "everyday problem solving," many researchers began testing variables such as problem context (which could be physical or emotional), intuition, motivation, and intention. Many people became interested in everyday problem solving results, which were scattered through the psychological, educational, gerontological, marketing, and other literatures. Duplication of effort was common. This book was conceived of as a resource to pull together some of the key approaches in everyday problem solving studies, and to give the many interested readers some directions as they formulate new studies. The main ideas, approaches, and questions in everyday problem solving are in these chapters.

THE INTENDED AUDIENCE

When some of us first talked about creating such a book as this, we imagined the audience to be (as we were) researchers interested in new approaches in either problem solving or adult development. It soon became clear that many other categories of persons were in this audience. Clinicians, philosophers, marketing persons, administrators, artificial intelligence scientists, educators, and guidance counselors were as interested as cognitive and developmental psychologists were. Both researchers and practitioners had an interest, as did lay persons. Graduate students in many fields sensed a new source for thesis and dissertation topics. Undergraduates found the link between laboratory and life, represented by these tasks, to be compelling

The book is intended to give all of these potential users access to parts of the everyday problem solving literature they do not normally encounter. It is also meant to provide an overview of key everyday problem solving areas, for example, the models that have been used. We have concentrated on the psychological/educational areas and, since space is limited, therefore have neglected the organizational/clinical domains. However, many of the references cited in various chapters (e.g., Sinnott 1984a in Chapter 6) will lead readers to those literatures. Those interested in clinical aspects of this area will probably find the book edited by Kramer and Bopp (in press) useful and thought-provoking.

GOALS OF THE AUTHORS

Although each author has his or her specific goal, the authors have some missions in common. First, they are addressing some aspect of naturalistic problem solving, as opposed to purely laboratory work. Second, they are focusing on salient issues that are addressed in the field, such as the influence of problem context. Third, they lean heavily toward the study of mature or older adults and toward valuing ecological validity. The authors generally are not trying to summarize all the literature in their part of the field.

ISSUES IN EVERYDAY PROBLEM SOLVING RESEARCH

The issues that have been most salient in everyday problem solving research are similar to key issues in other areas of psychology:

—What model do we use?

—Do we consider perception/attitude or actual behavior?

—How does problem solving skill change (improve or diminish) over time, especially for mature humans?

—Can a more complex stage of thought be formed here?

—How can tasks be made ecologically valid?

—Is this sort of problem solving an adaptive skill?

—How do tasks relate to other information processing or psychological components identified in basic research?

—How does this part of the person's psychological makeup relate to physical dynamics and social dynamics?

Although each author has his or her own approach to these issues, there is a general approach that typifies this book. The overall model is one from general systems theory (GST) (Miller 1978; Sinnott in press) within an information-processing, cognitive, developmental, and psychometric framework. GST views the human system as unified and adaptive, with all functions serving the goal of individual continuity. Cognitive systems control stimulation and information flow for the organism, thereby optimizing it. Physical systems "nested" inside the person system, and social systems in which person systems are "nested," also strive for continuity and exchange "information" (in a broad sense) with the person system. Problem solving, then, is seen in this model as optimizing the dynamics, survival, and growth of the person system as it survives in interaction with other systems.

Some additional biases are apparent. The bias in this book is toward the study of behavior, rather than toward predictions or perceptions of or attitudes toward one's own behavior. There is something of a bias toward interview, think-aloud, or standard scenario methods. We are biased toward considering what improves over the lifespan, or (more neutral) changes, rather than what skills decline from an arbitrary young adult standard. We do not struggle, here, with the questions of whether our respondents are in one stage or another of development; rather, we examine how they do what they do. We seek ecological validity, without always addressing the limits that such a stance imposes. We spend less than enough time relating problem solving to other psychological skills, for example, memory and emotional maturity. Finally, we focus some—but again, not enough—on the complex interrelations between the person and his/her body, and his/her society.

SUMMARY OF CHAPTERS

The first portion of the book contains chapters that strongly address concepts, theories, models, and tasks used by researchers in the field.

Meacham and Emont define "problem solving" and what is meant by "everyday," relating both to the larger interpersonal context, the multiperson system. Luszcz examines theoretical models derived from the two major areas chosen by us: information-processing theory and post-formal cognitive developmental theory. She considers ways to unite the two conceptualizations. Sinnott and Cook collect the tasks used in everyday problem solving research so that this wide-ranging group of measures will be available to readers of this book. Sebby and Papini attempt to use Labouvie-Vief's model as a main framework for research integrating adaptivity and problem solving. Sinnott applies a model integrating GST, information-processing theory, and Piagetian theory to describe the thoughts and emotions of older and younger adults thinking aloud as they solve ill-structured problems. Planning is the focus of Rebok, who brings the transactional opportunistic, information-processing, and artificial intelligence models to bear on one planning experience, a grocery shopping task. Finally, Blanchard-Fields discusses everyday reasoning in the social-emotional context of attribution theory.

In the second part of the book, each author focuses on a particular problem, issue, or test. Kramer looks at the ways adults resolve conflicts, a frequently encountered social problem. She uses the realm of marital conflict to analyze conflict resolution dynamics. Consumer behavior, specifically consumer reasoning, is the problem area chosen by Capon, Kuhn, and Carretero. They examine the wide variation in categorization behavior by adults who succeed in solving the consumer problem. Leadbeater and Kuhn examine the process of interpretation as it impacts on understanding narratives, specifically discrepant narratives, another common problem. Levels of cognitive processing complexity seemed to influence behavior here. The measurement of intelligence concerns Cornelius, Kenny, and Caspi as they compare academic intelligence, everyday intelligence, self-concept, and performance on ability tests. They find that problem solving and verbal abilities are important to both academic and everyday intelligence. The chapter by Camp, Doherty, Moody-Thomas, and Denny, concerned with practical problem solving, contains a "generic" scoring system for efficacy of solutions, analyses of responses to social problems, and an analysis of relations between the fluid-crystallized intelligence dimension and practical problem solving. Arlin addresses the nature of the problem-as-a-problem. Krauss's chapter offers a set of materials (playing cards) that can be used to test for a number of different skills in an ecologically appropriate way. Her card task correlates with performance of traditional psychometric instruments.

The final chapters involve memory and intervention. Lee extends problem solving ideas to the realm of teaching and teacher preparation, a domain in which intervention is made in many lives. Cavanaugh,

Morton, and Tilse connect one component of information processing—memory—to problem solving processes and suggest some interesting intervention strategies drawn from clinical domains. Finally, Ventis concentrates on intervention strategies useful for improving problem solving and cognitive skills among the aging. The book closes with suggestions for future research.

This book as a whole, then, provides useful tools for researchers and others to continue work in theory and applications in everyday problem solving.

REFERENCES

Kramer, D., & Bopp, M. (in press). *Movement through form: Transformation in clinical and developmental psychology*. New York: Springer.

Commons, M., Kohlberg, L., Richards, F., Armon, C., & Sinnott, J. D. (Eds.). (in press). *Beyond formal operations, Volume 3: Models and methods in the study of adolescent and adult thought*. New York: Praeger.

Commons, M., Richards, F., & Armon, C. (Eds.). (1984). *Beyond formal operations: Late adolescent and adult cognitive development*. New York: Praeger.

Commons, M., Sinnott, J. D., Richards, F., & Armon, C. (Eds.). (in press). *Beyond formal operations II: Comparisons and applications of adolescent and adult developmental models*. New York: Praeger.

Miller, J. (1978) *Living systems*. New York: McGraw-Hill.

Sinnott, J. D. (in press). General systems theory: A rationale for the study of everyday memory. In L. Poon, D. Rubin, & B. Wilson (Eds.), *Everyday cognition in adulthood and late life*. New Rochelle, N.Y.: Cambridge University Press.

2

The Interpersonal Basis of Everyday Problem Solving

John A. Meacham
Nancy Cooney Emont

Billy Bigelow: On a night like this I start to wonder What life is all about.
Julie Jordan: And I always say two heads are better than one, to figger it out.
Richard Rogers and Oscar Hammerstein II, "If I loved You," *Carousel**

A research participant—an undergraduate at the University of Chicago—
is presented with two strings hanging from the ceiling of the psychology
laboratory, one near the wall, the other in the center of the room, and
is told, "Your problem is to tie the ends of those two strings together."
The participant soon learns that if one of the strings is grasped, the other
string is too far away to be reached. The experimenter explains that the
participant in this classic study of reasoning in humans (Maier 1931)
may use any of several objects in the room.

What is a reasonable solution to this problem? Wouldn't a reasoning
human, especially a verbal Chicago undergraduate, say, "Would you
help me by grasping this string and bringing it toward me, while I grasp
the other and bring it toward you?" Yet the experimenter was not at all
concerned with this potential solution to the problem, a solution that,
we will argue, directs our attention to the interpersonal basis of everyday
problem solving. By this we mean not merely that individuals solve
interpersonal problems or that individuals solve problems in interpersonal contexts, but that problem solving itself, in its essence, is best
understood in terms of interpersonal dialogue and cooperation.

In considering the issues surrounding everyday problem solving, we have drawn upon the rapidly expanding literature concerned with what Baltes, Dittman-Kohli, and Dixon (1984) have termed the "pragmatics of intelligence." Similarly, Sternberg (1985) has argued for increased attention to the practical aspects of intelligence concerned with adaptation and motivation. One of the earliest seminal efforts in this regard was Sinnott's (1975) substitution of familiar materials for traditional Piagetian tasks.

Our thesis regarding interpersonal problem solving is intended to be consistent with a rejection of individual cognition and consciousness as a basis for individual and societal development in favor of interpersonal relations, communication, and cooperation as that basis (Meacham 1984). Arguments in support of this perspective have been made by a number of writers. Vygotsky (1978), for example, emphasizes that all cognitive abilities appear first in social interaction, and only subsequently at the intrapsychological level (Wertsch 1985). Similarly, Habermas rejects intrasubjectivity as the starting point in understanding the individual and society, arguing instead for basing the individual and society in intersubjectivity, in the community of subjects in dialogue (Habermas 1984; McCarthy 1981, p. 326). Harre argues that the primary reality is the array of persons in conversation, with the psychological realities of human minds being brought into being as secondary realities (Harre 1984, p. 64). Thus our intention is to locate the basis for everyday problem solving not within the mind of the individual, but within interpersonal relations.

WHAT IS EVERYDAY PROBLEM SOLVING?

What Is a Problem?

Our suggestion for focusing on the interpersonal basis of problem solving calls for a brief consideration of what is meant when we say that one has a problem and that one has solved a problem. Davis (1973), after considering a number of possibilities, defines a problem as "a stimulus situation for which an organism does not have a ready response" (p. 13). We should agree, Davis notes, that if the organism has the option of avoiding or ignoring the problem, then, strictly speaking, there is not a problem. The organism must be motivated, through some feeling of discomfort or disequilibrium, for instance, to solve the problem. Further, Davis notes, we should not consider as problems those situations for which solutions are well known, for example, arithmetic problems. We should also exclude trial-and-error searching, for example, trying to discover an error in a checkbook that won't balance.

What is important in Davis's definition is the notion of an obstacle to response or action. Problems arise not in an abstract or theoretical context, but in the practical, motivating context of action. Problems are to be defined not according to intrinsic—logical or informational—qualities, but in terms of the organism's relations with and reactions to those qualities. In short, the essence of a problem is in the having of it.

Eysenck (1984), following Anderson (1980), sets forth some broader criteria in describing problem solving activities: First, the activities must be goal directed; second, a sequence of mental processes must be involved in attaining the goal; and third, cognitive processes should be involved. Eysenck remarks that the third "is a difficult criterion to apply in practice, but is intended to rule out such mundane activities as dealing a pack of cards" (p. 269). It is not clear, however, why mundane—everyday—activities should be ruled out, nor is it clear that dealing a pack of cards cannot be a problem. Dealing a pack of cards may indeed be a problem for a child first learning to play card games, or for an older adult suffering from arthritis. Learning new ways to hold the deck and handle the cards may be important solutions in these situations.

Eysenck's (1984) requirement that the learning of the solutions be cognitive seems arbitrary, and certainly inappropriate in the case of dealing a pack of cards. Instead, a more general requirement would seem to be that a problem entail an obstacle to response or action. Such a requirement is consistent with a dictionary definition: that a problem is "a question or situation that presents uncertainty, perplexity, or difficulty" (Morris 1969). Likely Eysenck desired to eliminate from consideration a mere task, that is, "a well-defined piece of work that is often imposed, of short duration, and burdensome" (Morris 1969), although this would appear to describe much traditional research on problem solving.

What Is Problem Solving?

What does it mean to solve a problem? Davis (1973) defines a problem solution as a creative idea or a new combination of existing ideas. A broad literature, ranging from experimental psychology to social and organizational psychology, is concerned with efforts to describe and prescribe the process of solving problems. Much of this literature documents various steps in problem solving. For example, Dewey (1933) describes two steps in problem solving: first, a state of doubt or difficulty, and second, an act of searching and inquiring to find information to resolve the doubt or difficulty. A more detailed description of the process is provided by Shulman (1965; cited in Davis 1973, p. 79): First, discomfort leads to the sensing of the problem; second, a particular problem is formulated or defined; third, information is gathered, hypotheses are generated, and so on; and fourth, the problem is resolved, thus removing the discomfort. Kingsley and Garry (1957) provide a longer but similar list of steps.

Why is problem solving a problem? What are the points in the steps outlined above that might be expected to present the least and the most difficulty? Once a solution has been adopted, one merely carries out the actions called for by the solution and, barring new problems, the original problem has been solved. More difficulty can be expected, however, in setting forth at the outset the nature of the problem and in generating various possible solutions. These are steps that call not for mechanical application of routines and skills, but for creative interpretation of situations and production of meanings and possibilities that previously were only latent in the situation.

Problem solving is difficult because there are obstacles to creative interpretation and production of new meanings. The obstacles have been touched upon in experimental psychology under such headings as rigidity, fixation and mental set. A well-known example of how prior sets can be obstacles to problem solving was provided by Maier's (1931) research, mentioned briefly above, in which individuals were asked to tie two strings hanging from the ceiling at a distance such that the two could not be grasped at once. Somewhat less than half of those tested were able to solve the problem by tying a weight—a pair of pliers was on a table in the room—to one of the strings and then setting this string swinging so that it could be grasped while holding the other string. The failure to recognize that the pair of pliers could function as a pendulum weight was termed functional fixedness. As Crovitz (1970) notes, when it comes to creativity and problem solving, "The natural tendency is to keep trying the same old thing when illumination requires more flexibility than that" (p. 80).

What, then, is at the heart of having a problem and solving it? One has a problem when one's mind is in a rut. Successful problem solving involves breaking out of the rut, or breaking the mental set that has impeded recognition and appropriate definition of the problem, and that has impeded the discovery and production of new and potentially successful solutions to the problem. To this extent, we agree with traditional conceptions of problem solving. But we can draw attention to the nature of our disagreement, and provide some anticipation of our conclusion, by asking how one's mind gets out of the rut, how mental sets are broken. The answer, we would argue, is not by means of individualistic, cognitive, problem solving routines, as Crovitz (1970) suggests, but through interpersonal, social, problem solving conversations. It is in dialogue with others that one's mental sets are broken, as friends suggest new ways of thinking about situations, point to inconsistencies in our logic, provide a counterbalance to our emotional attachments in the situation, and suggest new means for solving our problems.

What Is Meant by "Everyday?"

It is the study of problem solving in its everyday context that calls attention to the interpersonal basis of problem solving. For this reason, it is important to reflect upon the many meanings associated with the term "everyday," and to distinguish those which may be most important for present purposes. The dictionary suggests "ordinary, routine, commonplace, and usual" (Morris 1969). Concern with how people solve problems in an everyday context has often been expressed as an issue of the ecological validity of research in psychology. Typical laboratory research involves the testing of hypotheses derived from theories of how the mind works. To the extent that findings from such research may be generalized to or have applicability in settings outside the laboratory, they may be said to be ecologically valid.

A number of approaches may be pursued to answer the question of whether research findings are generalizable to or ecologically valid in everyday contexts. As Scheidt (1981) points out, typically researchers have approached this question from a measurement perspective, choosing measures that appear to possess ecological face validity in the real world, and then comparing findings with these measures against findings previously obtained in the laboratory. Scheidt observes that this measurement approach to ecological validity is not a certain one, and concludes by accusing many researchers of opting for "quick, convenient, 'real world' representations of tasks, stimuli, situations, and rules," thus producing merely "ecologically cosmetic" studies.

Ill-Structured Problems

In our view, understanding human action in everyday contexts requires two fundamental changes in perspective beyond the measurement approach to ecological validity. The first of these changes involves a consideration of how problems arise and the manner in which they are resolved (if they are resolved). In traditional research, the researcher defines the problem by setting forth the initial conditions and/or materials to be employed, the rules to be followed, and the goal to be achieved. Thus much problem solving research would appear to concern not problems but tasks, as defined above.

In contrast, as Riegel (1973), Eysenck (1984), and others have pointed out, in everyday life problems are rarely so well defined. We are continually coming upon, discovering, and inventing new problems that we haven't come across before, because of the unpredictability the human world presents to us. Often it is not apparent until well after the fact—sometimes too late—that we are facing a problem. The steps in problem solving that Dewey (1933), Kingsley and Garry (1957), Shulman (1965), and others have described as experiencing doubt or difficulty and then formulating, clarifying, or defining a problem are essential steps in the process of problem solving, for without them there is, in the everyday context, no problem to be solved. Thus research neglecting how people initially have or experience and define problems cannot provide a complete picture of everyday problem solving.

Furthermore, in laboratory research the temporal point of problem solution is generally quite clear: Not only is the problem structured so that there is only one correct solution, which can be quickly confirmed upon its discovery, but the researcher knows the solution in advance and can confirm for the participant that this is the correct solution. In contrast, for everyday problems there are often many alternative solutions, all workable but involving different combinations of costs and benefits. Once a particular solution has been decided upon, confirmation that this is the correct or best solution may take years, if such confirmation is possible. Consider, for example, the many possible solutions and the associated uncertainties in choice of an identity, career or spouse.

Everyday problems of this sort, having no single correct answer and lacking the structure for arriving at a single answer, form only one of several possible categories of problemlike situations. The following brief categorization will serve to define more narrowly the kinds of situations considered as everyday problem solving. Everyday problem solving is not concerned, in our view, with situations in which both the goal and the means are well defined, situations that may more properly be termed tasks rather than problems (such as balancing a checkbook). Everyday problem solving is not addressed by research in situations in which the goal is already defined and the problem solution consists in the discovery of the means to achieve the goal (finding a suitable birthday present for someone).

In contrast, everyday problem solving is best described by situations in which both the goal and the means are initially unclear, so that there are in a sense two aspects of ill-structured problems: the discovery and clarification of the end goal and the discovery and testing of the means for achieving the goal. It is not merely the case that in this third situation the problem definition has been taken out of the hands of the researcher and placed in the hands of the research participant; further, the issue of values has been raised, in the choice of goals for human action and in the need for justification of those goals as well as of the means for achieving the goals. Well-structured, laboratory research problems evade issues of value and responsibility; ill-structured everyday problems are invaded by these issues.

Ecologically Sound Inquiry

The second fundamental change in perspective required for understanding human action in everyday contexts involves a further consideration of what is meant by ecologically sound research. The invocation of this phrase should bring to mind not merely the generalizability or external validity of one's research findings, but also the interdependence of people and institutions in the human environment. This principle of interdependence—the ecological cycle—means that any intervention by researchers may potentially pollute the human environment. Such pollution should be guarded against.

Further, any research intervention may potentially enrich the human environment. The potential for enriching the human environment engenders among researchers a responsibility to strive to do so. As research in psychology moves from the laboratory to the everyday world, the responsibilities of researchers to safeguard the everyday world increase, just as in the case of genetic engineering, which in recent years has been moving from laboratory to real-world experiments. Participants in traditional psychological research may guard against its potentially polluting impact by discounting a laboratory experience as not real life, not relevant, not everyday; this discounting can be more difficult for participants when research is designed explicitly to mimic and provide an understanding of everyday processes.

How might research on problem solving pollute the human environment and so be ecologically unsound? At least two possibilities suggest themselves. First, the traditional paradigm for research on problem solving confirms a relationship of inequality in power between the researcher and the research participant. The researcher defines the problem and knows the answer in advance but withholds it from the subject in the research. The research participant must struggle to discover the solution to a problem that he or she is not intrinsically motivated to solve. Further, the constraints imposed by the researcher upon the participant—to follow certain rules that define the problem and thus limit the possible solutions to the problem, not to leave the laboratory to ask for help, and so on—merely add to the research participant's feeling of helplessness or powerlessness in the face of the problem (Meacham 1980).

The ideology that is confirmed by this traditional paradigm for both the researcher and the research participant is that science and psychology are authoritative and powerful. The researcher is superior to the participant in controlling the problem setting, in knowing the problem solution but not disclosing it, and in manipulating the research participant, as an object, into a less powerful, subordinate position. Whether the reinforcing of an ideology of power differentials in the human environment is polluting is, of course, a matter of point of view; some would argue that this is the natural state of things, in the same way that racism, sexism, and ageism are normative. We would argue strongly, however, that such pollution of the human environment is to be avoided.

The second way in which research on problem solving may be ecologically unsound is in neglecting to take advantage of the opportunity to strengthen and enrich processes that constitute the human environment. To get closure on this point, we must jump ahead of our argument somewhat: If our thesis is correct—the basis of problem solving is its interpersonal nature—then the most ecologically sound research on problem solving is that which reinforces the tendency and the skills within the research participants to call upon interpersonal resources in problem solving, that is, to ask a friend for help. Research that isolates the research participant and asks that he or she solve a problem without friends is not ecologically sound, for it inculcates in the participant precisely the opposite of the skills that can be so important in real life, everyday problem solving. Ecologically sound problem solving research leaves the research participants, at the conclusion of the research, with a stronger set of skills for everyday problem solving.

In summary, ecologically sound research on everyday problem solving should mean not merely doing research in a "natural" environment rather than in the laboratory, or research aimed more at describing what people do rather than at testing theory. It should also mean conducting research that doesn't pollute the human environment by further legitimizing an ideology that is oppressive to the research participants. Ecologically sound research should be research that has an emancipatory intent, that has as one of its aims the strengthening of existing problem solving processes and the introduction of new problem solving processes for the research participants. Our perspective here is not inconsistent with that of Howard (1985), who observes that psychologists ought "to consider what human beings might become in response to our research" (p. 262) and calls upon researchers to modify their ambitious pursuit of value-free knowledge.

Everyday Problem Solving: A Prescription

A prescription for what everyday problem solving entails, and for what features researchers could profitably explore, follows from integrating our separate discussions from a definitional standpoint of problem solving and of everyday contexts. The features of everyday problem solving are highlighted by contrasting them with those of traditional research on problem solving, as shown in Table 2.1. These features follow from the interpersonal basis of everyday problem solving. It is this uniquely human basis—problem solving not by isolated machines but by humans in cooperation with one another—that gives everyday problems their unpredictable, ill-structured nature; injects issues of value into matters of problem definition, and justification of means for ends; and raises for the researcher issues of responsibility for preserving and enriching the human world in which the research is conducted.

Table 2.1
Traditional Research versus Everyday Problem Solving

Traditional Research on Problem Solving	Everyday Problem Solving
Individualistic	Interpersonal
Well-defined tasks	Ill-structured problems
One task at a time	Several interwoven problems
Limited time frame	Extended time frame
Only one correct solution	Several possible solutions
No value issues	Inherent value issues
Power inequality between researcher and participant	Equality of power
Polluting	Enriching (skills, long-term interpersonal relations)
Better to strive to solve the problem alone	OK to ask for help

There are also a number of other features of everyday problem solving that distinguish it from traditional research on problem solving. In traditional research, the participant is presented with a single problem, for example, moving the missionaries and the cannibals to the other side of the river. In everyday contexts, one must simultaneously consider several interwoven problems with varying degrees of complexity, difficulty, importance, and urgency. A major issue in everyday problem solving is choosing which problem to attack now, and which to postpone for later consideration, if it is considered at all. This issue involves matters of style—resolving several minor problems first versus attacking the major one and of time management. The interweaving of problems also permits serendipitous fertilization of one problem domain by information from another, often leading to productive solutions. Of course, the potential for serendipity is greatest when the problem solving process is interpersonal. For this reason, we would argue that the greatest obstacle to problem solving is the mental set dictating that one ought to strive to solve the problem oneself; instead, the quickest route to problem solution can be, despite Maier's (1931) string-grasping participants not being permitted to do so, asking a friend for help.

PROBLEM SOLVING IN INTERPERSONAL CONTEXTS

Two Examples

Some support for our thesis on the interpersonal basis of everyday problem solving may be found by turning to two quite different examples of interpersonal or group problem solving, and asking whether they may direct our attention to aspects of problem solving, potentially important in everyday problem solving, that may be less apparent from the perspective of the individualistic research paradigm.

Prisoner's Dilemma

The first example of interpersonal problem solving is provided by Packer (1985), who divided groups of young adults, all friends, into two teams and asked them to play a modified version of Prisoner's Dilemma. Prisoner's Dilemma is a noncooperative, nonzero-sum simulation game, structured so that each player or team is tempted to play to win. If both teams compete, however, then both lose. The Prisoner's Dilemma is analogous to everyday problem solving in stimulating motives of both competition and cooperation. Packer's research questions were concerned not with the choices made by the teams (as with most Prisoner's Dilemma research), but with each team's actions and verbal rationales during the course of the game. Recordings of the conversations among the team members and between the teams provided the data for Packer's analyses.

The focus of the analyses was upon a particular event that occurred between some of the teams. Following the point at which an agreement to cooperate had been reached, so that the dilemma had apparently been resolved, the winning team (with the higher score at that point) deliberately broke the agreement, an action characterized by the losing team as "burning." It is at this point that Packer's study provides evidence on interpersonal, everyday problem solving, for the problem between the two teams is now not merely that of competition and cooperation as structured by the Prisoner's Dilemma game, but also the experience of the losing team that, having trusted the other team to act morally, it did not, and the experience of the winning team that, having acted in good faith, it is judged to be immoral. What has happened is consistent with Sarason's (1978) description of problem solving in the social arena: "The very process of formulating a problem, setting goals, and starting to act . . . begins to change [the] perception of problems, goals, and actions . . . " (p. 376).

Packer identifies three phases in the resolution of these problems between the teams. In phase one, the immediate reaction to the "burn-ing," the losing team reacts with strong emotions of outrage and indig-nation over the cheating, and refuses to cooperate further or to be involved in the game. Accusations against the winning team are inar-ticulate (Packer 1985, p. 51). In phase two, accusation and response, a gradual articulation by each team of its own position occurs; appreciation of the other team's grasp of events is lacking, however, until late in this phase, so that, for example, the winning team, "faced with the losing team's presentation of them as having been selfish, and as being morally inferior, . . . see the losing team as adopting an unfairly and inappro-priately morally superior attitude" (p. 88). In phase three, articulation or standoff, those teams able to resolve the conflict do so by granting the validity of the other team's account of what had happened (p. 105), acknowledging that there has been a misunderstanding (p. 106), and mutually recognizing the two ways of comprehending the situation (p. 108)—that not only had not everybody understood the situation in the same way, but there had been, in a sense, two situations (p. 130). In summary, the three phases might be characterized as first, strong emotions and unreflective action; second, a one-sided understanding of the situation; and third, a mutual understanding of the situation (p. 142).

Group Therapy

A second example of problem solving in an interpersonal context is group therapy. Following Rosenberg's (1984) distinctions, we will not be concerned with self-help or support groups, where the emphasis is primarily upon building group cohesion and providing support in coping with continuing problems. In group therapy, on the other hand, the emphasis is to a greater extent upon problem solving. We assume there to be similarities between problem solving in the context of group ther-apy and problem solving as it may occur in any everyday group of friends. MacKenzie and Livesley (1984) have suggested that a therapy group engaged in problem solving moves through a sequence of six steps; considering these will further distinguish traditional research on problem solving and everyday problem solving.

A first step in group therapy is engagement, involving recognition and acceptance of the problem (MacKenzie & Livesley 1984). In tradi-tional research on problem solving, this step is highly structured by the researcher; but in everyday problem solving, weeks or months may pass while a problem grows unnoticed or is not accepted by the individuals involved. The second step is one in which the group decides how to operate, that is, how to handle the diversity of opinions within the group and how to resolve conflicts. In traditional, individualized research this step would not be involved. But MacKenzie and Livesley's scheme alerts us to the fact that in everyday problem solving, individuals are engaged not only in problem solving but also in maintaining and strengthening long-term interpersonal relations. Indeed, the latter must usually be a more important goal than to solve a short-term problem. The third, fourth and fifth steps are concerned with information gathering and generation of solutions to problems. In the case of group therapy, these steps directly involve the individuals in the group, which would not typically be the case in everyday problem solving.

The sixth and final step involves termination of the group. In traditional research on problem solving, this is the debriefing of the participant, explaining the purpose of the research, and such. Although many participants may find such research interesting, it is likely that more than a few leave with a feeling of having been manipulated by the researcher, who knew the problem solution all along. The researcher typically does not tell the participant how well he or she performed, or whether the hypotheses of the research are confirmed, for the answers to these questions await participation by more people in the research. In the case of group therapy, termination involves recognition that the problem has been solved, that people's lives have been made better, and an expression of thanks for the mutual efforts of those who participated in the problem solving group. Beyond group therapy, in everyday problem solving there is typically not a termination of the group. Instead, the process of successful problem solving may facilitate a feeling of cooperation among the members of the group, so that they will be more willing to work together toward everyday problem solving at some point in the future.

Steps in Everyday Problem Solving

A recapitulation of some of the steps in everyday problem solving, as revealed by our brief review of problem solving in interpersonal contexts, is provided by Table 2.2. (Of course, our suggestion of a sequence of steps is intended merely as a heuristic, and is not to imply a rigid, nonoverlapping sequence.) Examination of this table makes clear the radical divergence between problem solving as conceptualized and revealed through traditional research, on the one hand, and everyday problem solving, on the other. The former provides merely a skeletal outline of the possible steps and processes, as well as the obstacles that may arise, in the course of everyday problem solving. More important for practical applications is that the sequence of steps outlined for everyday problem solving is rich in potential opportunities for overcoming obstacles and facilitating the problem solving process. Consistent with the thesis of this chapter, each of these opportunities depends upon understanding the problem solving process as an interpersonal one and

Table 2.2
Steps in Everyday Problem Solving

Traditional Research on Problem Solving	Everyday Problem Solving
Individualistic	Interpersonal
Well-defined tasks	Ill-structured problems
One task at a time	Several interwoven problems
Limited time frame	Extended time frame
Only one correct solution	Several possible solutions
No value issues	Inherent value issues
Power inequality between researcher and participant	Equality of power
Polluting	Enriching (skills, long-term interpersonal relations)
Better to strive to solve the problem alone	OK to ask for help
Alternative solutions generated in isolation	Alternative solutions generated with help of other people
	Other people help to break mental sets (emotional, perceptual, etc.)
Solution tested in isolation	Solution adopted, may be tested
Immediate validation of solution by experimenter	Solution may be validated only eventually, if at all
Debriefing	Maintain, strengthen interpersonal relations

thus calling upon friends for help in defining the problem, gathering information, breaking mental sets, generating solutions, validating solutions, and so on.

The sequence of problem solving steps gleaned from traditional research accounts gives insufficient attention to the role of emotions, including at times strong emotions, in both hindering and facilitating the resolution of problems. Although Dewey (1933), Kingsley and Garry (1957), and Shulman (1965) refer to minor feelings of doubt, difficulty, or discomfort, Packer (1985) describes the participants in his research as outraged, indignant, and even inarticulate; and MacKenzie and Livesley (1984) describe as an important part of the group therapy process the agreement upon procedures for resolving conflicts that arise in the course of group problem solving. No doubt such strong emotions and conflicts can be significant in preventing individuals from breaking mental sets and moving toward reconceptualizing situations and resolving problems. The most effective means of minimizing this deteriorative role of emotions is by making the problem solving process interpersonal, so that other persons with less strong emotional attachments to features of the situation may provide a counterbalancing influence and perhaps even channel the energies associated with strong emotions into productive work toward resolving problems.

THE INTERPERSONAL BASIS OF PROBLEM SOLVING

What makes everyday problem solving distinctive and worthy of study is that its basis is not individualistic but interpersonal. Everyday problem solving is not one person striving to solve a problem in his or her mind, but is two or more people cooperating and working together to define and solve a problem. It is this uniquely human, interpersonal basis that gives everyday problems their unpredictable, ill-structured nature, that injects issues of value into the process of defining and solving problems, and that places upon researchers the responsibility for preserving and enriching the human world in which their research on problem solving is conducted.

The greatest obstacle to successful problem solving is failure to break the mental set dictating that one ought to solve problems by oneself rather than asking a friend for help. Our perspective on problem solving is radically different from the traditional perspective on intelligence, with its aim of ranking individuals against one another in terms of reified abilities thought to exist within the minds of individuals (Gould 1981). Instead, the capacity for problem solving is located within the matrix of interpersonal relations between parent and child, teacher and student, supervisor and worker, and so on, so that the critical question becomes, as Vygotsky (1978) has pointed out, not what the child can do alone but what the child can do with the assistance of an adult, not what problems one person can solve alone but what one person can do with the support and help of friends. From this interpersonal perspective, efforts to teach problem solving routines to individuals are misguided, for they support an ideology that locates any deficit in problem solving abilities within the individual, an ideology of blaming the victim.

Worse, traditional research on problem solving, by implying that problem solving skills are located within individuals, so that it is individuals who should strive to solve problems alone, may discourage precisely those interpersonal behaviors that would be most conducive to successful everyday problem solving. Instead, problem solving processes can be improved by conducting research on and promoting skills in communication and cooperation, skills that serve to integrate individuals within groups that can be helpful in solving problems, skills that are consistent with an ideology not of self-sufficiency but of interdependence (Sampson 1977).

Of course, some concerns might be expressed regarding the interpersonal perspective advanced in this chapter. A first might be that everyday problem solving has merely been removed from the mind of the first individual, who has a problem, to the mind of a second, who provides a solution, so that the problem solving process remains individualized and not interpersonal in its basis. In reply, we note that the solution does not exist in the mind of the second individual apart from the problem being raised in conversation with the first. Further, we would argue against the view that the second individual must be better at breaking mental sets and thus seeing the potential solution. From our perspective, mental sets are broken not through the efforts of isolated individuals but through the clash of minds. As many of us will readily acknowledge, our common experience is that it is often easier to see the errors of another's reasoning than of our own. What is important in having a productive clash of minds is that there be equality of power among the individuals, so that the direction of the conversation follows not from consideration of tradition, status, or power but from the force of the better argument (Habermas 1984). In this regard, traditional research on problem solving, in further legitimizing relations of inequality between the researcher and the participant, undermines the conditions for successful problem solving.

A second concern regarding the interpersonal perspective is that it is inconsistent with well-known, classic examples of problem solvers in their everyday, applied work—scientists, for example. Here, we can reply that the well-known, classic examples are of a piece with our cultural ideal of self-contained individualism (Sampson 1977), as well as with a positivist conception of science, and may very well not conform to the reality of what scientists do in their work. Indeed, it is not difficult to find examples of scientists who proclaim the necessity of interpersonal relations for their work, as the following example from an interview by Bringuier (1980, p. 18) illustrates:

Bringuier: Do you think a researcher should work alone?

Piaget: Oh no; you must have contacts, and you must, especially, have people who contradict you. You have to have a group.

   In closing this chapter, we can touch briefly on the central focus of this volume, which is concerned with how individuals solve everyday problems. Our answer is that individuals don't solve everyday problems in their heads; they solve problems by communicating with and working cooperatively within a group of friends.

REFERENCES

Anderson, J. R. (1980). *Cognitive psychology and its implications*. San Francisco: W. H. Freeman.

Baltes, P. B., Dittmann-Kohli, F., & Dixon, R. A. (1984). New perspectives on the development of intelligence in adulthood: Toward a dual-process conception and a model of selective optimization with compensation. In P. B. Baltes and O. G. Brim, Jr. (Eds.), *Life-span development and behavior* (Vol. 6, pp. 33–76). New York: Academic Press.

Bringuier, J. C. (1980). *Conversations with Jean Piaget*. Chicago: University of Chicago Press.

Crovitz, H. H. (1970). *Galton's walk: Methods for the analysis of thinking, intelligence, and creativity*. New York: Harper & Row.

Davis, G. A. (1973) *Psychology of problem solving: Theory and practice*. New York: Basic Books.

Dewey, J. (1933). *How we think*. New York: Heath.

Eysenck, M. W. (1984). *A handbook of cognitive psychology*. Hillsdale, N.J.: Erlbaum.

Gould, S. J. (1981). *Mismeasure of man*. New York: Norton.

Habermas, J. (1984). *The theory of communicative action* (Vol. 1; *Reason and the rationalization of society*). Boston: Beacon Press.

Harre, R. (1984). *Personal being*. Cambridge, Mass.: Harvard University Press.

Howard, G. S. (1985). The role of values in the science of psychology. *American Psychologist, 40,* 255–265.

Kingsley, H. L., & Garry, R. (1957). *The nature and conditions of learning* (2nd ed.). Englewood Cliffs, N.J.: Prentice-Hall.

MacKenzie, K. R., & Livesley, W. J. (1984). Developmental stages: An integrating theory of group psychotherapy. *Canadian Journal of Psychiatry, 29,* 247–251.

Maier, N. R. F. (1931). Reasoning in humans. II. The solution of a problem and its appearance in consciousness. *Journal of Comparative and Physiological Psychology, 11,* 181–194.

McCarthy, T. (1981). *The critical theory of Jurgen Habermas.* Cambridge, Mass.: MIT Press.

Meacham, J. A. (1980). Research on remembering: Interrogation or conversation, monologue or dialogue? *Human Development, 23,* 236–244.

Meacham, J. A. (1984). The social basis of intentional action. *Human Development, 27,* 119–124.

Morris, W. (Ed.). 1969. *The American Heritage dictionary of the English language.* Boston: Houghton Mifflin.

Packer, M J. (1985). *The structure of moral action: A hermeneutic study of moral conflict.* Basel: Karger.

Riegel, K. F. (1973). Dialectic operations: The final period of cognitive development. *Human Development, 16,* 346–370.

Rosenberg, P. P. (1984). Support groups: A special therapeutic entity. *Small Group Behavior, 15,* 173–186.

Sampson, E. E. (1977). Psychology and the American ideal. *Journal of Personality and Social Psychology, 35,* 767–782.

Sarason, S. B. (1978). The nature of problem solving in social action. *American Psychologist, 33,* 370–380.

Scheidt, R. J. (1981). Ecologically-valid inquiry: Fait accompli? *Human Development, 24,* 225–228.

Shulman, L. S. (1965). Seeking styles and individual differences in patterns of inquiry. *School Review, 73,* 258–266. (Cited in Davis 1973, p. 79.)

Sinnott, J. D. (1975). Everyday thinking and Piagetian operativity in adults. *Human Development, 18,* 430–443.

Sternberg, R. J. (1985). *Beyond IQ: A triarchic theory of human intelligence.* New York: Cambridge University Press.

Vygotsky, L. S. (1978). *Mind and society.* Cambridge, Mass.: Harvard University Press.

Wertsch, J. V. (1985). *Culture, communication, and cognition: Vygotskian perspectives.* Cambridge, Mass.: Cambridge University Press.

3

Theoretical Models of Everyday Problem Solving in Adulthood

Mary A. Luszcz

Wood (1983) states, "Post-adolescent development differs from previous development in that it deals with ability to solve ill-structured as opposed to well-structured problems" (p. 261). This claim implies an interconnection between theoretical models of practical problem solving and the issue of whether further cognitive development occurs beyond that postulated to characterize Piaget's stage of formal operations. In the course of arguing that the essential difference between formal and postformal thinking is that the former is analytical and the latter is synthetic, Kramer (1983) unifies the various approaches to postformal operational thought by postulating a set of features they share. These features concern the way knowledge is structured: knowing becomes more relativistic, contradictions are acknowledged and accepted as an integral part of knowing, and knowing becomes more integrative, extending across domains or disciplines that may have discrepant, but equally valid, perceptions of the nature of truth. Analogously, everyday problem solving subsumes these principles. It will be argued that these insights guide adults' solving "real-life" or "wicked" (Churchman's [1971] term) problems.

Before this conclusion is reached, some background will be outlined to establish a schema for comprehending the proposal. The schema must contain slots pertaining to the definition of a problem; the role of context; and parameters of traditional problem solving situations. Then the nexus between everyday problem solving and broader theories of high-level cognitive processes will be examined.

Theoretical models of everyday problem solving are in an early stage of ontogeny. Rather than explicit theories or models, a host of approximations to theories is a more apt description of the collection of ideas and conceptual issues that pertain to the topic, but clarity with respect to defining features is lacking (Cavanaugh et al. 1985). Thus it is important to acknowledge at the outset that this attempt to sketch what is known about such models is likely to contain some misperceptions, broad leaps, and overgeneralizations that stretch the notions introduced by others beyond their intended boundaries. The problem of characterizing theoretical models of everyday problem solving in adulthood is itself ill-structured; therefore "solutions" are better thought of as approximations to the goal of describing such theories. Before discussing theories of problem solving, the nature of problems will be treated briefly.

CLASSIFYING PROBLEMS TO BE SOLVED

Problems can be conceived as falling along a continuum of structuredness, from well-structured to ill-structured. The structuredness of a problem has been defined in terms of the presence or absence of certain parameters of decision theory (Wood 1983). By considering the extent to which a problem provides values for each parameter, it is possible to differentiate among well-structured and ill-structured problems, as well as to propose alternative paths to their solution. Well-structured problems entail relatively specific values for each of these parameters, while for ill-structured problems the value of one or more of the parameters is not known.

Well-structured problems might be thought of as "puzzles" (Kitchener 1983; Neisser 1976) with a single correct answer, arrived at through application of explicit rules comprising part of a production system (Simon 1978, 1979) within a problem space conceived of as a necessarily closed system (Newell & Simon 1972). Ill-structured problems are more amorphous dilemmas, open to multiple solutions; any particular solution is in large part dependent on the breadth of the problem space.

Simon (1978) offers a list of features that distinguish between well-structured and ill-structured problems. The latter differ from the former in that the criterion for establishing goal attainment is more complex and less definite; instructions alone provide incomplete information for problem solution; the boundaries of what might be considered relevant information are vague; and movement from step to step in the solution process is not readily predictable.

One could also speculate that the type of knowledge required for solution of well-structured problems differs from that invoked to solve ill-structured problems. Ohlsson (1983) suggests that even in semantically rich problem solving domains, the knowledge tapped is largely technical, a point also made by Simon (1981). That is, it is externalized and codified, including a notation system that is acquired through an explicit learning experience. Technical knowledge may be contrasted with "natural" knowledge, which lacks a notation system and usually is acquired incidentally. This distinction has implications for solving real-life or everyday problems, in that such problems are more likely to draw on natural knowledge domains for their solution. If natural knowledge is itself "ill-structured," then applying it to ill-structured problems suggests a qualitatively different solution process than that used in solving mathematical or formal operational problems.

Implicit in this discussion is some correspondence between ill-structured and everyday problems. While it is the case that some everyday problems are well-structured (e.g, how to orchestrate the timing in meal preparation or coordinating schedules of individual family members), real life increasingly confronts us with more open-ended problems. Well-structured and ill-structured everyday problems share the feature of entailing a multitude of solution paths, but for the latter the destination is often unclear or one of several alternative end points. It is such labyrinthine problems that seem to have occupied the thinking of writers on everyday problem solving and to which conceptualizations of adult thinking speak.

The Role of Context

The concern with everyday problem solving has arisen in conjunction with an increasing concern with the role of contextual factors in cognitive activities (Rogoff & Lave 1984). The thrust of this concern is an appreciation of the fact that thinking is constrained by the context in which it occurs. The impact of context on everyday problem solving is pervasive, and is likely to increase with an individual's acknowledgment of the relativity, arbitrariness, and contradictions inherent in any problem and its solution.

The context of the problem is part of its definition and, necessarily, part of its solution (cf. Labouvie-Vief 1982; Simon 1979; Sinnott 1984a; Wood 1983). Part of the context of problem definition is the nature of the underlying inquiring system or epistemology of problem solving. Churchman (1971) delineates five inquiring systems aligned to major philosophical views in an attempt to place qualitatively different kinds of problems into suitable contexts. The inquiring systems are the Leibnizian, the Lockean, the Kantian, the dialectical or Hegelian, and the Singerian/Churchmanian. The first two relate to problems at the well-structured end of the continuum, while the latter three focus on increasingly ill-structured problems.

The Leibnizian inquiring system is the "archetype of formal, symbolic systems" (Motroff & Sagasti 1973, p. 120). It is suited to well-structured problems where solutions can be generated deductively, according to explicit transformational rules. The Lockean inquiring system applies to problems that can be solved empirically through an inductive process of experimentation and elaboration of "facts." Kantian inquiring systems are synthetic, multimodal systems wherein representations of problems can be constructed in at least two alternative ways. The major dilemma for the problem solver is to consider which conceptualization is optimal, or best represents the context in which the problem is to be solved. These systems are used for moderately ill-structured problems (Churchman 1971). A dialectical or Hegelian inquiring system is suited to problems for which it is possible to derive completely antithetical representations. The conflicting representations arise from differing underlying assumptions that the same data may be used equally well to support. They can be used effectively with problems of low to moderate structure. If conflict results in some synthesis, the problem may become better-structured and amenable to one of the earlier inquiring systems. The final inquiring system is the Singerian/Churchmanian, which has the function of transforming "wicked" problems into structured ones and vice versa. It may be considered a metalevel inquiring system that can be used to study the other inquiring systems or to address ethical principles and the teleological significance of problem situations.

These inquiring systems highlight the range of phenomena that "problem" entails. Indeed, different theories may be required to account for solving problems occupying different conceptual spaces. Newell and Simon's (1972) seminal model of problem solving seems to be concerned with Leibnizian and Lockean inquiring systems, while those of Arlin (1984), Basseches (1984a, b) Kramer (in press a), Labouvie-Vief (1982), and Sinnott (1984a) are more applicable to Kantian and Hegelian inquiring systems. Analyses of contributions to this volume may set the groundwork for Churchmanian inquiries. The next portion of this chapter will consider the relation of these models to everyday problem solving.

Information-Processing Models Of Problem Solving

Newell and Simon's (1972) model is decidedly circumscribed and unabashedly linked to three specific problem solving tasks: chess, symbolic logic, and algebraic puzzles, which could be considered "everyday" only by chess masters, logicians, and mathematicians. Their theory was put forth as a general one, but the boundaries of its applicability have yet to be fully explored.

In 1973 Simon

proposed that in general , the processes used to solve ill-structured problems are the same as those used to solve well-structured problems. In working on ill-structured problems, however, only a small part of the potentially relevant information stored in long-term memory and external reference sources plays an active role in the solution processes at any given moment in time. (Simon 1978, p. 287)

Thus it is purported that the notion of problem space and use of production systems would in principle apply similarly to ill-structured and well-structured problems. One exception might be in the more fluid character of the problem space, which will undergo "gradual and steady alteration" in the course of everyday problem solving.

While it seems reasonable to expect that across subjects and tasks, problem solvers will rely on long-term memory and a set of operators within a problem space to logically solve everyday problems, the solution of the latter, unlike solution of the abstract puzzles traditionally studied by Simon and his colleagues, demands consideration of allied domains that may lie outside the immediate problem space. A major difficulty in extending Simon's theory to everyday problem solving rests on the assertions about the problem space: that it is closed, that the set of operators within it is small and finite, and that it contains the correct solution, which merely must be distinguished from all the other possibilities. In solving everyday problems, the problem space is manifestly open to knowledge states pertaining to, for instance, social, emotional, moral, and interpersonal corollaries of the problem and its solution. The permeability of the problem space to these elements weakens considerably the feasibility of explicitly specifying it. Introduction of these ancillary considerations necessarily multiplies the number of operators and states of knowledge they might produce.

A second distinguishing feature relates to the relatively greater contribution of long-term memory to the search through the problem space while solving ill-structured as compared with well-structured problems (Simon 1981). Efficient movement through long-term memory will enable the problem solver to detect relevant information and consider successive knowledge states until the problem is solved (Newell & Simon 1972). Bowden (1985) emphasized that time constraints on this search may limit successful solutions. Rabbitt (1982) suggests that with age one becomes not only slower and less flexible in active control of search, but also less efficient in maintaining comprehensive tallies of sequences of responses. Thus both authors mark ways in which everyday problem solving is vulnerable to changes accompanying aging, while at the same time denying them status as immutable barriers to problem solving.

Cavanaugh et al. (1985) question Newell and Simon's (1972) emphasis on how subjects decide which part of the knowledge content and processes to introduce into the problem space prior to solving a problem. Within highly specifiable task domains dealing with well-structured problems, the selection of elements is constrained, finite, and well-defined. In solving everyday problems, criteria for inclusion of information in a problem space would be much more complex, as potential candidates for inclusion are numerous, and those selected will color the nature of the final solution.

Perhaps most problematic is the notion of a singular solution. While ultimately one solution must be enacted (Labouvie-Vief 1985), its correctness may be difficult, if not impossible, to assess objectively.

Nonetheless, at a conceptual level Newell and Simon's (1972) model offers a host of well-defined constructs and processes within which to generate theories dealing with everyday problems. In order for the Newell and Simon model to apply directly to everyday problem solving, it would be necessary to expand notions concerning the definition of the problem space, identification of operators within production systems, and specification of criteria for successful solutions.

Another benefit derivable from the Newell and Simon approach is careful consideration of methodologies that might be used to study everyday problem solving. Models of cognitive processes require data of high density (Simon 1979); through the use of informationally dense verbal protocols generated while people think aloud about a task, research on everyday problem solving would no doubt be enhanced (see also Ericsson & Simon 1984; Giambra & Arenberg 1980).

Another concept within mainstream cognitive psychology that offers insight into the nature of everyday problem solving is that of schemata (Braune & Foshay 1983). Schemata use encapsulates the tendency to bring to new problems old solutions based on past experience. Over time these experiences cumulate to provide useful heuristics whereby strategies for problem solving are invoked. Schemata may facilitate the recognition of information that provides a basis for seemingly intuitive solutions (Simon 1981). As yet a model specifically elaborating the role of schemata in everyday problem solving has not been forthcoming. The incomplete account of practical problem solving provided by information processing notions may profitably be complemented by theoretical statements concerning the nature of changes in cognitive functioning that occur in adulthood.

Contextual/Dialectical Models of Problem Solving

Klaus Riegel's (1973, 1979) discussion of dialectic operations marked a watershed in reconceptualizations of the nature of thought in adulthood (Basseches 1984a; Kramer 1983). Variations on the theme of the possible emergence of structures falling under the rubric of "postformal" operations owe much to his early writings. Dialectic operations concretized the utility of acknowledging contradiction as an inherent quality of thinking activities that go well beyond the domain of "cold cognition" (Zajonc 1980), and are subsumed as part of a holistic approach to everyday problem solving that incorporates social psychological and affective dimensions.

Considerable debate surrounds the issue (which exceeds the scope of this chapter) of whether further structural change occurs beyond that of formal operations (see Kramer 1983; Labouvie-Vief 1980). Emerging models of everyday problem solving seem to tacitly assume that further cognitive change occurs in adulthood, and thereby seek to reduce the gap between extant knowledge of adult cognitive functioning and everyday problem solving (Cavanaugh et al. 1985). They have evolved inductively as a by-product of trying to come to terms with data that conflict with expectations based on decline models of adult cognitive change. For example, Charness (1982) reports the paradoxical findings of age-related declining memory accompanied by increased problem solving efficiency in semantically rich domains. Accordingly, the present discussion will begin with a performance model and progress to those with a decidedly more dialectical flavor.

Denney (1984) has proposed a performance model of cognitive development across the life span to account for observed differences in the ability of adults to solve practical, as opposed to traditional, problems. The crux of Denney's model is a distinction made between an individual's unexercised potential and his or her optimally exercised potential. "Unexercised potential" refers to the performance level anticipated in the absence of exercise or training, while "optimally exercised potential" refers to a higher level resulting from regular use or practice of a particular ability. Both are inextricably linked to one's biological potential, thereby allowing individual differences and declines seen late in adulthood to be interpreted as reflections of a biologically constrained diminution of one's optimally exercised potential.

This model would make two predictions regarding problem solving: first, that greater facility would be expected in solving problems akin to those with which one has become familiar through exercise or training; second, that providing opportunities for such exercise would enhance performance levels. Studies from Denney's lab (Denney & Palmer 1981; Denney et al. 1982), as well as from that of Charness (1981, 1982), provide empirical support for such predictions. Denney's model implicitly suggests that experiential factors, especially practice, are crucial in determining problem solving across domains. Yet in the absence of a plausible model of *how* practice facilitates problem solving, the utility of Denney's essentially descriptive model is circumscribed. Most of the interpretations in practice terms could be recast using the notion of schemata. Wider issues must be dealt with that pertain to the nature of experiential factors and the processes whereby they are incorporated into the cognitive repertoire of maturing adults. Kramer (in press a, b) offers a way out of this dilemma.

Kramer (in press a) proposed a model of social-cognitive development that is the union of concepts derived from the vast literature on further cognitive development in adulthood. Her underlying claim is that social cognition is a form of real-life problem solving. Here she concurs with Reese and Rodeheaver (1985), who contend that through solving problems and making decisions, adults link themselves cognitively to their environment. To meet social cognitive environmental demands, adults use cognition as a means to an end, not as an end in itself. The elusive end might be resolution of real-life problems, but the means become prominent as adults adapt dynamically to the vagaries of everyday living.

A precursor of this view is that of Schaie (1977–78). He argues that adulthood brings with it demands for which the cognitive structures and functions acquired in childhood through early adulthood may be irrelevant or inadequate. His approach suggests qualitative changes in cognitive structures associated with environmental pressures brought on by major transitions in adulthood. While his model deals mainly with an increasing selectivity in application of cognitive effort to deal with the demands of adulthood, Schaie also purports that these changes are associated with increased ability to solve complex problems that retain meaning and purpose for the individual. His model foreshadows those of Kramer, Sinnott, and Labouvie-Vief in highlighting the interpersonal, social nature of cognition in adulthood, where intelligence becomes at once more practical and more abstract.

Kramer (in press b) argues for an adult-centered model of cognitive development that not only takes into account the context in which cognitive activities occur but also suggests a cyclical expansion and contraction of evolving knowledge systems. She does not see relativistic and dialectical thinking as exclusively adult activities. She maintains and illustrates that they are emergent in children's negotiations within social cognitive domains.

Kramer distinguishes between relativistic reasoning, which "involves an awareness that all things are in a state of flux" and dialectical reasoning. The latter also incorporates the notion of continual change, but has the added dimension of viewing these changes as part of an evolutionary process in which contradictions within a system can be resolved to achieve new systems of increasingly adaptive knowledge. The ultimate system may be an ideal that is rarely attained. In it, as the child progresses cognitively and comes to a fuller understanding of self, others, and societal institutions, the nonabsolute nature of these entities is appreciated. By tying these developments to what is known of adult social cognition, an integrated life-span perspective can be attained (Kramer in press a).

Kramer's conceptualization has ramifications for theory. This development in the area of problem solving can be viewed from two vantage points. First, it highlights the contextual embeddedness of cognitive activities by focusing on their use in social domains, beginning during childhood and continuing thereafter. Second, it suggests that rudimentary forms of relativistic and dialectic reasoning are applied in social domains, offering a point of continuity between thought processes required for everyday problem solving in childhood, adolescence, and adulthood. An isomorphism between early and later forms of relativistic and dialectic reasoning remains to be established.

The work of Sinnott (1984a) has been proceeding within a framework that sees relativistic operations as comprising a further stage of postformal cognitive development. The contrast between Sinnott's and Kramer's approaches illustrates the dynamic dialectical nature of efforts to solve the problem of how cognitive changes impact on everyday problem solving in adulthood. Ultimately a life-span perspective is desirable. By "jumping out" of a strictly postformal operational view, Kramer offers a means to this end via extensions from social cognition. Sinnott's tactic is a synthetic approach invoking notions stemming from Einsteinian physics and a explicit statement of a hierarchically superordinate category of relativistic cognitive operations. Sinnott sets out to extend notions of Piaget (1972) and Riegel (1979) to describe further cognitive development that she says "*may* be unique to adults" (p. 298). As these demands are allegedly the stuff of adults' everyday problem solving (Kramer in press a), her position is especially relevant to the present discussion.

Sinnott questions whether the knowledge that allows us to understand and deal with physical relations is a sufficient basis for understanding and dealing with interpersonal relations that adults report to be an important domain of intellectual endeavor (Scheidt & Schaie 1978; Kramer & Dittman-Kohli 1984; Sinnott 1984b). These two relations differ in terms of necessary subjectivity, wherein the object of knowledge cannot be separated from the individual's subjective interpretation of that knowledge. Interpersonal relations are especially prone to being affected by change resulting from being understood or interpreted in different ways by the participants in them. Sinnott goes on to suggest that knowledge of interpersonal relations must include operations for understanding necessary subjectivity and the inseparability of subject and object. Such operations she terms "relativistic."

Relativistic operations (see Table 3.1) offer a system that subsumes formal operations and permits selection from among internally consist-

Table 3.1
Examples of Relativistic Operations

1. Metatheory shift	changing a priori considerations from one set to a conflicting set
2. Problem definition	focusing on defining the problem
3. Process/product shift	deciding to solve for a dynamic or for a particular content solution
4. Parameter setting	defining the limits of the problem factors
5. Pragmatism	evaluating abstract and practical solutions separately for usefulness, difficulty
6. Multiple solutions	being aware that a multi-causal problem most likely has several correct solutions
7. Multiple causality	utilizing multifactorial explanations and probabilistic predictions
8. Paradox	being aware that a problem can be read in two conflicting ways

Source: Cavanaugh et al. 1985, p. 154.

ent but logically contradictory formal systems. They evolve in response to demands placed on adults to deal effectively with a reality that may present numerous logical scenarios for action. In solving everyday interpersonal problems, the use of relativistic operations to appreciate the necessary subjectivity in them would be highly adaptive.

Sinnott (1982) has developed a set of eight criteria for determining the presence of relativistic operations in the thinking of adults. Relativistic operations can be invoked at multiple points and levels in problem solving activities. They represent, to date, the best-articulated set of operations applicable in real life as well as in abstract problem solving.

Sinnott (1982) found strong evidence for the use of relativistic operations in the solution of problems by adults aged from 26 to 89 years, although their use varied according to the nature of the problem. They were most prevalent in attempts to solve problems with a prominent interpersonal component. Their greatest utility was in allowing one to consciously reconceptualize a problem during the solution process so that a new set of interpretive rules could assist in its resolution.

Sinnott describes a dynamic problem solving process that takes account of the necessity for reconceptualization as demanded by considerations of how the problem is defined, what pragmatic goals warrant various solutions, what elements contribute to the content of the problem, and so on. The particular relativistic operations utilized depend not only on the problem itself but also on an individual's style (Sinnott 1983, 1984a).

Evidence of relativistic operations elucidates the process of solving everyday problems, especially those in an interpersonal domain. Problem solving is seen as a dynamic cycle of conceptualization and reconceptualization in the context of one's necessary subjectivity in relation to the nominal problem. Relativistic operations suggest means whereby people define a problem space and elaborate a production system, containing relativistic operations as operators, for problem solution. Thus Sinnott's model complements the information-processing model of Newell and Simon (1972), especially at the point of defining the problem space and determining solutions. Fundamentally Sinnott's model merges problem, solver, and solution. She shows not only that most everyday problem solving ventures extend beyond the bounds of cold cognition, encompassing the pragmatics of life in its broadest sense, but also how people use relativistic operations to solve everyday problems.

Sinnott's model will need further verification because its empirical edifice is not vast. Nonetheless, converging evidence, such as Labouvie-Vief (1985), suggests that in solving problems, the interpretation given to the problem not only may diverge from that formally intended by the researcher but also may reflect a meshing of personal and social goals with those necessitated by a logical solution to an objective problem. Relativistic operations such as a metatheory shift, parameter setting, and pragmatism could underlie such reinterpretations. Labouvie-Vief (1982) would postulate that reconceptualizations reflect an "autonomous" logic, which emerges in adulthood at some unspecified point beyond mastery of formal operational thinking.

Labouvie-Vief's (1980, 1982) account of the dynamics of adult intellectual activity underscores the role of affect and a striving for self-regulation as central motivators of cognitive change. Intellectual development is seen to take place in an expanding social context that fosters an increasing awareness that autonomous self-regulation is the raison d'être of adult life.

Logic moves through three levels: intrasystemic, intersystemic, and autonomous. At the intrasystemic level one would operate as though knowledge or truth could be distinguished from nontruths, and the latter discounted or rejected. An allegedly coherent system of universal knowledge lacks functional self-reference. Labouvie-Vief states, "The self constructs but does not fully realize its constructions emanate from it" (1982, p. 182). In Sinnott's terms, necessary subjectivity is not realized as an element of thought. From Kramer's viewpoint, inherent contradictions cannot be assimilated. As one moves to intersystemic logic, logic becomes relativized and is seen as constrained by the system or domain used to construct it. The self becomes aware that although truth or knowledge is relative, actions are not, and only one course can be followed. In essence, the self or self-reference becomes more explicit and, in the pursuit of one's own truth, becomes aligned to commitments and pragmatic constraints that begin to regulate thinking.

With this emergence of the self, one embarks on an autonomous level of logic: "Autonomy is characterized by a shift in focus from the logic of formal systems to the logic of self-regulating systems" (Labouvie-Vief 1982, p. 183). Self-regulating systems encompass not only the self but also the self in relation to others; thus necessary subjectivity is full blown. Thinking and action are constrained by their relationship to each other; and pragmatic, social, ethical, and logical considerations define their relationship. Truth is fully contextualized as an integral part of one's overall life structure.

Labouvie-Vief's conceptualization is admittedly nonspecific, but it has broad implications for interpretations of many cognitive dimensions in later adulthood. In relation to problem solving, it would imply a shift from accepting and executing a task solely on the basis of an agenda set by an experimenter to one of constructing one's own agenda for solution. While an intrasystemic logic might predispose one to accept a problem at face value and solve it logically, autonomous logic would evoke consideration of the problem in the context of one's personal and social goals, thus engendering a multiplicity of solutions across individuals. Self-reference becomes a starting point rather than an afterthought in problem solving.

SUMMARY AND CONCLUSIONS

The search for a theoretical model of everyday problem solving in adulthood began with a consideration of a distinction between well-structured and ill-structured problems. Everyday problem solving as discussed in the literature routinely deals with the latter. Approaches to problem solving in these situations appears to be highly contextually constrained. Rather than being an exclusively or even predominantly logical exercise, everyday problem solving becomes enmeshed in the subjective social and affective world of adult adaptation. As adults attempt to solve everyday problems, they are confronted by the relative nature of truth, contradictions within and between knowledge systems, and a need to integrate across domains to arrive at workable, if not "correct," solutions. Dialectical inquiring systems offer a framework within which to explore this process.

Leibnizian and Lockean systems, such as that exemplified by Newell and Simon, are at present insufficient to account for the complex task faced by adults negotiating real-life problems under less than ideal conditions. The views of Kramer, Sinnott, and Labouvie-Vief share a contrasting orientation focusing on the individual in relation to self and to others. The social context of problem solving alters and is altered by cognitive structures at the disposal of mature adults. Thus a dialectic is established wherein problem solving entails emotions and pragmatic, as well as logical, dimensions. As the problem space expands to incorporate these features, the operations used to solve problems must diversify and become increasingly sophisticated.

Sinnott's model is most explicit in proposing the nature of relativistic operations that orchestrate adult solving of everyday problems. Nonetheless, Kramer and Labouvie-Vief implicitly address similar issues, also acknowledging the relativistic nature of knowing and the crucial role of self-reference in regulating adult social cognition. Everyday problem solvers evince an awareness of the inherent contradictions of solutions serving various spheres (Sinnott 1982). Their task is to work through these contradictions from a perspective of necessary subjectivity, drawing on an autonomous logic in which self-regulatory goals guide solutions. The task clearly exceeds the bounds of cold cognition, as pragmatics and commitments intrude on logical actions. The contradictions separating Leibnizian or Lockean inquiring systems from Kantian or dialectical ones are not so much at the level of exploitable cognitive processes as at the interface between implementation of these processes and subjective awareness of their insufficiency as mechanisms for adaptation.

Theoretical models of everyday problem solving are in their formative stages of development. One would have to agree with Chi, Glaser, and Rees's (1981) suspicion that there may not exist a general problem solving process but, rather, a plethora of strategies whose use depends on the nature of the problem as well as on characteristics of the problem solver. Research and theorizing on everyday problem solving in adulthood, then, are on the right track: Qualities of problems and people feature prominently in these early efforts.

Existing conceptualizations fall short of adequately meeting the formal criteria for status as theories, and they do not enjoy vast empirical support. This situation is indeed fortuitous, in that the opportunity exists to continue the inductive approach, bootstrapping from theories of postformal operations, with which theory building in this domain has begun. Thus it may be possible to avoid a situation in which theory obstructs research progress (Greenwald et al. 1986) and original work is stifled (Rabbitt 1982).

REFERENCES

Arlin, P. K. (1984). Adolescent and adult thought: A structural interpretation. In M. L. Commons, F. A. Richards, & C. Armon (Eds.), *Beyond formal operations: Late adolescent and adult cognitive development* (pp. 258–271). New York: Praeger.

Basseches, M. A. (1984a). Dialectical thinking as a metasystematic form of cognitive organization. In M. L. Commons, F. A. Richards, & C. Armon (Eds.), *Beyond formal operations: Late adolescent and adult cognitive development* (pp. 216–238). New York: Praeger.

Basseches, M. (1984b). *Dialectical thinking and adult development.* Norwood, N.J.: Ablex.

Bowden, E. M. (1985). Accessing relevant information during problem solving: Time constraints on search in the problem space. *Memory and Cognition, 13,* 280–286.

Braune, R., & Foshay, W. R. (1983). Towards a practical model of cognitive/ information processing task analysis and schema acquisition for complex problem-solving situations. *Instructional Science, 12,* 121–145.

Cavanaugh, J. C., Kramer, D., Sinnott, J. D., Camp, C. J., & Markley, R. P. (1985). On missing links and such: Interfaces between cognitive research and everyday problem-solving. *Human Development, 28,* 146–168.

Charness, N. (1981). Aging and skilled problem-solving. *Journal of Experimental Psychology: General, 110,* 21–38.

Charness, N. (1982). Problem solving and aging: Evidence from semantically rich domains. *Canadian Journal on Aging, 1,* 21–28.

Chi, M. T. H., Glaser, R., & Rees, E. (1981). *Expertise in problem solving* (Technical Report no. 5). Pittsburgh: University of Pittsburgh; Learning Research and Development Center.

Churchman, C. S. (1971). *The design of inquiring systems: Basic concepts of systems and organizations.* New York: Basic Books.

Denney, N. W. (1984). A model of cognitive development across the life span. *Developmental Review, 4,* 171–191.

Denney, N. W., & Palmer, A. M. (1981). Adult age differences on traditional and practical problem-solving measures. *Journal of Gerontology, 36,* 323–328.

Denney, N. W., Pearce, K. A., & Palmer, A. M. (1982). A developmental study of adults' performance on traditional and practical problem-solving tasks. *Experimental Aging Research, 8,* 115–118.

Ericsson, K. A., & Simon, H. A. (1984). *Protocol analysis: Verbal reports as data.* Cambridge, Mass.: MIT Press.

Giambra, L., & Arenberg, D. (1980). Problem solving, concept learning, and aging. In L. W. Poon (Ed.), *Aging in the 1980's: Psychological issues* (pp. 253–259). Washington, D.C.: American Psychological Association.

Greenwald, A. G., Pratkanis, A. R., Leippe, M. R., & Baumgardner, M. H. (1986). Under what conditions does theory obstruct research progress? *Psychological Review, 93,* 216–229.

Kitchener, K. S. (1983). Cognition, metacognition, and epistemic cognition: A three-level model of cognitive processing. *Human Development, 26,* 222–232.

Kramer, D. A. (1983). Post formal operations? A need for further conceptualization. *Human Development, 26,* 91–105.

Kramer, D. A. (in press a). A life-span view of social cognition. *Human Development.*

Kramer, D. A. (in press b). Social cognition in adulthood: Overview of an emerging perspective. *Human Development.*

Kramer, D. A., & Dittman-Kohli, F. (1984, November). A taxonomy of tasks in cognitive aging: An action-in-context approach. Paper presented at the meeting of the Gerontological Society, San Antonio, Texas.

Labouvie-Vief, G. (1980). Beyond formal operations: Uses and limits of pure logic in life-span development. *Human Development, 23,* 227–263.

Labouvie-Vief, G. (1982). Dynamics of development and mature autonomy: A theoretical prologue. *Human Development, 25,* 161–191.

Labouvie-Vief, G. (1985). Intelligence and cognition. In J. E. Birren & K. W. Schaie (Eds.), *Handbook of the psychology of aging* (2nd ed., pp. 500–530). New York: Van Nostrand Reinhold.

Mitroff, I. I., & Sagasti, F. (1973). Epistemology as general systems theory: An approach to the design of complex decision-making experiments. *Philosophical and Social Sciences, 3,* 117–134.

Neisser, U. (1976). General, academic, and artificial intelligence. In L. B. Resnick (Ed.), *The nature of intelligence.* Hillsdale, N.J.: Erlbaum.

Newell, A., & Simon, H. A. (1972). *Human problem-solving.* Englewood Cliffs, N.J.: Prentice-Hall.

Ohlsson, S. (1983). On natural and technical knowledge domains. *Scandinavian Journal of Psychology, 24,* 89–91.

Piaget, J. (1972). *The principles of genetic epistemology.* New York: Basic Books.

Rabbitt, P. M. A. (1982). How do old people know what to do next? In F. I. M. Craik & S. Trehub (Eds.), *Aging and cognitive processes* (pp. 79–98). New York: Plenum.

Reese, H. W., & Rodeheaver, D. (1985). Problem solving and complex decision making. In J. E. Birren & K. W. Schaie (Eds.), *Handbook of the psychology of aging* (2nd ed., pp. 474–499). New York: Van Nostrand Reinhold.

Riegel, K. F. (1973). Dialectic operations: The final period of cognitive development. *Human Development, 16,* 346–370.

Riegel, K. F. (1979). *Foundations of dialectical psychology.* New York: Academic Press.

Rogoff, B., & Lave, J. (Eds.). (1984). *Everyday cognition: Its development in social context.* Cambridge, Mass.: Harvard University Press.

Schaie, K. W. (1977–78). Toward a stage theory of adult cognitive development. *Journal of Aging and Human Development, 8,* 129–138.

Scheidt, R., & Schaie, K. W. (1978). A taxonomy of situations for an elderly population: Generating situational criteria. *Journal of Gerontology, 33,* 848–857.

Simon, H. A. (1973). The structure of ill-structured problems. *Artificial Intelligence, 4,* 181–202.

Simon, H. A. (1978). Information-processing theory of human problem solving. In W. K. Estes (Ed.), *Handbook of learning and cognitive processes* (Vol. 5). Hillsdale, N.J.: Erlbaum.

Simon, H. A. (1979). Information processing models of cognition. In M. R. Rosenzweig & L. W. Porter (Eds.), *Annual Review of Psychology, 30*, 363–396.

Simon, H. A. (1981). *The sciences of the artificial* (2nd ed.). Cambridge, Mass.: MIT Press.

Sinnott, J. D. (1982, August). Age-related adult strategies for solving combinatorial Piagetian problems. Paper presented at American Psychological Association meeting, Washington, D.C.

Sinnott, J. D. (1983, November). Examining individuals' strategies on everyday problems using a thinking out loud approach. Paper presented at the Annual Meeting of the Gerontological Society of America, San Francisco.

Sinnott, J. D. (1984a). Postformal reasoning: The relativistic stage. In M. L. Commons, F. A. Richards, & C. Armon (eds.), *Beyond formal operations: Late adolescent and adult cognitive development* (pp. 298–325). New York: Praeger.

Sinnott, J. D. (1984b). How adults define "intelligence in adulthood." Unpublished manuscript. Baltimore: Towson State University Psychology Department.

Wood, P. K. (1983). Inquiring systems and problem structure: Implications for cognitive development. *Human Development, 26*, 249–265.

Zajonc, R. B. (1980). Feeling and thinking: Preferences need no inferences. *American Psychologist, 35*, 151–175.

4

An Overview—If Not a Taxonomy—of "Everyday Problems" Used in Research

Jan D. Sinnott
Jennifer Cook

The purpose of this chapter is to offer the reader a brief review of the kinds of tasks that have been used in the past in cognitive naturalistic problem solving studies. The reader may then make a more informed judgment about whether to create new materials and tests. The tasks are summarized in Table 4.1.

Several decisions have an impact on the contents of the table or are reflected in its organization. These include the definition of a "problem," the definition of "everyday" or "naturalistic," and the extent of prior work to be reviewed. For this chapter a problem is defined as "any set of conditions that the problem solver perceives as needing resolution and that must be resolved in order to get to a goal state." This is a very broad definition that could include items ranging from disturbing emotional states to math problems. The element of perception is important, but the respondent's perception of an unresolved state can only be assumed in this review.

The definition of "everyday" or "naturalistic" must of necessity be a somewhat arbitrary one. It is easier to say what everyday is *not* than to describe what it *is*. Abstract math problems and abstract symbolically expressed syllogisms were not considered appropriate, even though they often dealt with trains or kitchen sinks . . . common objects. The basic principle with which discriminations were made seemed to be "Is this ever likely to happen to anyone, and if it did, would they care?" The problems in the table therefore represent situations that range from "possible, but not too likely" to "happening all the time," and from

The assistance of Lena Phillips is gratefully acknowledged.

Table 4.1
Types of Somewhat Naturalistic Problems Used in Problem Solving Cognitive Research

I. Classification and Comparisons

AUTHOR	TASK	RESULTS
Bruner & Potter (1964)	Ss asked to identify an object as it is being focused	Ss misidentified objects long after naive Ss (those who started with less defocusing) were able to readily identify the object in question.
Cantor & Mischel (1979)	can a person be both a fisherman and a father?	Role concepts were linked by "family resemblance" structures more than object concepts.
Coltheart & Evans (1981)	attributes of birds	This can depend on the context imposed by the set of items being evaluated.
Dolen & Bearison (1982)	solutions to interpersonal problems	Levels of social interaction were a significant predictor of cognitive decline.
Higgins, Rholes & Jones (1977)	morality of passing notes in class	It was viewed as helpful by one person and dishonest by another.
Kahneman & Tversky (1973)	evaluation and prediction based on description of freshman	Ss picked the most representative scores for both evaluation & prediction.
Lingle, Altom & Medin (1984)	are human beings a social or natural object category?	Classification depends on focus on behavior or relationship to other living things.
	persons classified	Categories served as attributes for classifying persons as athletes.
	describe the term "girl"	One could identify abstract attributes such as human, female, or perceptual features such as height, weight, and other physical characteristics.

Table 4.1 (continued)

AUTHOR	TASK	RESULTS
	concept of "fat"	The distinction between representational and identification attributes played an important role in social categories.
	inferences about truck drivers	The attributes inferred from a category membership were not always the attributes used to decide category membership in the first place.
	occupations classified	Worker gender might become salient as the basis for classification. Dimensions used to compare objects are likely to be specific to a particular context or set of stimuli.
	pet classification	Object categories were organized with different levels of abstraction.
	behaviors interpreted as friendly or unfriendly	Two people familiar with the same population had different impressions as to who is friendly and who is unfriendly, depending on context.
Luchins (1942)	water jar problem	One will follow same procedure and won't look at the problem on its own merits if one has done a similar problem earlier.
McCloskey & Glucksberg (1978)	are cows better examples of the concept "mammal" than are whales?	No single set of attributes could be used to determine category membership; members of a category vary in the degree to which they are typical members of that category.
McGuire, McGuire & Winton (1979)	children's self-descriptions	Children who were more likely to include gender in their self-description came from families in which their gender was in the minority.
McGuire & Padauer-Singer (1976)	children's self-descriptions	Children were more likely to mention personal characteristics if they had minority status relative to other members of their group.

42

Medin, Altom, Edelson & Freko (1982)	medical diagnosis	Ss tended to choose cases that maintained correlation between symptom values over cases that had more characteristic symptoms but did not maintain the correlation.
Rothbart, Fulero, Jenson, Howard & Birrell (1978)	impressions of New Zealanders	Interactions with one New Zealander were influential.
Rumelhart (1984)	looking for a telephone number	Search was not random; it was guided by schemata, find phone book, region of book, interpret symbols on page.
Spivack, Standen, Bryson & Garrett (received 1986)	does interpersonal problem solving ability decrease with age?	Elderly exhibited poorer ability, except in the area of consequential thinking.
Tversky (1977)	compare oneself with various stereotypes	If stereotypes weren't known, the self served as a reference point; stereotypes that were known were at least as prominent as reference points as was the self.
Tversky & Gati (1978)	Ss compare large and small countries	For some categories the general assumptions of a dimensional similarity model are not well supported.
Tversky & Kahneman (1973)	classification as a mammal	People based classification judgments on similarity to readily available exemplars.
Von Baeyer, Sherk & Zanna (1981)	how people categorize others	The way people categorize others influenced both the behavior they unconsciously elicited from the person as well as how they themselves behaved toward the person.
Wallsten & Budescu (1981)	categorizing people according to scores on subsections of the MMPI	Clinicians based their classifications on configurations of scores on the various subscales. Graduate students favored a simple additive rule.

II. Problem Solving (syllogisms and logic)

Arenberg (1982)	concept problems involving "poisoned foods"	Age differences were found.

Table 4.1 (continued)

AUTHOR	TASK	RESULTS
Ceraso & Provitera (1971)	invalid syllogisms	Ss performed more accurately on valid syllogisms than on invalid syllogisms; emotion was a factor.
Cheng & Holyoak (1985)	inferences about mailing letters, diagnoses	Subjects used pragmatic reasoning schemes.
Henle (1962)	logic questions concerning importance of talking about problems	Some Ss tried to evaluate the truth of the conclusion rather than the logical form of the argument.
Revlin, Leirer, Yopp & Yopp (1980)	questionnaire on logic and reasoning concerning the Russians; syllogisms involved politics	Most college students answered deductive reasoning problems successfully, especially if the problem involved emotionally laden material.
Revlis (1975)	syllogisms involving political parties; syllogisms--concrete and abstract	Ss' beliefs influenced the way in which they interpreted the controversial premise.
Scribner (1975)	syllogisms in different cultures	Kpelle nonliterates were correct 53% and they used empirical reasoning. Kpelle college students were correct 80% and American college students were correct 90%. Students used theoretrical reasoning.
Scribner (1977)	asking unschooled people in West Africa to reason logically with syllogisms	Schooling doesn't teach how to reason but when to reason.
III. Problem Solving		
Basseches (1980)	variety of real-life conflicts	More experienced persons used a broader range of dialectical schemata to resolve conflict.
Bowden (1985)	riddles	Ss could access the relevant information if enough time was given.
Duncker (1945)	tumor problem--how can a tumor be destroyed by X-rays without tissue around it being destroyed?	Ss solved problem in stages, from general to specific solution. Avoid contact between X-rays and healthy tissue, insert protective wall, insert a cannula.

Elo (1965)	playing chess	Peak age for skillfulness was 35 years old.
Kahneman & Tversky (1972)	subjective probability sex ratio in classes and families	Judgment was influenced by context.
Kaiser, Jonides & Alexander (1986)	predict path of bullet, water from hose	Physics training was not related to everyday problem performance.
Kuipers & Kassirer (1984)	reason about causal processes of disease	An expert model was created.
Laine & Butters (1982)	20 Questions game	Alcoholics did not initiate strategies for problem solving as efficiently as nonalcoholics of the same age and education.
Posner (1969)	physical match task and name match task	The name match task involved one more step than the physical match task.
Reitman (1965)	compose a fugue	A variant of a General Problem Solver Artificial Intelligence Program was created.
Restle & Davis (1962)	how can a prisoner escape from a tower using a rope half as long as needed?	Speed was analyzed.
Rothbart, Fulero, Jenson, Howard, & Birrell (1978)	*Ss* estimated the proportion of men over 6 feet tall	*Ss* used availability as a cue for frequency and overestimated the number of 6 footers in the group with extreme instances.

IV. Judgment and Decisions (simulated)

Bransford & Johnson (1973)	comprehension of ill-structured paragraph	*Ss* were confused by paragraph until they were told it is about washing clothes; then they were able to bring their clothes washing schema to the fore and make sense of the story.
Chomsky (1968)	are nonsense strings of words grammatical?	*Ss* judged sentence to be grammatical because it seemed to conform to the rules of English, though it didn't make sense.

Table 4.1 (continued)

AUTHOR	TASK	RESULTS
DeSoto (1961)	ordering and comparison of persons	People had a schema for ordering stimuli along single dimensions, a schema they tended to use even if the stimuli were inherently multidimensional.
Hamill, Wilson & Nisbett (1980)	the detailed presentation of a single welfare case vs statistics, and attitudes toward welfare recipients	Enhanced availability and memorability of detailed single case information made it disproportionally important in the judgment process.
Holyoak & Gordon (1984)	spatial comparisons of parts of a horse	People reported consulting a spatial image before making a decision.
Holyoak & Mah (1982)	judging how close cities are to the Pacific coast	Distance judgments were influenced by semantic context.
Kahneman & Tversky (1973)	likelihood each person described was a lawyer or engineer	Ss ignored prior probability in their judgments.
Kahneman & Tversky (1982a)	categorizing a woman	Given "contradictory" information, most judged her as an "active feminist", while others thought she was an "active feminist who worked as a bank teller."
Kahneman & Tversky (1982b)	magnitude of loss in a competitive situation and creativity	The closer to a goal, the easier to construct counterfactual scenarios and the less necessary the actual outcome appears.
King, Kitchener, Davison, Parker & Wood (1983)	justification of beliefs	Young adults showed significant increases in reflective judgment scores over a 2 year period.
Langer (1975)	influence of appearance of a person on chance outcomes	The belief that one has some control over the outcome led a judge to have higher expectations of success than actual probabilities warranted.
Mayer (1973)	comparisons of objects	Decisions are faster when size discrepancies are larger.

Reference	Task	Finding
McGuinness (1986)	relations among family members	Matrix or hierarchy representation strategy determined the number of mental steps needed.
Potts (1974)	comparison of boys	Decisions about who is taller were made more quickly the further apart the items were in the ordering. Ss were faster to compare items never previously paired than to compare items that were explicitly learned together.
Reyes, Thompson & Bower (1980)	judging guilt of a defendant	Evidence in a criminal case that was presented more vividly was recalled better and was used more as a basis for judgment than equally probable but less vivid evidence.
Rosch, Mervis, Gray Johnson & Boyes-Braem (1976)	picture verification task	Objects were identified first at the basic level; additional processing was required to go to super- or subordinate levels.
Ruch (1934)	recalling nonsense equations	Older people were poor at tasks that needed modification of old habits, e.g., suppressing algebraic skills.
Sanford & Maule (1971)	finding faults in machines	The young Ss used the best strategy: testing a frequently faulty machine every time.
Sherman & Corty (1984)	inferences from a general principle in psychology	People had a tendency to use concrete and vivid single case instances in making judgments.
Simon (1956)	chess	When people made decisions, they satisficed rather than maximized or optimized.
Trope (1978)	inferences about a target person's attributes	The neglect of awareness of reliability made people overconfident in their judgments.
Tversky & Kahneman (1980)	causal analysis of eye color	Causal analysis dominated over diagnostic information and led to characteristic errors in judgments.

Table 4.1 (continued)

AUTHOR	TASK	RESULTS
V. Judgment and Decisions (everyday examples)		
Borgida & Nisbett (1977)	course evaluations	It is likely the enhanced availability and memorability of the face-to-face information makes it important in the judgment process.
Botwinick (1969)	scenarios with life situation problems presented to subjects of both age groups; problems were unique to old and unique to young	Old were more cautious than young because all choices to solutions of problem were risky.
Capon & Kuhn (1979)	Ss in supermarket asked to determine which of 2 sizes of a common item sold in the store was a better buy	32% used proportional reasoning strategy when size ratio was simple (2:3); performance declined when ratio was more complex (20% correct).
Corcoran (1966)	proofreading	People used speech recoding even when the recoding actually hurt performance.
Fong, Krantz & Nisbett (1986)	housing, vacation, work dilemmas	Respondents did use abstract rules, and could be trained to do better.
Holyoak & Gordon (1984)	drawing an analogy between a failing marriage and one under evaluation	Pertinence of information influenced judgment.
Isen, Clark, Shalker & Karp (1978)	positive life events (winning lottery)	A positive mood made it easier to imagine positive events.
Kahneman & Tversky (1982b)	one asked why a couple were divorced	People view departures from normalcy as potential causes.
Kaplan (1980)	judging team performance	Fans judge a football team by abstract information; they judge differently when the identities are given.
Lichtenstein, Slovic, Fischhoff, Layman & Combs (1978)	estimating causes of death	Media coverage can create biases in judgments.
Ross, Greene & House (1977)	false consensus	People judged the number of others who shared a trait with them as relatively high.

Shanks (1985)	evaluate effectiveness of munitions during test taken on a computer terminal	Contingency judgments may be based on conditioning.
Sherman & Corty (1984)	judging people; baseball scenario; incidence of violent death; bridge game; exams	Judgments were based on stereotypical heuristics. Principles guided managerial strategy in baseball; rules to guide decisions may be very specific.
Wason & Johnson-Laird (1972)	checking sales receipt	20% of Ss answered correctly. When problems are "real life" situations, Ss can come to the correct conclusion more accurately than if Ss have no schemata into which to incorporate the problem.
Welford (1958)	judge consistency of real-life problem propositions	Task of providing personal answers was easier for all Ss than the task of logical analysis of propositions.

"sort of interesting" to "crucial." So to *some* degree they are naturalistic problems, although most are not common occurrences or of major importance.

How extensive was the search? We limited ourselves to published work from 1970 to present. A glance at the table, which forms the body of this chapter, shows how productive this was. We searched only the cognitive/intelligence/intellectual development literatures, which means that an equally large number of studies might be found in marketing, organizational dynamics, education, or clinical and counseling domains. We did not include tasks used by authors of chapters in this book, supposing that the reader could go directly to those chapters for more detailed descriptions and references. Finally, we do not claim to be exhaustive in covering all problems. The table is meant to suggest the various directions available to an investigator working in the area. If a direction looks promising, the researcher can be certain that more variants of the type of problem in the table have been used and can be found.

The choices of subsections for the table were difficult and proved to be somewhat arbitrary. Some investigators were exploring, not testing a hypothesis that fell under a single descriptor within a standard body of problem solving literature. Some created problems overlapping several processes that appear in standard problem solving literature. Some called memory tasks "problems," but these have been omitted from the table. With considerable humility we present five categories of problems that appear as subheads: classification problems; problem solving focused on logical and syllogistic reasoning; other problem solving; judgment/simulated decision making; and judgments/everyday examples. We suggest that readers scan all examples, and not remain bound by our heuristic categorizations.

We hope that additions to the table will be suggested to us, and that eventually a booklet of possible tasks will be available on request for any researcher.

REFERENCES

Arenberg, D. (1982). Changes with age in problem solving. In F. I. M. Craik & S. Trehub (Eds.), *Aging and cognitive processes* (pp. 221–235). New York: Plenum.

Basseches, M. (1980). Dialectical schemata: A framework for the empirical study of the development of dialectical thinking. *Human Development, 23,* 400–421.

Borgida, E., & Nisbett, R. E. (1977). The differential impact of abstract versus concrete information on decisions. *Journal of Applied Social Psychology, 7,* 258–271.

Botwinick, J. (1969). Disinclination to venture response versus cautiousness in responding: Age differences. *Journal of Genetic Psychology, 115,* 55–62.

Bowden, E. M. (1985). Accessing relevant information during problem solving: Time constraints on search in the problem space. *Memory and Cognition, 13,* 280–286.

Bransford, J. D., & Johnson, M. K. (1973). Considerations of some problems of comprehension. In W. G. Chase (Ed.), *Visual information processing.* New York: Academic press.

Bruner, J. S., & Potter, M. (1964). Inference is visual recognition. *Science, 144,* 424–425.

Cantor, N., & Mischel, W. (1979). Categorization processes in the perception of people. In L. Berkowitz (Ed.), *Advances in experimental social psychology,* (Vol. 10). New York: Academic Press.

Capon, N., & Kuhn, D. (1979). Logical reasoning in the supermarket: Adult females' use of a proportional reasoning strategy in an everyday context. *Developmental Psychology, 15,* 450–452.

Ceraso, J., & Provitera, A. (1971). Sources of error in syllogistic reasoning. *Cognitive Psychology, 2,* 400–410.

Cheng, P. W., & Holyoak, K. J. (1985). Pragmatic reasoning schemas. *Cognitive Psychology, 17,* 391–416.

Chomsky, N. (1968). *Language and mind.* New York: Harcourt Brace Jovanovich.

Coltheart, V., & Evans, J. St. B. T. (1981). An investigation of semantic memory in individuals. *Memory and Cognition, 9,* 524–532.

Corcoran, D. (1966). An acoustic factor in letter cancellation. *Nature, 210,* 658.

DeSoto, C. B. (1961). The predilection for single orderings. *Journal of Abnormal and Social Psychology, 62,* 16–23.

Dolen, L. S., & Bearison, D. J. (1982). Social interaction and social cognition in aging: A contextual analysis. *Human Development, 25,* 430–442.

Duncker, K. (1945). On problem solving. *Psychological Monographs, 58:5,* whole no. 270.

Elo, A. E. (1965). Age changes in master chess performance. *Journal of Gerontology, 20,* 289–299.

Fong, G. T., Krantz, D. H., & Nisbett, R. E. (1986). The effects of statistical training on thinking about everyday problems. *Cognitive Psychology, 18,* 253–292.

Hamill, R., Wilson, T. D., & Nisbett, R. E. (1980). Insensitivity to sample bias: Generalizing from atypical cases. *Journal of Personality and Social Psychology, 39,* 578–589.

Henle, M. (1962). On the relation between logic and thinking. *Psychological Review, 82,* 154–155.

Higgins, E. T., Rholes, C. R., & Jones, C. R. (1977). Category accessibility and impression formation. *Journal of Experimental Social Psychology, 13,* 141–154.

Holyoak, K. J., & Gordon, P. C. (1984). Information processing and social cognition. In R. S. Wyer, Jr., & T. K. Srull (Eds.), *Handbook of social cognition* (Vol. 1). Hillsdale, N.J.: Erlbaum.

Holyoak, K. J., & Mah, W. A. (1982). Cognitive reference points in judgments of symbolic magnitude. *Cognitive Psychology, 14,* 328–352.

Isen, A. M., Clark, M., Shalker, T. E., & Karp, L. (1978). Affect accessibility of materials in memory, and behavior: A cognitive loop? *Journal of Personality and Social Psychology, 36,* 1–12.

Kahneman, D., & Tversky, A. (1972). A subjective probability: A judgment of representativeness. *Cognitive Psychology, 3,* 430–454.

Kahneman, D., & Tversky, A. (1973). On the psychology of prediction. *Psychological Review, 80,* 237–251.

Kahneman, D., & Tversky, A. (1982a). On the study of statistical intuitions. *Cognition, 11,* 123–141.

Kahneman, D., & Tversky, A. (1982b). The simulation heuristic. In D. Kahneman, P. Slovic, & A. Tversky (Eds.), *Judgment under uncertainty: Heuristics and biases.* New York: Cambridge University Press.

Kaiser, M. K., Jonides, J., & Alexander, J. (1986). Intuitive reasoning about abstract and familiar physics problems. *Memory and Cognition, 14,* 308–312.

Kaplan, R. M. (1980). How do fans and oddmakers differ in their judgment of football teams? *Personality and Social Psychology Bulletin, 6,* 287–292.

King, P. M., Kitchener, K. S., Davison, M. L., Parker, C. A., & Wood, P. K. (1983). The justification of beliefs in young adults: A longitudinal study. *Human Development, 26,* 106–116.

Kuipers, B., and Kassirer, J. P. (1984). Causal reasoning in medicine: Analysis of a protocol. *Cognitive Science, 8,* 363–385.

Laine, M., and Butters, N. (1982). A preliminary study of the problem solving strategies of detoxified long-term alcoholics. *Drug and Alcohol Dependence, 10,* 235–242.

Langer, E. (1975). The illusion of control. *Journal of Personality and Social Psychology, 34,* 311–388.

Lichtenstein, S., Slovic, P., Fischhoff, B., Layman, M., & Combs, B. (1978). Judged frequency of lethal events. *Journal of Experimental Psychology: Human Learning and Memory, 4,* 551–578.

Lingle, J., Altom, M., & Medin, D. (1984). Of cabbages and kings: Assessing the extendibility of natural object concept models to social things. In R. S. Wyer, Jr., & T. K. Srull (Eds.), *Handbook of cognitive psychology* (Vol. 1). Hillsdale, N.J.: Erlbaum.

Luchins, A. S. (1942). Mechanization in problem solving. *Psychological Monographs, 54:6,* whole no. 248.

Mayer, R. S. (1973). Comparing objects in memory: Evidence suggesting an internal psychophysics. *Perception and Psychophysics, 13,* 180–184.

McCloskey, M., & Glucksberg, S. (1978). Natural categories: Well-defined or fuzzy sets? *Memory and Cognition, 6,* 462–472.

McGuinness, C. (1986). Problem representation: The effect of spatial arrays. *Memory and Cognition, 14,* 270–280.

McGuire, W. J., McGuire, C. V., & Winton, W. (1979). Effects of household sex composition on the salience of one's gender in the spontaneous self-concept. *Journal of Experimental Social Psychology, 15,* 77–90.

McGuire, W., & Padauer-Singer, A. (1976). Trait salience in the spontaneous self-concept. *Journal of Personality and Social Psychology, 33,* 743–754.

Medin, D. L., Altom, M. W., Edelson, S. M., & Freko, D. (1982). Correlated symptoms and simulated medical classification. *Journal of Experimental Psychology: Learning, Memory and Cognition, 8,* 37–50.

Posner, M. (1969). Abstraction and the process of recognition. In G. H. Bower & J. T. Spence (Eds.), *The psychology of learning and motivation* (Vol. 3). New York: Academic Press.

Potts, G. R. (1974). Storing and retrieving information about ordered relationships. *Journal of Experimental Psychology, 103,* 431–439.

Reitman, W. R. (1965). *Cognition and thought.* New York: Wiley.

Restle, F., & Davis, J. H. (1962). Success and speed of problem solving by individuals and groups. *Psychological Review, 69,* 520–536.

Revlin, R., Leirer, V. O., Yopp, H., & Yopp, R. (1980). The belief-bias effect in formal reasoning: The influence of knowledge on logic. *Memory and Cognition, 8,* 584–592.

Revlis, R. (1975). Syllogistic reasoning: Logical decisions from a complex data base. In R. Falmagne (Ed.), *Reasoning: Representation and process.* Hillsdale, N.J.: Erlbaum.

Reyes, R. M., Thompson, W. C., & Bower, G. N. (1980). Judgmental biases resulting from different availabilities of arguments. *Journal of Personality and Social Psychology, 39,* 2–12.

Rosch, E. H., Mervis, C. B., Gray, W. D., Johnson, D. M., & Boyes-Braem, P. (1976). Basic objects in natural categories. *Cognitive Psychology, 8,* 382–439.

Ross, L., Greene, D., & House, P. (1977). The false consensus phenomenon: An attributional bias in perception and social perception processes. *Journal of Personality and Social Psychology, 13,* 274–301.

Rothbart, M., Fulero, S., Jenson, S., Howard, J., & Birrel, P. (1978). From individual to group impressions: Availability heuristics in stereotype formation. *Journal of Experimental Social Psychology, 14,* 237–255.

Ruch, F. L. (1934). The differentiative effects of age upon human learning. *Journal of Genetic Psychology, 11,* 261–286.

Rumelhart, D. E. (1984). Schemata and the cognitive system. In R. S. Wyer, Jr., & T. K. Srull (Eds.), *Handbook of social cognition* (Vol. 1). Hillsdale, N.J.: Erlbaum.

Sanford, A. J., & Maule, A. J. (1971). Age and the distribution of observing responses. *Psychonomic Science, 23,* 419–420.

Scribner, S. (1975). Recall of classical syllogisms: A cross-cultural investigation of error on logical problems. In R. J. Falmagne (Ed.), *Reasoning: Representation and process.* Hillsdale, N.J.: Erlbaum.

Scribner, S. (1977). Modes of thinking and ways of speaking: Culture and logic reconsidered. In P. N. Johnson-Laird & P. C. Watson (Eds.), *Thinking: Readings in cognitive science.* Cambridge, Mass.: Cambridge University Press.

Shanks, D. R. (1985). Continuous monitoring of human contingency judgment across trials. *Memory and Cognition, 13,* 158–167.

Sherman, S. J., & Corty, E. (1984). Cognitive heuristics. In R. S. Wyer, Jr., & T. K. Srull (Eds.), *Handbook of social cognition* (Vol. 1). Hillsdale, N.J.: Erlbaum.

Simon, H. A. (1956). Rational choice and the structure of the environment. *Psychological Review, 63,* 129–138.

Spivak, G., Standen, C., Bryson, J., & Garrett, L. (received 1986). *Interpersonal problem solving thinking in an elderly group: A pilot study*. Philadelphia: Hahnemann Community Health/Mental Retardation Center, Department of Mental Health Sciences.

Trope, Y. (1978). Inferences of personal characteristics on the basis of information retrieved from memory. *Journal of Personality and Social Psychology, 36*, 93–106.

Tversky, A. (1977). Features of similarity. *Psychological Review, 84*, 327–352.

Tversky, A., & Gati, I. (1978). Studies of similarity. In E. Rosch & B. B. Lloyd (Eds.), *Cognition and categorization*. Hillsdale, N.J.: Erlbaum.

Tversky, A., & Kahneman, D. (1973). Availability: A heuristic for judging frequency and probability. *Cognitive Psychology, 5*, 207–232.

Tversky, A., & Kahneman, D. (1980). Causal schemas in judgment under uncertainty. In M. Fishbein (Ed.), *Progress in social psychology* (Vol. 1). Hillsdale, N.J.: Erlbaum.

Von Baeyer, C. L., Sherk, D. L., & Zanna, M. D. (1981). Impression management in the job interview: When female applicant meets the male (chauvinist) interviewer. *Personality and Social Psychology Bulletin, 7*, 45–52.

Wallsten, T. S., & Budescu, D. V. (1981). Additivity and nonadditivity in judging MMPI profiles. *Journal of Experimental Psychology: Human Perception and Performance, 7*, 1096–1109.

Wason, D., & Johnson-Laird, P. (1972). *Psychology of reasoning: Structure and content*. Cambridge, Mass.: Harvard University Press.

Welford, A. (1958). *Aging and human skill*. London: Oxford University Press.

5

Problems in Everyday Problem Solving Research: A Framework for Conceptualizing Solutions to Everyday Problems

Rickard A. Sebby
Dennis R. Papini

As a field of inquiry, everyday problem solving research has developed without the services of specific theoretical models. Much of the guidance in this area of research has been provided by the adaptation of general models of adult cognitive development (e.g., Baltes, Dittmann-Kohli, & Dixon 1984; Berg & Sternberg 1985; Denney 1984; Kramer 1983; Sinnott 1984; Schaie 1979). The major purpose of this chapter is to suggest that Labouvie-Vief's (1982) model of adult cognitive functioning provides a useful theoretical framework for research investigating everyday problem solving. This model's potential value for everyday problem solving lies in its integration of cognitive, self-knowledge and social-knowledge systems. The result of this integration is an ability to describe how contextual and structural adaptations may influence solutions to everyday problems. However, the uniqueness of this conceptualization for everyday problem solving is not simply the acknowledgment of contextual and structural variation as influences upon adult cognitive functioning. Instead, Labouvie-Vief's model allows for a fundamental redefinition of the goals, purposes, and results of adult cognitive change as it relates to the effective adaptation of a population. These points will be more fully explored in the following discussion.

This research was supported by a grant from the Grants and Research Funding Committee, Southeast Missouri State University, that was awarded to both authors. The preparation of this chapter was supported by funds provided by the Office of the Dean of Graduate Studies and Extended Learning, Southeast Missouri State University. The authors are grateful to David Cargle, Carol Lewis, Karen Brown, and Lisa Caceres for their help in collecting and analyzing the data.

LABOUVIE-VIEF'S THEORY

The distinction between Labouvie-Vief's (1980, 1982) model and those previously identified is a multifaceted one hinging on two interrelated points: the level of analysis used to evaluate successful cognitive adaptation, and whether adult cognitive development accelerates, declines, or remains stable. It is through an understanding of these interrelated points that the importance of Labouvie-Vief's theory for adult cognitive development and, more specifically, for everyday problem solving can be understood.

With respect to the first point, Labouvie-Vief (1980, 1982) argues that the failure of theories attempting to explain adult cognitive development partially lies in their tendency to define adaptation at the level of the individual rather than recognizing that individuals of different cohorts may perform specific and diverse functions in the service of efficient adaptation by an entire population. Labouvie-Vief postulates that young cohorts test the limits and established procedures of a culture, while older cohorts seek to preserve adaptive and worthwhile social mechanisms that have stood the test of time. By extension, individuals of the same cohort having diverse backgrounds and experiences may therefore evidence dissimilar modes of adaptation, based upon the particular environmental niche that they occupy (Labouvie-Vief & Chandler 1978).

Thus, a fundamental assumption of Labouvie-Vief's (1982) theory is that cognitive development does not proceed to a single end point specified by a linear, cumulative conception of development. Such an end point has been postulated, whether explicitly (e.g., Piaget 1970) or implicitly (Denney 1984), and often carries the added assumption that a particular set of cognitive strategies, components, and solution outcomes is needed in order to reach that end point. According to Labouvie-Vief (1980), confusion resulting from the tendency to equate cognitive progression with adaptation results in an expectation that some "best" stage of development, associated with specific cognitive strategies and skills, should necessarily characterize mature cognitive thought.

Although Labouvie-Vief's (1982) model of cognitive development does specify successive distinct stages characterizing adulthood, culminating in a "final" autonomous stage, Labouvie-Vief (1982, p. 187) has explicitly recognized that individual differences in the stage achieved, the rate of progression, and the means of achieving a particular stage may all depend upon the "dialectical interplay between individual and cultural evolution." Furthermore, the diverse end points reached by different individuals at different points in their development and within different stages may each be characterized as adaptive if viewed from the perspective of overall cultural adaptation.

The second point that serves to separate Labouvie-Vief's theory from others in this area concerns the assumption of cognitive decline. As generally perceived by most theorists (e.g., Baltes et al. 1984; Berg & Sternberg 1985; Denney 1984; Sinnott 1984), age-related differences in certain cognitive abilities (e.g., recall and recognition memory, classification, logical reasoning) increasingly described adult cognitive development. These cognitive components are thought to provide a foundation for the establishment and maintenance of other, more advanced cognitive abilities. As a case in point, Baltes et al. (1984) assume that adult development can be separated into two processes, cognition qua cognition, and the pragmatics of intelligence. The former is described as consisting of the mechanics of intelligence, whereas the latter is concerned with the "context-related application of the mechanics of intelligence" (p 63).

These authors emphasize that significant change, although not structural, does occur in the pragmatic intellectual arena during adulthood. Baltes and his colleagues (see also Berg & Sternberg 1985) restrict the development of the cognitive components to the first third of one's life: and, with the exception of peturbations in the system (e.g., decalage), most of the developmental change observed in these processes involves relatively mundane adjustments to losses inevitably resulting from biological aging.

In contrast with the views of Baltes et al. (1984) and others (Berg & Sternberg 1985; Denney 1984), Labouvie-Vief (1980, 1982) maintains that structural change in adult cognitive development is accomplished by logical "trade-offs." That is, movements from one stage to another are accomplished by the destructuring and restructuring of various logical systems, with the result that some levels of cognitive functioning appear to decline (or regress) in the service of adaptation. Labouvie-Vief specifically states that the elements of logical systems will be so restructured that only the examination of several levels of functioning will allow the actual relationship among elements to be fully explicated. This view is particularly relevant for our consideration here, as Labouvie-Vief's model provides an integrative framework for understanding the relationships among components (some decline, some remain stable, and some progress). In addition, the relationship between this componential complex and other systems (personality, environmental, cultural) may be better understood. An integration of this type would seem to be especially appropriate for the field of everyday problem solving, which was initiated in order to provide a more realistic and broader view of adult cognitive abilities (Cavanaugh et al. 1985).

On the basis of Labouvie-Vief's (1980, 1982) theory, an even more general point can be made relative to the notion that structural change does occur in adulthood. Theories that advance this notion assume that stability and decline essentially characterize adult development. We believe that this view is based upon at least one untested assumption: that structural change cannot be described by changing relationships among stable and declining elements. Such views acknowledge the occurrence of selected stability and progression of some cognitive processes (selective optimization) and postulate the existence of "trade-offs between alternative goals and domains of intellectual functioning" as part of the optimization and compensatory process (Baltes et al. 1984, p. 68). However, such views fail to fully acknowledge the interrelatedness existing among all of the elements affecting the cognitive functioning of adults. Concentration upon the performance characteristics of simple components or exclusively studying the pragmatic nature of the developing intellect falls prey to many of the same problems (e.g., lack of reference to the actual ecological context in which adults function) that plagued earlier research efforts in this area.

APPLICATIONS TO EMPIRICAL RESEARCH ON EVERYDAY PROBLEM SOLVING

The major objective of this section of the chapter is to explore the potential insights offered by the application of Labouvie-Vief's (1982) model of adult cognitive development to empirical investigations of everyday problem solving. Labouvie-Vief's stages of adult cognitive functioning suggest that the integration of self and logical regulatory systems allows for greater sensitivity to and awareness of the context in which problems are embedded. This developmental process is characterized by structural reorganizations that result in different levels of awareness concerning the truth of a problem's solution, the logical certainty of that solution, the role of the self in the interpretation of problems, and the recognition that logical systems are embedded in cultural, social, and personal contexts. Presumably, older adults should perform as well as or better than younger adults on everyday problems because the problems are embedded in familiar contexts. Empirical research to investigate this possibility has been facilitated by the development of a scoring scheme (Labouvie-Vief et al. 1983; Hakim-Larson et al. 1983) that incorporates these postformal structural developments. Thus, transitions in reasoning from adolescence to old age are conceptualized as occurring at three qualitatively distinct levels.

Methodological Issues

Scoring Scheme

Problem solving at the intrasystemic level is based on the more or less absolute certainty of logical truth, with the implication that there is only one truth to be constructed during problem solving. Intrasystemic reasoning is characterized by the individual's inability to recognize that the premises upon which truth statements are founded are subjectively interpreted, and that the development of cognitive structures is embedded in socialization processes. The self system is not integrated with formal logic during decision making, and this results in solutions to problems that are logically sensible but may not be pragmatically adaptive.

Intersystemic reasoning emerges as the late adolescent begins to establish mastery over the formal operations. Problem solving with intersystemic reasoning is evidenced by a transition from logical absolutism toward logical relativism. The adolescent and young adult recognize that logical truth may depend upon the embedding context of the problem. As this breakdown in logical certainty occurs, the individual begins to recognize that the self can integrate logical operations with pragmatic concerns. Thus, the relativism of truth contrasts with the many practical solutions to problems that the individual must select from, with the knowledge that the solution selected is not more truthful than another.

Autonomous reasoning reflects the most integrative form of problem solving in adulthood. At this level, structural reorganization integrates the regulatory systems of self and logic. The individual becomes consciously aware of the self's role in interpreting the premises of a problem and evaluating each potential solution in terms of pragmatic, social, cultural, and personal truth. Situated between each pair of these three levels of reasoning are two transitional levels, resulting in a five-point rating scale. Thus, this scheme emphasizes the individual's self-awareness of the contexts in which problems are embedded as a meaningful, even necessary, dimension for empirical study.

The scoring scheme described above has facilitated the development of two interrelated lines of research. The first line has examined age differences in the quality of reasoning, depending upon the context in which problems have been embedded (Hakim-Larson et al. 1983; Labouvie-Vief et al. 1983; Papini & Sebby 1986; Sebby & Papini 1985). The second major focus of this research has been on the relationship between contextual factors (e.g., demographic characteristics, social personality variables, and indices of formal operational abilities) and the level of reasoning exhibited on problems embedded in various contexts (Sebby & Papini 1986). Both of these lines of research share certain methodological practices that are especially useful to the study of everyday problem solving. Especially noteworthy are the use of "talking aloud" strategies and the use of verbal syllogism problems embedded in at least two kinds of framework, formal and contextual.

Thinking-Aloud Strategy

The collection of qualitative reasoning data is accomplished by the use of a thinking-aloud strategy (Giambra & Arenberg 1980), in which subjects are asked to verbally report thought processes as they solve problems. Subjects are probed by trained experimenters in order to fully ascertain the level of reasoning involved in the solution of problems. A review of the "talking aloud" strategy (Ericsson & Simon 1980) suggests that it is an appropriate means of maximizing the report of mental processes involved in problem solving. The value of this strategy is currently receiving increased attention and use in everyday problem solving research (see Cavanaugh et al. 1985).

Problem Solving Tasks

The use of verbal syllogisms that are embedded in various contexts has important implications for everyday problem solving research. Because contextual relevance can be empirically assessed and manipulated, these problems allow researchers an opportunity to study contextually induced variations in cognitive processes. These syllogisms are constructed using if-then statements, with the only difference between types of problems being the relevance or meaningfulness of the context in which they are embedded. The formal syllogisms are designed to minimize the potential relevance of the problem's embedding context. Conversely, contextual syllogisms maximize the potential relevance of the problem's embedding context. Listed below are examples of the different types of embedding contexts employed in this line of research to date:

Formal

Nancy shows Tom a stack of cards with numbers printed on both sides of each card. Nancy tells Tom that if there is a number 2 printed on one side of a card, then the number 9 and the number 4 are printed on the other side of the same card. Nancy hands Tom a card with the number 2 printed on one side.

Adolescent-Relevant

Jean does not keep her room clean, and it is especially messy by Friday. Sara, Jean's mother, warns her that if the room is not clean by the time she gets home from work, Jean will not be allowed to go to the basketball game at school that night. Jean does not clean her room. Sara arrives home from work.

Adult-Relevant

John is known to be a heavy drinker, especially when he goes to parties. Mary, John's wife, warns him that if he gets drunk one more time, she will leave him and take the children. Tonight John is out late at an office party. John comes home drunk.

Older-Adult-Relevant

Ellen, who has lived in the same house for the last 25 years, has almost fallen down the stairs on at least a half-dozen occasions. After her last near fall, Ellen promised that if it ever happened again, she would sell her house and move into another that had only one floor. Yesterday, Ellen had another near fall but avoided it by catching her balance on the handrail.

Labouvie-Vief and her colleagues developed the syllogisms embedded in formal and adult-relevant contexts, while the present authors generated the syllogisms embedded in adolescent- and older-adult-relevant contexts.

The embedding context of each problem was empirically assessed by having over 300 volunteers of all ages rate whether the syllogisms would be relevant for adolescents, young and middle-aged adults, older adults, or no age group in particular (formal tasks). Only syllogisms embedded in contexts rated as age-group-relevant or not relevant to any age group by 75 percent of these volunteers were included in the studies by the present authors. Thus, the syllogisms were perceived as being embedded in age-relevant contexts by lay persons. In addition, the personal relevance or meaningfulness of the syllogisms for each subject was also empirically assessed by having subjects rate personal relevance of the syllogisms on a five-point Likert scale. Collectively, these data may provide information about interindividual variability in the quality of reasoning employed during problem solving.

The research described below is presented in two segments. The first examines age differences in the quality of reasoning exhibited on syllogism problems that are embedded in different contexts; the second explores the relationship between quality of reasoning on syllogisms and personal context.

Research Investigating the Task's Embedding Context

Preliminary investigations guided by Labouvie-Vief's (1982) model have attempted to document the influence of the contexts in which problems are embedded on the quality of adult reasoning. The original research reported by Labouvie-Vief et al. (1983) and Hakim-Larson et al. (1983) described age differences in the quality of reasoning on problems embedded in formal and adult-relevant contexts (see examples described above). These authors employed a sample consisting of five age groups ranging from nine years of age through the early thirties. For syllogisms embedded in both types of contexts, the adult groups evidenced reasoning at higher levels of Labouvie-Vief's scoring scheme than the preadolescent and adolescent groups. The younger age groups tended to give solutions to the problems that were logical but exhibited little or no self-awareness of pragmatic constraints, and solutions generated by these subjects were aired with absolute certainty of their truth.

There were no appreciable differences in reasoning among the three adult groups. The solutions generated by these subjects were more variable and usually reflected at least some awareness that the self plays a role in assessing the certainty or truth of any given solution. In addition, subjects' reasoning level on syllogisms embedded in adult contexts was significantly higher than the reasoning level observed on formal syllogisms for all age groups. Thus, the adult syllogisms were found to enhance the level of reasoning employed by all subjects, presumably because they were embedded in more relevant contexts.

These results provide support for Labouvie-Vief's (1984) suggestion that the adaptive significance of mature cognition is the result of a trade-off between the adolescent's systematic or automatized application of formal logic and the adult's pragmatic reasoning that integrates logic with experience in contexts. The formal logical approach of adolescence and youth tends to be devoid of the self-awareness that solutions to problems may have pragmatic constraints, while the approach of adult-hood is characterized by the self's realization that problem solving involves personal and contextual considerations. This original study generated several questions that are related to the competence-performance issue. While it is not our intention to address this issue here (see Overton & Newman 1982 for a review), the research that follows begins to explore the limits of performance across different age groups of subjects.

In the research by Labouvie-Vief et al. (1983) and Hakim-Larson et al. (1983), adolescent subjects evidenced lower reasoning level scores than did the adult groups. This difference in performance may be due to age-related changes in cognitive functioning, or it could be due to the fact that syllogisms embedded in adult contexts are not as relevant for adolescents as they are for adults (Piaget 1972). Perhaps if syllogisms were generated that accurately reflected contexts relevant to adolescents, the age differences in reasoning would be minimized. In addition, by generating syllogisms embedded in contexts relevant to older adults, it may be possible to examine age differences during adulthood that were not detected by Labouvie-Vief et al. (1983). We attempted to address both of these issues in a series of studies (Papini & Sebby 1986; Sebby & Papini 1985).

Papini and Sebby (1986) examined whether, given problems embedded in relevant contexts, adolescents would employ a reasoning style that reflects an integration of purely logical solutions with pragmatic considerations. The sample consisted of adolescent (13–16 years of age, N = 36), youth (17–19 years of age, N = 34), and young adult (20–29 years of age, N = 30) groups. Each subject was presented with syllogisms embedded in formal, adolescent, and adult contexts. Participants were also asked to complete demographic questionnaires and measures of formal operations (Tomlinson-Keasey & Campbell, cited in Hopper et al. 1984; Sinnott & Guttmann 1978) that will be discussed later. Subjects were asked to "think aloud," and tape recordings of responses to the syllogisms were scored by two independent raters (.82 interrater agreement) using Labouvie-Vief's scheme.

The results of this study are presented in Figure 5.1. Subsequent chi-square analyses were performed for each type of syllogism, with age group and level of reasoning constituting the rows and columns of the matrix. There were significant age differences on the formal (X^2 (4, $N=100$) = 23.06, $p < .0001$), adolescent (X^2 (4, $N=100$) = 20.31, $p < .001$), and adult (X^2 (4, $N=100$) = 31.43, $p < .0001$) syllogisms. Visual inspection of Figure 5.1 reveals a clear progression from the automatic use of formal logic that is characteristic of adolescence, to greater awareness of the self's role in problem solving evident in young adult reasoning. The youth in this study are clearly transitional on the formal syllogisms and split when the syllogisms are embedded in more relevant contexts. Adolescent reasoning shows a similar pattern in that reasoning on the formal syllogisms is primarily level 1 (corresponding to the intrasystemic level in Labouvie-Vief's theory), while reasoning on adolescent and adult syllogisms is slightly more variable.

Notice, however, that level 1 reasoning is predominant among adolescents, regardless of syllogistic context. This finding provides additional support for the research of Labouvie-Vief et al. (1983), in that adolescents do not engage in higher levels of reasoning even when problems are embedded in relevant contexts. These findings are also interesting in that autonomous reasoning was not found at all in the adolescent and youth groups, and so infrequently in the young adult group as to prohibit further analysis. In order to explore autonomous reasoning in greater detail, a study employing a broader sample of the adult ages was conducted.

Sebby and Papini (1985) employed the same basic methodology reported earlier, with the exception that the syllogisms were embedded in formal, adult-relevant, and older-adult-relevant contexts. The sample was comprised of young adult (18–25 years of age, $N=25$), middle-aged adult (26–44 years of age, $N=23$), and older adult (59–78 years of age, $N=22$) groups. Interrater agreement was uniformly high across all types of syllogisms (average .86). The mean level scores and standard deviations for each age group by type of syllogism are presented in Table 5.1. These data depict higher levels of reasoning on the syllogisms embedded in adult- and older-adult-relevant contexts than on formal syllogisms across all age groups (t-tests revealed $p < .01$ for all of these analyses). Both middle-aged and older adults employed higher levels of reasoning

Figure 5.1
Number of Subjects in Each Age Group Exhibiting Different Reasoning Levels on Each Type of Problem

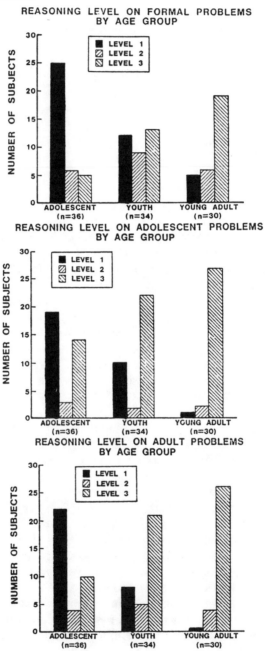

Table 5.1
Means and Standard Deviations of Qualitative Level Scores by Subjects in Each Age Group on Each Task Type

Age Group	Task Type		
	Formal	Adult-Relevant	Older Adult-Relevant
Young	1.90 (0.73)	2.32 (0.80)	2.72 (0.71)
Middle-age	3.02 (1.07)	3.61 (0.91)	3.67 (0.73)
Older	2.16 (0.97)	3.06 (0.94)	3.11 (0.79)

on adult- and older-adult-relevant syllogisms than did young adults. However, the reasoning levels of these two adult groups did not differ significantly.

Taken as a whole, these findings illustrate the importance of considering contextual factors in cognitive adaptation during problem solving. When subjects of all ages are confronted with a problem that is relatively devoid of contextual relevance (i.e., a formal syllogism), the most efficient adaptation may be to use formal logic. However, when problems emerge that are inextricably interwoven with personal knowledge and pragmatic considerations, there is a persistent tendency for young adults and adolescents to attempt solutions through the systematic application of formal logic. Middle-aged and older adults recognize that logic must, at times, be integrated with experience, lest logical solutions to real problems be confused with sensible solutions. The similar pattern of findings that emerged in these research projects does demonstrate replicability. However, there was sufficient variability in reasoning within age groups to warrant investigations of the demographic, formal operational, and social-personality correlates of this variability.

Research Investigating the Individual's Personal Context

In addition to age differences in reasoning on syllogisms embedded in different contexts, several studies have begun the difficult task of identifying features of the personal context (see Hooper et al. 1984) that influence reasoning during adulthood (Papini & Sebby 1986; Sebby & Papini 1986). Features of the personal context have been assessed by collecting demographic information (e.g., age, gender, educational level, health status, and influence of others on decision making), as well as measures of formal operational ability and social-personality characteristics. The formal operational measures included the Isolation of Vari-

Table 5.2
Beta Values, F Statistics, and Associated Probability Values for Each Variable Selected in Each Stepwise Regression Analysis Conducted for Each Task Type

	Beta Value	F	p > F
Formal Task Variables			
Age Group	0.58	13.96	.001
Educational Level	-0.25	3.91	.05
Gender	0.31	3.49	.06
Isolation of Variables	0.12	12.44	.001
Proportional Reasoning	0.17	6.49	.01
Adolescent Task Variables			
Age Group	0.48	19.50	.0001
Systematic Search	0.03	4.31	.05
Adult Task Variables			
Age Group	0.39	12.36	.001
Gender	0.54	9.43	.01
Isolation of Variables	0.09	8.14	.01
Systematic Search	0.04	5.86	.05

ables Task and the Systematic Search Task developed by Tomlinson-Keasey and Campbell (in Hooper et al.) and the Cake and Paint Proportional Reasoning Task developed by Sinnott and Guttmann (1978). Included in the set of social-personality measures were Levenson's (1972) Locus of Control Scale, MacDonald's (1970) Ambiguity Tolerance instrument, Bem's (1974) Sex-Role Inventory, the Rosenberg Self-Esteem Scale (Rosenberg 1965), and the Defining Issues Test (Rest 1979). The general strategy in both of these studies (Papini & Sebby 1986; Sebby & Papini 1986) has been to examine the relationship between personal context variables and reasoning on the different types of syllogisms.

In a study partially described earlier, Papini and Sebby (1986) explored the relationship among demographic variables, measures of formal operations, and level of reasoning. The results of this initial effort are presented in Table 5.2. As previously discussed, age differences emerged in the stepwise regression analyses for each type of syllogism, with adolescents exhibiting reasoning characterized as intrasystemic (level 1) and young adults exhibiting intersystemic (level 3) reasoning. Examination of the demographic variables revealed that higher reasoning levels were associated with increased age, a tendency for subjects with more education to employ level 1 reasoning on formal syllogisms, and a tendency for females to use higher levels of reasoning on the formal and adult syllogisms. The measures of formal operational ability were differentially related to level of reasoning. In general, the logical skills required for these tasks were more strongly related to higher-level reasoning on the formal syllogisms than on the adolescent and adult syllogisms. Thus, formal operations appear to be a necessary but not a sufficient explanation of the different levels of reasoning in Labouvie-Vief's model. This conclusion is similar to that drawn by Kramer (1983) in an examination of relativistic versus formal logic.

Sebby & Papini (1986) also addressed the role of personal context in everyday problem solving during adulthood. The sample consisted of young adult (20–40 years of age, N = 21), middle-aged (41–66 years of age, N = 21), and older adult (67–83 years of age, N = 22) groups. These subjects were presented with both formal and contextual (adolescent, adult, and older adult) syllogisms, along with assessments of demographic information, formal operations, and social-personality characteristics.

Canonical discriminant analysis revealed that personal context variables were differentially associated with level of reasoning on the syllogisms. In general, three demographic variables were found to consistently discriminate between levels of reasoning on the syllogisms. Age was related to level of reasoning: younger subjects were again found to engage primarily in intrasystemic and intersystemic reasoning on the syllogisms, regardless of the embedding context. Middle-aged and older adults were most likely to engage in intersystemic and autonomous reasoning, especially on contextual syllogisms. Autonomous reasoning was associated with an awareness that others (e.g., friends, parents) may influence decision making. Finally, subjects reporting poorer health status tended to respond with less integrative reasoning than subjects reporting good health.

Three social-personality variables consistently discriminated levels of reasoning on the syllogisms. Autonomous reasoning was related to higher moral reasoning state scores, greater externality, and higher self-esteem. This set of findings has special merit, given Labouvie-Vief's assertions that autonomous reasoning is characterized by a consolidation of logic within the self system that allows for an awareness of the many pragmatic concerns that may affect a problem's solution. The formal operational measures revealed that the Paint Proportional Reasoning Task consistently discriminated between intrasystemic and intersystemic reasoning levels on the formal, but not on the contextual, syllogisms. The use of autonomous reasoning was associated with higher scores on the Isolation of Variables Task, an indication that autonomous reasoning requires the cognitive ability to identify and account for relevant variables during problem solving.

Thus, the empirical work to date suggests that contextual factors have important influences upon adult problem solving behavior. Factors deemed relevant include the embedding task context and the individual's sociopersonality and cognitive characteristics. As can be observed, on the basis of the investigations previously conducted, description and explication of the complex interrelationships characterizing adult cognitive development are in their preliminary stages. The results obtained to date enable us to suggest that Labouvie-Vief's model of adult cognitive development can be employed as a useful explanatory vehicle for everyday problem solving.

CONCLUSIONS

The usefulness of Labouvie-Vief's (1982) model for everyday problem solving can be summarized by a reexamination of the origins of this field of inquiry. The development of this field was, in many ways, a reaction against cultural myths that predicted the decline, senility, and uselessness of older members of our society. A realistic appraisal of the functioning of older adults was attempted by the introduction of problem contexts that were more relevant and ecologically valid.

This strategy has been strengthened by allowing older adults to define and select problem contexts and cognitive skills that they believe are ecologically relevant for their particular cohort. However, embedded within the frame of theoretical reference frequently used to interpret and explain behavioral aspects of cognitive development are implicit notions of decline.

For example, inherent in many theories is the notion of progression to some higher stage of thought, underscored by the maintenance of certain select cognitive components. When contextual demands exceed the reserve capacity of the organism to adapt, when contextual support does not provide the appropriate exercise, or when the componential underpinning of higher (more adaptive) cognitive structures fails, decline is predicted. These assumptions continue to uphold the functioning of the prototypical young adult as the criterion by which the behavior of older adults is selectively or generally evaluated. Thus, the inherent qualitative uniqueness potentially characteristic of adult thought is indirectly recognized at best.

Labouvie-Vief's model of adult development clearly departs from this trend. Ecological niches are filled by each member of the population according to the ability to adapt individually to the demands of that context. At whatever level of cognitive functioning (intrasystemic, intersystemic, autonomous), adaptation is a function of one's particular affective, cognitive, physical, and biological characteristics interacting with cultural values, attitudes, and sociocultural institutions. Labouvie-

Vief posits that individuals increasingly structure these various influences in qualitatively different ways; initial reliance on formal logic constraints are imposed on solutions and that efficient adaptation is accomplished only by adherence to a self-referential system that integrates these other influences. In this way a complete and utter escape from even subtle influences of decline may be accomplished.

However, this conception of development should not be interpreted to rule out decline (or regression) as a phenomenon of interest. In fact, a more complete understanding of such decline, based on a reinterpretation guided by parameters established in Labouvie-Vief's model, may be made possible. In the final analysis a more realistic assessment of the actual strengths and weaknesses of adult cognitive functioning may eventually result. This was, as stated previously, the impetus for the development of the field of everyday problem solving. It is our view that a truly realistic understanding of the cognitive abilities of older adults cannot be accomplished unless all adaptive possibilities are fully examined. We believe that Labouvie-Vief's model offers researchers such a possibility.

REFERENCES

Baltes, P.B., Dittmann-Kohli, F., & Dixon, R.A. (1984). New perspectives on the development of intelligence in adulthood: Toward a dual-process conception and a model of selective optimization with compensation. In P.B. Baltes & O.G. Brim, Jr. (Eds.), *Life-span development and behavior* (Vol. 6, pp. 33–76). New York: Academic Press.

Bem, S. (1974). The measurement of psychological androgyny. *Journal of Consulting and Clinical Psychology, 42,* 155–162.

Berg, C. A., & Sternberg, R. J. (1985). A triarchic theory of intellectual development during adulthood. *Developmental Review, 5,* 334–370.

Cavanaugh, J. C., Kramer, D. A., Sinnott, J. D., Camp, C. J., & Markley, R. P. (1985). On missing links and such: Interfaces between cognitive research and everyday problem solving. *Human Development, 28,* 146–168.

Denney, N. W. (1984). A model of cognitive development across the life span. *Developmental Review, 4,* 177–191.

Denney, N. W., & Palmer, A. M. (1981). Adult age differences on traditional and practical problem-solving measures. *Journal of Gerontology, 36,* 323–328.

Denney, N. W., Pearce, K. A., & Palmer, A. M. (1982). A developmental study of adults' performance on traditional and practical problem solving tasks. *Experimental Aging Research, 8,* 115–118.

Denney, N. W., & Thissen, D. M. (1983). Determinants of cognitive abilities in the elderly. *International Journal of Aging and Human Development, 16,* 29–41.

Ericsson, K. A., & Simon, H. A. (1980). Verbal reports as data. *Psychological Review, 87,* 215–251.

Giambra, L. M., & Arenberg, D. (1980). Problem solving, concept learning, and aging. In L. Poon (Ed.), *Aging in the 1980's* (pp. 253–259). Washington, D.C.: American Psychological Association.

Hakim-Larson, J., Adams, C., Hayden, M., DeVoe, M., & Labouvie-Vief, G. (1983). Transitions of adult cognition. Presented at the annual meeting of the Gerontological Society of America, San Francisco.

Hooper, F. H., Hooper, J. O., & Colbert, K. K. (1984). *Personality and memory correlates of intellectual functioning: Young adulthood to old age.* New York: Karger.

Kramer, D. A. (1983). Post formal operations? A need for further conceptualization. *Human Development, 26,* 91–105.

Kramer, D. A., & Woodruff, D. S. (1986). Relativistic and dialectical thought in three adult age groups. *Human Development, 29,* 280–290.

Labouvie-Vief, G. (1977) Adult cognitive development: In search of alternative interpretations. *Merrill-Palmer Quarterly, 23,* 227–263.

Labouvie-Vief G. (1980). Adaptive dimensions in adult cognition. In N. Datan & W. Lohman (Eds.), *Transitions in aging,* (pp. 3–26). New York: Academic Press.

Labouvie-Vief, G. (1981). Proactive and retroactive aspects of constructivism: Growth and aging in life-span perspective. In R. M. Lerner and N. Busch-Rossnagel (Eds.), *Individuals as producers of their development.* New York: Academic Press.

Labouvie-Vief, G. (1982). Dynamics of development and mature autonomy. *Human Development, 25,* 161–191.

Labouvie-Vief, G. (1984). Culture, language, and mature rationality. In H. W. Reese & K. McCluskey (Eds.), *Life-span developmental psychology: Historical and generational effects.* New York: Academic Press.

Labouvie-Vief, G., Adams, C., Hakim-Larson, J., & Hayden, M. (1983). Contexts of logic: The growth of interpretation from pre-adolescence to mature adulthood. Paper presented at the biennial meeting of the Society for Research in Child Development, Detroit.

Labouvie-Vief, G., & Chandler, M. J. (1978). Cognitive development and life-span developmental theory. Idealistic versus contextual perspectives. In P. B. Baltes (Ed.), *Life-span development and behavior* (pp. 181–210). New York: Academic Press.

Levenson, H. (1972). Distinctions within the concept of internal-external control: Development of a new scale. Paper presented at the annual meeting of the American Psychological Association, Honolulu.

MacDonald, A. P., Jr. (1970). Revised scale for ambiguity tolerance: Reliability and validity. *Psychological Reports, 26,* 791–798.

Newman, J. L., Attig, M., & Kramer, D. A. (1983). Do sex-role appropriate materials influence the Piagetian task performance of older adults? *Experimental Aging Research, 9,* 197–202.

Overton, W. F., & Newman, J. L. (1982). Cognitive development: A competence-activation/utilization approach. In T. Field, A. Houston, H. Quay, L. Troll, & G. Finley (Eds.), *Review of human development.* New York: Wiley.

Papini, D. R., & Sebby, R. A. (1986). Contextual variation in cognitive processes:

Transitions from adolescence to young adulthood. Paper presented at the meeting of the Society for Research in Adolescence, Madison, Wis.

Piaget, J. (1970). Piaget's theory. In P. H. Mussen (Ed.), *Carmichael's Manual of Child Psychology* (Vol. 1, pp. 703–732). New York: Wiley.

Piaget, J. (1972). Intellectual evolution from adolescence to adulthood. *Human Development, 16,* 1–12.

Rest, J. R. (1979). *Development in judging moral issues.* Minneapolis: University of Minnesota Press.

Rosenberg, M. (1965). *Society and the adolescent self-image.* Princeton: Princeton University Press.

Schaie, K. W. (1979). Age changes in intelligence. In R. L. Sprott (Ed.), *Aging and intelligence.* New York: Van Nostrand Reinhold.

Sebby, R. A., & Papini, D. R. (1985). The influence of contextual variation on adult cognition. Paper presented at the meeting of the Gerontological Society of America, New Orleans.

Sebby, R. A., & Papini, D. R. (1986). Pragmatic reasoning as related to formal operations and social-personality factors. Paper presented at the meeting of the American Psychological Association, Washington, D.C.

Sinnott, J. D. (1975). Everyday thinking and Piagetian operativity in adults. *Human Development, 18,* 430–443.

Sinnott, J. D. (1984). Postformal reasoning: The relativistic stage. In M. L. Commons, F. A. Richards, & C. Armon (Eds.), *Beyond formal operations: Late adolescent and adult cognitive development* (pp. 298–325). New York: Praeger.

Sinnott, J. D., & Guttmann, D. (1978). Piagetian logical abilities and older adults' abilities to solve everyday problems. *Human Development, 21,* 327–333.

Tomlinson-Keasey, C., & Campbell, P. (1977). *Formal operations test and scoring manual.* Unpublished, University of California-Riverside.

6

A Model for Solution of Ill-Structured Problems: Implications for Everyday and Abstract Problem Solving

Jan D. Sinnott

The general question addressed in this chapter is whether a model can be created to describe adults' thought processes during solution of ill-structured logical problems similar to those encountered in life. We are often faced with situations, at work or at home, that seem to demand that we use our reason, logic, math abilities, analytical abilities. Often these same situations have unclear goals as we think about them further, and also demand creative, practical, and synthetic solutions. For example, in a work situation we might logically work toward maximizing productivity *or* logically work toward maximizing creativity. We might try to find the most practical solution or the most elegant logical/mathematical solution. Such ill-structured (Churchman 1971) problems have unclear goals and demand Kantian or dialectical inquiry systems. They seem to be more common in human experience than well-structured ones. Well-structured problems have single solutions, optimal solution paths, and structured goals, and demand Lockean inquiry systems. They are most frequently found in our problem solving studies, and seldom found in real life.

We *do* often solve everyday ill-structured problems. The question is how? We might assume that many of the processes used to solve well-

A portion of this chapter was presented at the annual meeting of the Gerontological Society, San Francisco, 1983, as part of the symposium "Understanding of Problem Solving from a Gerontological Perspective," L. Giambra, chair. This research was supported in part by a National Institute on Aging grant to the author. The author thanks David Arenberg, Ph.D., for his cooperation; the anonymous reviewers for their comments; and Robin Armstrong and Debbi Johnson for their assistance.

structured problems are used at some point. These processes are described in the growing literature on problem solving, problem solving models, and language comprehension. But investigators studying ill-structured everyday problems, such as understanding the point of discourse (Shank et al. 1982) and planning a day's activities (Hayes-Roth & Hayes-Roth 1979), described *additional* processes. They do not typically use *logical* problems in their studies.

Even investigators who are using logical problem of some kind often report processes that are, in Schoenfeld's (1983) words, "beyond the purely cognitive." Additional processes, such as emotion, seem necessary to a more complete model of problem solving that can address both well-structured and ill-structured problems. When we examine problem solving transcripts, there are too many steps that appear to be unexplained when traditional models are used. Typical models may miss processes that we can capture by describing everyday problem solving, especially everyday *logical* problem solving. This is what is attempted in this chapter.

This chapter is part of a description of a multiproject research program. One focus of this program is describing the information processing of adults of various ages who are solving everyday problems. Another focus is describing information processing in terms of Piagetian postformal operations (e.g., Sinnott 1987, in press). A third focus is analysis of compensatory mechanisms that maximize the efficiency of an information processing system at various points in the lifespan.

These studies are part of a larger program of research investigating positive changes in everyday intellectual abilities over the adult life span. The research results were first expressed as Piagetian postformal operations, but later were also expressed as artificial intelligence-like models of complex information processing and problem solving skills.

Results suggest that complex self-referential thinking processes like those needed to process truth statements in the "new physics" (relativity theory, quantum mechanics) are developed by mature adults, are postformal, and are used to compensate for changing demands and abilities by adults solving everyday problems. Such abilities may permit individuals to be more adaptive at various stages of life.

OBJECTIVES

In this chapter the primary focus will be on describing and modeling all the processes—purely cognitive and "impurely" cognitive—that enter into the solution of logical problems with everyday qualities, such as those in the problems and protocol analysis below. This chapter, then, is partly exploratory and descriptive. It will also address the way two specific processes, described in studies of well-structured logical problems, operate in everyday problem solving. The two to be examined are goal clarity and the availability of an algorithm or a heuristic. The question here is whether goal clarity and heuristic availability have similar roles in the solution of everyday, ill-structured problems, as they do generally in the literature on logical problem solving.

In two articles (Sweller 1983; Sweller & Levine 1982) Sweller discussed the impact of changes in goal specificity on strategies employed on a problem. For a problem *high* in goal specificity, means-end analysis was the strategy of choice. Little learning of general transferable solutions took place, and processing was more "top down." For a problem *low* in goal specificity, hypothesis testing was the more usual strategy. Learning was more likely to occur, history-cued rule induction was likely to take place, and "bottom-up" processing was more likely.

A problem may be seen as either a puzzle (which has a structured goal, an optimal solution path, and a single solution for which an algorithm exists, and which utilizes a Lockean inquiry system) or an ill-structured problem (for which there is no unequivocal single solution, and little certainty about the theoretical assumptions that fit the problem, and which utilizes a Kantian or a dialectical inquiry system) (Churchman 1971). A respondent's perception as to whether a problem is a puzzle or a less structured problem is part of his/her decision concerning goal clarity. Developmental differences in assumptions about the nature of knowable reality (e.g., "objective reality is knowable") influence the possibility that a person can consider that a problem is a one-goal puzzle *or* a problem that has potential for several goals (Toulmin 1958). Problems seen as having several potential solutions are frequently dealt with by satisficing (choosing the "good enough" answer) rather than maximizing strategies (Howard 1983). The problems in this study were hybrid problems, potentially treated either way or both ways by respondents. Respondent decisions about the nature of the problem were likely to be a systematic source of variation in the strategies employed.

Concerning a heuristic or algorithm, the respondent might start out with one or develop one during the course of solving several problems. Greeno, Magone, and Chaiklin (1979) found respondents applying available rules or approaches without reference to stated goals. Available heuristics were used no matter what. Expectations for this study concerning the effects of goal clarity and heuristic availability on strategy, size of problem space, and other factors are in Table 6.1.

The next section of this paper presents a thinking-aloud protocol analysis that contains the kind of thinking that needs to be modeled. A discussion of the methodology used in obtaining the protocol, and of assumptions underlying the thinking-aloud approach, follows. Next, a model to explain the behavior is described and discussed. The relations between goal clarity and heuristic availability and the respondent's processes are examined. The model and hypotheses consistent with Table

Table 6.1
Expected Relations of Perceived Goal Clarity and Availability of Heuristic to Some Dimensions of Strategy, Problem Space, Performance on Well-Structured Problems, and Skills Needed

Clarity of Any One Goal*	Availability of Learned Heuristic/Algorithm	Probable Stategy
(1) Clear	Available	Use learned heuristic or algorithm. Performance on well-structured problems should be good if persons prefer this approach. Seeing problems this way is related to youth and good skills. Small problem space.
(2) Clear	Unavailable	Use means-end analysis. Medium problem space. If performance is poor on well-structured problems by solvers who prefer this strategy, it is due to time-consuming nature of strategy to find a heuristic. Seeing problems this way is related to poor skills. Train for skills to improve performance.
(3) Clear	Available	Use learned heuristic/algorithm and assume that goal is "whatever is yielded by that process." Small problem space. If performance is poor on well-structured problems by solvers who prefer this strategy, errors probably are due to "not having the concept"; performance may be rapid. Seeing problems this way may be related to aging-related decline. Train for flexibility to improve performance.

Table 6.1 (continued)

Clarity of Any One Goal*	Availability of Learned Heuristic/Algorithm	Probable Stategy
(4) Unclear	Unavailable	Trial-and-error responding and search for positive feedback OR decision about nature of problem; hypothesis testing for positive feedback from system to verify rules/goal; problem "solved" when an elected goal produces usable results within an accepted belief system. Very large problem space. Solvers capable of these strategies may make errors on well-structured problems because (1) they see more options than the task designer did and (2) they take too long. Seeing problems this way is related to maturity. Those who can reach a logical solution under these conditions can also do so under any of the other conditions in the table.

* May be examined in terms of subgoals or overall problem goal.

6.1 are tested. The final discussion centers on individual problem solving styles, developmental considerations, belief systems, intentionality, and control processes.

METHODOLOGY AND RESULTING PROTOCOL

The sort of thinking that must be explained by any model of everyday logical problem solving is described below. The problems given to this respondent were everyday versions of Piaget's formal operational problems (Cavanaugh et al. 1985; Inhelder & Piaget 1958; Sinnott 1975, 1982, 1983, 1984a, 1984b, 1987, in press). Four of the six presented the possibility of combining six items in pairs, offering a good opportunity for learning a heuristic or a goal set. The six problems were given in random order, so any one might have been preceded by as many as five others. The problems were present in written form in the respondent's work area throughout the session. The respondent had paper and pencils available, and as much time as needed. The problems permitted step-by-step means-end movement toward a goal state, permitted the construction of subgoals, and permitted hypothesis formation and some testing of those hypotheses within the problem space selected. The goal was potentially conceptualized as specific and fixed, or could be seen as alterable into other specific or general, final or intermediary, goals. Rule induction was possible across the set of problems. Subjects could work either forward or backward, or, if they changed rules-about-rules, *both* forward and backward.

Respondents

Respondents were part of the Baltimore Longitudinal Study of Aging and ranged in age from 26 to 89 (details of sample in Shock et al. 1984). To date some 150 respondents, about one-third female, have answered the problems, using one form or other of the thinking-aloud approaches described below. Fifty respondents (age range 26–86) experienced the same testing approach as the respondent whose answers are about to be discussed at length. (In two additional studies, three of the problems and other problem solving and cognitive tasks were administered to college students working singly or cooperatively in pairs, and five of the problems and other problem solving tasks were administered to Mensa members. Thus a large data base is available for the problems.)

Three respondents' products are discussed in some depth in this paper. The three were selected to portray three styles of problem solving: youthful (age 26), mature (age 41), and old (age 69). They were the first respondents in those three age categories whose transcripts were transcribed. All three worked in professional/technical occupations. Responses of the "mature" respondent are discussed at length below.

Thinking-Aloud Approach

The thinking-aloud (TA) approach to the study of problem solving has been described and used by a number of researchers (see Ericsson & Simon 1984 for a complete bibliography). Giambra and Arenberg (1980) recommended its use in developmental and aging studies, in which it is proving helpful (Giambra 1983; Sinnott 1983, 1984b, 1985, 1987, in press). Ericsson and Simon (1984) addressed all significant aspects of TA protocol analysis, including assumptions, instructions, coding, hypothesis testing, and impact of the TA method on results obtained. In this study the administration of the problems and analyses of protocols were performed with the issues summarized by Ericsson and Simon in mind. TA approaches require a minimal set of assumptions about the nature of processing, chiefly that it occurs in an information-processing framework. Evidence suggests that instructions to think aloud do not alter the sequence of cognitive processes significantly. Verbal concurrent and retrospective reports provide a nearly complete record of the sequence of information needed during task performance, and verbally reported data seem as regular and valid as other types of data (Ericsson & Simon 1984).

Several TA strategies were used over the course of the studies summarized in this chapter. The simplest involved presenting a written problem and asking respondents to keep talking about their thoughts as they worked on it. Their comments were taped. Another version involved taking notes rather than taping, and asking questions. In a more complex version the same request to think aloud was made, but when the respondent finished, additional questions necessary to clarify comments made while he or she was thinking aloud were asked. This last approach was the one used to elicit the responses described at length below. Respondents were asked to "Think aloud as you work on the problems. Say whatever comes to mind, even if it doesn't seem important. When you've finished with the problem, I'll ask you about anything you said that seems unclear to me." Therefore both TA and retrospective data were gathered, and both are reported as TA below.

Taped protocols were typed verbatim, and sections were segmented by meaning and numbered by problem and statement. Although it is customary to eliminate statements that seem to miss the problem's cognitive demands or that include the subject's analyses of his/her own processes, *all* the respondent's statements were retained. The model of the process that appears in the next section is generally congruent with the real-time order of the respondent's statements. (Transcripts of responses are available from the author.)

Protocol statements were analyzed by seeing them in several ways: as episodes—for example, choice of a subgoal (Newell & Simon 1972); as a series of solution steps—for example, a working forward path *vs.* a working backward path (Simon & Simon 1978); and as a series of processes—for example, processing a column in cryptarithmetic (Newell & Simon 1972). The entire protocol for a problem was considered as one unit at some levels of analysis; at other levels a single statement was considered to be one unit. This will become apparent below in the discussion of a protocol. As a point of clarification, "goals," "solutions," and "essences" differ. Several solution processes may be used to reach a goal, and several goals may serve one essential belief (essence) of the nature of the problem. One solution process may serve several goals, and one goal may serve several beliefs. This all implies the author's belief that no one level of analysis can be sufficient for understanding this process, and that a parsimonious explanation demands use of several levels.

Sample Description of Problem Solving Processes from a Protocol

The first problem was ill-structured but not combinatorial. The respondent first read the written problem, clarified instructions, and immediately alluded to his personal history, experience, and emotional reactions to this type of problem. He stopped those reactions and refocused his attention on the task, partly using repetitious behavior (reread the problem). A pause occurred while his face demonstrated concentration. During this concentration (often a period of silence during TA reports—see Ericsson & Simon 1984), he sought any disconfirmation of an emerging response, reviewed some information, and gave an answer. He verified his answer, looking relaxed during verbal play.

Retrospective thinking focused on his conflict with himself over solving the problem at all, and also showed self-monitoring of personality and cognitive style. He talked about his first step of generating ideas about the potential real purpose of the problem, and deciding on an official purpose. He reviewed his next step of accepting a major essential purpose of "good utilization of employee resources," monitoring his consistency and ideational productivity. He was aware that other solutions would meet the same goal even if they were different from the essential purpose he selected. He viewed the adequacy of a solution as dependent on intent of the audience/experimenter—that is, many criteria or purposes could be possible. He described his own personal criterion, and the ill-structuredness of the problem demands that permitted alternative interpretations and goal or essence choices. Some definition of "what's possible" and "what's silly" further parameterized his choice of goal and solution. He monitored his use of rules; not *all* aspects of this solution were relevant. He recalled his emotional reaction and his need to focus to circumvent that.

These events, put into a time-ordered flow, appear in Figure 6.1. (The flow of two other solutions appears in Figures 6.2 and 6.3.)

From the respondent's words it appeared that he sometimes worked forward and sometimes backward. He worked out the essence of the problem, the goals, the criteria for selection of goals and solutions, the solutions, and ways around difficult emotional and cognitive points. Many of his statements dealt with emotions, his past cognitive or emotional history, or his present roles in life; all these factors became part of the decisions about problem parameters or strategies for proceeding in the task. He seemed uncertain about the "real" goal (overall), and did not appear to have a usable heuristic, which would place him in category (4) of Table 6.1. His responses were category (4) for three other problems and category (1) for two more. He did act as predicted in that table.

A Model for Solution of Ill-Structured Problems

A model of the components in the solution of ill-structured problems was created from the respondent's first two solutions. That model set of processes was hypothesized to exist in the remaining solutions of this subject, and in the solutions of other subjects. The model was supported for this subject, and can be found in summary form in Figure 6.4, representing a state during problem solving, and in Table 6.2.

The model has five main points of special interest in regard to solution of ill-structured everyday problems: processes to construct problem spaces; processes to choose and generate solutions; monitors; memories; and noncognitive elements. While these elements probably are present in all problem solving activities, they are emphasized here because they were so prominent in protocols but are not emphasized in the literature.

Processes to Construct Problem Space

Newell & Simon (1972) and others have discussed the set of processing rules and content items that make up the problem space in which the subject works out a solution. Problem space is often explicitly described by the investigator doing task analysis (Ericsson & Simon 1984). Implied parameters of problem space usually demand "relevance" of the problem space element to the goal of the problem *as perceived by the task creator*. Therefore, when starting with a predetermined problem space, the analysis of the problem solving process must, of necessity, preclude some of the processes we saw in the respondent's protocol. Therefore, if all

Figure 6.1
Process Steps for Respondent A: Magazine Problem, Administered First

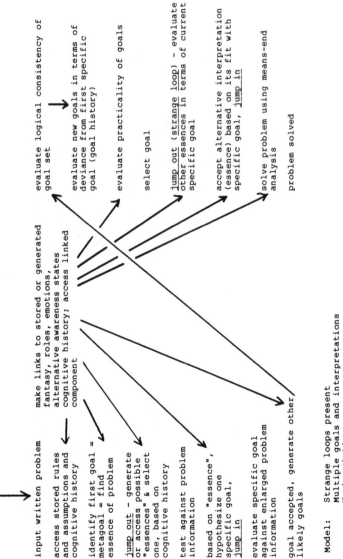

input written problem

access stored rules and assumptions and cognitive history

identify first goal = metagoal = find essence of problem

jump out - generate or access possible "essences" & select one, based on cognitive history

test against problem information

based on "essence", hypothesize one specific goal, jump in

evaluate specific goal against enlarged problem information

goal accepted, generate other likely goals

make links to stored or generated fantasy, roles, emotions, alternative awareness states cognitive history; access linked component

evaluate logical consistency of goal set

evaluate new goals in terms of deviance from first specific goal (goal history)

evaluate practicality of goals

select goal

jump out (strange loop) - evaluate other essences in terms of current specific goal

accept alternative interpretation (essence) based on its fit with specific goal, jump in

solve problem using means-end analysis

problem solved

Model: Strange loops present
         Multiple goals and interpretations
         No heuristic
         Use of "intrusive" components

Figure 6.2
Process Steps for Respondent A: Power Problem, Administered Third

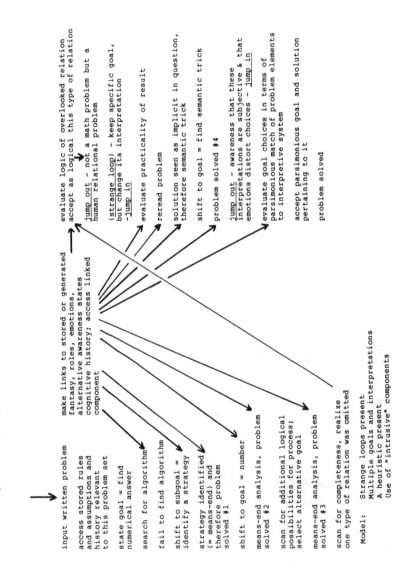

input written problem

access stored rules
and assumptions and
history relevant
to this problem set

state goal = find
numerical answer

search for algorithm

fail to find algorithm

shift to subgoal =
identify a strategy

strategy identified
(= means-end) and
therefore problem
solved #1

shift to goal = number

means-end analysis, problem
solved #2

scan for additional logical
possibilities for process;
select alternative goal

means-end analysis, problem
solved #3

scan for completeness, realize
one type of relation was omitted

Model: Strange loops present
        Multiple goals and interpretations
        A heuristic present
        Use of "intrusive" components

make links to stored or generated
fantasy, roles, emotions,
alternative awareness states
cognitive history; access linked
component

evaluate logic of overlooked relation
accept as logical this type of relation

jump out - not a math problem but a
human relational problem

(strange loop) - keep specific goal,
but change its interpretation
-jump in

evaluate practicality of result

reread problem

solution seen as implicit in question,
therefore semantic trick

shift to goal = find semantic trick

problem solved #4

jump out - awareness that these
interpretations are subjective & that
emotions distort choices - jump in

evaluate goal choices in terms of
parsimonious match of problem elements
to interpretive system

accept parsimonious goal and solution
pertaining to it

problem solved

82

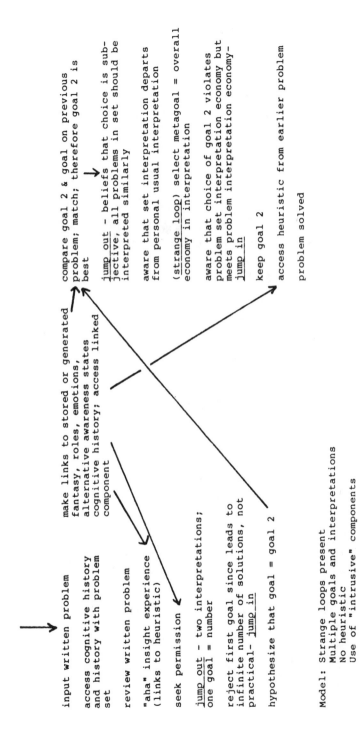

Figure 6.4
Basic Components in Solution of Ill-Structured Problems

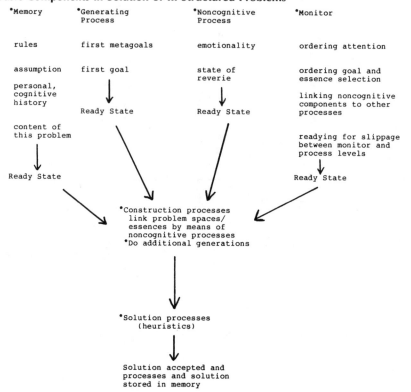

Table 6.2
General Steps in the Everyday Problem Solving Process

1. Decisions about the essence or nature of the problem.

2. Generation of goals and metagoals.

3. Evaluation processes.

4. Similarity testing process.

5. Processes to associate thought and feeling states.

6. Processes to "slip" levels of processing during processing.

7. Accesses processes.

8. Solution processes such as means-end analysis, hypothesis testing, and hill climbing to reach goals.

9. Memory.

10. Monitors.

11. Output processes.

NOTE: In everyday problems seen as well-structured, omit steps 1, 2, 6.

elements are considered, problem space may be said to be larger for solutions to ill-structured everyday problems, or it may be that there are multiple problem spaces available to the solver, who then accesses his/her desired number of spaces. This latter view appears in Figure 6.4. The access may be through cognitive or noncognitive associations between the spaces, or it may be by virtue of a more complex mechanism, a "strange loop" (Hofstadter 1979) using processes *within* a given space to select a new space and continue working in that new space.

The respondent frequently bridged between problem spaces when working on the first problem. He sometimes found a new "essence" of the problem by use of humor. He consciously noted that selection of a space to use was an arbitrary decision. He did the same on problem 2. Checking later problems to see if the respondent continued to select a problem space clearly reveals that he did so. Even in the last problem, which was well-structured in comparison with the rest, it's evident that the respondent left what would be considered the usual focused problem space. Without considering his digression into other spaces, anyone scoring his response on the problem would have to score it as illogical and incorrect: he gave the wrong number.

After examining the nature of his digression, one must admit that he was very logical in his approach. He did not "fail" the logical problem—he just worked in a larger space. He selected a space we might label "this is a rotational problem" and another we might label "this is a pairing-combinatorial problem," and moved within both to solve, finally, within one. He used the problems as a whole to decide the general nature of the *test* of which space to use more fully, and then to solve a version of the problem in that space accordingly. This complex shift across levels to a new problem space can be termed a "strange loop" (Hofstadter 1979). It is changing the rules of the game, by virtue of the game rules, during a game (a "self-modifying game") or slipping levels while in process. Table 6.3 contains a number of ways respondents might "change the rules," extrapolated from the subject's responses. Table 6.4 contains a summary of elements in the subject's larger problem space.

The idea of a "strange loop" is a useful one because it not only explains some behavior that is less than logical in appearance, but also seems to provide a mechanism for explaining relativistic thinking (as in relativity theory and quantum physics; Sinnott 1981). The respondent was aware that his choice of problem space was subjective, and also knew that it was necessarily so. This was a situation of truth uncertainty in which one sees that truth cannot be known both completely and with certainty (Gödel 1962). At the very least it called for jumping out of the process for a moment to decide what kind of game was being played (as opposed to deliberately changing the game rules by virtue of the game rules),

Table 6.3
Logically Derived Procedures Available to the Problem Solver Who Moves to "Change the Rules of the Game as It Is Being Played"

1. Unconsciously make the decision "I had a feeling" (spoken in retrospect).

2. Consciously decide, based mainly on experience with these problems, "This looks like the ABC problem I did first."

3. Consciously decide, based on examination of alternatives, "I had a feeling this could be either a math problem or a people problem, and I decided it was a people problem."

4. Step 3, with supposition that this is a _logical_ nonarbitrary decision.

5. Step 3, with awareness that this a necessarily _arbitrary_ decision (outside bounds of logic) that determines whether logic is used in reaching goal: "I'm just going to treat this like a math problem, although there's no way to tell if it is. So I'll calculate the number of pairs according to a formula I know...."

Table 6.4
Summary of Elements/Representations/Operators Apparently Available in Respondent A's Problem Space: Magazine Problem

1. Initial state

2. Goal state

3. Operators to perform chosen set of mathematical, move-related, or logical functions

4. Rules and assumptions that modify states and processes

5. Forms of individual's history, especially cognitive history, that modify processes and states

6. Emotional states

7. Operators to alter awareness, to monitor, and to alter levels of processing (e.g., metaoperators; epistemic operators)

8. Evaluation processes to test goal appropriateness, interpretation appropriateness

9. Subroutines to generate multiple goals and interpretations

10. "Task-unrelated" thoughts that are used in the problem

11. Operators to permit controlled slippage between levels of processing during processing

thereby letting the process be governed by belief systems of a broad sort.

Schoenfeld (1983) pointed out a number of ways that such control-level processes as belief systems influence intellectual performance. Solvers might express a belief system or metaprocessing constraints that arose from their experience with the problem and that also *changed* their experience with the problem. They might use what Kitchener (1983) or Lauer (1982) called epistemic cognition, or what Kuhn (1983) called "executive 2 strategies." They may be allowing their attention to control their consciousness, which, in turn, controls their attention (Csikszentmihalyi 1978). They perhaps are operating "as if" one must construct the world and truth as one lives it, and then live by that construction, a very self-referential type of truth (Landfield 1977). They perhaps are using metalevel reasoning that, in Piagetian terms, appears to be post-formal operational (Commons et al. 1984; Kitchener 1983; Sinnott 1984b), or synthetic modes such as those discussed by Bastick (1982). The respondent seemed to agree with Polanyi (1977) that an expression of truth, in every case, involves some sort of "passionate commitment" to a choice of beliefs amid ultimate uncertainty. This commitment seemed to take the form of choice of problem space and slippage of levels by means of strange loops. The knowingly arbitrary construction of problem space by the solver is a relatively unexplored dimension of the problem solving process.

Processes to Choose and Generate Solutions

The solutions to ill-structured problems also seemed to include processes to generate and select specific solutions. Clearly, construction of problem space, discussed above, is involved in this set of activities. But the respondent, even after selection of larger problem spaces (or problem essences), spent some energy generating several goals and specific solutions. The essence of a problem must be selected; then the goal or goals must be selected; and finally a solution or solutions must be generated and selected. Sometimes a goal or solution is selected first, and then a new essence is chosen to conform to that chosen goal and solution.

The generation of possible goals and solutions is a creative exercise that could be said to take advantage of previous learning or unconscious processes. For our respondent it seemed to be accomplished by bridges of associations or of task-unrelated thoughts or emotions. The larger the number of generated possible goals, the more the solver needs a mechanism for selection of the best goal or solution. One mechanism mentioned by our respondent was to select goals that were suitable to the decided-upon problem essence. Another was to select goals that he knew were reachable, or specific solution paths for which he had a heuristic available. He did this for the well-structured problem, too, which would make him appear to have failed it.

Monitors

Our respondent frequently monitored his own processes, shifts, choices and style. He also monitored his emotional reactions. The monitoring process sometimes helped him stay on track and deal with his limitations, and also let him decide about the nature of the problem and the goal to choose. Sometimes monitoring distracted him from the goal and slowed the process. The monitor therefore controls more than the flow of the process through a restricted problem space; it links other problem spaces, regulates choice of problem essence, and maintains continuity. The monitor probably has numerous specialists to handle subtasks.

Memory

Memory was predictably a component, but the sort of memories evoked were less predictable. Much of the protocol dealt with memories of school performance, emotions, job-related factors, and other personal historical data. Memory as repository for elements of the solution *while* working on the problem was also important. Lack of memory did not seem to be a serious problem for this respondent, and the personal history elements were useful in making available alternative interpretations of problem essence and in offering heuristics.

Noncognitive Elements

The presence of emotional reactions was obvious in this subject's responses throughout the protocol. Emotions and task-unrelated thoughts often were the impetus for choice of goal or problem essence. They kept the solver going, motivating him to continue through the process even when he was temporarily stalled on "hills." This and the other four components are certainly apparent in the protocol, and might appear more frequently in well-structured problem solving, too, if reports were not edited to remove this information. The reader might see Sinnott (1987, in press) for more extensive data on noncognitive processes in a larger sample and experimental induction of noncognitive effects.

Goal Clarity and Heuristic Availability

The predications in Table 6.1 concerning goal clarity and heuristic availability were supported by the responses of the first respondent, as described above. Responses of two additional respondents, a 26-year-old technician (young) and a 69-year-old professional (older) to the same problems were also a focus and will be discussed below. (They are not included here verbatim to save space.) For all three respondents the strategy predictions in Table 6.1 were supported. There were 15 clear instances where a goal was considered and use of some heuristic was possible. Fourteen of the 15 identified goal clarity/heuristic availability instances were associated with a strategy on that portion of the problem which was predictive of the solver's strategy on later problems in the set and on the well-structured problem at the end of the set.

Responses of Representatives of the Young and the Old

Responses of young and old respondents to one problem are diagrammed in Figure 6.5 (26-year-old's response) and Figure 6.6 (69-year-old's response). The importance of the five components (problem space construction, etc.) was clear in their responses, giving support to the model. Predictions (Table 6.1) based on goal clarity and heuristic availability were supported, and respondents were consistent across the problem set.

The responses of the young subject had a straightforward analytical quality and occupied a relatively small problem space. This respondent avoided multiple goals as well as unrelated thought and emotion. The responses of the older subject were very different, in that this subject described goals that were the identification of a process, not the creation of a product. The older respondent used task-unrelated thoughts and emotional processes.

The contrasting world views and truth systems (in a nontechnical sense) of the three problem solvers (middle-aged, young, old) were also interesting. Respondent A (middle-aged) appeared to live in a world of many truths and options that could be effectively monitored and shifted. A saw that world as partially created by the knower. A not only could synthesize but also could analytically test propositions about reality. Respondent B's (young) world was more analytical and focused, one with less complicated truths and single specific answers. In C's (old) world, good process (rather than answers) constituted truth. The right answer was a "right process" or template. Content of the problem helped determine the process. The "good process truth" for C was very much in touch with everyday social reality. The three contrasting world views therefore were truth as relative fact; truth as single fact; truth as good process. These world views and styles correspond in an interesting way to aspects of three of the "inquiring systems" described by Wood (1983) and by Churchman (1971).

Figure 6.5
Process Steps for Respondent B: Power Problem, Administered Fourth

```
input written problem
            ↓
access history of problem
set - combinations
            ↓
goal = combinations
            ↓
reread problem demands to
confirm goal
            ↓
begin pairing:  use heuristic
            ↓
search for further definition  ←──────────────→  shift to thoughtful,
of goal         |                                 unfocused state
                ↓
jump out - aware that further
goal definition is a subjective
decision - jump in
            ↓
evaluate for thoroughness
            ↓
problem solved


Model:   Strange loops absent
         Single goal and interpretation
         Heuristic available
         Little use of "intrusive" components
```

Predictions Based on the Model: Support and Age Differences

Table 6.1 summarized the predicted effects of goal clarity and heuristic availability (two factors discussed in the literature) on respondents' strategy and apparent success on the problems. Some confirmation of those predictions was discussed earlier. This section will summarize how successfully one can use the young, middle-aged, and old adults' models developed from the Power problem and Table 6.1 hypotheses to predict three things: the same respondents' success on other problems; the same respondents' errors on other problems; and the same respondents' steps to solution of other problems. Age differences will then be discussed. The steps to solution used by other young, middle-aged, and old respondents will be explored in another paper.

Figure 6.6
Process Steps for Respondent C: Power Problem, Administered Fourth

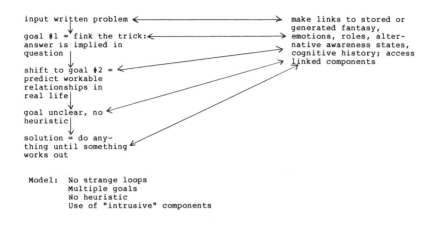

```
input written problem  <───────────────────────>   make links to stored or
                                                    generated fantasy,
goal #1 = fink the trick:<──────────────────>      emotions, roles, alter-
answer is implied in                                native awareness states,
question                                            cognitive history; access
                                                    linked components
shift to goal #2 = <
predict workable
relationships in
real life

goal unclear, no <
heuristic

solution = do any-
thing until something
works out
```

```
Model:   No strange loops
         Multiple goals
         No heuristic
         Use of "intrusive" components
```

Success on Problems (Seen as Well-Structured)

The six problems were scored "Pass" if respondents gave the correct numerical answer after treating the problems as mathematical, combinatorial, or proportionality problems, which was what they were intended to be in Piagetian formal operations studies. Results are in Table 6.5. Based on models of responses to the ill-structured combinatorial Power problem, and on Table 6.1, it would be expected that the young respondent would pass all other problems, while the other two respondents might possibly pass the well-structured problem but would probably fail the ill-structured ones. The younger respondent did pass the others except for the Bedroom problem; the older respondent failed all other problems; and the middle-aged respondent failed all but the Vitamin C problem.

Errors on Problems

Responses to the six problems by the three subjects were examined for crucial errors if the problem was not passed. On the basis of Table 6.1 and the Power problem response model, the younger respondent would be expected to pass all other problems. Actually one was not passed because of use of an incorrect heuristic, but this is a peripheral error and not one that would invalidate the model. On the basis of Table 6.1 and the Power problem response models, the middle-aged and older respondents would be expected to make errors by using too large a problem space on ABC (the well-structured problem); they did so. They also would be expected to use too large a problem space on the four

Table 6.5
Success, Crucial Errors, and Number of Solutions, Goals, Essences for Each Respondent, by Problem

Power

Young: Pass; no errors; two solutions, two goals, one essence.

Middle: Fail; error due to adopting large problem space; four solutions, four goals, two essences.

Old: Fail; error due to adoption of large problem space, poor input; two solutions, two goals, two essences.

ABC

Young: Pass; no errors; one solution, goal, essence.

Middle: Fail; adoption of large problem space; two goals, solutions, essences.

Old: Fail; adoption of large problem space; one solution, two goals, two essences.

Bedroom

Young: Fail; erroneous heuristic; one solution, two goals, two essences.

Middle: Fail; adoption of large problem space; six solutions, one goal, one essence.

Old: Fail; adoption of large problem space and no heuristic; two solutions, one goal, one essence.

Magazine

Young: Pass; no errors; two solutions, one goal, one essence.

Middle: Fail; too large problem space; four solutions, four goals, two essences.

Old: Fail; goal was equal to a process; one solution, two goals, two essences.

Vitamin C

Young: Pass; no errors; two solutions, one goal, one essence.

Middle: Pass; no errors; two solutions, one goal, one essence.

Old: Fail; no heuristic; two solutions, one goal, one essence.

Camp

Young: Pass; no errors; one solution, goal, essence.

Middle: Fail; large problem space; one solution, two goals, two essences.

Old: Fail; no heuristic; five solutions, one goal, one essence.

remaining problems; the middle-aged respondent did this on three of them and the older respondent on two.

Steps to Solution

Twelve steps to solution that were almost always present were to input material, monitor, remember, generate an "essence of problem," generate goals, generate solutions, slip levels, use "noncognitive" processes, select, evaluate, move to goal, and output.

The mean number of solutions, goals, and problem essences for each of the three respondents reflected the number of solutions, goals, and essences in their Power problem responses. The middle-aged respondent had the largest number ($\bar{X}_s = 3.3$; $\bar{X}_g = 2.3$; $\bar{X}_e = 1.7$), while the older and younger respondents had fewer (O:$\bar{X}_s = 2.2$, $\bar{X}_g = 1.3$, $\bar{X}_e = 1.3$; Y:$\bar{X}_s = 1.5$, $\bar{X}_g = 1.3$, $\bar{X}_e = 1.2$). These data suggest an age difference in ideational productivity, association, and flexibility in responding to ill-structured problems.

These data are in accord with data for errors. The middle-aged respondent, with too large a problem space to "succeed" on abstract problems and with a capacity to shift attention, had the greatest number of solutions, goals, and essences, and most often slipped levels; the younger, with little productivity and very focused attention, succeeded well in the abstract, but only in the abstract.

If success were redefined as "finding a solution, by some criterion, when the problem is *not* seen as abstract combinatorial or proportional," the younger respondent would be a dismal failure and the middle-aged would shine. This is an important consideration in a world where many practical and political problems can be framed as abstract well-structured *or* as everyday ill-structured.

The older respondent had the unfortunate experience of having too large a problem space and a poor grasp of problem information with absence of a heuristic. Without the latter two drawbacks, which could be related to memory loss, the older respondent might have done better than the younger or even the middle-aged. The solutions finally produced by the older respondent also were equivalent to general processes, and therefore were potentially very useful to that respondent in a number of situations.

Looking more closely at the steps in light of Table 6.1, we would predict, on the basis of the Power problem responses, that the younger respondent would, overall, have more category (1) responses. This was the case for four of the five remaining problems. More category (4)'s were predicted for the middle-aged and older respondents. This was the case for four of the five remaining problems for the middle-aged respondent; but four of five were category (2) for the older respondent.

The older respondent's data here run counter to hypotheses, while the remaining data support them.

DISCUSSION

This very short discussion will serve to recapitulate the results of this study and to focus on belief systems and intentionality as control processes, compensatory mechanisms, and the possibility of age-related styles for solving ill-structured problems. Many other topics could be addressed but are not, due to space limitations. For additional data concerning use of this model during cooperative problem solving, see Sinnott (1984a); for effects of experimental manipulations of emotion, daydreaming, intention, context, and postformal thought demands, see Sinnott (1987, in press). More extensive data on noncognitive processes in a larger sample of solvers is in Sinnott (1987, in press)

In the work just reported, a model of the processes used in the solution of potentially ill-structured, everyday problems was created. This model, although parsimonious, contained features not usually included in problem solving models. It explained many more of the actual rambling statements made by respondents than would any model without levels slippage, noncognitive processes, and processes for generation. The basic steps that are part of the model were found across the problems and in respondents of three different age groups. Hypotheses focused on the effects of goal clarity and availability of a heuristic also were formulated and supported, suggesting additional mechanisms and research.

This model and these analyses point out the central controlling role that phenomenological variables such as belief systems, intentionality, and creativity may have in problem solving. As Polanyi (1977) says, in every act of knowing there is a passionate contribution of the knower. We might substitute "problem solver" for "knower." Even science, the most objective form of problem solving, involves a personal commitment (Polanyi 1977). These personal commitments might take the form of beliefs or judgments about problem essence. Beliefs and syntheses may be part of the regulatory process that defines problem space and focuses attention, allowing for modifications in the structure of the rules *during* a process done *by* the rules. Therefore, they may serve the same function that recombinations of DNA serve: introducing variety and range into the process. The same could hold true for the function of noncognitive variables: they might provide the bridges between problem spaces that effectively enlarge problem space. These two mechanisms—bridging and recombination—introduce variety into an active system. The system is bounded or limited or parameterized by other processes, such as memory and heuristics. These complementary processes are, then, both enlarging and narrowing, and together, and only together, provide the maximum number of useful options to the solver during complex ill-structured problem solving.

From a system theory point of view (Miller 1978), any problem solving system must encompass enough disorganization (openness, entropy) to meet adaptational demands plus sufficient organization to maintain continuity. Only systems that have means to handle fuzzy sets in interpretation of situations will be able to be innovative in somewhat new situations while still making sense of those situations. What had been missing in past studies was a way to conceptualize those many problems that, unlike math or logic, are not strictly constrained in meaning. What had been missing was a way to describe how a problem solving system can broaden its expertise, adaptivity, and creativity, and how it can do old things in new ways. This model is one step in such a description. A desirable future step is the implementation of an Artificial Intelligence program to execute this sort of solution.

The three age-related styles of problem solving described above were also found in other sets of responses. They were not reported here because of space considerations. They would constitute another level of proof for the utility of the model. The three age-related styles appear to be consistent with potential strategic compensatory mechanisms for cognitive deficits at various levels of age/experience. They also appear to be consistent with the adult life periods as described by Erikson (1982) and Schaie (1977–78).

The "youthful" style seemed best for data gathering, learning, and bottom-up processing. Attention was focused and narrow; memory content was readily available. Past experience, monitoring, and products of unconscious processes were not important to the solution. There was a tendency to view the problem in abstract, noncontextual terms. This, of course, could be the most useful style for the concrete-inexperienced solver who has relatively few structures of knowledge available. The young solver may compensate for lack of structures, monitoring skills, and experience by staying close to the data and marching in a straight line toward solution.

The "mature" style seemed best for data gathering and optimal organization of information experienced in context. Top-down and bottom-up processing both seemed prevalent. Attention varied from focused to diffuse, memory contents were richer and were available. Monitoring and unconscious processes were important to the solution. This could be the most useful strategy for the executive, generative, responsible, mature adult active in the worlds of work and family. The mature thinker seemed to compensate for the high difficulty level of his/her environment, full of ill-structured problems, by strategically utilizing large problem spaces, syntheses, and monitoring-related decisions.

The "old" style seemed best for rapid, low-energy-demand solutions done by an experienced solver with many available structures of knowledge. It was top-down in style, with little attention to data, probably because of poor memory capacities. Attention was diffuse, possibly because of limited arousal capabilities. This style, then, seemed to compensate for low memory and energy, and overextensive stored data and structure. Solution was seen as "finding the best process or heuristic," and other steps (like actually reaching a concrete solution) were minimized. While this style was still useful because it was enough in touch with the reality of the problem that the processes made sense, it was less useful than a style that permitted choice of a process *and* carried it to completion. One can imagine that a subject with even less energy might simply impose a heuristic quickly, top-down, whether or not it fit the problem at all. Such an idiosyncratic style (which does occur) is better labeled a "decline" style. That style compensates inadequately for the deficient system seen in very old problem solvers or those with limited capacities who are, however, experienced enough to have any structures to impose.

It has been suggested (Salthouse, private communication) that older respondents may produce protocols of the style described above as an artifact of their inability to *both* monitor and process (speak and think) because of limited resources. Salthouse suggested that protocols would appear more limited than necessary because they captured only parts of a larger, more complex thought process. While this is an argument to consider, it does not appear to be a compelling reason to reject this model or any protocol, even that of the older respondent. The protocol of the oldest of the three subjects was just as long as that of the youngest, but the style was very different. If omissions did occur, there would be no reason to expect them to be systematic. The older respondent's protocol, however limited, still contained elements (listed in the steps) that add to our understanding of the process of solving ill-structured problems. Much work remains to be done on everyday ill-structured problem solving models.

In general, these analyses suggested the following: (1) ill-structured/everyday problems and thinking-aloud analyses should be used more frequently; (2) their use leads to understanding of additional processes and mechanisms important to understanding problem solving in general; (3) additional mechanisms should be incorporated into models of problem solving; (4) such complex models can aid our understanding of potentially age-related compensatory mechanisms in problem solving; (5) some mechanisms useful in understanding abstract logical problem solving seem to apply to ill-structured/everyday problem solving as well.

REFERENCES

Bastick, T. (1982). *Intuition: How we think and act*. New York: Wiley.
Cavanaugh, J., Kramer, D., Sinnott, J. D., Camp, C., & Markley, R. (1985). On missing links and such: Interfaces between cognitive research and everyday problem-solving. *Human Development, 28,* 146–168.
Churchman, C. (1971). *The design of inquiring systems: Basic concepts of systems and organization*. New York: Basic Books.
Commons, M., Richards, F., & Armon, C. (Eds.). (1984). *Beyond formal operations*. New York: Praeger.
Csikszentmihalyi, M. (1978). Attention and the holistic approach to behavior. In K. Pope & J. Singer (Eds.), *The stream of consciousness*. New York: Plenum.
Ericsson, K. A., & Simon, H. (1984). *Protocol analysis*. Cambridge, Mass.: MIT Press.
Erikson, E. (1982). *The lifecycle completed*. New York: Norton.
Giambra, L. (1983). An idiographic, in depth approach to complex concept identification in adulthood. Paper presented as part of the symposium "The Understanding of Problem Solving from a Gerontological Perspective: Today's Status, Tomorrow's Research, and Some New Ideas," L. Giambra, chair, sponsored by the Gerontological Society, San Francisco.
Giambra, L., & Arenberg, D. (1980). Problem solving, concept learning, and aging. In L. Poon (Ed.), *Aging in the 1980's: Psychological issues* (pp. 253–259). Washington, D.C.: American Psychological Association.
Gödel, K. (1962). *On formally undecidable propositions*. New York: Basic Books.
Greeno, J., Magone, M., Chaiklin, S. (1979). Theory of constructions and set in problem solving. *Memory and Cognition, 7,* 445–461.
Hayes-Roth, B., & Hayes-Roth, F. (1979). A cognitive model of planning. *Cognitive Science, 3,* 275–310.
Hofstadter, D. (1979). *Gödel, Escher, & Bach: An eternal golden braid*. New York: Random House.
Howard, D. (1983). *Cognitive psychology*. New York: Macmillan.
Inhelder, B., & Piaget, J. (1958). *The growth of logical thinking from childhood to adolescence*. New York: Basic Books.
Kitchener, K. (1983). Cognition, metacognition, and epistemic cognition. *Human Development, 26,* 222–232.
Kuhn, D. (1983). On the dual executive and its significance in the development of developmental psychology. In D. Kuhn & J. Meacham (Eds.), *On the development of developmental psychology*. Basel: Karger.
Landfield, A. (1977). *Personal construct psychology*. Lincoln: University of Nebraska Press.
Lauer, R. (1982). Epistemic cognition. Paper available from author.
Miller, J. (1978). *Living systems*. New York: McGraw-Hill.

Newell, A., & Simon, H. (1972). *Human problem-solving.* Englewood Cliffs, N.J.: Prentice-Hall.

Polanyi, M. (1977). *Personal knowledge.* Chicago: University of Chicago Press.

Schaie, K. W. (1977–78). Toward a stage theory of adult cognitive development. *International Journal of Aging and Human Development, 8,* 129–138.

Schoenfeld, A. H. (1983). Beyond the purely cognitive: Belief systems, social cognitions, and metacognitions as driving forces in intellectual performance. *Cognitive Science, 7,* 329–363.

Shank, R., Collins, G., Davis, E., Johnson, P., Lytinen, S., & Reiser, B. (1982). What's the point? *Cognitive Science, 6,* 255–275.

Shock, N., Andres, R., Arenberg, D., Costa, P., Greulich, R., Lakatta, E., & Tobin, J. (1984). *Normal human aging: The Baltimore Longitudinal Study of Aging.* Washington, D.C.: U.S. Government Printing Office.

Simon, D. P., & Simon, H. (1978). Individual differences in solving physics problems. In R. S. Siegler (Ed.), *Children's thinking: What develops?* Hillsdale, N.J.: Erlbaum.

Sinnott, J. D. (1975). Everyday thinking and Piagetian operativity in adults. *Human Development, 18,* 430–443.

Sinnott, J. D. (1981). The theory of relativity: A metatheory for development? *Human Development, 24,* 293–311.

Sinnott, J. D. (1982). Do adults use a postformal "theory of relativity" to solve everyday logical problems? Paper presented as part of the symposium "On Missing Links: Interfaces Between Cognitive Research and Everyday Problem Solving," J. Cavanaugh & D. Kramer, chairs, sponsored by the Gerontological Society, Boston.

Sinnott, J. D. (1983). Individual strategies on Piagetian problems: A thinking aloud approach. Paper presented as part of the symposium "Understanding of Problem Solving from a Gerontological Perspective: Today's Status, Tomorrow's Research, And Some New Ideas," L. Giambra, chair, sponsored by the Gerontological Society, San Francisco.

Sinnott, J. D. (1984a). *Effects of goal clarity and presence of a partner on problem solving performance.* Technical report available from the author at Towson State University, Baltimore, MD 21204.

Sinnott, J. D. (1984b). Postformal reasoning: The relativistic stage. In M. Commons, F. Richards, & C. Armon (Eds.), *Beyond formal operations* (pp. 288–315). New York: Praeger.

Sinnott, J. D. (1987). Experimental evidence for relativistic, self-referential postformal thought: The roles of emotion, intention, attention, memory, and health in adaptive adult cognition. Paper presented at the Third Beyond Formal Operations Symposium at Harvard University: "Positive Development During Adulthood," Cambridge, Mass.

Sinnott, J. D. (in press). Lifespan relativistic postformal thought: Methodology and data from everyday problem solving studies. In M. Commons, J. D. Sinnott, F. Richards, & C. Armon (Eds.), *Adult development: Comparisons and applications of developmental models.* New York: Praeger.

Sweller, J. (1983). Control mechanisms in problem solving. *Memory and Cognition, 11,* 32–40.

Sweller, J., & Levine, M. (1982). The effects of goal specificity on means-end analysis and learning. *Journal of Experimental Psychology: Learning, Memory, and Cognition, 8,* 463–474.

Toulmin, S. (1958). *The uses of argument.* Cambridge: Cambridge University Press.

Wood, P. (1983). Inquiring systems and problem structure: Implications for cognitive development. *Human Development, 26,* 249–265.

7

Plans, Actions, and Transactions in Solving Everyday Problems

George W. Rebok

A primary everyday problem solving activity is planning, with planning being defined as the conscious or deliberate predetermination of a sequence of actions aimed at accomplishing a problem goal (Hayes-Roth & Hayes-Roth 1979; Pea 1982). Planning entails selecting and coordinating actions as well as monitoring and guiding the execution of a plan to a successful conclusion. The major aims of the present chapter are to review extant theoretical models of planning and problem solving, artificial intelligence, and transactional approaches, and to describe a recently proposed model of planning called the transactional opportunistic model. Several focal issues guided the formulation of this synthesized approach: How does transactional planning differ from other types of planning activity? What are some of the major differences between planning in informal, everyday life situations and in formal, problem solving tasks? What role do contextual factors play in planning in realistic problem situations? Are some contexts more supportive of planning efforts than others?

Context is, of course, not the only factor that affects the nature and direction of planned actions. Problem solver characteristics and the structure of the task itself must also be taken into account. Good planners must be able to establish suitable decision criteria, flexibly allocate their cognitive resources, review and evaluate previous decisions, carry out alternative plans as necessary, and formulate plans at high levels of abstraction. Individual (and developmental) differences in knowledge structures, component cognitive processes, motivational levels, and problem solving styles may explain some of the widespread variations in planning effectiveness. We will discuss individual differences in planners and planning by citing data from a recent series of experiments in our laboratory on a routine, everyday cognitive activity, grocery shopping.

CURRENT THEORETICAL PERSPECTIVES

Planning's relevance to most everyday cognitive activities has been acknowledged by cognitive psychologists of diverse theoretical persuasions (Forbes & Greenberg 1982). Perhaps the most influential contemporary conceptualization of planning is the information-processing perspective. In information-processing theories, planning is usually viewed as a multistep sequence of problem solving that involves plan representation, plan construction, plan execution, and planning process remembering. These steps do not occur independently, but are functionally integrated into an organized planning series.

Artificial intelligence approaches to planning derive from information-processing models and share the latter's emphasis on the conceptualization of plans as isomorphic to computer programs. However, artificial intelligence approaches generally focus more on the development of "intelligent" machine programs that can get a computer to plan a simplified task as efficiently as possible.

Transactional approaches to planning, which encompass the work of Piaget, Flavell, Vygotsky, and Leont'ev, view the capacity to anticipate the consequences of planned actions and to reflect on and understand their impact as the main foci of planning activity. More than information-processing and artificial intelligence approaches, transactional models view plans as "internalized actions which both direct and are derived from problem-solving activities" (Meyer & Rebok 1985, p. 50). The above approaches form the theoretical basis for the transactional opportunistic model of planning discussed below. Particular attention will be paid to the model's applicability to human planning in everyday problem solving contexts.

Major Tenets of the Transactional Opportunistic Model of Planning

The transactional opportunistic model of planning builds on the information-processing approach proposed by Hayes-Roth and Hayes-Roth (1979), but includes a transactional, thinking-in-action component not emphasized in their model. Meyer and Rebok (1985) have outlined three major tenets of the transactional opportunistic approach to planning and problem solving:

1. Initial plans are only partially elaborated prior to the execution phase of a problem solving task, assuming they are elaborated at all.

2. Problem solving is a process involving a dynamic, rather than a static, relationship (transaction) between plans and actions.

3. Subsequent plans are very much dependent on *feedback* from prior executions and *reflections* on the relative efficiency of those executions.

We will now review each of the above notions to show how it extends and clarifies previous assumptions about planning and problem solving.

Tenet 1 contrasts with the assumptions of traditional hierarchical approaches, in which planning is seen as a primarily hypothetico-deductive process proceeding from top-down abstractions. In this view high-level, or more abstract, plans are *successively refined* at progressively lower levels of abstraction until the problem goal is attained. Although most planning, especially in everyday contexts, may not operate in this orderly, top-down manner, it is not completely bottom-up and purely inductive either. Rather, planning can be characterized by a dynamic transaction between lower and higher levels of decision making.

This transactional view is consistent with data showing that plans rarely are fully formulated at the highest level of abstraction but often require considerable feedback from completed actions for subsequent elaboration and successful execution. Lesgold, Feltovitch, Glaser, and Wang (1981), for example, have shown that expert problem solvers have more completely elaborated planning schemata than novices, but experts also possess a rapid perceptual recognition skill involving an interaction of lower and higher levels of representation. In contrast with novices, expert problem solvers seem to rely on context and data-driven rules rather than high-level, fully elaborated plans (Rose 1985). Thus, experts are at once both more structured and more flexible than novices in controlling their planning activity.

There are several reasons why incomplete elaboration seems to be especially characteristic of plans in everyday problem solving contexts. In contrast with laboratory problems having clearly defined goal criteria, everyday problem goals are often vague and the problem solver must frequently infer the goals and generate plans for reaching them (Dörner 1983, 1985; Wilensky 1981, 1983). Furthermore, the goal states in everyday problems are multiple, interactive, and flexible, and conflicts among contradictory goals are not uncommon (Newman & Bruce 1986; Wilensky 1983). In laboratory problem solving, subjects must find the solution to a single, complex problem (e.g., choosing the best chess move, solving a cryptarithmetic problem), but in everyday problem solving (e.g., running an errand) individuals must often synthesize solutions to several rather simple interacting problems.

Incomplete plan elaboration may also result from a lack of information about present and future states of the problem and from a lack of knowledge about permissible operators for moving through the planning space. For everyday problems, problem solvers often do not have at their disposal the means (the operators) by which a situation can be altered. Even if the operators are known in advance, the planner may not be able to mentally project the consequences of those moves because of various limitations on mental representation and working memory. These limitations may become very apparent with everyday problems involving distant goals and long-range planning because the number of unknown variables increases dramatically (Frese & Stewart 1984). There- fore, the everyday problem solver faces a trade-off between the desire for a more complete and elaborated plan and the need for flexibility of action.

Tenet 2's assumption about planning as a dynamic, transactional op- portunistic process involving plans and actions contrasts with previous models of planning as a preliminary organizing stage of problem solving. In information-processing and artificial intelligence models, planning is seen as the initial stage in a two-stage problem solving sequence; the second, or control, stage involves monitoring and guiding the execution of the plan to a successful conclusion. In the transactional opportunistic model, no strict separation is maintained between the planning and execution stages of problem solving. In the course of executing actions, novel plans emerge as previous goals are revised and replaced with new ones. These emergent constructions arise from immediate feedback on the success of completed actions as well as from the problem solver's reflections on the outcomes of those actions, or what Piaget (1976, 1978) has termed "reflected abstraction."

Because the transactional component is an essential feature of our model, we need to examine it in greater detail. From a transactional perspective, the key issue is how plans and goals are transformed in learning to adapt to changing problem and task conditions. In some instances, plans are sufficiently elaborated and/or the problem situation is sufficiently well-defined that plans are maintained in their original form through the final problem solution. However, on many laboratory and everyday tasks, the majority of individuals substantially modify their plans (see, e.g., Meyer & Rebok 1985), and these modifications have major implications for the subsequent achievability of planned actions.

Individuals may make a number of different moves and decisions in modifying their initial plan while trying to execute its action. They may redefine the goal of the problem and replace it with a set of goals or subgoals requiring different plans for their attainment (Dörner 1983, 1985).

Redefining a goal and replacing a plan to attain it with a new one of course implies that the problem solver had a plan with clearly specified goals in the first place. Many times, however, people enter the execution phase of problem solving with no clear goal or plan of action in mind.

Instead, problem solving is carried out on a pragmatic, plan-as-you-go basis, which we have termed planning-in-action (Meyer & Rebok 1985). This approach to problem solving can be observed among persons of all ages and levels of experience, but is found most commonly in very young children and inexperienced planners.

According to the third tenet of the transactional opportunistic model, plans are modified on the basis of opportunistic actions taken in executing a problem and/or on the basis of reflections on the relative effectiveness of previous solution attempts. While a plan of action is being executed, individuals may make use of positive and negative feedback cues to inform themselves about the effects of an action and the necessity of refining or abandoning their original plan. As noted in tenets 1 and 2 above, the need for refinement greatly depends on the degree of elaboration and goal relevance of the original plans.

The central role of feedback from performance in elaborating previous plans and in devising new ones cannot be overemphasized. Feedback lies at the heart of the dynamic between plans and actions. For example, a person with limited knowledge about the task domain may be insensitive to the full range of feedback cues available in the problem environment. He or she may be more likely to employ predominantly top-down planning strategies and less likely to edit plans in response to negative feedback (see, e.g., Karmiloff-Smith 1984). On the other hand, individuals with more background knowledge or experience may respond to negative feedback cues by trying alternative plans until goal conflicts are eliminated (Wilensky 1981).

Not only do people use feedback to modify subsequent plans, but they also consciously reflect on the successes or failures of their actions before, during, and after the completion of problem solving efforts. With increasing age and task experience, individuals seem better able to metacognitively reflect on past actions in an effort to produce a more adequate plan for future actions. Although problem solvers may not always be able to report on their mental activity or describe their planning knowledge, they use their metacognitive awareness to monitor and evaluate what they did (Lefebvre-Pinard 1983). As Rogoff (1982, p. 159) remarked, "People demonstrate metacognitive understanding through their management of real situations."

To summarize, I have argued for the usefulness of a transactional opportunistic approach to describe the way people go about planning and solving problems in everyday life. This perspective has much in common with contextualistic approaches, which view the transaction between the active organism and the changing context as the basis for understanding psychological functioning. The transactional opportunistic view is also congruent with general systems theory approaches to cognition (see Sinnott, Chapter 19 of this volume), with their emphasis on networks of interactive processes functioning as a whole, the importance of feedback for coordinating activity, and the focus on processes underlying change over time. We will now review two currently active areas of theory and research to illustrate how our model builds upon and clarifies notions of planning and problem solving used in each of these areas.

Information-Processing and Artificial Intelligence Models of Planning

The information-processing model of planning originated in Miller, Galanter, and Pribram's (1960) seminal work *Plans and the Structure of Behavior*. Underpinning information-processing approaches is the view of planning as a fundamentally top-down process, with plans being successively refined at progressively lower levels of abstraction. Newell and Simon (1972) embodied this successive refinement, or problem decomposition, approach to planning in a computer program called the General Problem Solver (GPS). In developing the GPS, Newell and Simon created a program with extremely powerful and general heuristic methods such as means-ends analysis and planning ahead. Means-ends analysis compares the initial state of the problem with the desired end state (goal) and finds a means of reducing or eliminating those differences. Because means-ends analysis results in a rather rigid, one-step-at-a-time approach to problem solving, GPS was endowed with an overall plan for the use of means-ends analysis and other heuristics, such as subgoal decomposition.

According to Newell and Simon (1972), the major feature of planning is to simplify the search for a problem solution through a complex problem space. This planning-by-simplification process involves omitting the details surrounding the original problem, forming a more general, abstract problem, and using the solution to provide a plan for solving the more restricted problem. In the original GPS system, this planning process rigidly proceeded by solving the most general problem first and then more specific and detailed subproblems, sub-subproblems, and so on. In later versions (those developed in the mid–1960s), tree structures of alternative goals and operators can be built that flexibly allow for local increases in plan complexity while maintaining the overall top-down direction.

Sacerdoti (1977) has developed a computer model of planning that more fully takes into account the need for some form of planning-in-action. His model, called Nets of Action Hierarchies, or NOAH, constructs an abstract preplan that can be revised or improved during its execution, depending on the consequences of various actions. However, as with planning systems like GPS, NOAH is basically a top-down planner, with high-level plans guiding and constraining the formulation and execution of lower-level plans. In addition, NOAH assumes that initial plans are relatively complete and require little or no elaboration for their successful execution.

More recently, Barbara and Frederick Hayes-Roth (1979) have proposed an information-processing model of planning that departs from previous models in two significant ways. First, the Hayes-Roths conceptualize planning as a multidirectional, opportunistic process that includes both top-down and bottom-up abstractions. As the problem solver works down the hierarchy of abstraction, low-level concrete plans may suggest abandonment, revision, or updating of high-level plans into successively more detailed subplans. Second, the Hayes-Roths propose the existence of several specific levels of abstraction and operationalize the differences among them. Plans at one level of the hierarchy may influence decision sequences higher or lower in the hierarchy.

The Hayes-Roths tested their opportunistic planning model (OPM) by analyzing think-aloud protocols of adults performing an errand-planning problem (Goldin & Hayes-Roth 1980; Hayes-Roth & Hayes-Roth 1979). The subjects' job was to plan the route for a day's errands in a fictitious town. The subjects received scenarios listing the errands, the starting and ending locations and times, and sometimes additional temporal and spatial constraints. Subjects also received a map of the town. Because the time allotted for performing the errands was insufficient, subjects needed to establish priorities for accomplishing the most important errands first and for planning the most efficient route.

The Hayes-Roths categorized subjects' verbal descriptions of their planning activities into five conceptual planes or levels: plan, plan abstraction, world knowledge, executive, and metaplan. Planning decisions at the first three levels involve statements about the main features of the developing plan, whereas those at the executive and metaplan levels involve the executive control of the plans generated. Each conceptual plane is further partitioned into several levels of abstraction. For example, the executive plane has three levels involving decisions for allocating general cognitive resources, prioritizing cognitive activities, and scheduling plans. The levels of the metaplan plane involve plan definition, choosing a problem solving model, setting cognitive policies, and evaluating problem criteria.

The OPM model has proved to be quite robust and has been adopted by artificial intelligence researchers and other investigators for use in a variety of problem domains (Smith 1985; Thorndyke & Wescourt 1984). The model seems to be particularly well suited to real-life knowledge domains for which plans are continuously developed and carried out in a complex, changing environment (Hayes-Roth & Thorndyke 1985). Future work on information processing and artificial intelligence will likely witness an increased concern for more flexible, abstract, and powerful representations of planning and problem solving architecture.

Transactional Perspectives on Planning

Broadly speaking, transactional perspectives on planning emphasize the importance of the constantly changing relation between plans and actions, and especially the effects of executed actions on subsequent planning and problem solving. Two major directions in the study of planning from a transactional perspective can be discerned. First, the increased emphasis on studying the strategies people use to solve problems has produced a shift in concern to the processes by which people monitor and evaluate their cognitive activity. This area of investigation, which falls under the rubric of metacognition, has become popular among developmental psychologists and artificial intelligence researchers. The second stream of investigation, which has been inspired by the research of the Soviet psychologists Vygotsky and Luria, is concerned with the self-regulating function of private speech. A related line of work, which also derives from Soviet research, especially Leont'ev's (1979) activity theory, examines the coordination of means-goals relationships in intentional activity.

Probably the most active area of investigation in the 1980s comes from within a subfield of developmental psychology known as metacognition. In general, metacognition is a form of cognition that encompasses an awareness of the goals of cognitive activity as well as the plans and procedures for reaching them (Brown & DeLoache 1978). During the ongoing attempts to reach the goal, the problem solver must engage in planning-in-action, which involves monitoring, evaluating, testing, and revising the outcomes of one's cognitive efforts. Initially, most of the work on metacognition focused on the nature and development of metacognitive knowledge about memory, its capacities and its limitations (Flavell & Wellman 1977; Kreutzer, Leonard, & Flavell 1975). However, research on metacognition has been increasingly extended to such diverse areas as reading comprehension (Baker & Brown 1984; Myers & Paris 1978), attentional processes (Miller & Weiss 1981), and referential communication (Yussen & Bird 1979).

A second major thrust in transactional approaches to planning is found in the work of Soviet psychologists (Leont'ev 1979; Luria 1961; Vygotsky 1962, 1978). Vygotsky (1962) was among the first investigators to postulate a direct connection between awareness of one's cognitive processes and the ability to self-regulate them, and to raise the issue of how children acquire an awareness and mastery of intentional thought (Lefebvre-Pinard 1983). Vygotsky also initiated work on verbal self-regulation in children by focusing on the issue of how speech-for-self progressively assumes the role of organizer of behavior. Vygotsky's contemporary, Luria (1961), attempted to clarify and expand Vygotsky's point on the self-regulatory role of language in a series of well-known experiments on self-produced verbalization on a simple discrimination learning task.

Contemporary efforts have dealt with issues more directly relevant to the development of planning skills, such as the use of problem solving strategies to enhance self-control (Meichenbaum & Asarnow 1979; Mischel 1979). Mischel's work bears a close resemblence to Luria's work on the development of verbal self-regulation, but is less concerned with strictly verbal aspects of control. Rather, Mischel attempts to understand how both verbal and nonverbal cognitive strategies lead to increased self-regulation in various situations involving delay of gratification and resistance to temptation. He is particularly interested in identifying those aspects of cognitive strategies about which children have developed a conscious awareness (e.g., plans, self-monitoring). Meichenbaum's work applies the theoretical notions of Luria and Vygotsky to a treatment paradigm involving self-instructional training with children and adults (Meichenbaum & Goodman 1979). Developing self-control, improving reading comprehension, and increasing creative problem solving are among the problem domains he has examined. More recently, Meichenbaum and his colleagues (Meichenbaum, Burland, Gruson, & Cameron 1985) have focused on metacognitive skills such as goal setting, strategy planning, and self-monitoring for improving the efficiency, maintenance, and generalization of self-instructional training.

A related line of planning research from a transactional perspective has roots in the activity theory of Leont'ev (1979). Leont'ev, a student of Vygotsky, distinguishes three levels of abstraction. The first level involves motives (e.g., hunger) that energize an organism's activity but have little to do with selecting goals and plans of action. In contrast, the second level involves what Leont'ev terms an "action," an aspect of cognitive and behavioral functioning aimed at a conscious goal. This level of abstraction is most directly relevant to the concept of planning and is implicated in action theoretic accounts of cognition (Chapman 1984). The third level of abstraction involves operations, the means by which actions are carried out under various limiting conditions of the task environment. Operations, which are often unconsciously triggered by the contextual conditions of a task, first appear as goal-directed actions, and then, through ceaseless repetition, become sufficiently automatic to be used as a means in planning and solving problems. Applications of Leont'ev's activity theory can be found in Meacham's (1977, 1982) work on remembering planned actions, or prospective remembering, and Paris's (Paris 1978; Paris, Newman, & McVey 1982) research on the coordination of means and goals in mnemonic activities.

CONTEXTUAL FACTORS IN EVERYDAY PLANNING

Psychologists often treat cognition as something that can be isolated from the context and content of what is being processed, that is, they try to minimize the effects of the task environment so that performance will reflect "pure process" (Rogoff 1982; Scribner 1986). This tendency is reflected, for example, in the division of problem solving activity into two discrete and consecutive phases: planning and execution. During the execution phase, only one problem state is considered important at a given time—the one that is being executed—and each action executed according to plan moves the problem solver further along through the problem space. If a plan is sufficiently elaborated, with full attention to all the relevant details in the task environment, then execution can be fully predicted and this phase of problem solving becomes merely an uninteresting "mop-up" activity.

However, in task domains that interact with real-world contexts, plans rarely are fully elaborated, so that the execution phase plays an indispensable part in the problem solving process. Thus, models of planning not only must incorporate selected opportunities for revising decisions in planning (opportunism) but also must allow for the execution and modification of those plans in action (transactionalism).

The position we espouse is that plans can never be separated from the problem solving context in which they are implemented. Thus, in real-life situations, as in laboratory situations, there is no such thing as "pure planning" and no such thing as "context-free" problem solving. Rather, planning reflects a continual interplay between plans and actions and the contexts that afford (or do not afford) various opportunities for their execution. This interplay can be found in Leont'ev's (1979) activity theory and the interdependence of subject and object; it is also evident in Vygotsky's (1962, 1978) sociocultural theory of adaptation. The notion of affordances has direct links to the work of the Gibsons, who have argued that perception and action occur as adaptations to the environment, and therefore cannot be understood without reference to that environment. We can extend the Gibsons' observations to the realm of everyday problem solving with one critical addendum. Consistent with a Piagetian constructivist position, we would argue that the properties of the environment do not exert an automatic or deterministic influence on problem solving, but assume a functional role only through the initiating and interpretive activities of the planner (Scribner 1986).

DESCRIPTION OF THE GROCERY-SHOPPING TASK

In developing a task for assessing the parameters of real-life planning efforts, five important plan-related criteria were taken into account. We first sought to identify tasks that would create a face-valid context for what might be considered "meaningful planning activity." Specifically, we focused on the question of what happens in the course of an everyday situation that may become problematic to the individual and that would stimulate effortful planning activity.

Our choice of a planning task was also governed by the perceived familiarity of the task to subjects. Ideally, the task should be familiar to all subjects, but differentially familiar so that the effects of subjects' background knowledge and experience with the task can be assessed (Goodnow 1986). In other words, our concern is with how knowledge (both tacit and explicit) interacts with the planning process.

In addition, the task needed to be of sufficient complexity to subjects that several different courses of action would be considered in selecting means for reaching the desired goal. However, the task could not be so complex as to prevent subjects from mentally simulating their plan's execution and its results, and revising when necessary. A good everyday task also allows you to study the transaction between a planner's skills and knowledge and the problem at hand. The task therefore should permit some preplanning before action as well as planning in the action of solving the problem. Finally, the task environment should circumscribe a problem domain for the exercise of a clearly delimited, highly structured planning activity. Evidence from script theory (Schank & Abelson 1977) and the organization of environments around scripted activities (e.g., elementary classrooms, the drugstore) suggests that human activity is organized in terms of segments on the order of ten minutes to two hours (Lave, Murtaugh, & de la Rocha 1984). These "proximal" activities are smaller in scope than more "distal" and empirically intractible activities, such as planning a career or deciding on a long-range financial plan.

In summary, it is necessary to choose from among everyday problem-solving tasks those which clearly call for planning activity, possess a high degree of familiarity, and offer alternative paths to solution. The tasks must also allow for planning-in-action and circumscribe a limited domain of cognitive activity. Thus, we have argued that the task environment must be designed with a transactional approach in mind.

After examining several candidate tasks, we decided that a grocery-shopping problem met the five criteria outlined above. The ubiquity and familiar character of shopping qualify it as an appropriate arena for studying planning in everyday life (Lave et al. 1984). Although most people are familiar with grocery shopping, their knowledge about the activity may well vary as a function of budget, nutritional concerns, family size, available stores, and so on. Grocery shopping is also an activity that is routinely associated with a number of planning generation activities (e.g., making a shopping list, meal planning), so people rec-

Figure 7.1
Sample Grocery-Shopping Scenario

```
You are having three couples over for brunch on Sunday

morning.  Because of work obligations, you have left

everything until the last minute.  It is now Saturday

evening at 8:45 pm, and the store closes at 9:00 pm.

You remember on your way to the store that you are low

on cash because you paid the telephone bill yesterday.

You look in your wallet and find only $35.00.  Do the

best you can to purchase the items you need for brunch

tomorrow.
```

ognize the value of planning in that context even if they themselves do not engage in planning activities. In addition, grocery shopping involves a highly structured interaction between the planning activity and the setting (the supermarket), so there exist many alternative paths for proceeding through the store (Lave et al. 1984).

Despite the fact that many shoppers see themselves engaged in a routine activity and making habitual purchases, shopping is an activity that affords rich transactional opportunities for plan revision and updating. Consider the case when the shopper decides to backtrack to buy an item not originally planned (e.g., eggs) because an item in another part of the store that goes with that item (e.g., bacon) is on sale. Finally, shopping occurs within a specifiable time-space matrix that imposes certain constraints on planners' decisions regarding the number of items that can reasonably be purchased, the amount of money that can be spent, and the time that can be spent in the store.

The grocery-shopping task we designed involves planning a series of shopping trips through a hypothetical supermarket. Subjects are given a map of the supermarket, some planning aids (e.g., a shopping list, coupons), and a scenario depicting a typical shopping situation. The scenarios are varied in terms of the amount of money subjects may spend and/or the time allowed. The allotted money or time is invariably insufficient, so that subjects are forced to set priorities about which items to purchase and to organize their trip through the store in the most efficient manner. A typical shopping scenario involving both monetary and time constraints is shown in Figure 7.1.

The Grocery-Shopping Task and Experimental Procedures

In this section we discuss some preliminary explorations of grocery-shopping planning and describe some empirical evidence that is consistent with the proposed transactional opportunistic model (Rebok et al. 1986). Although these data are incomplete, they lead us to the conclusion that good planners can be distinguished from poor planners, and that this difference most likely resides in the degree to which planners consciously monitor and control their plans. Good planners seem to be able to make decisions at a higher level of abstraction and to shift attentional focus between various levels of the planning hierarchy.

Subjects and Materials

To test the assumptions of the transactional opportunistic model, we asked 20 young adults (14 females and 6 males, mean age = 18.30, *SD* = .57) from the introductory psychology subject pool at the State University of New York, Geneseo, to perform the grocery-shopping task. Each subject was given a map of a hypothetical grocery store and two shopping scenarios. All subjects received scenario 1, which included a list of ten possible items to purchase at the store (e.g., oranges, milk, fabric softener). The scenario was given as a demonstration exercise and was used to compare planning efficiency across subjects. Subjects then received one of four shopping scenarios involving either monetary and/or temporal constraints. In scenarios 2 and 3, subjects were limited to spending $20, in scenario 5 they could spend up to $35, and in scenario 4 no dollar limit was placed on the amount they could spend. The scenarios also varied in terms of the time allowed subjects to make their purchases. In scenario 2, subjects had less than three hours to shop, in scenario 4 about a half hour, and in scenario 5 only 15 minutes. In scenario 3 they could plan to shop anytime during an entire day and take as much time as desired. Scenarios thus varied from relatively constrained in terms of money and time to relatively unconstrained.

For all five scenarios, subjects were instructed to go through the supermarket and plan out loud which items to purchase and to trace their route through the store by drawing lines from item to item on the map. All verbal responses were tape-recorded for subsequent protocol analysis.

Immediately following the planning task, the Picture Arrangement subtest from the Wechsler Adult Intelligence Scale-Revised (WAIS-R) was administered. The Picture Arrangement task was chosen as a marker measure of planning ability because it involves arranging actions and events in a logical sequence to tell a story. The mean score on the Picture Arrangement test was 15.5 out of a possible 20 (*SD* = 3.58). Finally, all subjects completed a biographical information form on their age, sex, and year in college, and answered a question about their typical grocery-shopping habits.

Results

Two principal analytic procedures were used to examine the results. The first procedure treated plans as products, with the main focus on the efficiency or economy of the planned routes produced. We operationalized efficiency on a 100-point scale, using the following formula, based on Goldin and Hayes-Roth (1980):

Route
Efficiency $= 100-100 \times \dfrac{\text{(planned route length } - \text{ optimal route length)}}{\text{optimal route length}}$
Score

Optimal route estimates were provided by two independent raters who agreed on the shortest route length. Because not all subjects received the same second scenario, we used route efficiency scores derived from scenario 1 to conduct the analysis. Efficiency scores could theoretically range from 0 to 100, but the actual range was considerably less (range $= 48.52$ to 100.00, mean $= 78.32$, $SD = 14.52$).

In order to test for interindividual differences in planning efficiency, we contrasted the protocols of good and poor planners. We defined "good" planners as subjects who achieved a route efficiency score of 90 or better, and "poor" planners as those with an efficiency score under 70. Using this criterion, we were able to reliably distinguish five good protocols from six poor protocols. Mean route efficiency scores were 98.01 ($SD = 4.44$) for the good planners and 62.63 ($SD = 7.71$) for the poor planners, $t(9) = 31.47$, $p < .005$. Thus, significant individual variation in planning can be identified even on a routine, everyday task and in a small sample of relatively experienced planners.

In the second phase of the analysis, each subject's think-aloud protocol was divided into segments that represented the planning processes they used to make their purchasing decisions. The average number of segments for all plans produced on the four test scenarios was 15.3, with a range from 11.4 (scenario 2) to 22.2 (scenario 5). Each segment was then coded according to the five content categories developed by Hayes-Roth and Hayes-Roth (1979):

1. *Plan*. Statements about specific actions the planner intends to take (e.g., "I'm going to get a dozen oranges")
2. *Plan abstraction*. General statements about intentions, strategies, and tactics that summarize statements in the plan category (e.g., "I'll go past the deli to the meat and fish")
3. *World knowledge*. Statements about relationships in the problem environment

Table 7.1
Percentages of Responses in Each Content Category Across Scenarios

	Scenario			
Level	Scen 2	Scen 3	Scen 4	Scen 5
Plan	64.9	54.9	55.2	45.0
Plan Abstraction	3.5	1.4	6.0	7.2
World Knowledge	12.3	21.1	19.4	27.0
Executive	12.3	16.9	16.4	17.1
Metaplan	7.0	5.6	3.0	3.6

that might influence the planning process (e.g., "Dairy products will be next because they are closest")

4. *Executive.* Statements determining the allocation of attentional resources during planning (e.g., "I'll wait to get the frozen foods last because they may thaw")

5. *Metaplan.* Statements about problem definition, planning and problem-solving methods, and evaluation criteria (e.g., "I'll make a list so I can go through [the store] and take the shortest route").

A trained research assistant performed the initial coding for all 20 protocols, and the author independently checked this coding, with over 95 percent agreement.

The percentage of responses falling into each of the above content categories for scenarios 2–5 are shown in Table 7.1. The table shows that while "low-level" plans accounted for the majority of responses across the four scenarios, rather sizable percentages (> 10 percent) of "high-level" responses occurred in the world knowledge and executive categories. The overall percentages for the five categories across scenarios are 53.3 percent (plans), 4.9 percent (plan abstraction), 21.2 percent (world knowledge), 16.0 percent (executive), and 4.6 percent (metaplan). To determine the effect of planning context on plan decisions, we looked at the percentages of responses in each of the above decision categories as a function of the degree of constraint in each of the scenarios. A 4×5 chi-square analysis revealed that the scenarios differed significantly from each other across the five decision categories: X^2 (12) = 360.53, $p < .001$. Note that scenario 2 (one of the least constrained in terms of time) has a much higher percentage of plans than scenario 5 (the most constrained scenario). Thus, it appears subjects will produce more concrete plans when they feel unconstrained by the planning context.

A correlational analysis was carried out to determine whether the abstraction level of the plans was related to route efficiency scores. Intuitively, it would be expected that better planners employ a greater number of higher-level planning categories (plan abstraction, world knowledge, metaplan, executive) than poorer planners. As expected, higher route efficiency scores were positively correlated with plan abstraction: $r(18) = .53$, $p < .05$; the correlations between efficiency scores and world knowledge, executive, and metaplan decisions were in the expected direction but nonsignificant ($rs = .14, .14$, and $.13$, respectively).

According to the transactional opportunistic model, not only should better planners make more decisions at higher levels of abstraction than poor planners, but they should also be more able to shift attentional focus between different levels of the planning hierarchy (see Goldin & Hayes-Roth 1980 for a similar argument). To test our assumption about attentional flexibility, we measured the number of planning decisions whose level in the planning hierarchy differed from the level of the preceding decision. We found that planners shifted their attentional focus an average of 9.45 times on scenarios 2–5. A correlational analysis then revealed that better planning (as indicated by route efficiency scores) was positively associated with a greater number of attentional shift decisions: $r(18) = .31$, $p < .05$.

This seems to be a reasonable result, inasmuch as more efficient planners should be able to switch rapidly from a lower-level to a higher-level plan (or vice versa) than less efficient planners. It is also reasonable to suggest that planners who make a greater number of executive decisions (reflecting allocation of attentional resources) should show greater attentional flexibility. Strong support was found for this suggestion by correlating the number of executive decisions on scenarios 2–5 with the number of attentional shift decisions on those scenarios: $r(18) = .80$, $p < .01$.

Finally, we examined whether there were significant relationships between the product measure (route efficiency) and WAIS-Picture Arrangement scores and between the process measures (plan abstraction, world knowledge, executive, and metaplan decisions) and WAIS scores. Contrary to our expectations, no significant relationship was found between route efficiency and WAIS scores. As expected, metaplan processes showed a significant correlation with WAIS scores: $r(18) = .45$,

$p < .05$. However, WAIS scores failed to correlate significantly with the frequency of plan abstraction, world knowledge, or executive decision processes.

Discussion

The preliminary results of the research reported here provide additional empirical support for the major tenets of the transactional opportunistic model of planning. Only weak support could be found for the proposition that better (more efficient) planning is related to greater usage of high-level, abstract decision categories. Although highly efficient planners did rely more heavily on plan abstraction than less efficient planners, they showed only a slightly greater tendency to use world knowledge, executive decisions, and metaplanning. It is of interest to note that most of our planners, regardless of the problem situation, employed more concrete decision categories, such as plans and world knowledge, than the abstract categories of plan abstraction and metaplan decisions. This greater reliance on concrete data in the task situation has been reported by other investigators in planning studies with children (Pea & Hawkins 1987) and young adults (Goldin & Hayes-Roth 1980). Unless subjects are asked to perform their shopping tasks in an unusual or nonroutine manner, they may rely on the most concrete approach to the problem.

An alternative interpretation for reliance on concrete decision criteria involves the cognitive characteristics of the planners. Previous research by the author and his colleague Jerome Meyer has shown that children carry out planning on a largely pragmatic, concrete basis, that is, "planning-in-action" (Meyer & Rebok 1983, 1985). By young adulthood, individuals can engage in more reflective processing and abstract from previous and projected actions in formulating a subsequent plan. However, as Meyer and Rebok (1985) noted, even younger and older adults generate insufficiently elaborated plans that require considerable planning-in-action. The reasons underlying this type of planning behavior are not immediately clear, but they may involve, among other things, the inability to mentally represent the "problem-as-solved" or incomplete knowledge about the task environment and the appropriate operators. In any event, the end result is a preference for more concrete-level decisions.

Consistent with the assumptions of the transactional opportunistic model, we found some evidence for greater attentional flexibility among more proficient planners. Compared with poorer planners, better planners make more level transitions from concrete to abstract and from abstract to concrete plans. This finding suggests that not only do better planners maintain more focused attention (as shown by their efficient route planning), but they also can flexibly redirect their attention up and down the planning hierarchy.

With regard to the cognitive and metacognitive components of planning, we found little evidence for a systematic relationship between WAIS Picture Arrangement Test performance and planning efficiency and quality. Given that the Picture Arrangement Test involves a logical sequencing of actions in a story problem, the lack of an overall relationship is somewhat puzzling. Perhaps everyday problem solving depends more on abilities related to problem definition, subgoal, decomposition, and metacognitive monitoring and evaluation than laboratory-based problem solving.

DIRECTIONS FOR FURTHER RESEARCH

Given the major tenets of the transactional opportunistic model of planning, we suggest that future research on everyday problem solving proceed in three important directions. In this section, we briefly discuss each of these directions and the implications of our transactional opportunistic view for conducting everyday problem solving research.

First, the transactional opportunistic approach to planning emphasizes the view that problem solving is an activity spanning the roles of the person and the problem context (Rogoff 1982). A central part of this view is that planning is a functionally adaptive activity that continually changes to fit the problem state and the goal situation. If we adopt the transactional position that change is given, not derivative, then serious questions are raised about the usefulness of problem solving models that focus solely on the correctness or incorrectness of the end product or solution. Rather, investigators should study the cognitive system in operation, or "in flight," to borrow Vygotsky's (1978) phrase, rather than study processes that are already completely formed or fully automated (Berg & Sternberg 1985; Smyth, Morris, Levy, & Ellis 1987).

Consistent with the transactional opportunistic view, we encourage the sophisticated use of methodologies that join traditional information-processing analyses with naturalistic descriptive methods (see Agar & Hobbs 1983). Microgenetic studies, which examine the short-term quantitative and qualitative changes in people's problem-solving skill, would be particularly welcome (Catán 1986). The microgenetic approach has been applied to study events such as learning to solve a novel problem or developing expertise in a specific cognitive domain (see, e.g., Scribner 1986).

Finally, we have discussed the important role of conscious reflection, or metacognition, in regulating and controlling thinking during problem solving. Reflective activity can modify and direct the course of future planning and action. A necessary research step is to look at plan execution and executive monitoring in problem solving, rather than merely to focus on plan generation. Such research efforts might not only inform us about the self-regulatory aspects of planning but also suggest ways in which the search for a problem solution in a dynamically changing environment could be improved. In a series of experiments, Reither (Reither & Stäudel, 1985) has reported modest success in improving problem solving on a computer-simulated management problem by training adult subjects to reflect on their thought processes. We believe that training studies involving complex forms of realistic problem solving under controlled laboratory conditions offer a fruitful research avenue for investigating the relationship between planning and acting (see Kluwe 1987; Kluwe & Friedrichsen 1985).

CONCLUDING REMARKS

The transactional opportunistic perspective on planning and problem solving bridges information-processing, artificial intelligence, and trans-action-oriented points of view. This perspective (1) regards incomplete plan elaboration as characteristic of everyday forms of problem solving, (2) views problem solving in real life as a spontaneously dynamic process involving a transaction between plans and actions, and (3) emphasizes the importance of feedback from action and conscious reflection on action for the formulation and execution of subsequent plans.

The exploratory and descriptive character of the research supporting the transactional opportunistic approach makes it likely that assumptions of the model will need to be modified as more data are collected. It is also likely that other aspects of problem solving important to transactional opportunism remain to be discovered. These limitations notwithstanding, studies of problem solving under everyday conditions clearly demand a reconsideration of traditional laboratory analyses focusing on static plans, unambiguous goal states, and familiar operators. Everyday problem solving is an open-ended system requiring both planning and acting in a continuous, dynamic fashion.

REFERENCES

Agar, M. H., & Hobbs, J. R. (1983). Natural plans: Using AI planning in the analysis of ethnographic interviews. *Ethos, 11*, 33–48.

Baker, L., & Brown, A. L. (1984). Metacognitive skills and reading. In P. D. Pearson, M. Kamil, R. Barr, & P. Mosenthal (Eds.), *Handbook of reading research* (pp. 353–394). New York: Longman.

Berg, C. A., & Sternberg, R. J. (1985). A triarchic theory of intellectual development during adulthood. *Developmental Review, 5*, 334–370.

Brown, A. L., Bransford, J. D., Ferrara, R. A., & Campione, J. C. (1983). Learning, remembering, and understanding. In J. H. Flavell & E. M. Markman

(Eds.), *Handbook of child psychology: Cognitive development* (Vol. 3, pp. 77–166). New York: Wiley.

Brown, A. L., & DeLoache, J. S. (1978). Skills, plans, and self-regulation. In R. S. Siegler (Ed.), *Children's thinking: What develops?* (pp. 3–35). Hillsdale, N.J.: Erlbaum.

Bruce, B. (1986). Robot plans and human plans: Implications for models of communication. In I. Gopnik & M. Gopnik (Eds.), *Studies in cognitive science from the McGill workshops* (pp. 97–114). Norwood, N.J.: Ablex.

Catán, L. (1986). The dynamic display of process: Historical development and contemporary uses of the microgenetic method. *Human Development, 29,* 252–263.

Chapman, M. (Ed.). (1984). Intentional action as a paradigm for developmental psychology: A symposium. *Human Development, 27,* 113–144.

Dörner, D. (1983). Heuristics and cognition in complex systems. In R. Groner, M. Groner, & W. F. Bischof (Eds.), *Methods of heuristics* (pp. 89–107). Hillsdale, N.J.: Erlbaum.

Dörner, D. (1985). Thinking and organization of action. In J. Kuhl & J. Beckmann (Eds.), *Action control: From cognition to behavior* (pp. 219–235). New York: Springer-Verlag.

Flavell, J. H., & Wellman, H. M. (1977). Metamemory. In R. V. Kail, Jr., & J. W. Hagen (Eds.), *Perspectives on the development of memory and cognition* (pp. 3–33). Hillsdale, N.J.: Erlbaum.

Forbes, D. L., & Greenberg, M. T. (Eds.). (1982). *Children's planning strategies.* San Francisco: Jossey-Bass.

Frese, M., & Stewart, J. (1984). Skill learning as a concept in life-span developmental psychology: An action theoretic analysis. *Human Development, 27,* 145–162.

Goldin, S. E., & Hayes-Roth, B. (1980, June). *Individual differences in planning processes.* Rand Note (N–1488-ONR). Santa Monica, CA: Rand Corporation.

Goodnow, J. J. (1986). Some lifelong everyday forms of intelligent behavior: Organizing and reorganizing. In R. J. Sternberg & R. K. Wagner (Eds.), *Practical intelligence: Nature and origins of competence in the everyday world* (pp. 143–162). New York: Cambridge University Press.

Hayes-Roth, B., & Hayes-Roth, F. (1979). A cognitive model of planning. *Cognitive Science, 3,* 275–310.

Hayes-Roth, B., & Thorndyke, P. W. (1985). Paradigms for intelligent systems. *Educational Psychologist, 20,* 231–241.

Karmiloff-Smith, A. (1984). Children's problem solving. In M. E. Lamb, A. L. Brown, & B. Rogoff (Eds.), *Advances in developmental psychology* (Vol. 3, pp. 39–90). Hillsdale, N.J.: Erlbaum.

Kluwe, R. H. (1987). Executive decisions and regulation of problem-solving behavior. In F. E. Weinert & R. H. Kluwe (Eds.), *Metacognition, motivation, and understanding* (pp. 31–64). Hillsdale, N.J.: Erlbaum.

Kluwe, R. H., & Friedrichsen, G. (1985). Mechanisms of control and regulation in problem solving. In J. Kuhl & J. Beckmann (Eds.), *Action control: From cognition to behavior* (pp. 183–218). New York: Springer-Verlag.

Kreutzer, M. A., Leonard, S. C., & Flavell, J. H. (1975). An interview study of children's knowledge about memory. *Monographs of the Society for Research in Child Development, 40* (1, serial no. 159).

Lave, J., Murtaugh, M., & de la Rocha, O. (1984). The dialectic of arithmetic in grocery shopping. In B. Rogoff & J. Lave (Eds.), *Everyday cognition: Its development in social context* (pp. 67–94). Cambridge, Mass.: Harvard University Press.

Lefebvre-Pinard, M. (1983). Understanding and auto-control of cognitive functions: Implications for the relationship between cognition and behavior. *International Journal of Behavioral Development, 6,* 15–35.

Leont'ev, A. N. (1979). The problem of activity in psychology. In J. V. Wertsch (Ed.), *The concept of activity in Soviet psychology* (pp. 37–71). White Plains, N.Y.: Sharpe.

Lesgold, A. M., Feltovich, P. J., Glaser, R., & Wang, Y. (1981). *The acquisition of perceptual diagnostic skill in radiology* (technical report). Pittsburgh: University of Pittsburgh, Learning Research and Development Center.

Luria, A. R. (1961). *The role of speech in the regulation of normal and abnormal behaviors.* New York: Liveright.

Meacham, J. A. (1977). A transactional model of remembering. In N. Datan & H. W. Reese (Eds.), *Life-span developmental psychology: Dialectical perspectives on experimental research* (pp. 261–283). New York: Academic Press.

Meacham, J. A. (1982). A note on remembering to execute planned actions. *Journal of Applied Developmental Psychology, 3,* 121–133.

Meichenbaum, D., & Asarnow, J. (1979). Cognitive modification and metacognitive development: Implications for the classroom. In P. Kendall & S. Hollon (Eds.), *Cognitive behavioral interventions: Theory, research, and procedures* (pp. 11–30). New York: Academic Press.

Meichenbaum, D., Burland, S., Gruson, L., & Cameron, R. (1985). Metacognitive assessment. In S. R. Yussen (Ed.), *The growth of reflection in children* (pp. 1–30). New York: Academic Press.

Meichenbaum, D., & Goodman, S. (1979). Clinical use of private speech and critical questions about its study in natural settings. In G. Zivin (Ed.), *The development of self-regulation through private speech* (pp. 325–360). New York: Wiley.

Meyer, J. S., & Rebok, G. W. (1983, April). Acting to plan and planning to act in children's problem solving. Paper presented at the meeting of the Society for Research in Child Development, Detroit.

Meyer, J. S., & Rebok, G. W. (1985). Planning-in-action across the life span. In T. M. Shlechter & M. P. Toglia (Eds.), *New directions in cognitive science* (pp. 47–68). Norwood, N.J.: Ablex.

Miller, G. A., Galanter, E., & Pribram, K. H. (1960). *Plans and the structure of behavior.* New York: Holt.

Miller, P. H., & Weiss, M. G. (1981). Children's attention allocation, understanding of attention, and performance on the incidental learning task. *Child Development, 52,* 1183–1190.

Mischel, W. (1979). On the interface of cognition and personality: Beyond the person-situation debate. *American Psychologist, 34,* 740–754.

Myers, M., & Paris, S. G. (1978). Children's metacognitive knowledge about reading. *Journal of Educational Psychology, 70,* 680–690.

Newell, A., & Simon, H. A. (1972). *Human problem-solving*. Englewood Cliffs, N.J.: Prentice-Hall.

Newman, D., & Bruce, B. C. (1986). Interpretation and manipulation in human plans. *Discourse Processes, 9,* 167–195.

Paris, S. G. (1978). Coordination of means and goals in the development of mnemonic skills. In P. A. Ornstein (Ed.), *Memory development in children* (pp. 259–273). Hillsdale, N.J.: Erlbaum.

Paris, S. G., Newman, R. S., & McVey, K. A. (1982). Learning the functional significance of mnemonic actions: A microgenetic study of strategy acquisition. *Journal of Experimental Child Psychology, 34,* 490–509.

Pea, R. D. (1982). What is planning development the development of? In D. Forbes & M. Greenberg (Eds.), *Children's planning strategies* (pp. 5–27). San Francisco: Jossey-Bass.

Pea, R. D., & Hawkins, J. (1987). Planning in a chore-scheduling task. In S. L. Friedman, E. K. Scholnick, & R. R. Cocking (Eds.), *Blueprints for thinking: The role of planning in cognitive development* (pp. 273–302). New York: Cambridge University Press.

Piaget, J. (1976). *The grasp of consciousness: Action and concept in the young child.* Cambridge, Mass.: Harvard University Press.

Piaget, J. (1978). *Success and understanding.* Cambridge, Mass.: Harvard University Press.

Rebok, G. W., Krusemark, D. S., Griffith, R. B., & Meyer, J. S. (1986, April). Individual differences in planning on a real-life problem-solving task. Paper presented at the meeting of the Eastern Psychological Association, New York.

Reither, F., & Stäudel, T. (1985). Thinking and action. In M. Frese & J. Sabini (Eds.), *Goal directed behavior: The concept of action in psychology* (pp. 110–122). Hillsdale, N.J.: Erlbaum.

Rogoff, B. (1982). Integrating context and cognitive development. In M. E. Lamb & A. L. Brown (Eds.), *Advances in developmental psychology* (Vol. 2, pp. 125–170). Hillsdale, N.J.: Erlbaum.

Rose, R. (1985). The black knight of artificial intelligence. *Science, 6,* 46–53.

Sacerdoti, E. D. (1977). *A structure for plans and behavior.* New York: Elsevier.

Schank, R. C., & Abelson, R. (1977). *Scripts, plans, goals, and understanding.* Hillsdale, N.J.: Erlbaum.

Scribner, S. (1986). Thinking in action: Some characteristics of practical thought. In R. J. Sternberg & R. K. Wagner (Eds.), *Practical intelligence: Nature and origins of competence in the everyday world.* New York: Cambridge University Press.

Sinnott, J. D. (in press). General systems theory: A rationale for the study of everyday memory. In L. W. Poon, D. Rubin, & B. Wilson (Eds.), *Everyday cognition in adulthood and late life.* New Rochelle, N.Y.: Cambridge University Press.

Smith, J. (1985, November). Wisdom as a growing expertise in the fundamental pragmatics of life: The sample case of life planning. Paper presented at the meeting of the Gerontological Society of America, New Orleans.

Smyth, M. M., Morris, P. E., Levy, P. M., & Ellis, A. W. (1987). *Cognition in action.* Hillsdale, N.J.: Erlbaum.

Thorndyke, P. W., & Wescourt, K. (1984). *Modeling time-stressed situation assessment and planning for intelligent opponent simulation* (Technical Report PPAFTR–1124–84–1). Woodland Hills, Cal.: Perceptronics.

Vygotsky, L. S. (1962). *Thought and language*. New York: Wiley.

Vygotsky, L. S. (1978). *Mind in society: The development of higher psychological processes*, M. Cole, V. John-Steiner, S. Scribner, & E. Souberman (Eds.). Cambridge, Mass.: Harvard University Press.

Wilensky, R. (1981). *A model for planning in complex situations*. Berkeley Electronics Research Laboratory Memorandum no. UCB/ERL/M81/49. College of Engineering, University of California, Berkeley, CA.

Wilensky, R. (1983). *Planning and understanding: A computational approach to human reasoning*. Reading, Mass.: Addison-Wesley.

Yussen, S. R., & Bird, J. E. (1979). The development of metacognitive awareness in memory, communication, and attention. *Journal of Experimental Child Psychology, 28*, 300–313.

8

Everyday Reasoning and Adult Development from an Attributional Framework

Fredda Blanchard-Fields

Current research and theorizing in adult cognitive development have supported an adaptive view of intelligence and aging. For example, Labouvie-Vief (1985, 1986) argues that adult cognition represents a major reorganization in thinking that has profound adaptive significance. She discusses two modes of knowing. The first reflects objective, analytical, and rational thought freed from subjectivity and error. The second represents concrete and contextually embedded thought and feelings that focus on the subjective significance of reality. Labouvie-Vief believes that the major developmental task in adulthood is the integration of these two modes of knowledge, as complementary and irreducible processes. This integration leads to what she calls a prototypical or ideal state of healthy adult functioning.

The purpose of the present chapter is to discuss how this conceptualization of adult cognition and current research in socioemotional reasoning suggest an alternative direction for examining everyday reasoning in adulthood, specifically, in the area of attributional processes. Therefore, first I would like to briefly discuss a developmental dimension that may underlie this process: self-other differentiation. Second, I would like to review several research contexts related to this dimension and discuss their implications to attribution research. Finally, I would like to apply this conceptual focus within an attributional framework and discuss implications for the understanding of everyday reasoning in adult development.

SELF-OTHER DIFFERENTIATION AND ADULT COGNITION

There has been a growth of research attempting to delineate cognitive dimensions that surpass those of traditional formal operational models (see Commons, Richards, & Armon 1984). It is in this context that I have been primarily interested in investigating dimensions involving self-other differentiation. This concerns the ability to adopt a relativistic point of view in which self and other are accepted as independent and valid self-regulating systems. As a result, subjective processes of thinking can be differentiated from the product of thinking itself. The individual is aware that the thinker influences the object of thought and that subjectivity must be included in any analysis.

A number of studies indicate that this dimension of adaptive cognition becomes particularly evident in adulthood, when cognitive tasks focus on socioemotional domains (Armon 1984; Blanchard-Fields 1986; Cavanaugh et al. 1985; Gilligan & Murphy 1979).

Therefore, in order to study the developmental implications of progressions in self-other differentiation, I examined developmental differences in reasoning in the context of emotionally salient social dilemmas. Three ambiguously structured tasks consisting of text ranging from high to low emotional saliency were presented to adolescents, college-age students, and middle-aged adults. Each task consisted of two divergent accounts of the same event sequence. Subjects were questioned as to how they perceived the discrepancies (see Blanchard-Fields 1986 for a complete description). The scoring scheme assessed progression along the dimension of self-other differentiation described above. A significant upward progression of mean scores was found over the three age groups. However, what was interesting about this finding was an interaction between age group and emotional saliency of the task. Adolescents performed as well as young adults on the least emotionally salient task. However, they performed at lower levels of reasoning on the more emotionally salient tasks. This discrepancy was not evident in young and middle-aged adult performances.

The more emotionally salient context appeared to be more disruptive for younger than for older thinkers, thus affecting performance, particularly their ability to differentiate an event from its interpretation. The less mature thinkers expressed a strong, externally based belief in the objective, asserting a right-versus-wrong conception of reality. As a result, these individuals were more likely to create distortions in the text accounts (i.e., to construe only one perspective as correct). In contrast, mature adults were aware that the differing accounts were inherently interpreted; therefore, they produced each party's perspective more accurately and with less distortion.

In contrast with the outcome measures (levels of reasoning) assessed in this study, similar findings have been demonstrated in studies that concentrate on a text-processing analysis. For example, in a study by Cynthia Adams (1986), text-processing style was examined from adolescence through older adulthood. Results demonstrated a shift from a literal, text-dependent processing mode in youth to a more interpretive and integrative mode in maturity. What is interesting in this study is that mature adults not only produced the sequence of action in the story (the propositional structure of the story) but also elaborated the line of action through the integration of the story's deeper psychological and metaphoric meanings (Adams 1986).

In the context of self-other differentiation, mature readers demonstrated a differentiation between the conventionalized meaning of the text (text-based propositions) and one's personal psychological perspective. One of the conclusions Adams draws from these findings is the importance of adopting a "reader-oriented" approach to the developmental study of adult cognition. In other words, the transaction between reader and text needs to be considered, given that each reader brings a psychological perspective to the task. In this case, text comprehension was accounted for by more than the propositional content alone.

These findings suggest the need to study everyday reasoning in an adult developmental context that takes into consideration how the individual structures reality and approaches everyday problems. Whether or not it involves how adults transform text (Adams 1986), expand the problem space in problem solving situations (Arlin 1984; Sinnott 1985), or resolve interpretive discrepancies in interpersonal dilemmas (Blanchard-Fields 1986), adaptive functioning needs to be defined in terms of the problem solver or information processor rather than in terms of experimenter-imposed manipulations of the task itself. However, this approach has been relatively ignored in traditional social and cognitive psychology.

The findings and implications of the research approaches discussed thus far suggest that (a) if a major reorganization in thinking occurs in adulthood, progression in self-other differentiation may represent a developmental dimension underlying its; (b) in order to tap this dimension, the methodology of choice needs to consider the individual's role in structuring reality or experience, that is, the way the individual approaches problem solving situations, decision making, interpersonal dilemmas, and so on; and (c) future research could profit from a text-processing approach, that is, how individuals process text information and distort its contents as a function of developmental indices. These concerns become particularly evident when focusing on attributional processes in a developmental context. At this point, I would like to briefly review some of the relevant research in and criticisms of attributional processes, and then to discuss some ongoing research I am conducting in this area.

ATTRIBUTION THEORY AND RESEARCH, AND ADULT DEVELOPMENT

A major focus of the attributional literature is the kinds of attributional biases individuals make in assessing causal relations. This is exemplified in story comprehension and memory research. For example, college students demonstrate state-dependent retention resulting in text distortions due to emotional and motivational processes (Bower 1978, 1981; Pichert & Anderson 1977). Similarly, social psychologists have demonstrated college students' tendency to produce informational distortions when making causal attributions.

One such distortion is the fundamental attribution error (Jones 1979; Jones & Harris 1967; Kelley & Michela 1980), where the individual underestimates the role of situational factors in controlling behavior in favor of personal dispositional factors. For example, Nisbett and Ross (1980) report a number of studies that attribute this bias to the application of schemata to the situation. In particular, social schemata are used as tentative guides for perception and behavior. If relied on too heavily, they may result in inferential errors. For example, Owens, Bower, and Black (1979) found that by presenting characters' motives to the reader prior to his/her reading of the text guided, to some extent, the kinds of inferences drawn, comprehension, and recall of the text.

However, most of these studies involve experimenter manipulation of consensus information, availability of information, or representativeness of information. The experimenter determines the "true" cause or explanation of an event, in this case situational factors. Thus, subjects may "wrongly" attribute the author's view in a position paper to the author's personal view, ignoring the fact that the substance of the essay was dictated by another person (Jones & Harris 1967); underestimate the strong situational factors that influenced a character's behavior in an obedience study à la Milgram (Bierbrauer 1973); or rate the degree of responsibility of a primary character in an action sequence as high for negative, as opposed to positive, outcomes (Nisbett & Ross 1980).

A more recent attempt to account for these types of biases can be found in the cognitive processing approach to attributions. This has produced a research emphasis on encoding, representation, and retrieval functions in making attributions (Harvey & Weary 1985; Taylor & Fiske 1981). A result has been studies examining such dependent variables as visual attention (McArthur 1980; Taylor & Fiske 1978) or quantity and errors of recall to index the effects of social schemata (Hansen 1985; Owens et al. 1979; Wimer & Kelley 1982).

Although the traditional social psychology and more current cognitive processing approaches have provided experimental rigor to the study of attributional processes in adulthood, there are several limitations that deserve consideration. First, as Taylor and Fiske (1981) point out, the emphasis on cognitive processing has resulted in the use of problems and methods that have become increasingly cognitive and less social.

Second, most studies represent an experimenter manipulation that determines, a priori, the processing mode to be expressed, thus not allowing the subject to process the information in his or her own way. Again, processing ability needs to be defined in terms of the information processor rather than in terms of the predesigned task demands, in order to achieve a better understanding of adult social cognition.

Third, most of the research on attributional errors has focused on the notion of "error" in response to a single correct answer. The postformal cognition literature emphasizes that most problem situations do not result in one correct answer independent of the particular perspective imposed on the problem (Basseches 1986; Commons et al. 1984). This is especially characteristic of social tasks or problems. Given the complexity of the social environment and the different frames of reference of the participating individuals in that environment, a methodology is needed to capture the full extent of social understanding exhibited by the problem solver. The criterion of accuracy may not be appropriate in this case. What may be more important would be such outcomes as serving an adaptive function, facilitating future functioning, and promoting mental health.

This leads to a fourth limitation, the nondevelopmental nature of attributional research. Inasmuch as the bulk of attributional studies demonstrating such biases as the fundamental attribution error were documented primarily on college youth samples, a developmental perspective suggests a number of interpretations for this finding. First, the fundamental attributional error may result from a tendency by the youthful thinker to accept a dualistic, right-versus-wrong structure of reality and knowledge. Thus, causal explanations are partitioned into either-or categories pitting internal causes, such as personality traits, against external environmental factors. Over attribution toward personal dispositional factors has been shown to be a potent source for social judgment bias (Nisbett & Ross 1980; Tversky & Kahneman 1982). In his research on marital conflict, Doherty (1981) found that individuals were more likely either to externalize blame to the spouse or to internalize blame to themselves, as opposed to examining the relationship. This is similar to the research reviewed above in which reality is objectified into right-versus-wrong, in contrast with the integration of both perspectives.

Second, this attributional error could involve an overreliance on pre-conceptions of doubtful validity. For example, such factors as perceptual and motivational biases of the self system may be operating and the individual may not be aware of it, especially in emotionally salient contexts. This has long been suggested by the perceptual defense literature, in which personal values not only direct but also distort perception (Buner & Postman 1947; Gibson 1969). This would be particularly evident in the individual who ignores the relative contribution of both self characteristics and external agencies operating on the situation. Whereas the attribution literature labels this "self-serving biases" or "defensive biases," the developmental literature would consider it a lack of differentiation between subject and object or the neglect of more psychological and subjective factors and perspectives.

Although there is considerable research concentrating on attributional processes, the informational biases and distortions made by individuals were documented primarily on college-aged youth. Thus, again, this limitation relates to the fact that is is not typically studied systematically from a developmental perspective. In combination with the results pertaining to progressions in self-other differentiation suggested above and in the developmental literature, it is suggested that a developmental perspective may shed more light on attributional processes.

A number of researchers have suggested that the area of attributions could benefit from the perspective of an adult developmental context. For example, Blank (1984) argues that as you move from the relative homogeneity of college students to the variety of individuals who live in the nonacademic world, the meaning and motivation in the process of attribution may be quite different. Blank argues that attributions are more realistically analyzed as individual constructions in which reality is negotiated rather than as stable factors. Thus, individuals may expand as well as constrict the boundaries of possible causes and reasons for what they and others do. In fact, Blank found that in nonacademic adult populations, attributions of success and failure were related to outcomes in socially verifiable ways. In other words, the definition of success or failure must be related to the context of the individual. This is much like the relativistic operations espoused by current researchers in adult cognitive development. Once again, how the individual constructs reality becomes an important methodological issue in examining adaptive reasoning in adulthood.

With this in mind and with the advantages of a developmental approach to the study of attributions, I was prompted to begin a program of research in this area. As a result, a pilot study was undertaken to examine attributional processes in an adult developmental context. The initial goal of this study was to establish adult and older adult developmental trends and patterns of committing causal attributional errors.

In addition to a traditional attributional assignment procedure, a think-aloud procedure modeled after Ericsson and Simon (1984) and Rowe (1985) was used. Location of causality (internal versus external) and assignment of responsibility were the primary attribution dimensions of reasoning assessed. Heider's (1958) five levels of causality were represented in ten vignettes presented to subjects, each consisting of a sequence of events involving one or more characters whose actions result in a particular outcome. The levels of causality are characterized by varying degrees of ambiguity of social information given (on the nature of the interactions between persons and their environment). Thus, a highly ambiguous vignette would involve a situation where the intentions and foreseeability of the primary character with regard to the final outcome are unclear. By contrast, an unambiguous action sequence would make clear the intentions and foreseeability of the primary character.

With regard to attributional assignment, it was hypothesized that causal attributional biases, such as underestimating the role of external factors in controlling behavior (fundamental attribution error), would decrease with developmental maturity. The more ambiguous the information (the degree to which different agents share a causal role in an action situation), the greater may be the tendency for youthful thinkers to hold actors, as opposed to external environment factors, more responsible for the event.

From a more "constructivist" approach to the analysis of attributions, the product of attributional assignment may or may not differ between individuals. Instead, the process or meaning behind those assignments may differ. In fact, what became most interesting in the preliminary analyses of this data was the assessment of the on-line processing involved in making attributional assignments. Preliminary findings suggest that adolescents tend to use very absolutist, text-based reasons and a narrowly defined problem space in making their attributional assignments. For example, participants responded to an action sequence where a man was approached frantically by the father of a drowning child. Because the father could not swim, he threatened to kill the man if he did not save his son. The man brought the boy to safety. The participant was then asked: "To what degree is Adam (the man) responsible for the boy's life being saved?"

One adolescent's response was: "He's 100% responsible, since the boy couldn't swim. He had to save him." There was not much elaboration beyond this kind of response in the talk-aloud procedure for the majority of adolescents. They reached a conclusion with explanations tied exclusively to the text.

Older adults showed more variability in their responses than the adolescents. They tended to include more metastatements suggesting a more relativistic approach to the situation as well as a tendency to go beyond the information given. They used alternative ways of viewing the situations, such as moralistic versus legalistic, as well as including more self-monitoring statements, such as "I know I am seeing the situation this way due to my perspective on life."

Consequently, it may be the case that youthful thinkers display a more constricted causal analysis of socially ambiguous contexts than more mature thinkers. The increased power of causal analysis in older adults may be due to their ability to incorporate subjective perspectives in their analysis, as exemplified in an expanding problem space.

CONCLUDING COMMENTS

A number of implications for research in this area of everyday reasoning in adults are suggested by the research discussed above. First, research on "misattributions" or biases, such as those made by college students, can be applied to an adult developmental context. In this way, the issue of whether or not these biases function similarly across the life span can be assessed. Second, there is converging support for the application of methodologies that take into account how the subject structures a problem solving, decision-making, or (in this case) causal attributional task (Adams 1986; Blanchard-Fields 1986; Sinnott 1983). In this way, a distinction can be made between the use of adaptive modes of causal reasoning based on systematic use of psychological subjective decision criteria and new biases involving more personalistic, distortive modes of reasoning.

Finally, I have argued that developmentally mature adults are able to account for subjective factors in their thinking. This is in contrast with youthful thinkers, who assumed that thinking is based on an objective structure of reality that is juxtaposed to subjectivity. Instead of resulting in more "objective" conclusions and resolutions of reasoning dilemmas, this form of thinking tends to maximize the chances of subjective errors. Therefore, maturity in thinking is not just a return to more subjective modes of thinking. Instead, by accounting for subjectivity, the mature adult becomes a more objective and powerful thinker. If these conclusions are to be further corroborated or refuted in the literature, methods must clearly move away from a right-versus-wrong analysis and toward the development of methodologies, such as the think-aloud procedure, and respective coding schemes that have the potential to capture these developmental differences.

REFERENCES

Adams, C. (1986). Qualitative changes in text memory from adolescence to mature adulthood. Unpublished doctoral dissertation, Wayne State University.

Arlin, P. (1984). Adolescent and adult thought: A structural interpretation. In M. L. Commons, F. A. Richards, and C. Armon (Eds.), *Beyond formal operations* (pp. 258–271). New York: Praeger.

Armon, C. (1984). Ideals of the good life and moral judgment: Ethical reasoning across the lifespan. In M. L. Commons, F. A. Richards, & C. Armon (Eds.), *Beyond formal operations*. New York: Praeger.

Basseches, M. (1986). Comments on social cognition in adulthood: A dialectical perspective. *Educational Gerontology, 12,* 327–338.

Bierbrauer, G. (1973). Effect of set, perspective, and temporal factors in attribution. Unpublished doctoral dissertation, Stanford University.

Blanchard-Fields, F. (1986). Reasoning on social dilemmas varying in emotional saliency: An adult developmental perspective. *Psychology and Aging, 1,* 325–333.

Blank, T. (1984). Meaning and motivation in adult perceptions of causality. *Basic and Applied Social Psychology, 2,* 111–120.

Bower, G. (1978). Experiments on story comprehension and recall. *Discourse Processes, 1,* 211–231.

Bower, G. H. (1981). Mood and memory. *American Psychologist, 36*(2), 129–148.

Bruner, J., & Postman, L. (1947). Emotional selectivity in perception and reaction. *Journal of Personality, 16,* 69–77.

Camp, C. (1986). I am curious gray: Information seeking and depression across the adult lifespan. *Educational Gerontology, 12,* 375–384.

Cavanaugh, J., Kramer, D., Sinnott, J., Camp, C., & Markley, R. (1985). On missing links and such: Interfaces between cognitive research and everyday problem-solving. *Human Development, 28,* 146–168.

Commons, M., Richards, F. A., & Armon, C. (Eds.). (1984). *Beyond formal operations.* New York: Praeger.

Doherty, W. J. (1981). Cognitive processes in intimate conflict: I. Extending attribution theory. *American Journal of Family Therapy, 9,* 3–13.

Ericsson, K. A., & Simon, H. A. (1984). *Protocol analysis.* Cambridge, Mass.: MIT Press.

Gibson, E. (1969). *Principles of perceptual learning and development.* New York: Appleton-Century-Crofts.

Gilligan, C., & Murphy, M. (1979). Development from adolescence to adulthood: The philosopher and the dilemma of the fact. In D. Kuhn (Ed.), *New directions for child development, no. 5, Intellectual development beyond childhood.* San Francisco: Jossey-Bass.

Hansen, R. D. (1985). Cognitive economy and commonsense attribution processing. In J. Harvey & G. Weary (Eds.), *Attribution: Basic issues and applications.* Orlando, Fla.: Academic Press.

Harvey, J. & Weary, G. (1985). *Attribution: Basic issues and applications.* Orlando, Fla.: Academic Press.

Heider, F. (1958). *The psychology of interpersonal relations.* New York: Wiley.

Jones, E. E. (1979). The rocky road from acts to dispositions. *American Psychologist, 34,* 107–117.

Jones, E. E., & Harris, V. A. (1967). The attribution of attitudes. *Journal of Experimental Social Psychology, 3,* 1–24.

Kelley, H. H., & Michela, J. L. (1980). Attribution theory and research. In M. R.

Rosenzweig & L. W. Porter (Eds.), *Annual Review of Psychology, 31*, 457–501.

Labouvie-Vief, G. (1985). Intelligence and cognition. In J. E. Birren & K. W. Schaie (Eds.), *Handbook of the psychology of aging* (2nd ed., pp. 500–530). New York: Van Nostrand Reinhold.

Lavouvie-Vief, G. (1986, November). Modes of knowing and life-span cognition. Paper presented at the meeting of the American Psychological Association, Washington, D.C.

McArthur, L. Z. (1980). Illusory causation and illusory correlation: Two epistemological accounts. *Personality and Social Psychology Bulletin, 6*, 507–519.

Nisbett, R., & Ross, L. (1980). *Human inference: Strategies and shortcomings of social judgment*. Englewood Cliffs, N.J.: Prentice-Hall.

Owens, J., Bower, G. H., & Black, J. B. (1979). The "soap opera" effect in story recall. *Memory and Cognition, 7*, 185–191.

Pichert, J. W., & Anderson, R. C. (1977). Taking different perspectives on a story. *Journal of Educational Psychology, 69*, 309–315.

Rowe, H. (1985). *Problem solving and intelligence*. Hillsdale, N.J.: Erlbaum.

Sinnott, J. D. (1983). A model for solution of illstructured problems: Implications for everyday and abstract problem solving. Paper presented at the Gerontological Society annual meeting, San Francisco.

Taylor, S. E., & Fiske, S. T. (1978). Salience, attention, and attribution: Top of the head phenomena. In L. Berkowitz (Ed.), *Advances in experimental social psychology* (Vol. 11). New York: Academic Press.

Taylor, S. E., & Fiske, S. T. (1981). Getting inside the head: Methodologies for process analysis and social cognition. In J. H. Harvey, W. Ickes, & R. F. Kidd (Eds.), *New directions in attribution research*. Hillsdale, N.J.: Erlbaum.

Tversky, A., & Kahneman, D. (1982). Causal schemas in judgments under uncertainty. In D. Kahneman, P. Slovic, & A. Tversky (Eds.), *Judgments under uncertainty: Heuristics and biases*. Cambridge: Cambridge University Press.

Wimer, S., & Kelley, H. H. (1982). An investigation of the dimensions of causal attribution. *Journal of Personality and Social Psychology, 43*, 1142–1162.

9

A Developmental Framework for Understanding Conflict Resolution Processes

Deirdre A. Kramer

The present chapter concerns developmental influences on the conflict resolution of adults. It is proposed that social cognitive developmental level influences how individuals construe conflict and its resolution. In the conflict resolution literature, social cognitive processes have not been studied in a developmental framework. Much of the work in that area has been conducted on young adults generally, and college students in particular. When a broader age-range sample is used, age differences are not usually analyzed. Recent developments in the area of adult development and aging that suggest continued cognitive growth in adulthood may shed new light on conflict resolution. Conclusions drawn from research with young adults may not generalize to the rest of the adult life span.

In this chapter, social cognitive development will be construed in terms of developing world views or naive theories about the social world. The first section will outline this framework. In the second section, conflict resolution will be discussed, with particular emphasis on constructive versus destructive strategies. The third section will focus on the effect of attributional style on conflict resolution and the final section will attempt to subsume attributional style and conflict resolution within the developmental framework, using marital conflict as the focus of analysis.

THE DEVELOPMENTAL FRAMEWORK

The present conception sees people as lay theorists, or lay epistemologists, who construct naive theories about the social world. According to Kelly (1955), people act as lay scientists, collecting data, making predictions, and testing them. These result in naive theories or construction systems, also referred to as personal constructs.

A construct is a way of organizing reality, much like a map or a template, allowing one to chart a course of action. While the fit may not be accurate, it allows one to order the continual flux of events in the world; it acts like a working hypothesis. When the predictions one makes are met with failure, constructs may be adjusted to provide a better, more adequate representation of reality, provided the person is not highly resistant to change.

Kelly suggested that lay theories might mirror philosophical and scientific theories, and that they can be shared, or public. The present chapter focuses on views believed to be shared (though not always explicit) and to mirror philosophical theories. Development is construed as a series of successive transformations in one's world view, as problems are encountered that cannot be adequately resolved within the current one. Since each successive world view in the model is believed to be capable of solving a broader range of interpersonal problems, development to a higher level occurs as a result of the dialectic between the individual's cognitive level and problems or obstacles encountered in the environment. According to the present conception, these developing world views influence the kinds of attributions one makes about relationships and the actions one undertakes within relationships, such as conflict resolution behaviors.

The lay theories presented in this paper were originally derived from Pepper's (1942) four world views: *formism*, which yields an absolute form of thinking; *mechanism*, which yields a systematic, scientific form of thinking; *contextualism*, which yields a pragmatic, here-and-now form of thinking; and *organicism*, which yields an integrated, evolution-oriented form of thinking. These lay theories are believed to form a developmental sequence in which the former two predominate in early and middle adolescence, contextualism (i.e., relativism) develops in late adolescence and early adulthood, and organicism (i.e., dialecticism) evolves in middle and old age (Basseches 1980; Blanchard-Fields 1986; Kramer 1983; Kramer & Woodruff 1986; Labouvie-Vief 1984; Pascual-Leone 1983; Sinnott 1984).

Both formistic and mechanistic world views are analytic, meaning that they assert an unchanging, stable external world that must be reduced to its constituent components if it is to be understood. Change, when it occurs, is not inherent to the organism but is produced from the outside. The absolute, or formistic, world view, which is based on a Platonic ideal, asserts that external reality is but a manifestation of, and hence can be reduced to, an underlying plan or blueprint. These forms have objective, universal reality apart from their external manifestation. In addition to being universal, they are static or unchanging, are unrelated to one another, and all phenomena can be reduced to them. Translated into social reality, an individual manifesting an absolute world view would see others as fitting neatly into self-evident types or categories, and would construe moral and interpersonal decisions in terms of absolute principles or codes of behavior. Contradiction is seen to be logically impossible, so when two or more parties conflict in their perspectives, only one can be right.

Mechanistic reasoning, which is presumed to follow absolute reasoning developmentally, also construes the world as essentially stable and seeks to understand complex reality by reducing it to its basic components. However, in this case the basic components are not ideal plans but material building blocks of the complex unit. For behavior theory, they might be S-R units; for the cognitive realm, memory components, such as short-term and long-term memory; for a relationship, they might refer to each autonomous agent (individual) comprising that relationship. In the latter instance, each individual is seen as having independent, objective existence that is not significantly altered in the context of the relationship. Thus, in interpersonal conflict it is meaningful to talk of "blame." All social phenomena are produced by external events or forces. Further, individuals are not inherently developing; they need that outside "push." Thus, in order to understand a social event, it is necessary to analyze its causal antecedents, which then combine to produce the event.

Contextualism and organicism have been described as synthetic world views, in that they do not seek to analyze the whole into its basic components in order to understand a phenomenon. Each "element" will take on a different meaning in the context of the whole. The extreme relativistic or pragmatic reasoning that emerges from a contextualist world view involves an awareness that there is no one right way of construing reality; that the reality one constructs is influenced by the tools of his or her sociocultural and historical context, his or her specific experiences, personality, and so forth. One cannot separate knowledge from its historical and contemporary context. Contradiction would be seen as an inherent feature of reality, since different contexts can produce incompatible, yet equally valid, conceptions of reality (e.g., different moral values stemming from disparate cultures or different cohorts). Finally, change or flux is an inherent feature of reality. As the world changes, so does one's conception of it. However, there is no necessary connection between different contexts, or between past, present, and future. In a contextualist or relativistic world view, anything is possible, including total chaos (Pepper 1942).

Dialectical or integrated reasoning, which emerges from an organismic world view and is believed to be rare before middle age (Basseches 1980; Blanchard-Fields 1986; Kramer 1983; Kramer, Melchior, & Levine 1987; Kramer & Woodruff 1986; Labouvie-Vief 1984; Pascual-Leone 1983), involves an awareness as well that knowledge is in a state of flux and must be embedded in its broader context. Therefore, it subsumes relativity; but relativity is not seen in its extreme form, in which one context randomly replaces another. Rather, change occurs in a systematic way, and the relationship between contradictory elements is a systematic one (Kramer in press). In such a view, the part is subordinated to the whole or system, which defines and gives functional meaning to that part. A change in any one part of the system necessitates changes in every other part. Socially, the characteristics, behaviors, or roles any individual takes on in the context of some system (such as a family or a marital relationship) are influenced by those of the other individuals. Conflict is a natural feature of social reality and is seen as the impetus for continued growth.

It is important to note that while these lay theories are believed to represent a developmental sequence, and that there is mounting evidence to this effect, they probably reflect individual differences as well. There is undoubtedly considerable individual variation within a given age group and across domains. Many people probably never reach the integrated level; and, in keeping with the idea that one's lay theory is constructed as a result of adaptation to particular real-life demands, none would be expected to demonstrate it across all domains. Furthermore, thinking is dynamic and not likely to manifest itself in consistent ways across or even within situations. This is especially true in emotionally stressful situations, which may result in the simultaneous use of multiple levels of thinking in order to resolve a problem (Kramer & Haviland 1987). It is better to think in terms of the greater flexibility that development affords. The higher the level of development, the greater the number of reasoning tools at one's disposal. Elsewhere I have elaborated on the adaptive role that lower levels of thinking may play as a special case of the higher ones (Kramer in press).

CONFLICT RESOLUTION

Conflict is generally defined as the perception of incompatible goals. Conflict resolution is the negotiation of a solution that will satisfy each of the conflicting parties—that is, a fair "contract" that will benefit all parties involved (Deutsch 1969). This latter point is an important one, as a distinction has been made in the literature between cooperative and noncooperative modes of dealing with conflict. Scanzoni (1979) reserved the label "conflict *resolution*" for cooperative modes exclusively, contrasting it with "conflict *regulation*," or the exercise of nonlegitimate (coercive) power, resulting in injustice. However, coercion is likely to generate further conflict and thus does not result in true resolution. Conflict *resolution* must by definition be cooperative. Deutsch (1969) made a similar distinction, labeling cooperative resolution "constructive" and noncooperative resolution "destructive." According to Scanzoni, conflict resolution leads to a stronger relationship between the conflicting parties, characterized by greater equality and interdependence:

The process of resolution has the effect of increasing solidarity or cohesion within the system. . . . The reasons for increased solidarity owing to resolution are several. One is the removal of the injustice; another may be the increase of trust relations accomplished through negotiation of the struggle. Finally, a new set of exchanges or patterns often has the effect of making system members more interdependent subsequent to the struggle than they were prior to it. For instance, there may be more sets of rewards and costs present than before; and their distribution may occur within a more complex set of reciprocities in which more enduring sets of obligations are generated to a greater degree than was the case previously. (Scanzoni 1979, p. 310)

Scanzoni's analysis of conflict resolution is easily captured in dialectical[1] terms, whereby conflict is the impetus for the construction of a more integrated system that is characterized by increased mutual understanding and communication. Thus, internal contradiction or conflict (thesis and antithesis) results in a struggle to achieve a synthesis that allows each party to maintain its own integrity—that is, to achieve some of its stated objectives, yet to become transformed in the process. The synthesis has emergent features, such as the achievement of new rewards and qualitatively different modes of relationship than previously existed.

Failure to achieve such a synthesis—one party defeats the other—often leads to continued attempts at retaliation, perhaps even violence (Scanzoni 1979). According to Deutsch, "Destructive conflict is characterized by a tendency to expand and to escalate. As a result, such conflict often becomes independent of its initiating causes and is likely to continue after these have become irrelevant or have been forgotten" (1969, p. 11). The further the escalation, the lower the chances for adequate resolution, because of a breakdown of strategy. The ensuing strategy is one that minimizes in-group distinctions, maximizes in-group versus out-group distinctions, places pressure on members of the in-group to conform, and relies on coercion, deception, and threat, rather than mutual understanding and cooperation. Thus, this strategy will serve only to further escalate the conflict, resulting in a spiraling trend toward continual conflict (Deutsch 1969). Conflict *without* resolution results in escalated conflict, and is thus destructive, following dialectical principles. It will be argued, therefore, that integrated, dialectical reasoners should better be able to recognize this self-defeating circle and attempt cooperative forms of resolution.

According to Deutsch, conflict resolution strategies deteriorate under extreme stress. A consequence of this is a concomitant breakdown in communication processes, resulting in "a suspicious, hostile attitude which increases the sensitivity to differences and threats, while minimizing the awareness of similarities" (Deutsch 1969, p. 13). Such an attitude can result in a breakdown of normal codes of behavior or morality, as such codes are not generally considered applicable to those different from oneself.

One of the causes of this communicative breakdown, according to Deutsch, is a breakdown in cognitive processes, most notably seen in the decrease in the range of available cues. The effects of threat, anxiety, and, generally speaking, emotional arousal on restricting consideration of available cues is a well-documented fact (e.g., Easterbrook 1959; Janis & Mann 1977). Deutsch describes this breakdown of cognitive processes as follows:

It reduces the range of perceived alternatives; it reduces the time-perspective in such a way as to cause a focus on the immediate rather than the over-all consequences of the perceived alternatives; it polarizes thought so that percepts tend to take on a simplistic cast of being "black" or "white," "for" or "against," "good" or "evil"; it leads to stereotyped responses, it increases the susceptibility to fear- or hope-inciting rumors; it increases defensiveness; it increases the pressures to social conformity. Intensification of conflict is the likely result as simplistic thinking and the polarization of thought pushes [*sic*] the participants to view their alternatives as being limited to "victory" or "defeat." (Deutsch 1969, p. 15)

The polarized thinking described above is also a description of absolute and mechanistic reasoning; thus, what Deutsch may be describing is a regression to a lower cognitive level, characterized by absolute and/or mechanistic reasoning during stress. Individuals who regularly adopt these modes of thinking may show maladaptive conflict resolution strategies even in nonstressful situations.

In the present chapter it will be argued that developmental level will mediate these effects in a number of ways. Generally speaking, this mediation will occur via (a) qualitatively different definitions of conflict and conflict resolution, depending on the world view one adopts; (b) the lower likelihood that more advanced reasoners will perceive conflict as threat; (c) different attributions about the source of the conflict and different efficacy expectations; and (d) greater automatization of cognitive processes pertaining to productive conflict resolution among higher-level reasoners, which would reduce the information-processing demands on their systems and, hence, result in less likelihood of a breakdown of cognitive and decision-making strategies under conditions of high stress. Taken together, these four processes should make the developmentally more advanced reasoner less prone to destructive forms of conflict resolution. Since individuals at different epistemological levels would make different attributions about the source of a conflict or possibilities for resolution, let us first consider the relationship between attributional style and conflict resolution.

ATTRIBUTIONAL STYLE IN INTIMATE RELATIONSHIPS

According to Charney (1980), conflict is an inherent feature of human relationships, particularly marriage. "Many personality and family problems grow out of our not knowing how to process an intricate network of dualities, contradictions, dilemmas, paradoxes, and momentums that are intrinsic to the human condition rather than resulting from 'disturbance' or pathology" (Charney 1980, p. 37). Charney is describing the dialectical process, and if his characterization of marriage is a valid one, the integrated, dialectical reasoner would be best equipped to recognize this feature of marriage and act accordingly. He or she should be more prepared to deal with conflict in an open and constructive manner.

Many of the characteristics described by Lewis and Spanier (1979) of high-quality marriages are those likely to be exhibited by persons who reason relativistically or integratedly: mutual respect, equality of decision making, open channels of communication, acceptance of opposing perspectives. They also differentiate marriages that continue to strengthen and grow over the years from those that do not (Aldous 1978; Reedy, Birren, & Schaie 1981). Relativistic and integrated reasoning both result in an acceptance of the validity of mutually contradictory perspectives as implicit features of reality, and realize the necessity for tolerance of these. Integrated reasoning takes this idea a step further to realize the benefit of open communication in transforming the relationship to a higher level of equilibrium (through the resolution of the conflict). Thus, couples who use these modes of thinking should continue to grow (Kramer in press).

If we are to understand how different levels of reasoning influence conflict resolution, we must explore how couples make attributions about the source of the conflict and its resolvability. A fair amount of work has been conducted that explores attributions of the source of conflict and its resolution in married and nonmarried couples. The following section describes these efforts.

Causal Attributions and Efficacy Expectations

Doherty (1981a, 1981b) has presented a model of the relationship between attributional style and locus of control, and its effect on family conflict. He proposes that two cognitive processes, causal attributions and efficacy expectations, operate during ongoing and stressful conflict, and influence possibilities for adequate resolution.

Causal attributions are inferences about the cause of behaviors or events—or, in the case of conflict, causes of the conflict. In Doherty's model, causal attributions can fall into one of six categories, representing attributions implicating (a) the self, (b) other family members, (c) the relationship, (d) the external environment, (e) theological causes, and (f) luck, fate, or chance. He distinguishes four other attributional dimensions as well: (a) intent (positive or negative; intentional or unintentional), (b) stability (e.g., a permanent trait versus a statelike mood); (c) voluntariness, and (d) specificity (does the action reflect the issue at hand or more general issues?).

Research has found that young dating and married couples attribute more benign intent to themselves and less to their partners (Fletcher 1983; Harvey, Wells, & Alvarez 1978; Madden & Janoff-Bulman 1981; Orvis, Kelley, & Butler 1976). Couples also tend to commit the fundamental attribution error, attributing their own behavior to situational and statelike factors and that of their partners to dispositional factors (Orvis et al. 1976). This suggests that when observing the behavior of others, subjects in these studies typically invoke absolute traitlike explanations of behavior.

Efficacy expectations refer to the perceived expectation that the couple or individual will be able to resolve the conflict, that is, has the ability to bring about a solution (Doherty 1981b). Doherty proposes that people with high efficacy expectations are "more apt to initiate, persist in, and cooperate with attempts to resolve the family conflict . . . [because] individuals are more apt to pursue goals perceived as achievable through personal effort than ones perceived as unachievable" (1981b, p. 27). In his model, both attribution and efficacy responses will influence the nature of attempts to resolve interpersonal conflict in intimate relationships. For example, a person with a high internal locus of control and a high sense of efficacy will be likely to attempt the requisite changes in himself or herself that will resolve the conflict. A person with low efficacy, regardless of locus of causality, is likely to feel helpless.

Of special interest is the person who makes an external causal attribution—that is, blames the other person for the conflict—and also has a high sense of efficacy. Such a person is likely to try to change the partner; and if the attribution is negative in nature, this can result in persistent strategies, including blame and coercion, aimed at attempting to change the partner. This strategy is destructive, as mentioned earlier, since it typically leads to escalation of conflict with potentially violent results. That such a strategy has detrimental consequences for marital relations is evident in the high degree of conflict escalation reported by subjects in Harvey et al.'s (1978) study involving recently separated couples.

To extrapolate from Deutsch's writings, the more escalated the conflict, the more the couple loses sight of the original issues, which results in restricted cognitive and problem solving strategies and, ultimately, less adequate solutions. Therefore, failure to adequately and productively—or, in Deutsch's terms, constructively—resolve the conflict initially means less likelihood of doing so later. Thus, since externalizing blame, a common phenomenon, according to research cited above, is likely to lead to attempts at coercion, which is destructive, the role of attributions in understanding the escalation of conflict is a crucial one.

In support of Doherty's model, research has shown that low trust orientations (generalized attributions about the negative intent of the partner), coupled with a high sense of internal efficacy, are related to the use of coercive attempts at changing the partner (Doherty 1981b). Furthermore, external attributions about the source of conflict (blaming the spouse) have been found to be related to low marital satisfaction (Madden & Janoff-Bulman 1981). Madden and Janoff-Bulman also found that perceived efficacy in producing solutions was positively related to marital satisfaction. Thus, while scant, these findings do support the efficacy of Doherty's predictions.

Toward a Broader Conception of Attributions

As noted above, those who blame themselves *and* have a high sense of efficacy may be able to effect changes without escalating the conflict. However, internal attributions coupled with *low* efficacy are likely to lead to helplessness, probably coupled with feelings of shame and guilt. Thus, it is important to note, since Doherty does not address this point, that internal blame may not always be adaptive. It needs to be accompanied by a high sense of efficacy. Even when it is, there can still be the danger that changing the self will not adequately alter existing problems in the relationship. In fact, it may intensify the problems if the spouse feels threatened by the change and escalates his or her attempts to maintain the status quo (Scarf 1987). Systems theorists stress the importance of the relationship unit itself as a source of the conflict, and the importance of reorganizing the relationship in resolving the dilemma. If such is the case, then blaming either locus or party, and attempting to effect all the changes in that one party, is unlikely to result in real resolution. What happens when attempts to change the self, no matter how successful, do not lead to changes in the conflict, because the problems do not reside solely within the self? This might result in feelings of failure and, hence, guilt, or even lowered expectations for efficacy. Along these lines, Blanchard-Fields and Robinson (1987) found that internal attributions for the *cause* of relationship stress were associated with greater self-blame.

Unfortunately, Madden and Janoff-Bulman do not address the issue of marital satisfaction in those who assign equal blame to both parties. Doherty (1981a) includes a category for causal attributions geared toward the relationship itself, but reports that such attributions were rarely made by the subjects. The other studies that, combined, show greater blame attributed to the other party versus the self (e.g., Fletcher 1983; Harvey et al. 1978; Madden & Janoff-Bulman 1981; Orvis et al. 1976) would also tend to cast doubt on the prevalence of relationship attributions. However, it must be kept in mind that in all of these studies the subjects were predominantly young adults, many of them college students. It is argued here that such attributions are more likely to be made by integrated reasoners, who are likely to be older.

Those reasoning in an integrated manner cannot isolate a single "cause" of a problem. There is a greater emphasis on contextual factors influencing conflict in both relativistic and integrated reasoning. The more mature thinker would be likely to place the conflict in the broader relationship and cultural-historical context. Thus, by studying mature adults, we might find a greater prevalence of relationship and situational attributions. Further, as pointed out by Fletcher (1983), people do attribute a substantial portion of the conflict to situational factors (approximately one-fourth to one-fifth), and to themselves (approximately one-third of the blame, across studies). So even in young adults, the blame is not entirely reduced to one causal factor. What is lacking in this research is an analysis of *how* the subjects conceptualize the interaction among such sources. The cognitive level of the individual would likely influence how such an interaction is conceptualized (e.g., the dialectical reasoner would assert that one cannot isolate blame to the self, the other, or situational factors, but that all form a unified whole).

It is important to stress, however, as do Orvis et al. (1976), that the conflict is not merely a cognitive process. In relationships many emotional factors are involved, and failure to resolve the discrepancies can result in the escalation of conflict that only serves to enhance such emotional intensity. Since emotional arousal can affect cognitive processes (Easterbrook 1959; Janis & Mann 1977), result in regression to lower cognitive levels (Rosenbach, Crockett, & Wapner 1973), and lead to destructive modes of dealing with conflict (Deutsch 1969), it is an important factor to incorporate in models of conflict resolution. It is especially important, since a personal construct or lay theory of reality represents a global perspective on reality, one that encompasses both affective and cognitive processes, which may make the construct highly resistant to change.

COGNITIVE LEVEL, ATTRIBUTIONAL STYLE, AND CONFLICT RESOLUTION

Overview of the Model

It is argued that the developmental model presented earlier, in which individuals construct different lay theories with each succeeding level of development, represents a useful organizing framework for understanding how conflict resolution strategies might evolve over the course of the life span. It will be argued that the world view one adopts will result in (a) different definitions of conflict and power, (b) different attributions about the source of the conflict, and (c) different efficacy expectations regarding its resolution. These differing constructions of the conflict situation will, in turn, result in the adoption of particular strategies for resolving conflict. Consequently, the amount of conflict will be either reduced or escalated.

Reduction of conflict will reinforce one's lay theory, necessitating little or no change in the social cognitive structure. However, if there is continuation or escalation of conflict, the individual may reevaluate his or her lay theory, possibly resulting in a reorganization of the cognitive structure. In other words, according to Kelly's (1955) theory of personal constructs, if the predictions one makes about the source of the conflict and how to reduce it do not prove successful, they are likely to be reevaluated; changing them will necessitate a reorganization of the cognitive structure in order to make more adequate predictions about the source of the conflict and choose a more realistic conflict resolution strategy. The existing structure will not be able to accommodate these changes, which is why a cognitive reorganization is needed. However, it is important to keep in mind that change does not always occur, as Kelly (1955) argued, because the individual may, for a variety of reasons, defensively cling to an inadequate construct or lay theory (e.g., Kramer & Haviland 1987). This model is depicted in the diagram in Figure 9.1. Finally, it will be argued that emotional arousal will differentially affect the conflict resolution strategies of individuals at different social cognitive levels.

In general, relativistic and, to an even greater extent, integrated thinking are expected to facilitate constructive, as opposed to destructive, conflict resolution. Each contains basic assumptions that are commensurate with constructive modes of resolution. This is due to the greater ability to accept opposing viewpoints and the realization that there is no one right way to view reality, which come with these modes of

Figure 9.1
Developmental Model of Conflict Resolution

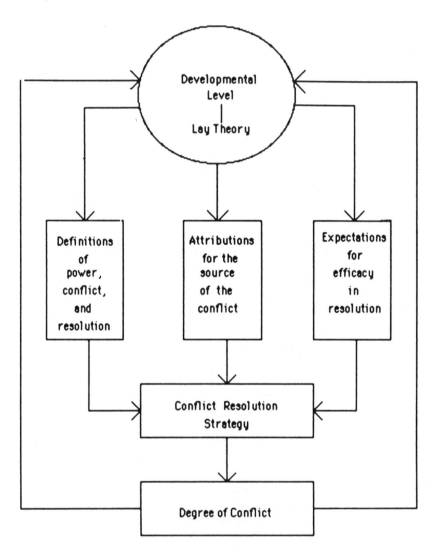

thinking. However, even with relativistic reasoning, it could be argued that under conditions of stress, it would be possible to decide pragmatically to exert force and one's own viewpoint, for the sake of ease, convenience, and profit. Since there is no implicit awareness of the interrelatedness of all phenomena and the greater adequacy of achieving integrated solutions, there would be no logical necessity to the idea of achieving constructive conflict resolution. However, because of relatively high conceptual complexity, under nonstressful conditions, relativistic reasoning would allow for a more constructive conflict resolution than absolute reasoning, especially since absolute thinking—especially when found in adults—may be a manifestation of a defensive personality structure (Kramer & Haviland 1987).

Integrated, dialectical reasoning would not only allow for the validity of opposing viewpoints but would also recognize the logical necessity of cooperation. This would be due to the dialectical assumptions of (a) "movement through forms," where progress is defined in terms of the resolution of contradiction, and (b) "reciprocity," where all events and people are interrelated, and therefore any attempts to impose one's will on another party will result in problems for the self as well—due to the other party's continual search for resolution or satisfaction. Thus, the person reasoning integratedly would inherently understand the distinction between conflict resolution and conflict regulation, and would recognize that regulation leads to attempts at retaliation and escalated conflict. No real progress will be made unless a real resolution is achieved, whereby the conflicting elements become subordinated to a new system. To the integrated reasoner, there would be a logical necessity for cooperative conflict resolution. Let us now take a closer look at the model.

Definitions of Power and Conflict

Power is a central feature of many models of conflict resolution (Rubin & Brown 1975; Scanzoni 1979). Scanzoni defines it as "the capability to achieve intended effects" (p. 302). Since the intended effect may be cooperative action, power need not be dictatorial. In fact, people thinking at different levels may construe in either competitive or cooperative terms, depending on how they conceive of conflict.

Predictions about what kinds of definitions about conflict and power, and what kinds of attributional styles, are associated with each of the four lay theories are presented in Table 9.1. One's level of reasoning will influence what one considers an adequate definition of conflict resolution. Absolute and mechanistic reasoning would likely lead one to define conflict resolution in competitive terms. To an absolute reasoner, resolution would be a matter of the "correct" party imposing his or her will on the "wrong" party; and to the mechanistic reasoner, it would consist of the stronger party overpowering the weaker. Any attempts at coercion that might arise from this will result in escalation of conflict, attempts at retaliation, eventual loss of sight of the original issues, and attempts to degrade the other party. Thus, a win-lose situation is set up, and power is seen as the ability to emerge the winner.

Relativistic reasoning will likely lead one to shy away from power, in

Table 9.1

Definitions of Power and Conflict, and Attributional Style as a Function of Lay Theories

Lay Theory	Definition of Power	Definition of Conflict	Causal Attributions	Efficacy Expectations
Absolute	submissive	disruptive -- to be ignored or eliminated via triumph of right over wrong	dispositional, enduring traits in self or other fate	low
Mechanism	coercive	disruptive -- to be eliminated via coercion of weaker by stronger	manipulable behaviors of self or other environmental events	high
Relativism	laissez-faire, avoidant	inherent feature of reality -- to be tolerated	clashing points of view context chance,luck	low
Integrated	cooperative	inherent feature of reality -- to be used as an impetus for growth	relationship interaction of individual and environment	high

the realization that there is no absolutely correct side and that each party has a legitimate right to his or her own perspective. Alternatively, power would be reconceptualized as the ability to coexist without any attempt at coercion or real resolution, setting up a "nobody wins/nobody loses" situation. Integrated reasoning is likely to result in a definition of conflict resolution as cooperative, recognizing the inherently vicious circle that arises when one attempts to impose his or her way on the other. Integrated reasoning would also likely result in a definition of power as the ability to achieve a solution that will satisfy both parties, thus setting up a win-win situation. Further, such a solution would be seen as involving progress, through a creative synthesis of opposing perspectives, resulting in greater equality, reciprocity, and interdependence among the parties. In this conception, power is achieved by moving the system itself forward and not merely the individual (who, in the dialectical view, could not move forward if the system did not move forward).

Attributional Style

In terms of attribution theory, absolute and mechanistic thinking would be most likely to lead to attributing conflict to isolated causes in the self or the other. From an absolute perspective, these causes would be represented by enduring personality traits; from a mechanistic perspective, by manipulable behavior. However, absolute reasoning is expected to yield low efficacy expectations, because of the belief in the inherent stability of personality traits and dispositions, and the belief in the idea of fate, while mechanistic reasoning is expected to yield high efficacy expectations, because of the belief that reality can be altered through strong outside forces. Unfortunately, when high efficacy is coupled with internal causal attributions, efforts to change the self may be successful but unable to resolve the conflict effectively unless the system itself changes. External attributions about the source of the conflict, coupled with high efficacy expectations, are likely to result in coercive attempts, which will escalate conflict and thus are maladaptive. Low efficacy expectations, coupled with either internal or external attributions, are likely to result in submission and may ultimately erupt in rage and violence toward either the self or the partner (Doherty 1981b). Thus, an attributional style that in the proposed model is related to either an absolute or a mechanistic world view is not likely to be an adaptive style of construing intimate-relationship conflict.

Relativistic reasoning will likely result in attributions to chance and situational factors, but without any attempts at real control. This is due to the assumption in relativism that change is an inherent feature of reality, and one cannot predict what changes will occur—they occur randomly and without explanation. Thus, relativistic reasoning will probably result in a laissez-faire or distant strategy—or, conversely, adoption of resolution or regulation tactics merely for pragmatic purposes (i.e., involving a regression to a more mechanistic level).

It is integrated reasoning that should yield attributions to the relationship system or to the interaction between the individual and the environment. However, whereas the relativistic reasoner is expected to have low expectations for efficacy, the integrated reasoner is expected to have high expectations and thus to see conflict as an impetus for moving the relationship forward. Unfortunately, research on attribution does not typically involve mature samples, and thus no definitive conclusions can be made regarding the attributions of integrated reasoners. One exception to this is a study by Blanchard-Fields (1986b), who found that older adults assigned less certainty to their attributions about whether a character was responsible for the outcome of some event, indicating their awareness of the subjective nature of attributions. It is expected that integrated reasoners would make fewer self- and other-attributions, and more relationship attributions, and that they would experience a greater amount of marital satisfaction than nondialectical reasoners.

Stress and Affect Intensity

Since stress has been found to detrimentally affect the conflict resolution strategies adopted (Deutsch 1969; Janis & Mann 1977), and to
adversely affect cognitive processing (Easterbrook 1959), resulting in a
regression to lower cognitive levels (Rosenbach et al. 1973), the author
proposes that stress will differentially affect the processing of absolute,
mechanistic, relativistic, and integrated reasoners.

First, it is expected that absolute and mechanistic reasoning will result
in simplistic attributions and poorer conflict resolution strategies under
all conditions. Nevertheless, since these forms of thinking probably serve
a defensive function (Kramer & Haviland 1987), individuals displaying
them are expected to feel highly threatened in conflict situations. Under
conditions of extreme stress, relativistic or integrated reasoning may also
break down, resulting in competitive forms of problem solving. However, this regression is expected to be more apparent in relativists than
in integrated reasoners. First, integrated reasoners are aware of the logical necessity of cooperative conflict resolution strategies, and thus may
be able to more effectively use such a model to guide their actions, even
in stressful situations. Second, with the advent of a dialectical structure,
the ability to integrate contradiction into a meaningful structure is likely
to have developed to a greater degree of automatization in integrated
reasoners than in relativistic ones, and thus will require fewer attentional
demands (e.g., Pascual-Leone 1983, 1984). Therefore, it will take a
greater amount of stress to reduce the range of available cues to the
point that stress will interfere with the conflict resolution. Consequently,
an interaction between social cognitive level and stress on conflict resolution is expected.

Empirical Support for the Model

To assess the validity of the model, it is necessary to test for age
differences in the lay theories, in the definitions of conflict and power,
and in attributional style. One would also have to test for the relationship
among these processes, and the effects of emotional arousal on the
reasoning and conflict resolution strategies of individuals manifesting
different world views. Little work has been done to date. There is evidence for developmental shifts in these world views, with a shift toward
relativistic thinking in late adolescence and early adulthood (King et al.
1983; Kramer & Haviland 1987; Perry 1970), and a further shift toward
integrated reasoning in later life (Basseches 1980; Blanchard-Fields 1986;
Kramer, Goldston, & Kahlbaugh 1987; Kramer, Melchior, & Levine 1987;
Kramer & Woodruff 1986). Longitudinal work is needed, however, to
substantiate these later-life findings.

To date, there is no work that directly addresses age differences in definitions of conflict and power, and no work that directly assesses attributions for interpersonal conflict. Research on attributional style and aging has focused primarily on the generalized domain, the intellectual domain, or the health domain (Lachman 1986). One exception to this is a study by Blanchard-Fields and Robinson (1987) on attributions about the source and controllability of relationship stress. Adolescents and young adults were more likely than middle-aged or older adults to attribute the source of relationship stress to themselves (i.e., make internal causal attributions). The results regarding internal attributions of controllability, however, were not as clear-cut. However, they cite a study by Aldwin and Revenson (1985), which found that older adults perceived themselves as less responsible for the occurrence of a stressful event, but equally capable of coping with that event. Furthermore, Blanchard-Fields and Robinson found that high internal locus of causality was associated with increased self-blame.

These findings, therefore, support the distinction between locus of causality (causal attributions) and outcome (efficacy expectations) made by Doherty and elaborated in the present model. Unfortunately, Blanchard-Fields and Robinson did not study interactive attributions. Work in other domains shows evidence for increased external locus of control in later life (Lachman 1986), without a corresponding decrease in internal locus of control, which suggests that older adults may be more aware of the joint operations of multiple levels of "causality."

My own research shows significant relationships between our scale of paradigm beliefs and the Levenson generalized locus-of-control scale. Relativism was significantly associated with attributions to chance, while absolute and mechanistic beliefs were significantly and positively correlated with both internal and external locus of control, suggesting that absolute and mechanistic reasoning results in a view of events in the world as isolatable and controllable, while relativistic reasoning does not. Integrated beliefs were slightly, but significantly, associated with both internal and chance attributions, which suggests a possible awareness of the interaction between internal efficacy and a nondeterministic environment.

Further support for the model comes from a study on communication in dating couples, where relativistic and integrated thinkers reported more effective problem solving and were more open to reciprocal patterns of communication (Kramer & Levine 1987). Finally, there is some tentative evidence in support of the hypothesis of differential responses to emotional arousal by people at different cognitive levels. When subjects who were classified as being highly integrated, according to our questionnaire of paradigm beliefs, were compared with those who were highly absolute on the questionnaire, integrated reasoners did not experience the debilitating effect of age-relevant content material on an interview assessing paradigm beliefs that was found in the general sample (Kramer, Melchior, & Levine 1987). In contrast, absolute reasoners performed more poorly on the same-age dilemma, which suggested that they may have succumbed to the effects of emotional arousal that might have been produced by the more relevant dilemmas.

CONCLUSIONS

Recent conceptualizations of cognitive shifts in adulthood have much to contribute to existing knowledge in the social psychological domain. In particular, it is argued that cognitive level influences (a) definitions of conflict and power (b) attributions regarding the source of conflict in relationships, and (c) efficacy expectations regarding the possibility for resolution of such conflict. These processes, in turn, influence the kind of conflict resolution strategy adopted. The degree of conflict in the situation feeds back into the individual's cognitive level, where he or she may reassess his or her lay conception of social interaction. However, the process is a dynamic, ongoing one that does not follow a neat, linear path (Kramer in press). Rather, one struggles to continually adapt to changing interactions, some of which may threaten the integrity of the individual's self system. Thus, the individual is involved in an ongoing dynamic to construct, maintain, and reconstruct his or her social-cognitive structure in the context of multiple, sometimes conflicting, sometimes novel interpersonal situations, many or all of which are emotionally imbued. Preliminary evidence provides support for this model; however, much more systematic investigations with fine-grained measures of attributional style and a broader-based age range are needed.

NOTE

1. The dialectic is being used in two manners here. The first sense is as a metatheoretical perspective, a general model for conceptualizing developmental change and conflict resolution processes. The second is as a level of reasoning—a way of conceptualizing social reality by lay people. It will be argued that if conflict resolution processes conform—at a theoretical or metatheoretical level—to dialectical principles, then an individual at the integrated, dialectical level of reasoning will be better equipped to understand conflict resolution processes.

REFERENCES

Aldous, J. (1978). *Family careers: Developmental change in families*. New York: John Wiley & Sons.

Aldwin, C. M., & Revenson, T. A. (1985). Cohort differences in stress, coping, and appraisal. *The Gerontologist, 25* (special issue), 66.

Basseches, M. (1980). Dialectical schemata: A framework for the empirical study of dialectical thinking. *Human Development, 23,* 400–421.

Blanchard-Fields, F. (1986a). Reasoning on social dilemmas varying in emotional saliency: An adult developmental perspective. *Psychology and Aging, 1,* 325–333.

Blanchard-Fields, F. (1986b). Attributional processes in adult development. *Educational Gerontology, 12,* 289–300.

Blanchard-Fields, F., & Robinson, S. L. (1987). Age differences in the relation between controllability and coping. *Journal of Gerontology, 42,* 497–501.

Charney, I. W. (1980). Why are so many (if not really all) people and families disturbed? *Journal of Marital and Family Therapy, 6,* 37–47.

Deutsch, M. (1969). Conflicts: Productive and destructive. *Journal of Social Issues, 25,* 7–41.

Doherty, W. J. (1981a). Cognitive processes in intimate conflict: I. Extending attribution theory. *American Journal of Family Therapy, 9*(1), 3–13.

Doherty, W. J. (1981b). Cognitive processes in intimate conflict: II. Efficacy and learned helplessness. *American Journal of Family Therapy, 9*(2), 35–44.

Easterbrook, J. A. (1959). The effect of emotion on cue utilization and the organization of behavior. *Psychological Review, 66,* 183–201.

Fletcher, G. J. B. (1983). The analysis of verbal explanations for marital separation: Implications for attribution theory. *Journal of Applied Social Psychology, 13,* 245–258.

Harvey, J. H., Wells, G. L.,& Alvarez, M. D. (1978). Attribution in context of conflict and separation in close relationships. In J. H. Harvey, W. Ickes, & R. F. Kidd (Eds.), *New directions in attribution research* (Vol. 2, pp. 235–260). Hillsdale, N.J.: Erlbaum.

Janis, I. L., & Mann, L. (1977). *Decision making: A psychological analysis of conflict, choice, and commitment.* New York: The Free Press.

Kelly, G. A. (1955). *The psychology of personal constructs.* New York: W. W. Norton.

King, P. M., Kitchener, K. S., Davison, M. L., Parker, C. A., & Wood, P. K. (1983). The justification of beliefs in young adults: A longitudinal study. *Human Development, 26,* 106–116.

Kramer, D. A. (1983). Post-formal operations? A need for further conceptualization. *Human Development, 26,* 91–105.

Kramer, D. A. (in press). Change and stability in marital interaction patterns: A developmental model. In D. A. Kramer & M. J. Bopp (Eds.), *Transformation in clinical and developmental psychology.* New York: Springer-Verlag.

Kramer, D. A., Goldston, R. B., & Kahlbaugh, P. E. (1987, November). Age differences in paradigm beliefs, personality/attitudinal measures, and affect intensity. Paper presented at the 40th annual meetings of the Gerontological Society of America, Washington, D.C.

Kramer, D. A., & Haviland, J. M. (1987, June). Emotion-cognition links in Anne Frank's diary. Paper presented at the Third Beyond Formal Operations Symposium: Positive Development During Adolescence and Adulthood, Harvard University.

Kramer, D. A., & Levine, C. B. (1987, June). Cognitive development and conflict resolution. Paper presented at the Third Beyond Formal Operations Symposium: Positive Development During Adolescence and Adulthood, Harvard University.

Kramer, D. A., Melchior, J., & Levine, C. B. (1987, May). Age-relevance of content material on relativistic and dialectical reasoning. Paper presented at the 17th annual symposium of the Jean Piaget Society, Philadelphia.

Kramer, D. A., & Woodruff, D. S. (1986). Relativistic and dialectical thought in three adult age groups. *Human Development, 29*, 280–290.

Labouvie-Vief, G. (1984). Logic and self-regulation from youth to maturity: A model. In M. L. Commons, F. A. Richards, & C. Armon (Eds), *Beyond formal operations: Late adolescent and adult cognitive development* (pp. 158–179). New York: Praeger.

Lachman, M. E. (1986). Locus of control in aging research: A case for multidimensional and domain-specific assessment. *Psychology and Aging, 1*, 34–40.

Lewis, R. A., & Spanier, G. B. (1979). Theorizing about the quality and stability of marriage. In W. R. Burr, R. Hill, F. I. Nye, & I. L. Reiss (Eds.), *Contemporary theories about the family* (Vol. 1, pp. 268–294). New York: The Free Press.

Madden, M., & Janoff-Bulman, R. (1981). Satisfaction: Wives' attributions for conflict in marriage. *Journal of Marriage and the Family, 43*, 663–674.

Orvis, B. R., Kelley, H. H., & Butler, D. (1976). Attributional conflict in young couples. In J. H. Harvey, W. Ickes, & R. R. Kidd (Eds.), *New directions in attribution research* (Vol. 1, pp. 353–386). Hillsdale, N.J.: Erlbaum.

Pascual-Leone, J. (1983). Growing into human maturity: Toward a metasubjective theory of adult stages. In P. B. Baltes & O. Brim (Eds.), *Life-span development and behavior* (Vol. 5, pp. 117–156). New York: Academic Press.

Pepper, S. C. (1942). *World hypotheses*. Berkeley: University of California Press.

Perry, W. G. (1970). *Forms of intellectual and ethical development in the college years: A scheme*. New York: Holt, Rinehart & Winston.

Reedy, M. N., Birren, J. E., & Schaie, K. W. (1981). Age and sex differences in satisfying love relationships across the adult lifespan. *Human Development, 24*, 52–66.

Rosenbach, D., Crockett, W. H., & Wapner, S. (1973). Developmental level, emotional involvement, and the resolution of inconsistency in impression formation. *Developmental Psychology, 8*, 120–130.

Rubin, J., & Brown, B. R. (1975). *The social psychology of bargaining and negotiation*. New York: Academic Press.

Scanzoni, J. (1979). Social processes and power in families. In W. R. Burr, R. Hill, F. I. Nye, & I. L. Reiss (Eds.), *Contemporary theories about the family* (Vol. 1, pp. 295–316). New York: The Free Press.

Scarf, M. (1987). *Intimate partners: Patterns in love and marriage*. New York: Random House.

Sinnott, J. D. (1984). Postformal reasoning: The relativistic stage. In M. L. Commons, F. A. Richards, & C. Armon (Eds.), *Beyond formal operations: Late adolescent and adult cognitive development* (pp. 298–325). New York: Praeger.

10

Consumer Reasoning

Noel Capon
Deanna Kuhn
Mario Carretero

Despite a long history of study of intelligence, until very recently little was known about the ways in which people behave intelligently in real-world activities. The most obvious place we might look for people to exhibit intelligence in real-world settings is in their vocational roles, and a majority of the studies of practical intelligence have been devoted to the investigation of intelligence in work-related settings (Frederiksen 1986; Scribner 1984; Sterberg & Wagner 1986). In the series of studies described in this chapter, we investigate practical intelligence outside a work setting. How and to what extent do individuals display intelligence in simple, everyday activities common to most people, and how great is individual variation in this regard? The investigation of practical intelligence in a nonvocational setting is particularly important from a life-span developmental perspective (Dixon & Baltes 1986). Intelligence in the work place is confined to a particular context and segment of the life span, and may depend on specific acquired knowledge and expertise that are hard to separate from intellectual operations. From a developmental perspective, it is important to know not only the extent of interindividual variability but also the extent of intraindividual variability in performance of the same intellectual task at different points across the life span (Kuhn et al. 1983).

THE CONSUMER TASK

The everyday task we investigate is one that is not thought of as intellectually demanding but in fact could involve a good deal of cognitive processing—examining and evaluating a set of similar items and selecting one to be purchased. How do people function cognitively in their role as consumers? There is of course an existing literature on consumer behavior, but for the most part researchers in that field have followed the tradition of social and cognitive psychologists, basing their work on laboratory tasks that involve symbolic stimuli and are not intended to reflect the subject's activity as it occurs in a natural context. The few researchers undertaking studies of shoppers in a natural setting have relied on a nonintrusive observational methodology and have found it difficult to unravel the complexity of the behavior being observed (Bettman 1979; Lave et al. 1984). Our objective in our studies was to constrain the range and complexity of the stimuli encountered by the subject, and thereby to reduce the complexity of the stimuli encountered by the subject, and thereby to reduce the complexity of the observed behavior to a manageable level, while at the same time preserving to a considerable degree the naturalness of the shopping situation.

In some early work (Capon & Kuhn 1979), we explored how one traditional reasoning competency—the formal operational scheme of proportionality—was exhibited in a consumer context by asking consumers to calculate which of two sizes of a product was the better buy. The significant finding from this work was a wide individual variability in skill level, even within educational and SES groups. From there, we went on to focus on the consumer situation itself—how do people approach a set of consumer products that vary on multiple dimensions? We wished to avoid reenactments of habitual consumer choices (such as might occur in a grocery store). For this reason, we constructed a set of items that would be new to subjects but nevertheless come from a general product class with which they would be familiar. In each of the studies described in this chapter, we constructed a set of products that varied along several dimensions (typically four, with two levels of each dimension), and each combination of dimensions was represented. The set was presented to the subject in a randomly arranged array, which she/he was free to manipulate.

CONSUMER PREFERENCE

In the first study (Capon & Kuhn 1980), the objects were a set of pocket-size notebooks of the type that might be purchased in a low-priced variety store. The dimensions were color (red or green), surface (dull or shiny), shape (long/thin or short/wide), and fastening (side or top). Each of the 16 possible combinations was represented in 2 identical notebooks, yielding a total set of 32 notebooks. In this study, we focused on the extent to which subjects' expressed preferences regarding each of the four dimensions were reflected in their preferences regarding the notebooks themselves. In other words, was the subject able to take into account and integrate his or her individual dimension preferences into preference judgements regarding the notebooks in a consistent way? Such consistency arguably might be regarded as one reflection of practical intelligence in the consumer context. The consistency criterion is a particularly salient one when considering the behavior of individuals as consumers. Though there exists no systematic evidence in support of it, the stereotype is prevalent that consumers, particularly those of lower education and SES levels, are likely to behave in an impulsive way. Rather than weigh all of the dimensions of the objects they are contemplating and integrate their preferences with respect to these dimensions into an overall evaluation of the object, the individual is more likely (the stereotype suggests) to fix on a single dimension of the object, ignoring others she/he in fact cares about equally, or to base selection on only a global impression of the object, with no analysis of its dimensions. In either case, the implication is that the individual has not necessarily selected as best the object she/he "really" prefers.

This initial study was a developmental one. Cognitive processing of the sort just referred to could be complex and exceed the capacities of younger subjects, making it important to examine performance developmentally. Moreover, we anticipated that developmental data would be of use in interpreting individual variation that might be observed in adult samples. Subjects in this study were 20 kindergarteners, 20 fourth graders, and 20 eighth graders from a middle-income elementary and junior high school, and 20 young adults from a large state university in the same community. The university was a commuter school, so students were from the local community.

Performance of the young adult subjects indicated considerable cognitive sophistication. Correlation coefficients in notebook preference ratings across replications, that is, the 2 identical sets of 16 notebooks, were computed for each subject. The average coefficient was .72. Fourteen subjects had coefficients above .75 and only two had coefficients below .40. In the dimension ratings, 95 percent of adult subjects preferred one value over the other on either three or all four dimensions. Considerable consistency was found between main effects in the object ratings and preferences in the dimension ratings: In only two instances did a subject show a main effect for a dimension in the object ratings while indicating no preference in the rating of that dimension. In no instance did a subject show a main effect in the object ratings while indicating a contradicting preference in the dimension ratings. Thus, subjects were able to articulate accurately in the dimension ratings the preferences they were taking into account in the object ratings.

When the relation between object and dimension ratings was viewed in the opposite direction, however, the picture was different. Though the preferences indicated by subjects' object ratings were reflected as well in their dimension ratings, the reverse was not true. In their dimension ratings, subjects indicated preferences with respect to more dimensions than those for which significant effects emerged in their object ratings. A typical case was a subject who expressed preferences on three dimensions in the dimension ratings, but in the object ratings showed effects for only two of these. Thus, despite the sophistication shown by adult subjects in their ability to integrate preferences with respect to multiple dimensions in a systematic manner, and their ability to accurately articulate these preferences in independent dimension ratings, in making object ratings these subjects typically did not take into account all the dimensions on which they had preferences.

A comparison of the performance of younger subjects with that of adults revealed both similarities and differences. Most subjects at all age levels expressed preferences for one value over the other for either three or all four of the dimensions. In object ratings, however, substantial differences among the age groups appeared. Consistency coefficients dropped to .50 for eighth graders, .40 for fourth graders, and .04 for kindergarteners. In contrast with the adults, who tended to show two or three main effects (with about half of those also showing some interactions between dimensions), eighth graders modally showed only a single main effect, fourth graders showed either a single main effect or no effects, and kindergarteners modally showed no effects. Thus, younger subjects had as many dimension preferences as older ones, but in making object ratings took even fewer of these dimensions into account. Some additional data were presented in this study supporting the interpretation that the youngest subjects used a "shifting-single-dimension" strategy (i.e., the subject attended to only one of his or her dimension preferences in judging a notebook, with the dimension attended to fluctuating frequently). Among older subjects, this fluctuation disappeared and a single dimension was attended to as the basis for notebook preference judgments, but not until adulthood were subjects able to integrate their preferences on two or more dimensions in making preference judgments regarding the objects embodying those dimensions.

Relations to Cognitive Ability Measures

The preceding pattern of results suggested an interpretation within the Piagetian framework of concrete and formal operations—the decline of the shifting-dimension strategy and the resulting focus on a consistent single dimension with the decline of preoperational and development of concrete operational reasoning during the early school years, and the appearance of multiple-dimension strategies with the development of formal operations during adolescence. This possibility was explored in a second study (Capon & Davis 1984). Subjects were of a single age group—adults—to avoid common variation of measures with age. They consisted of 60 female members of a church group (median age 44, with a range from 20 to 76); modal educational level was high school, though 13 reported some college and 10 had college degrees. Four measures of formal operations were administered: isolation of variables, systematic combination, proportion, and correlation. Tasks were adapted from the original Inhelder and Piaget (1958) tasks to involve everyday content familiar to subjects. Results indicated performance on the consumer (notebooks) task to be related to formal operations, but not uniformly. Significant associations were obtained for the isolation of variables and combination tasks, but not for the proportion or correlation tasks. This result is congruent with much of the research literature on formal operational reasoning, indicating absence of a tight interlinking among different formal operational reasoning strategies. It is also congruent with the nature of this consumer task. Like the consumer task, isolation of variables and systematic combination tasks focus on the processing of multivariable data, while the proportions and correlation tasks do not have this emphasis.

Results of the Capon and Davis (1984) study thus anchor our consumer task to existing measures of cognitive ability. In so doing, the results suggest it is more likely that the performance variability across subjects observed in the consumer task is variability of a cognitive rather than of a dispositional or motivational nature. Relations between performance on the consumer and two formal operations tasks, however, were moderate rather than perfect. Such "partial overlap" with established ability measures, it should be noted, is probably the best outcome one can expect in studies of practical intelligence. If the new measures correlate very highly with established measures of mental ability, the argument can be made that they are "nothing but" alternative measures of those abilities; conversely, if the new measures show no such correlation, a question might be raised regarding their validity.

Consumer Reasoning Across the Life Span

In another follow-up study (Capon, Kuhn, & Garucharri 1981), we examined performance on the consumer task across the life span. The task was the notebook task described above; subjects were 20 adults in their thirties, 20 in their fifties, 20 in their sixties, and 20 in their seventies. A central question, of course, in the life-span literature has been the extent to which intellectual functioning declines or remains stable during later years. A major problem in addressing this question has been the limited relevance of existing tasks for assessing intellectual functioning in the lives of middle-aged and older adults (Kuhn et al. 1983). We were thus interested in how older adults would perform on this task more relevant to their everyday activities.

The standard of comparison was the sophisticated performance of the college subjects in the Capon and Kuhn (1980) study. Results supported the position that a high level of performance on such a task is maintained throughout the adult years and well into old age: A substantial proportion of subjects (40 percent or greater) demonstrated an ability to integrate their preferences on a number of dimensions into consistent preference judgments regarding objects embodying those dimensions, using either a simple linear model or one that incorporated interaction effects. Performance of subjects in their thirties and fifties was, if anything, superior to that of college students. The performance of subjects in their sixties and seventies was also of a very high level, though there were some modest differences between the elderly and middle adult subjects in consistency of object ratings, consistency between object and dimension ratings, and patterns of effects in the object ratings. Inspection of the data indicated that the slightly lower group performance of the elderly was due to decidedly inferior performance of a few individuals. Thus, it is the generally high level of performance of all adult subjects, rather than the modest differences between the middle adult and elderly subjects, that should be stressed.

CONSUMER SELECTION

Another result that should be emphasized is that within each age group, especially the adult age groups, in the preceding studies there appeared substantial individual variation. It is to an examination of this variation that we have turned in more recent work. Our attention in recent work has also turned more directly to the consumer choice task itself: How does an individual structure the task of choosing an item to purchase from a multivariable array? In the current study (Capon, Kuhn, and Carretero unpublished), we included the tasks from the earlier research, but we preceded them with a choice task in which the subject was asked simply to "think aloud" as she went about making a purchase choice among the randomly arranged array of alternatives. This task brings us much closer to the consumer's activity in a natural context, and it was this activity that we attempted to simulate.

We changed the product from notebooks to skirts, which we thought would be more significant to subjects. Subjects were 41 Hispanic women, members of a Catholic church in a lower SES urban neighborhood in a large eastern city. All spoke Spanish as their first and primary language, and little or no English. All interviews were conducted in Spanish by the third author. Subjects ranged in age from 18 to 69; median age was

45. Two subjects had no formal education; 21 had completed elementary school; 17 had completed high school; and 1 had some college experience. In choosing this population, our intent was to study subjects who were unlikely to be functioning at high levels with respect to traditional academic intelligence and who for the most part had no special vocational expertise, but who nevertheless would be highly experienced and possibly skilled in the activity that was to be the focus of our investigation. Would such subjects exhibit intelligence in the familiar activity in which we asked them to engage? In particular, would individual differences be observed despite the restricted range of this sample with respect to traditional academic intelligence?

The session took place in a specially outfitted room in the church where the subjects were members. The setting was designed to simulate as far as possible the conditions a woman might encounter in choosing a skirt for purchase in a clothing store. The room contained a clothing rack, on which the skirts hung, a full-length mirror, adequate overhead lighting, a table, and several chairs. The 24 skirts were hung in random order on the rack. The subject was free to move skirts along the rack, to reorder them on the rack, to remove them from the rack for examination, and, if desired, to try them on. The skirts had been tailored by a skilled seamstress especially for the study. They were of a quality that might be found in a medium-priced clothing store. The 24 skirts represented all possible combinations of one trichotomous and three dichotomous dimensions: color (navy, tan, green), fabric (polyester, corduroy), front pockets (present or absent), and hem ruffle (present or absent). The skirts were all of an identical, average size. The subject was told that the purpose of the study was to learn about how women select clothing. She was then engaged in a few minutes of casual conversation with the interviewer as a warm-up. The three segments of the study—skirt choice task, skirt rating task, and dimension rating task—were always conducted in that order. Though order effects could exist, this constant order was chosen so as not to risk contaminating the main task (skirt choice), on which protocol analysis is based. In the main task, the subject was shown the rack of skirts and told that she was to select the skirt that she liked best, just as she would if she were buying one in a store. She was told that she should take as long as she liked and that it was important to choose carefully, for at the conclusion of the study a drawing would be held (like the raffle drawings sponsored frequently by the church), and the three winners would each receive the skirt she had chosen, custom-made in her size. Following the choice task, the subject was asked to give preference ratings for each skirt and for each of the four dimensions. About six months later, 29 (71 percent) subjects returned for a second session during which the entire interview was repeated.

Processing Strategies

Half of the transcribed verbal protocols from the skirt selection task were examined as the basis for construction of a coding scheme, which was then applied to all of the protocols. In developing the coding scheme, an iterative process was used in which a trial scheme was constructed, a portion of the protocols coded, the scheme revised, and the process repeated. The result was a microscheme that classifies each evaluative judgment made by the subject. Results of the microscheme coding were then used as the basis for global classification of subjects, as reported below. An evaluative judgment was chosen as the most coherent unit of analysis, rather than each individual utterance. Such a judgment could consist of multiple utterances, for example, "I like this skirt—the fabric is nice and the color is good on me." After construction of the scheme was completed and applied to all protocols, half of the protocols were selected randomly for independent coding by a second coder. Percentage agreement for identification and coding of an evaluative judgment was 91 percent.

The object of the coding scheme was to assess evaluative judgments with respect to the apparent complexity of the cognitive operations involved. An initial dichotomy that was examined, therefore, was whether a subject's judgment pertained only to a single skirt or whether it pertained to a set of skirts that the subject had grouped together on some basis. In the former case, which we shall refer to as a single-alternative evaluation, the subject made a judgment regarding a single skirt, either globally or with respect to one or more of its dimensions. Evaluations involving more than one skirt we observed to be of three types. In one, which we shall refer to as a multiple-alternative evaluation, the subject identified a set of skirts based on one or more dimensions and made an evaluative judgment of the set as a whole. In the other two, the subject either compared two skirts with each other (a simple comparative evaluation) or a set of skirts with another skirt or set of skirts (a multiple-alternative comparative evaluation). Each of these judgment types was also examined with respect to another aspect of complexity, the number of dimensions of the skirts taken into account and whether these dimensions were integrated in an additive manner ("I like both the color and the ruffles") or a compensatory manner ("I like the color but not the ruffles"). These distinctions are summarized with examples in Table 10.1.

Overall, 414 evaluative judgments were identified, an average of 10 per subject. The majority of these, 306, were single-alternative evaluations (shown by all 41 subjects). There were only 29 multiple-alternative evaluations, 52 simple comparative evaluations, and 10 multiple-alternative comparative evaluations. Notable, then, is the fact that though

Table 10.1
Microscheme Coding of Evaluative Judgments

Single-alternative evaluations

    Global   This skirt is pretty.

    Global with qualification   I like this skirt except for the pockets.

    Unidimensional   I don't like the color of this shirt.

    Bidimensional

      Additive   The color and pockets are nice.

      Compensatory   I like the color but not the pockets.

    Tridimensional

      Additive   The color and fabric are nice, and I like the ruffle.

      Compensatory   I like the color and fabric but not that ruffle.

Multiple-alternative evaluations

    Global*   *

    Unidimensional   I like the color of these skirts.

    Bidimensional

      Additive   I don't like the polyester or ruffle on these.

      Compensatory   I like these tan skirts but not the pockets.

    Tridimensional

      Additive   I like the color and fabric of these, and the pockets are nice.

      Compensatory   I like the color and fabric of these but not the pockets.

Simple comparative evaluations

    Global   I like this skirt better than that one.

    Unidimensional   This is a better color than that one.

    Bidimensional

      Additive   This is a better color and fabric than that one.

      Compensatory   This has a better color but that's a nicer fabric.

    Tridimensional

      Additive   This one's a better color and fabric than that one, and it has ruffles.

      Compensatory   They're both a nice color, but I prefer the fabric and ruffles on this one.

Multiple-alternative comparative evaluations

    Single-to-group

      Unidimensional   I don't like this skirt as much as the blue ones.

Table 10.1 (continued)

Bidimensional	I like this skirt's color and fabric better than those over there.
Group-to-group	
Unidimensional	I like the polyester skirts better than the corduroy.
Bidimensional*	*

* Did not occur

subjects had been instructed to think aloud as they went through the process of selecting a skirt, most of the time they simply expressed judgments about individual skirts, with no indication of how these judgments related to selection.

We did, however, observe a transition point in the protocols of some subjects. Toward the end the protocol, after a number of evaluative judgments of one or more of the types described had been made, some subjects verbalized a restricted choice set of specific alternatives from which selection was to be made. They then proceeded to make a choice from among this restricted set. Of the 41 subjects, 18 (44 percent) displayed this two-phased approach. For 16 of the 18, the restricted choice set consisted of only 2 alternatives; for the other 2, it consisted of 3 alternatives. During phase 2, over half of the evaluations (53 percent) were simple comparative; the remainder were single-alternative. During phase 1 (the only phase for 23 of the subjects), in contrast, most evaluations (81 percent) were single-alternative, and other types were infrequent.

Global classification of subjects is presented in Figure 10.1, in the form of a tree diagram. Phase 1 behavior is portrayed in the top half of the diagram, and phase 2 behavior in the bottom half. The number of subjects falling into each classification is shown. The first and second branchings yield four groups: those who (in their phase 1 behavior) showed only single-alternative evaluations, showed some simple comparative evaluations, showed some multiple-alternative evaluations, and showed both simple comparative and multiple-alternative evaluations. As reflected in Figure 10.1, most subjects who showed one of these two types of more complex processing also showed the other. Presence of simple comparative evaluations without multiple-alternative evaluations was particularly rare.

The third branching refers to the type of single-alternative evaluations used: no more than unidimensional, some bidimensional, and some tridimensional. Presence of bi- or tridimensional evaluations did not differ significantly as a function of presence of multiple-alternative eval-

Figure 10.1
Classification of Subjects

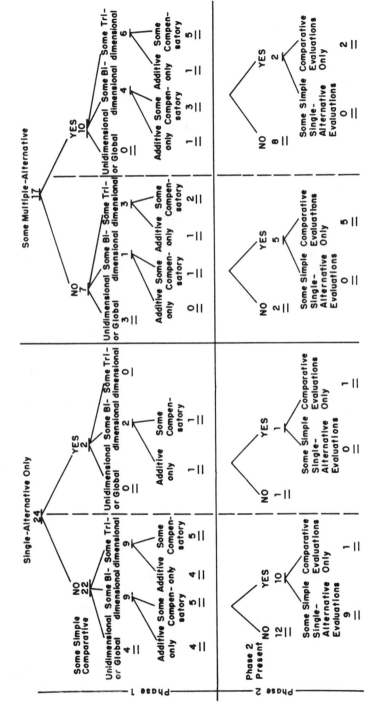

uations or as a function of presence of comparative evaluations. The final branching distinguishes those subjects who showed some compensatory evaluations from those who did not. There was a weak but nonsignificant trend toward more frequent occurrence of compensatory evaluations among multiple-alternative subjects.

Only the first two branchings were related to phase behavior. As reflected in Figure 10.1, subjects showing multiple-alternative but not comparative evaluations were highly likely to display a second, restricted-choice phase, subjects showing both types of more complex processing were unlikely to do so, and single-alternative subjects were about equally likely to do so or not. Differences also appeared with respect to type of phase 2 behavior. Among the 18 subjects who showed a second phase (final branching in Figure 10.1), half made only comparative evaluations during the second phase, while half also made single-alternative evaluations during the second phase. As reflected in Figure 10.1, subjects showing exclusive comparative evaluations in the second phase were much more likely to be in the multiple-alternative group: All seven subjects in this group showed exclusive use of comparative evaluations during phase 2, whereas only 2 of 11 (18 percent) of the single-alternative group did so, suggesting that the phase 2 behavior of the multiple-alternative group was different in quality and may have been more skilled or efficient. A further difference suggestive of this conclusion pertains to the degree of similarity among the alternatives in the phase 2 choice set. The implication of a choice set in which the alternatives differ on few rather than many dimensions is that the subject's phase 1 behavior has been more effective in narrowing down the alternatives. Two of five (40 percent) of the multiple-alternative-without-comparisons group and two of two (100 percent) of the multiple-alternative-with-comparisons group had a single dimension level difference in their phase 2 choice set, contrasted with only 3 of 11 (27 percent) of the single-alternative group. Finally, all subjects in the first two groups constructed a phase 2 choice set of only two skirts, which they then chose between.

Another aspect of behavior on the selection task that was examined was the relation between skirts examined and the skirt chosen—that is, did subjects show a tendency to choose the first skirt examined, the last skirt examined, or a skirt in the middle of the examination sequence? One subgroup of subjects chose proportionately more polar skirts (those examined first or last) than would have been expected by chance. Eight of the 13 single-alternative single-phase subjects chose the first skirt examined, three chose the last skirt examined, and the remaining two did not choose a polar skirt.

Finally, total number of skirts examined and total time taken in the selection process differed across subgroups. The multiple-alternative-without-comparisons subjects examined the fewest number of skirts (mean of 4.0) and took the least time (mean of 4 minutes, 39 seconds). These were the subjects who, while displaying only multiple-alternative and no comparative evaluations in phase 1, were highly likely to show a second phase that appeared to be highly efficient. Subjects who examined the largest number of skirts (mean of 12.5) and took the most time (mean of 7 minutes, 30 seconds), in contrast, were the multiple-alternative-with-comparison group. These subjects displayed both comparative and multiple-alternative evaluations in their phase 1 behavior and were unlikely to display a second phase. Intermediate were the single-alternative subjects (whose phase 2 behavior, if they did display a second phase, appeared not as efficient as that of the multiple-alternative subjects): They examined a mean of 7.6 skirts and took a mean of 5 minutes, 51 seconds. The difference in number of skirts examined by these three groups was significant.

Rating Data

Each of the subject's skirt ratings was treated as an independent judgment to be entered into an analysis of variance (ANOVA) for that subject, following the procedure used in the earlier studies. A considerable range of information integration patterns was displayed. Including both main and interaction effects, 13 subjects took all 4 dimensions into account, 13 took 3 into account, 6 took 2 into account, 8 took 1 into account, and 1 subject displayed no effects. In the dimension ratings, of the 41 subjects, 39 indicated a preference of one level of a dimension over the other(s) for all four dimensions; the remaining subjects indicated preferences for three of the four dimensions. Subjects showed considerable consistency between object ratings and their explicit dimension preferences, expressed directly in the dimension ratings. Of the 38 subjects who exhibited main effects in their ANOVAs, 25 exhibited dimension preference scores that were consistent with all of their main effects. Of the remaining 13 subjects, 10 had only a single dimension preference score inconsistent with a main effect. Overall, subjects thus showed considerable ability to integrate dimension preferences into preference ratings of the objects. However, despite the considerable consistency between the implicit preferences for levels of the skirt dimensions revealed as main effects in the ANOVAs and the preference scores obtained directly from the dimension ratings, there were far fewer significant right-direction main effects in the ANOVAs than there were nonzero preference scores for dimension: 71 versus 158. In other words, as found in the earlier studies, subjects did not take into account in the skirt ratings all those dimensions of the skirts with respect to which they had preferences.

Consistency Across Tasks and Time

Subjects were divided into two groups based on their performance on the rating tasks: strong and weak integrators. Three criteria were employed, all of which had to be met for a subject to be classified as a strong integrator: (1) integration of preferences for at least two dimensions was demonstrated by the appropriate significant effects in the subject's ANOVA; (2) 50 percent or more of all moderate, strong, and very strong dimension preferences resulted in right-direction main effects in the subject's ANOVA; (3) no moderate, strong, or very strong dimension preference resulted in a wrong-direction effect in the subject's ANOVA. Application of these criteria produced 16 subjects who were classified as strong integrators and 25 who were not. A strong relationship was found between this dichotomy and the groups developed on the basis of the choice task. Of the 24 single-alternative subjects, just 5 (21 percent) were strong integrators. Those subjects who showed some simple comparatives or a second phase (Figure 10.1) were no more likely to be strong integrators. In contrast, six of the ten (60 percent) multiple-alternative-with-comparisons and five of the seven (71 percent) multiple-alternative-without-comparisons subjects were strong integrators. With the two multiple groups collapsed, this association was significant.

Other measures of consistency were also moderate to high. A set of analyses was undertaken to investigate the degree of consistency exhibited by subjects within and across the skirt choice, skirt rating, and dimension rating tasks, both within and across the two sessions (six months apart). In each case, comparisons were made of the single-alternative, multiple-alternative-with-comparisons, and multiple-alternative-without-comparisons groups. The correlation between the first and second replications of the skirt rating task was uniformly high, with the lowest coefficient for any individual group in either session .61. The two within-session across-task measures were the relationships between skirt choice and dimension preferences, and between skirt choice and skirt ratings. The former consisted of the mean number of preferred dimension levels (obtained directly from the dimension ratings) that were present in the chosen skirt, that is, if the subject indicated a preference for corduroy over polyester in the dimension-rating task, was the skirt chosen in the choice task corduroy? Consistency was uniformly high on this measure, a mean of over 3 in every case. Consistency between skirt choice and skirt ratings was measured by the proportion of times that the skirt selected in the choice task was also the most highly rated skirt in the rating task. Once again there was high consistency, overall 79 percent and 88 percent agreement for the first and second sessions, respectively.

The three across-session measures were each derived from within-task comparisons, one each for the dimension rating, skirt rating, and skirt choice tasks. The dimension-rating measure consisted of the mean number of dimensions (of four) for which the preferred level (e.g., corduroy over polyester) was the same across sessions. The skirt-rating measure was the mean of the four possible correlation coefficients between the first and second replications of the skirt-rating task at the first session and the first and second replications of the skirt-rating task at the second session. The choice measure consisted of the mean number of dimensions of the chosen skirt for which the preferred level (e.g., corduroy) was the same at both sessions. All of these measures of consistency were high for all three groups. There was somewhat greater variability across groups in the last two measures, but these differences were not statistically significant. All subjects, then, performed all of the tasks with considerable consistency.

Global Strategy Types

Results of the choice task allowed us to classify subjects into four overall groups.

Single-Alternative Evaluation without Comparisons

The 12 subjects in this group (see Figure 10.1) showed the minimal form of behavior consistent with the task demand to examine the skirts and choose one. They examined a number of skirts, on average about a third of them, and made evaluative judgments about each as it was examined. No more complex judgments were expressed, either comparing skirts with one another or evaluating a set of skirts grouped together on some basis. After a series of single-alternative evaluations, the subject chose a skirt, almost always the first or last one examined.

Single-Alternative Evaluation with Some Comparison

The 12 subjects in this group likewise examined about a third of the skirts and showed a predominance of simple single-alternative evaluation, but they also showed some comparative evaluations, either during the first phase (n = 2) or a second, reduced-choice phase (n = 10). This second-phase behavior, however, differed from that of subjects in the multiple-alternative groups: Subjects continued to make single-alternative, as well as comparative, evaluations of the skirts in the second-phase reduced choice set (in contrast with multiple-alternative subjects, whose second-phase behavior was confined to comparative evaluations). Furthermore, the reduced choice set was different, likely to differ on more than one (sometimes as many as three or four) dimensions. Sub-

jects in this group, relative to those in the first group, showed evidence
of having imposed some higher-order strategic framework on the task,
either in explicitly comparing skirts with one another or in constructing
a reduced choice set. The variability among the two or three skirts in
the reduced choice set suggests that this effort may not have been particularly effective.

Multiple-Alternative Evaluation with Phase 1 Comparison

The ten subjects in this group, unlike those in the two previous groups,
showed evidence of having imposed a higher-order strategic framework
on the task by implicitly grouping skirts together on the basis of some
defining feature, usually one or more of the four dimensions on which
they varied, and making an evaluative judgment of them with respect
to the defining dimension(s). Subjects in this group, however, mixed
these judgments with simple comparisons of one skirt with another.
They rarely constructed a reduced choice set and were the slowest of
all groups in making a selection, examining the most skirts in the process.

Multiple-Alternative Evaluation with No Phase 1 Comparison

The higher-order strategic framework imposed on the task by the
seven subjects in this group consisted during phase 1 exclusively of
multiple-alternative grouping and evaluation with respect to defining
dimension(s). Most then used these evaluations as the basis for construction of a reduced choice set, differing on one or at most two dimensions, from which a selection was made. This reduced choice set
never contained more than two skirts, and only comparative judgments
were made once the reduced choice set has been constructed. These
subjects examined the fewest individual skirts and completed the selection process most rapidly. It thus appears that they imposed a framework
of higher-order strategies on the task with a greater degree of success
and efficiency than did subjects in the preceding group.

Generality of Strategies

In a dissertation by Martin (1987), the present study was replicated
using two different products, sweaters and coffee mugs, with each subject encountering both products (in counterbalanced order across subjects). Martin also manipulated the product array to be either random
(as in the previous work) or hierarchical (arranged in a matrix). This
manipulation had no effect on performance. Martin's study does, however, show the strategy types described above to be general across these
two kinds of products: Subjects tended to be classified as showing the
same type for both products. This finding, however, leaves unanswered

a number of important questions about these types, which we consider below.

CONSUMER REASONING AND EVERYDAY COGNITION

Of the series of studies we have described, the latter studies, in which subjects are asked to select a skirt or sweater or mug in the way they might do in a store, bear most directly on the topic of everyday cognition and problem solving. The results of the skirt study, like the earlier studies, provide evidence of intelligent performance on the part of all of the subjects examined but also evidence of significant individual variation. All subjects in the skirt study showed intelligent performance with respect to consistent selection of an identical or very similar skirt on two separate occasions six months apart, and also with respect to consistency in their ratings of the skirts, both within and across sessions; in their ratings of the dimensions; and in the relations among skirt choice, skirt ratings, and dimension ratings. Where notable individual variation occurred was in the relation between skirt and dimension ratings, that is, the extent to which a subject integrated her dimension preferences into preference judgments regarding the skirts themselves and, most important, in the think-aloud behavior exhibited in the selection task. Examination of the protocols from the latter suggested the four different groups described above.

To what extent is it valid to regard the four preceding types as constituting an ordinal scale with respect to intelligent performance of the activity we observed? Alternatively, are they better regarded simply as different styles of carrying out a common, everyday activity, some more analytic in nature, perhaps, but not necessarily less effective? An argument can readily be made for the last of the four types described as the most intelligent, efficient way to execute the task: Items are grouped conceptually on the basis of the dimensions in terms of which they vary. This categorization is used as the basis for narrowing the original set down to those having the preferred characteristics.

Arguments in favor of the second alternative, however, also can be made. Subjects in the first two groups, who did not show categorization by dimension, were no less consistent than subjects in the latter groups with respect to choice of skirt on the two separate occasions. One could argue that since they chose the same skirt, or nearly the same skirt, on the second occasion, it must have been the one they indeed liked best, and who is to criticize the way they went about selecting it? One might in fact make the even stronger argument that one-by-one examination of individual skirts reflects a "configural" approach that is the most intelligent—indeed, the only feasible—way of carrying out the task in the case in which the subject's dimension preferences are highly inter-

t is, preferences regarding one dimension are conditional on
of other dimensions. The limiting case of such a configural
of course, is the one in which all four dimensions interact
and each unique combination of dimensions therefore must be judged
as a separate entity.

Diminishing the likelihood of this "configural" interpretation, however, is the fact that if subjects in the first two groups had such configural,
or interactive, preferences, they did not display them in the skirt rating
and dimension rating tasks. No subject expressed any difficulty in making simple preference judgments for each of the dimensions in isolation
from the others (as would be reflected, for example, in judgments such
as "Blue is a better color, but only in the corduroy skirts.") More important, subjects in the first two groups rarely displayed more than a
single two-way interaction effect in the skirt rating task—fewer, on the
average, than the number of interacting effects displayed by subjects in
the two latter groups. It is unlikely, then, that their preferences were
configural to an extent that would have made it difficult for them to
engage in evaluation by dimension.

The temporal consistency argument is also vulnerable to a counter-
argument that subjects' consistency in this regard may have been at-
tributable not to any consistency in the selection process itself over the
two occasions but to the subject's memory of having selected a particular
skirt on the first occasion. In other words, the act of making the initial
choice may have been salient enough for subjects that they remembered
their choice on the second occasion and felt constrained to reaffirm it.
To the extent that this possibility is correct, second-occasion process is
constrained by first-occasion choice, in which case the replication no
longer provides a pure assessment of the consistency with which a
particular process yields the same choice on repeated occasions.

Temporal consistency of choice, then, may not be the most valid indicator of the consistency with which the subject carried out the task.
A more process-sensitive assessment of consistency, it can be argued,
may be found in the consistency between dimension ratings and skirt
ratings. In their ratings of the individual skirts, subjects often failed to
integrate all of the dimensions on which they expressed preferences in
a way consistent with those expressed preferences. Differences in this
regard, we also found, were related to the differences observed in the
skirt selection task: Subjects in the two single-alternative-evaluation
groups in the skirt selection task were unlikely to show successful integration of their dimension preferences in their ratings of the skirts.

Results of the skirt and dimension rating tasks, then, support the
interpretation of an ordinal ranking of the groups formed on the basis
of the skirt selection task, with the initial groups regarded as displaying
less skill or efficiency than the later ones. In rating the individual skirts,

subjects in the first and second groups did not exhibit the interaction effects that would have justified configural, item-by-item processing, nor was their performance likely to reflect integration of all of their dimension preferences in a consistent way. What this interpretation does not tell us, however, particularly if one discounts the configural possibility, is very much about how these subjects accomplished selection of a skirt. Though subjects in the first of the four groups described above exhibited only a series of evaluative statements regarding individual skirts, something presumably determined the selection the subject made. At one extreme, it might be argued that the subjects who appeared less skilled in fact engaged in categorization and comparison processes similar to those of subjects in the latter groups, and that this processing dictated choice, but the process was not accessible to the subject and therefore did not appear in the think-aloud protocol. The likelihood, however, that this assertion is correct in any strong form is diminished by the facts that (a) subjects in the first group, who showed only single-alternative evaluations, typically chose the first or last skirt examined; and (b) subjects in the second group, who showed construction of a restricted choice set (second phase), typically constructed a set that differed on several dimensions. Thus, the additional performance indicators available suggested that the selection process of these subjects differed substantially from that of subjects in the third and fourth groups.

Study of individual protocols supports this interpretation. Characteristic of subjects in the two single-alternative groups was a long series of single-alternative evaluations, often global in nature. For example, one typical subject said about four successive skirts on the rack: "This one is very nice; this is nice, too; I like this one too; this one is very pretty." Two-phase single-alternative subjects then typically turned to a comparison of two skirts, from which they ultimately chose one, but the basis for focusing on these two was not clear, that is, it was not clear that all others had been consciously eliminated as less desirable. One subject, for example, began the second phase by saying, "Well, these two, I like them very much because they are very similar, except one has pockets and the other doesn't." (In fact, the only commonality between the skirts was color; they were of different fabric, one had pockets and no ruffles, and the other had ruffles and no pockets.) She then chose one of the two, saying, "Well, these two, I like them very much because they are very similar, except one has pockets and the other doesn't." (In fact, the only commonality between the skirts was color; they were of different fabric, one had pockets and no ruffles, and the other had ruffles and no pockets.) She then chose one of the two, saying, "Well, I like this one very much so I would like to buy it." Single-alternative subjects who did not show a second phase simply chose one of the skirts examined, usually the first or last. One such subject, for example, chose the first skirt she had examined, saying: "I think that I'm not going to continue looking because I'm almost decided and I don't have too much time, so I would buy this one because my idea was to buy a simple skirt for the spring." These protocols thus appeared very different from those in which the subject went through a systematic evaluation by dimension and then chose the skirt that had the combination of favored dimensions.

What can be said more broadly about the individual variation observed in this study? The comparison and categorization operations absent in some protocols and present in others are very simple ones that are within the competence of adult subjects from the population sampled. It is unlikely, then, that fundamental differences in competence are involved. Subjects most likely differed in their disposition to actively impose the organizing structure these operations offer when the narrow task demands could be met without doing so. We believe it likely that the differences observed reflect broad cognitive/personality styles that characterize an individual's approach to a range of activities. In this respect, they no doubt relate to a number of other style constructs, described in previous cognitive style and personality literature, having to do with analytic versus holistic or linear approaches. A fundamental issue in studies of cognitive style has always been whether it is valid to impose any order on the styles identified, regarding one as more advanced or desirable than another. The task investigated in the present study might be regarded as one with respect to which it is particularly difficult to regard any approach as better than another. The choice of a particular skirt rather than the others cannot be regarded as better or worse than another choice would have been. No skirt was better than any other in any objective sense. Each woman presumably chose the skirt she liked best. How can a researcher impose value judgments on the way she went about it?

We deliberately chose to study a task that involved a relatively inconsequential choice for the subject, as we wanted to examine an activity that she engaged in often. One need only change the item being selected, however—say, to an insurance policy—and the variations in approach that we have identified take on a much different tone. The existence of subjects showing the more analytic types of processing is as important in its implications as is the existence of subjects showing the simpler linear types. Subjects who approached the task in a highly analytic way showed no tendencies to differ in age or amount of education from subjects who did not. The fact that the sample as a whole represents a restricted range with respect to educational attainment and traditional academic intelligence supports the view that intelligent behavior may be evident in other than traditional academic domains, and warrants being searched for and examined in those domains.

The individual variation we observed also assumes considerable significance from a life-span development perspective. In the Capon, Kuhn, and Garucharri (1981) study, we found that the proportion of subjects who showed high consistency in integrating their dimension preferences in ratings of the objects themselves dropped only slightly among the elderly. Subjects using more analytic approaches, then, may be highly likely to maintain them into old age, which suggests that the kind of activity examined in our studies may represent a fruitful domain in which to investigate the cognitive skill of the elderly. Life-span developmental psychologists have proposed that it may be the "pragmatics of intelligence" (Dixon & Baltes 1986), rather than the "mechanics," that shows patterns of stability and even progressive change throughout adulthood. While consonant with such a view, the present results strongly support the view that adult intellectual functioning is characterized by wide individual variation. Such variation must figure prominently in any account of adult intellectual functioning or development.

REFERENCES

Bettman, J. (1979). *An information processing theory of consumer choice*. Reading, Mass.: Addison-Wesley.

Capon, N., & Davis, R. (1984). Basic cognitive ability measures as predictors of consumer information processing strategies. *Journal of Consumer Research, 11*, 551–563.

Capon, N., & Kuhn, D. (1979). Logical reasoning in the supermarket: Adult females' use of a proportional reasoning strategy in an everyday context. *Developmental Psychology, 15*, 450–452.

Capon, N., & Kuhn, D. (1980). A developmental study of consumer information-processing strategies. *Journal of Consumer Research, 7*, 225–233.

Capon, N., Kuhn, D., & Carretero, M. (unpublished). Shopping styles and skills: Everyday cognition in a "noncognitive" task. Columbia University.

Capon, N., Kuhn, D., & Gurucharri, M. (1981). Consumer information-processing strategies in middle and late adulthood. *Journal of Applied Developmental Psychology, 2*, 1–12.

Dixon, R., & Baltes, P. (1986). Toward life-span research on the functions and pragmatics of intelligence. In R. Sternberg & R. Wagner (Eds.), *Practical intelligence: Nature and origins of competence in the everyday world*. New York: Cambridge University Press.

Frederiksen, N. (1986). Toward a broader conception of human intelligence. *American Psychologist, 41*, 445–452.

Inhelder, B., & Piaget, J. (1958). *The growth of logical thinking from childhood to adolescence*. New York: Basic Books.

Kuhn, D., Pennington, N., & Leadbeater, B. (1983). Adult thinking in developmental perspective. In P. Baltes & O. Brim (Eds.), *Life-span development and behavior*, (Vol. 5). New York: Academic Press.

Lave, J., Murtaugh, M., & de la Rocha, O. (1984). The dialectic of arithmetic in grocery shopping. In B. Rogoff & J. Lave (Eds.), *Everyday cognition: Its development in social context* (pp. 67–94). Cambridge, Mass.: Harvard University Press.

Martin, E. (1987). Consistency in individual consumer choice strategies. Unpublished Ph.D. dissertation, Columbia University.

Scribner, S. (1984) Studying working intelligence. In B. Rogoff & J. Lave (Eds.), *Everyday cognition: Its development in social context.* Cambridge, Mass.: Harvard University Press.

Sternberg, R., & Wagner, R. (Eds.). (1986). *Practical intelligence: Nature and origins of competence in the everyday world.* New York: Cambridge University Press.

11

Interpreting Discrepant Narratives: Hermeneutics and Adult Cognition

Bonnie Leadbeater
Deanna Kuhn

Addressing the question "Can fictional narratives be true?," Ricoeur (1983, p. 3) reminds us that "the term history in most of our Indo-European languages has the intriguing ambiguity of meaning both what actually happened and the report of those happenings." The distinction between fact and interpretation or, more broadly, between objectivity and subjectivity, is particularly problematic when we are faced with discrepant "histories" or narratives, as in eyewitness testimonies or newspaper and television reports.

Consider, for example, the importance of differentiating and reconciling fact and interpretation in the following accounts from the *New York Times* (June 18, 1985, p. B1). The reporter describes the controversy facing jurors who are considering an appeal contesting the will of J. Steward Johnson: Johnson died at 87, leaving most of his fortune to his third wife of 11 years and excluding his 6 children from a former marriage. Mrs. Johnson's position is explained by the reporter as follows:

A devoted woman from an educated, fervently anti-Communist, Polish family brings a rush of youthfulness into an old man's life. The woman, who had studied art in Poland, stands by her husband not only during the good times, when his money and her purchases revolutionize the art market, but also as prostate cancer overtakes him. Out of gratitude and affection, he drafts a series of wills in which he bestows upon her an increasingly larger share of his fortune.

This research was partially funded by a doctoral fellowship to the first author from the Social Sciences and Humanities Research Council of Canada. Mary Tramontin also contributed to this work in assisting in data collection and in the development of the scoring system. Thanks also to Larry Aber, who helpfully commented on drafts of this chapter.

That decision is spurred on by the disappointment he feels for his children who, he believes, have been ruined by the wealth that he lavished on them 40 years earlier: separate trust funds made up of Johnson & Johnson stock that, simply left alone, would have been worth $110 million each at the time of his death. Some of the trusts are now worth considerably less than that, although each of the children remains a multimillionaire.

Mr. Johnson's children offer this version:

An opportunistic, young domestic insinuates herself into an elderly man's confidence, and then charms, bamboozles and bullies him for her own ends. Through a combination of fraud, duress, coercion and undue influence, she and her lawyers become the sole beneficiaries of Mr. Johnson's final will. The Johnson children contend that when their father signed this last will, he was barely able to lift his head from his pillow or recognize some of them. Several days earlier, they assert, their stepmother asked a priest to administer last rites to him. He was confused, even hallucinatory, they say, more prone to fantasize about phantom Nazi submarines or Soviet invasions than to dispose of his estate as he would have wanted.

The problem presented both to the jurors and to us as newspaper readers is a familiar one: to construct from the ambiguous and conflicting narrative accounts an interpretation of what happened. We will argue that the problem of constructing an interpretation of what "actually happened" from discrepant narratives involves a hermeneutic process, and that central to this are the abilities to differentiate and reconcile the dialectic between fact and theory. We will also present evidence that both suggests an age-linked progression in the coordination of these abilities and raises questions about the end point of adult cognitive development.

While little empirical study has addressed the specific question of how individuals interpret discrepant narrative accounts, the work of developmental theorists suggests that the seemingly requisite ability to distinguish between fact and interpretations of facts is a relatively late development. Studying the intellectual and ethical development of Harvard College students longitudinally, Perry (1970) presents evidence of a progression from dualism to multiplicity (skepticism) to relativism. The dualist in Perry's scheme is embedded in the facts, making no distinction between fact and interpretation. Absolute, right answers exist for everything, and the facts are known by an authority. The multiplicity position is that of the radical relativist or skeptic, who emphasizes the subjectivity of all perception and sees no possibilities for judging among these opinions. In contrast, the relativist believes that reasonable, valid differences in the interpretation of facts exist, and that these stem from differences in points of view, value systems, or interpretations. Findings of subsequent researchers (Basseches 1980; Broughton 1978; King et al. 1983; Kitchener & King 1981, 1985) have supported the existence of this progression in college students.

Methodological problems have, however, hampered this empirical study (Kramer 1986). Researchers typically have asked subjects to describe, reflect on, and justify their epistemological beliefs when presented with controversial issues in complex, semistructured individual interviews. Efforts to score protocols using multidimensional scoring systems that assess broad philosophical concepts such as views of mind, self, and dialectical thinking have proved challenging for the establishment of adequate interrater agreement. The almost exclusive use of college student populations limits the generalizability of findings and also makes it difficult to assess the separate influences of age, education, and life experiences on development (Kitchener & King 1985).

In the research discussed here, we have proceeded in a different way. We have taken as a starting point the everyday reasoning problem of interpreting discrepant narrative accounts of events. Our investigation focuses on development of the ability to differentiate and coordinate fact and interpretation in dealing with such problems. Using a refinement of an instrument developed by Kuhn, Pennington, and Leadbeater (1983), we have undertaken to observe subjects of various age levels actually applying their epistemological understanding to an everyday task, rather than attempting to articulate and reflect on this understanding.

Kuhn et al. (1983) presented to 34 adults who were serving jury duty, and thus were reasonably representative of the general adult population, two fictitious accounts of the "Fifth Livian War" (Table 11.1). The jurors were then asked, in individual interviews, to "describe what the Fifth Livian War was about and what happened" and to respond to several questions: Who was victorious in this war? Why did the wars end? Are there important differences in the two accounts? Could both of the historians' accounts of the Fifth Livian War be right? Analysis of the jurors' responses focused on their ability to distinguish statements about the accounts (metastatements) from statements about the events themselves, and on their ability to differentiate and reconcile discrepancies in the two historians' perspectives.

Salient differences (Table 11.2) appeared in the jurors' ability to differentiate the historians' "points of view" and to reconcile them: Levels 0 and 1 represented positions in which no acknowledgment was made of the differences in the historians' interpretations and the accounts of the events were not distinguished from the events themselves. In contrast, level 2 subjects were greatly disturbed by the dichotomies in the two historians' idiosyncratic perspectives and had difficulties reconciling the two accounts. Level 3 subjects resolved these discrepancies by at-

Table 11.1
The Livia Task

A brief account of the Fifth Livian War
by J. Abdul
National Historian of North Livia

On July 19th 1878, during a period set aside by North Livia to honor one of their national leaders, the ceremonies were interrupted by a sneak attack from the South Livians, beginning the Fifth Livian War. Because the North Livians were caught by surprise, they were unprepared at first and the South Livians won a few early battles. But then the tide turned heavily in favor of the North Livians. Before the North Livians could reach a final victory, however, a neighboring large country intervened to prevent further bloodshed.

Despite their early setbacks, the later sweeping victories of the North Livians showed that they would have won, had the fighting continued. As a result of this war, the South Livians finally recognized that anything they gained from the North Livians would have to be worked out through peaceful negotiations. Thus ended the Livian Wars.

A brief account of the Fifth Livian War
by N. Ivan
National Historian of South Livia

In the last war, North Livia had beaten South Livia, taken some of its land and refused to leave. South Livia could no longer tolerate this situation and spent large sums of public funds to strenghten its military defenses. On July 20th 1878, the Fifth Livian War began. The war took place with rapid, dramatic victories for South Livia, resulting in great national celebration. After these dramatic victories, the South Livians suffered some minor losses. But then a neighboring large country intervened to prevent further bloodshed.

Despite their later setbacks, the final victory of South Livia seemed assured because of its overall position of strength. As a result of this war, the South Livians felt a new self-respect. They had always felt embarrassed by their previous defeats, but now they had proven that they were the equals of the North Livians on the battlefield. Because the South Livians had achieved military respect, they were willing to work out future differences through peaceful negotiations, thus ending the Livian Wars.

tributing them to minor differences in the historians' subjective emphases. These were seen as overlying but not obscuring the underlying facts, thus enabling the subject to reconcile the two accounts and construct his or her own reasonably certain, integrated account of what probably happened. Level 4 subjects attributed the discrepancies to differences in each historian's frame of reference. The subject was unable to reconcile these differences but saw both as valid interpretations of what happened.

The progression observed by Kuhn et al. resembles, in many respects, the developmental stages reported by Perry (1970) and Kitchener and King (1981, 1985), but it raises questions about what can be seen as the end point of such a sequence. Like Kitchener and King's highest-level subjects, the level 3 jurors used criteria of justification (e.g., affirming points of agreement and rejecting contradictions) to critically evaluate the internal consistency of the two historians' accounts and to synthesize a single, integrated, objective account of what happened. A higher level is, however, suggested in the jurors' interpretations of the discrepant narratives. The level 4 jurors did not reconcile discrepancies in the two accounts. Their interpretations appeared to be more open, inclusive, and creative than the level 3 jurors' analytic or deductive syntheses of the accounts. In level 3 responses to the question of what happened, discrepancies in the two accounts are abolished as mere subjectivity; level 4 subjects assert the validity of both historians' accounts. For example, one level 4 subject says:

Whose side you are on will determine what the Fifth Livian war was about. Apparently, each side had its version of the cause of the war.... Each side looked at its defeats and victories as proof that they were noble warriors, which enabled them to settle peacefully in arbitration.

The discrepancies between the two accounts are neither attributed to individualistic subjectivity, as at level 2, nor reduced to a single perspective, as at level 3. At level 4, the historian's embedment in his particular historical, cultural context is seen to reveal two plausible interpretations of what happened. It can be argued that this hermeneutic effort is a more adequate response to the interpretive demands of the task.

HERMENEUTICS AND THE INTERDEPENDENCE OF FACT AND INTERPRETATION

The hermeneutic task of interpreting narrative accounts is elaborated by the philosopher Paul Ricoeur (1983, p. 3) as a dialectic of objective "distantiation" and subjective "appropriation" of texts. Historians do not merely report a succession of events. Belonging to the history they communicate, they construct narratives to be told by someone to someone. Ricoeur (1978 pp. 153–155) argues that the narrative, mediated by this "communicative intention," gains an objectivity from the mind of the individual historian. Because of this distantiation, the narrative is not merely an expression of historians' thoughts, to be empathically or deductively understood. It is, rather, a codified text. On the other hand, the "conditions of intelligibility" of the narrative—the possibility of understanding the text—demand that it be interpreted by a reader, but this, in turn, necessitates the "subjective appropriation" of the narrative by the reader. The processes of constructing and interpreting narratives are then dialectically centered on the text itself. The narrative functions as a kind of medium for the transfer of meaning, which refers back to real events (or literal meanings) but at the same time conveys new meanings via the reader about our self and the world (Ricoeur 1981). Our attention is drawn to the reversal implicit in this dialectic. The problem of understanding what the historian meant or what actually happened shifts to become a problem of understanding the meaning of the work itself, of opening up the worlds of possible meaning conveyed by the text (Ricoeur 1978, p. 144).

We can infer from Ricoeur's views that the problem of interpreting discrepant narratives does not merely involve empathic understanding of multiple viewpoints, nor an analytic or deductive synthesis of competing perspectives. Interpretation is, rather, a problem of recognizing the dialectical interdependence of facts and reports of the facts. It is a problem of being open to possible worlds evidenced in texts and of reconstructing new narratives that must retain the same openness to future revision.

The differentiation and reconciliation of fact and theory in interpreting narrative accounts seems to be represented best by a dialectical position in which neither fact nor subjective interpretation is subordinated. From a hermeneutic perspective, their interdependence is seen as the condition of intelligibility for the interpretation of narratives. While these issues are central to epistemological debates among philosophers of science and history (Broughton 1983; Freeman 1984, 1985; Leadbeater 1986a, 1986b), there is little empirical knowledge of how individuals do in fact construct intelligibility from discrepant narratives, knowledge that might inform these philosophical debates. Here, we investigate the performance of subjects engaged in interpreting discrepant narrative accounts. We have assessed responses to the Livia Task made by sixth, ninth, and twelfth graders, as well as groups of adult graduate students and nonstudents of equivalent chronological age.

Participants were Caucasians from middle- to upper-middle-class socioeconomic backgrounds. The graduate students were recruited from a large urban private university. The nonstudent adults were recruited from members of New York City peace-movement organizations and their network of friends. This latter group is perhaps most representative of individuals with liberal political views. However, their life experiences afford them opportunities to discuss conflicting belief systems more than the general population, which perhaps stimulates their interest and ability in such tasks. As they represented a range of educational levels, we anticipated that this would allow for a preliminary assessment of the differential effects of education based on a group whose age and life experiences were similar to those of the graduate students. Their educational levels were as follows: one had a high school diploma only, eight had a two-year college associate degree or some two-year college courses, five had a bachelor's degree or some university courses, and six had a graduate degree or some graduate courses. Ten "recent attenders" had attended school (taken some courses at an educational institution) in the last four years but not within the last six months, and ten "nonrecent attenders" had not attended school within the last five years (range 5 to 15 years). The age of "recent attenders" was not significantly different from that of the "nonrecent attenders."

PRESENTATION AND ANALYSIS OF THE LIVIA TASK

The Livia Task was presented to each participant individually. It was introduced as follows: "North and South Livia are two small countries that existed in the nineteenth century in central Asia. During the latter part of the century there were a series of conflicts between the two countries, termed the Livian Wars. The following are two brief accounts of the Fifth Livian War, which took place in 1878."

The prerecorded accounts (Table 11.1) were played in counterbalanced order, and subjects were encouraged to read along on two typed copies. Subjects were told in advance that following the readings, they would be asked to "describe in your own words what the Fifth Livian War was about and what happened." They were also told that the two typed accounts would be left with them to refer to at any time. When the subject indicated readiness to proceed, the interviewer asked all of the following questions and probes:

1. Describe in your own words what the Fifth Livian War was about and WHAT HAPPENED. Probe: Can you tell me any more of the details? (Subsequently referred to as "What Happened?") 2. Are the two historians' accounts of the war DIFFERENT in any IMPORTANT ways? Probe: In what ways are they different? (Subsequently referred to as "Important Differences?") 3. Could BOTH of the historians' accounts of the Fifth Livian War be RIGHT? Probes: If NO—Why not? If YES— How can that be? Is one of the historian's accounts of the Fifth Livian War more TRUE than the other? How could you be CERTAIN of what happened in the Fifth Levian War? (Subsequently referred to as "Both Right")

Subjects' responses were audio-taped and transcribed. The protocols were classified into one of six global levels (0 to 5).[1] A summary of the critical differences between each of the levels is given in Table 11.2 and will be elaborated below. The initial step in the analysis of the protocols was to code whether facts and the historians' interpretations of the facts were differentiated in the subject's protocol. This assessment is aided by the identification of "metastatements" in the subject's responses. Following Kuhn et al. (1983, p. 178), a metastatement is defined as "a statement about one or both of the accounts," in contrast with a simple statement that is a "statement about the events described in the accounts." For example, "According to the North Livian historian, the tide turned heavily in favor of the North" is a metastatement, while "The tide turned heavily in favor of the North" is a simple statement. The

Table 11.2
Summary of Critical Differences Among Levels of Responses to the Livia Task

Level	Differentiate fact and interpretation	Discrepancies attributed to	Reconciles discrepancies	Nature of epistemological justification
0	no	characteristics of countries or events	does not apply	REALIST right is interpreted as plausible or moral
1	no	differences in what historians mention	yes	PREDUALISTIC adding stories together gives you more of the truth
2	yes	historians' distortions of the facts	no	DUALISTIC one's right & one's wrong
3	yes	historians' idiosyncratic opinions	no	RADICAL RELATIVIST everyone has a right to his or her own opinion
4	yes	historians' subjective emphasis	yes	OBJECTIVE RELATIVIST underlying facts can be detected through critical inquiry
5	yes	historians' ideological perspectives	no	CONCEPTUAL RELATIVIST accounts are both valid interpretations of the events

presence of metastatements implies the subject's recognition that interpretation plays a role in the historians' construction of the two accounts, and thus distinguishes levels 0 and 1 from levels 2–5.

The next step in coding the protocol involves making a level assignment for each of the following criterion questions:

1. To what are the differences in the accounts attributed?
2. Are the differences in the accounts seen as reconcilable?
3. What is the nature of the epistemological justifications given concerning the reconcilability of the two accounts?

While data answering these criterion questions may be found throughout the protocols, data for criterion question 1 are generally found in responses to WHAT HAPPENED and IMPORTANT DIFFERENCES; data for criterion question 2 are found in responses to IMPORTANT DIFFERENCES and BOTH RIGHT. Scores for the criterion questions were at the same levels for 52 percent of the protocols and at two adjacent levels for the remaining 48 percent of protocols. The global score represents the modal score given for the protocol. Reliability figures for the global scores, based on independent ratings of two judges for half of the protocols, were 71 percent for one pair of judges and 82 percent for the other (Leadbeater et al. 1982). Disagreements were resolved by discussion. Descriptions of each level and examples of the participants' responses for each question follow.

Level 0

At this level, the interpretations of facts are not differentiated from the facts themselves. No differences in the historians' perspectives are noted and few differences, even at the level of facts, are perceived. Any discrepancies that are cited are attributed to differences in the characteristics of the two countries (e.g., in their strength) or are rendered insignificant by temporal or factual distortions (e.g., historians are not seen as reporting on the same war or on simultaneous events). Since differences are not noted and the question "Can both of the historians be right?" suggests differences, the subjects frequently do not understand the question. Subject A04, for example, says: "What do you mean? Like, if the North won both wars, that they could take over the land, would that be right?" Here "right" is understood to mean "morally justified." Alternatively, level 0 subjects interpret "right" to mean believable or possible, as subject A06 says: "They *could* be right. . . . It doesn't seem to be nonfiction."

Level 1

As at level 0, no differences between facts and the historians' interpretations are noted at level 1. Superficial points of agreement are emphasized, and the perspective of only one historian is usually presented. The two accounts are seen to be telling pretty much the same story. Any discrepancies noted are considered to be differences in the completeness of what each side reports (e.g., one mentions an event the other doesn't). Discrepancies in facts are, thus, easily reconciled. One historian merely didn't see, experience, or write about something the other did. The two accounts thus can be combined or "put together" to literally add up to a more complete, inclusive story. For example subject, A16 says:

One is saying something the other person didn't say. But it wasn't the opposite of what they said, so if you put this together, it might be all the same. . . . This has a little that this doesn't have, and if they would be put together, like two plus two equals four, it would give more information than just reading one paper.

Level 2

At this level, and all remaining levels, facts and interpretations of the facts are distinguished. At level 2, however, only the discourse of objective, material facts has validity. The accounts are regarded as discrepant in the sense that each historian gives a different rendering of the facts. Differences in interpretation are understood as the result of subjective bias that distorts their presentations of what actually happened. Subjects do not attempt to reconcile the discrepancies; rather, differences are attributed to the historians' intentional or implicity prejudicing, distorting, or misrepresenting of the facts. In the case of widely discrepant reports of the facts, someone must be wrong or lying. A third, neutral party who doesn't have an interest in distorting the facts could give a truthful account or provide additional, more accurate information about what happened. Asked whether both historians' accounts could be right, subject A07 says:

No, because they're so different, it's hard to be right. THEY COULDN'T BOTH BE RIGHT? Maybe some parts of them could. Here it's exaggerated where it says some minor reverses, and here it says it turned out heavily in favor for them; so that's pretty exaggerated one way or the other. WHY WOULD THE ACCOUNTS BE EXAGGERATED? To make their country seem better. That way they would make the claim that they were right and the others were wrong. WHY MIGHT THEY DO THAT? I don't know, they're wrong not to admit they were wrong, and they just didn't want to be embarrassed.

Level 3

As at level 2, facts and interpretations are distinguished. In contrast with level 2, at level 3 and the remaining levels, subjects show awareness that theoretical interpretations have played a leading role in the construction of the two accounts. However, different importance is attributed to this role at each level. At level 3, the subject sees the accounts as involving the discourse of interpretations only. The historians are seen as holding very different "opinions" of what happened. Here the terms "points of view", "opinion," and "interpretation" are used in the sense made distinct by Perry's term "multiplicity." They refer to the individual historians' idiosyncratic perceptions of the events of the war. The accounts are seen as devoid of facts, as almost all opinion. The historians' subjective use of modifiers like "beaten badly," "sneak attack," and "minor victories" is emphasized. Differences in the two accounts cannot be reconciled, since there is no way to judge between them. The accounts could both be right, since each person sees things from his own point of view and "everyone has a right to his own opinion." Each is right in his own mind. For example, subject 001 says: "It depends on to whom it's right. They could both be wrong to the third party, or they could both be right in some ways."

Level 4

At this level, theoretical interpretation is recognized as having played a role in the construction of the accounts. Two distinct realms of discourse are addressed: one of subjective perspective and one of objective fact (in contrast with level 3, in which recognition of the subjective realm leads in effect to a renunciation of the objective, or to level 2 and below, in which only the objective realm is recognized as valid). At level 4, the subjective realm is clearly subordinated to the objective. The accounts are seen as telling much the same story or facts. Discrepancies are regarded as superficial ones of opinion, perspective, or subjective emphasis relative to an underlying factual reality. These minor differences of subjective emphasis are easily reconciled with respect to the realm of underlying objective fact. Subjects refer to criteria of justification, such as the assessment of the points of agreement, internal consistency, or points of noncontradiction in the accounts, which enable them to critically evaluate what probably happened. When asked whether both historians' accounts could be right, subject 012 says:

Yes, the accounts are subjectively written. If a third, objective party wrote the account, it might take into account. . . . All the facts listed in both accounts could be included. The facts are not contradictory; only some are omitted, deemphasized, and emphasized. The subjective opinions of both could be included if it were explained: "Some Southern Livians thought that . . . and some Northern Livians thought that. . . . "

Level 5

At this level, a coordination and balancing of the objective realm of fact and the subjective realm of interpretation is achieved. The recognition of subjectivity does not lead the subject to renounce objectivity, as at level 3, nor is subjectivity reduced to a superficial superimposition of perspective, as at level 4. Each historian's view is contrasted as expressing a different but potentially valid interpretation of what happened in his nation during the war. Differences in interpretations are attributed to the point of view or frame of reference of the particular culture or belief system of the people of North and South Livia, and each historian reports the perspective of his country. Differences are not easily reconciled in the sense of erasing differences between the two accounts. The realm of facts exists only as it is interpreted by a human observer

Table 11.3
Crosstabulation of Livia Task Performance and Educational Groups

Livia Task Levels	Educational Groups				Non Student Adults	Totals
	6th	9th	12th	Grads		
Level 0	7	2	1	0	0	10
Level 1	8	5	2	1	0	16
Level 2	5	7	5	3	2	22
Level 3	0	4	9	3	6	22
Level 4	0	0	7	9	10	26
Level 5	0	0	1	3	2	6
Totals	20	18	25	19	20	102

who is embedded in a particular historical/cultural context. Thus, multiple interpretations of events are to be expected and can themselves be critiqued. For example, subject 032 says:

Yes. How they saw it could have been right. How they saw it in their eyes, in their thinking. . . . If these men are from two different cultures, how they were brought up, I think, is very important. How they live, how their government is set up, is different. You know, how they look at things. HOW WOULD YOU KNOW IF THEY WERE RIGHT? I guess you really wouldn't know. I guess you have to depend on them to tell the right story. . . . It's interpretation. . . .

As reflected in the crosstabulation displayed in Table 11.3, findings support the expected age-linked progression in subjects' levels of responses. Older subjects were more highly represented at levels 3–5. While no sixth or ninth graders were classified at levels 4 and 5, 32 percent of the twelfth graders, 63 percent of the graduate students, and 60 percent of the nonstudent adults were classified at these levels. In contrast, 75 percent of the sixth graders and 39 percent of the ninth graders were classified at levels 0 and 1, compared with 12 percent of the twelfth graders, 5 percent of the graduate students, and none of the nonstudent adults. A chi-square analysis, with levels 0 and 1, levels 2 and 3, and levels 4 and 5 collapsed, shows the association between age group and level to be significant ($X = 58.17$, $df = 8$, $p < .001$). There was no association between subjects' sex and levels of responses.

Considering the two adult groups alone, the performance of the nonstudent adults did not differ significantly from that of the graduate students. There was also no association between education and performance on the Livia Task within the nonstudent adult group (comparing those with [$n = 6$] versus those without [$n = 14$] some graduate courses or a graduate degree). The length of time since last school attendance also was not significantly related to level of performance on the Livia Task (comparing "recent attenders" [n = 10] with "nonrecent attenders" [n = 10]).

CONCLUSIONS

The results we have described show an age-linked progression in individuals' interpretations of discrepant narrative accounts. More mature subjects show ability to distinguish between facts and interpretations of the facts, and to coordinate the two. While these findings are not sufficient to establish definitively the sequence of levels of performance that has been described, the association between age group and level is consistent with this sequence. The skepticism of level 3 begins to appear by ninth grade, becomes most prevalent among twelfth graders, and then declines in prevalence among the adult groups. These age-trend data, however, leave unresolved a number of important questions: Do responses reflect a fixed developmental sequence? Might at least some individuals bypass level 3 skepticism and first recognize subjectivity in the more moderate form identified in level 4? Or could these two responses to the recognition of subjectivity occur in an order the reverse of the one reflected above? Answers to such questions require longitudinal data. We also might ask whether the described sequence is generalizable to other content.

Studies of reflective judgment (Kitchener & King 1985; Strange & King 1981; Lawson 1980) have uniformly found that the performance of non-college student adults falls behind that of same-age college students. This pattern was not supported in our research. No differences in the performance of politically active, nonstudent adults and adult graduate students were found. Nor did we find any within-group association between either educational level or recency of school attendance and Livia Task performance among the nonstudent adult group. The life experiences of this small group of politically active adults affords them opportunities for discussing discrepant viewpoints that may have enhanced their performance.

Because of the small number of subjects classified at level 5, the end point in the progression we have examined remains difficult to specify with certainty. The modal level among both the adult graduate students and nonstudent adults was level 4. A number of investigators concerned with the development of epistemological beliefs (Broughton 1978, 1983; Perry 1970; Kitchener and King 1985; Labouvie-Vief 1982; Sinnott 1981) have identified a stage of skepticism, multiplicity, or radical relativism as the initial response to the recognition of multiple viewpoints and the realization that knowledge is not static or absolute. The theories proposed by such investigators differ significantly with respect to the precise nature of the path of the eventual resolution of this radical relativism (see Leadbeater 1986a). The radical relativist sees facts as relative to the idiosyncratic beliefs and attitudes of a particular individual, reducing the concept of truth to an empty one. Very different is the notion of "conceptual relativism" (Mandelbaum 1982), in which the frame of reference is the historical, cultural, and ideological context in which a judgment is made. Because such frames of reference are not confined to the subjective beliefs of a single individual, they allow for critique of these judgments and beliefs.

We have argued that hermeneutic theory, particularly the work of Paul Ricoeur on the interpretation of narratives, supports the position that the epistemological beliefs at level 5 are more inclusive, objective, open, and creative than either level 3's empathic support of the historian's right to his own opinion or level 4's analytic synthesis of the two accounts. A level 5 hermeneutic epistemology more closely reflects a dialectical resolution of the opposition of fact and theory in its endorsement of the view that facts do not stand independently of the frames of reference created by the ideological, cultural, and historical contexts in which they arose. Our findings suggest that at least a few individuals develop a level 5 perspective in adulthood. It is possible that the predominance of level 4 objectivist, epistemological beliefs in our adult subjects reflects the positivist or rationalist tradition of Western culture, where the deductive mode of scientific reasoning predominates in education and industry over a more hermeneutic approach (Packer 1985). We might then infer that only the cultural valuing of epistemological beliefs of level 5 subjects would lead to the "development" of adult cognition along the path we have described.

NOTE

1. This coding system is a revision of the one reported by Kuhn et al. (1983); thus numbering does not correspond.

REFERENCES

Basseches, M. (1980). Dialectical schemata: A framework for the empirical study of dialectical thinking. *Human Development, 23,* 400–421.

Broughton, J. (1978). The development of concepts of self, mind, reality and knowledge. In Damon W. (Ed.), *New directions in psychology: Social cognition* (pp. 75–100). San Francisco: Jossey-Bass.

Broughton, J. (1983). Not beyond formal operations but beyond Piaget. In M. Commons, F. Richards, & C. Armon, (Eds.), *Beyond formal operations: Late adolescent and adult cognitive development.* New York: Praeger.

Freeman, M. (1984). History, narrative and life-span developmental knowledge. *Human Development, 27,* 1–19.

Freeman, M. (1985). Paul Ricoeur on interpretation. *Human Development, 28,* 295–312.

King, P. M., Kitchener, K. S., Davison, M. L., Parker, C. A., & Wood, P. K. (1983). The justification of beliefs in young adults: A longitudinal study. *Human Development, 26,* 106–116.

Kitchener, K., & King, P. (1981). Reflective judgement: Concepts of justification and their relationship to age and education. *Journal of Applied Developmental Psychology, 2,* 106–116.

Kitchener, K., & King. P. (1985) The reflective judgement model: Ten years of research. Paper presented to the conference Beyond Formal Operations 2: The Development of Adolescent and Adult Thought and Perception, Harvard University.

Kramer, D. (1986). Relativistic and dialectical thought in three adult age-groups. *Human Development, 29,* 280–290.

Kuhn, D., Pennington, N., & Leadbeater, B. (1983). Adult reasoning in developmental perspective: The sample case of juror reasoning. In P. Baltes and O. Brim (Eds.), *Life-span development and behavior* (Vol. 5) New York: Academic Press.

Labouvie-Vief, G. (1982). Dynamic development and mature autonomy. *Human Development, 25,* 161–191.

Lawson, J. (1980). The relationship between graduate education and the development of reflective judgment: A function of age or educational experience. Ph.D. dissertation, University of Minnesota.

Leadbeater, B. (1986a). The resolution of relativism in adult thinking: Subjective, objective, or conceptual? *Human Development, 29,* 291–300.

Leadbeater, B. (1986b). Qualitative and developmental differences in the relational processes of adolescent and adult dialogues: The dialectic of intersubjectivity. Ph.D. dissertation, Teachers College, Columbia University.

Leadbeater, B., Kuhn, D., & Meinke, L. (1982). The development of relativistic thinking. Paper presented to the 12th annual symposium of the Jean Piaget Society, Philadelphia.

Mandelbaum, M. (1982). Subjective, objective, and conceptual relativism. In J. W. Meiland and M. Krausz (Eds.), *Relativism, cognitive and moral.* Notre Dame, Ind.: University of Notre Dame Press.

Packer, M. J. (1985). Hermeneutic inquiry in the study of human conduct. *American Psychologist, 40,* 1081–1093.

Perry, W. (1970). *Forms of intellectual and ethical development in the college years.* New York: Holt, Rinehart & Winston.

Ricoeur, P. (1978). Explanation and understanding. In C. E. Reagan & D. Stewart (Eds.), *The philosophy of Paul Ricoeur.* Boston: Beacon Press.

Ricoeur, P. (1981). The metaphorical process as cognition, imagination, and feeling. In M. Johnson (Ed.), *Philosophical perspectives on metaphor.* Minneapolis: University of Minnesota Press.

Ricoeur, P. (1983). Can fictional narratives be true? In *Analecta Husserliana, 14,* 3–19.

Sinnott, J. (1981). The theory of relativity: A metatheory for development? *Human Development*, 24, 293–311.

Strange, C., and King, P. (1981). Intellectual development and its relationship to maturation during the college years. *Journal of Applied Developmental Psychology*, 2, 281–295.

12

Academic and Everyday Intelligence in Adulthood: Conceptions of Self and Ability Tests

Steven W. Cornelius
Sheryl Kenny
Avshalom Caspi

The construct of intelligence has been a focal point of investigation throughout the history of reseach in the psychology of aging (e.g., Woodruff 1983). Despite the considerable theory and data that have been generated in research on intellectual aging, fundamental questions about the nature of intelligence in adulthood and its assessment have been recurrently posed (e.g., Dixon, Kramer, & Baltes 1985; Flavell 1970; Schaie 1978; Willis & Baltes 1980). Demming and Pressey (1957) argued that traditional methods of ability assessment may be ill-suited for understanding adults' functioning because most ability tests were designed for children in academic settings, and may be irrelevant to the experience of adults in everyday life. More recently, Horn (1978) acknowledged that tests used to assess fluid and crystallized abilities "may be mainly only atavistic carryovers from ability definitions of childhood, not very good indications of adult intelligence" (p. 244).

In this chapter, people's implicit theories of intelligence are used to describe major aspects of everyday intelligence and highlight some aspects of intelligence that may have been neglected in explicit theories of adult intellectual development. Explicit and implicit theories of intelligence represent different methodological approaches to understanding the nature of intelligence (e.g., Sternberg 1985a, 1985b). In an explicit approach, theories are developed from and tested on data obtained from people's actual performance on ability tests or cognitive tasks that are

The authors gratefully acknowledge the assistance of Carolyn Croke, Julia Hannum Rose, Lee Ward, and Robert Yavits in various phases of the research reported in this chapter.

presumed to be indicative of intellectual functioning. For example, the theory of fluid and crystallized intelligence (e.g., Cattell 1971; Horn 1982) was developed on the basis of factor-analytic and age-comparative studies of people's performance on ability tests.

In an implicit approach, on the other hand, people's ideas or beliefs about intelligence and how it changes constitute the focal concern. Sternberg and his colleagues (e.g., Berg & Sternberg 1985; Sternberg, Conway, Ketron, & Bernstein 1981) have examined people's conceptions of intelligence. Their findings suggest that experts in the field of intelligence and lay persons without advanced training in psychology have remarkably similar views of the qualities characterizing an intelligent person. Different characteristics, however, are identified with everyday and academic kinds of intelligence. Everyday intelligence is associated with abilities to solve practical problems, function adaptively in practical situations, and display competent interpersonal behavior. People's conception of academic intelligence emphasizes components such as problem solving, verbal abilities, and motivation.

The research described in this chapter was conducted to examine similarities and differences between implicit and explicit theories. Objective measures of intelligence used in explicit approaches may correspond to people's implicit theories to the extent that ability tests tap attributes that people believe characterize intelligence. Thus, the primary goal of the research was to investigate the relation between concepts of adacemic and everyday intelligence and ability tests that have been designed from an explicit approach. The results of two experiments are described. In the first, we examine young, middle-aged, and older adults' actual ability performance and its relation to their self-conceptions of academic and everyday intelligence. In the second experiment, an investigation of the kinds of ability tests people believe are indicative of academic and everyday types of intelligence is reported.

EXPERIMENT 1: SELF-CONCEPTIONS OF INTELLIGENCE AND ABILITY PERFORMANCE

Neisser (1979) argued that a person may be considered intelligent to the degree that his or her behavior corresponds to attributes that characterize an ideal concept or prototype of intelligence. Following this orientation, Sternberg et al. (1981) compared adults' self-conceptions of behavior with experts' prototypes of academic and everyday intelligence. They found that people's self-conceptions showed a moderate resemblance to the prototypes, but they were more similar to experts' characterization of everyday than of academic intelligence. The range and variance in degrees of resemblance were quite large: Some individuals showed negligible correspondence with these prototypes, and others displayed substantial correspondence. Their results also indicated that objective performance on an IQ test was highly related to the resemblance measure of academic intelligence and to a smaller degree to people's self-conception of everyday intelligence. In particular, IQ performance was significantly correlated with self-reported interest in learning and culture, and somewhat less with self-assessed verbal ability. Self-ratings of problem solving ability and social competence showed negligible relations with test performance.

In Experiment 1, this research was extended to examine people's implicit theories of their own intelligence in adulthood and old age. Young, middle-aged, and older adults were administered the questionnaire compiled by Sternberg et al. (1981) and multiple fluid- and crystallized-ability tests. This experiment had two objectives. The first was to examine the relation between performance on standard ability tests and adults' self-assessments of their functioning. If traditional tests are more indicative of academic than of everyday kinds of intellectual abilities, as critics have charged (e.g., Willis & Baltes 1980), it was expected that objectively measured performance would be more highly related to adults' self-conception of academic intelligence. The second objective was to determine whether the correspondence between adults' beliefs about their abilities and prototypes of academic and everyday intelligence are related to age and education—two factors that have shown considerable importance in the analysis of objective test performance (e.g., Botwinick 1977).

Procedure

The sample consisted of 105 adults between the ages of 20 and 89 years, with an equal number of young (20 to 39 years; $M = 25.6$; $SD = 6.5$), middle-aged (40 to 59 years; $M = 49.4$; $SD = 6.8$), and older adults (60 to 89 years; $M = 70.7$; $SD = 7.5$). The sample included 33 males and 72 females, with 11 males and 24 females in each age group. The average level of education was 13.6 years for the total sample, and levels of education were similar for young ($M = 13.1$), middle-aged ($M = 13.9$), and elderly adults ($M = 13.9$). Participants were administered tests of fluid and crystallized intelligence, a questionnaire of intellectual behaviors, and a biographical information questionnaire.

Objective Test Performance

Seven ability tests were administered to obtain performance measures of intellectual functioning. Tests were selected on the basis of the factor-analytic structure of abilities reported in previous research (e.g., Horn 1982). Fluid-ability measures included tests of inductive reasoning (Letter Sets and Letter Series; Blieszner, Willis, & Baltes 1981) and matrix classification (Figural Relations Matrices; Plemons, Willis, & Baltes 1978).

Crystallized abilities were assessed by tests of verbal comprehension (Verbal Meaning; Thurstone 1962), practical judgment (WAIS Comprehension subtest; Wechsler 1955), and experiential evaluation (Social Situations; Horn & Cattell 1966). A test of semantic relations (Verbal Analogies; Guilford 1969) was also administered, and may be indicative of both fluid and crystallized intelligence.

Self-Conceptions of Intelligence

The questionnaire compiled by Sternberg et al. (1981) was shortened to reduce administration time, and included 105 of 170 intellectual behaviors. The majority of items (93) were retained because they loaded on one or more factors in analyses of experts' and lay persons' ratings and, according to Sternberg et al. (1981, p. 44), appeared to be central to people's conceptions of intelligence. An additional 12 items were randomly selected from the remaining pool. Participants rated how characteristic each behavior was of themselves on a seven-point scale (1 = highly uncharacteristic; 7 = highly characteristic).

Self-concept measures of academic and everyday intelligence were obtained by comparing participants' ratings with experts' ratings of these behaviors, following the procedure described by Sternberg et al. (1981, p. 49). Correlations were computed between each individual's response pattern and experts' profile of ratings for prototypes of academic and everyday intelligence. The possible range of scores was from -1.00 to $+1.00$; higher positive scores indicate closer resemblance between an individual's self-concept and the pattern of qualities characterizing an ideal prototype. For academic intelligence, scores ranged from $-.22$ to .62 ($M = .18$, $SD = .21$); for everyday intelligence, scores ranged from $-.21$ to .71 ($M = .31$, $SD = .21$). Estimated reliabilities for these scores were .79 for academic intelligence and .72 for everyday intelligence.

In addition to the prototypic resemblance measures, a factor analysis was conducted to identify specific dimensions underlying people's self-conceptions of intelligence. Because the number of items included in the questionnaire was too large, given the size of our sample, to conduct this analysis using individual items, items with similar content and meaning were combined to form 28 variable clusters ranging in size from 2 to 8 items. A principal-axis factor analysis with oblique rotation was then performed on these scores. Four factors were extracted with eigenvalues greater than 1.

The first factor was indicative of problem-solving ability. It included high loadings on items associated with objectivity (e.g., displays objectivity, interprets information accurately, appreciates truth), the quality of problem solving (e.g., solves problems well, poses problems in an optimal way, assesses well the relevance of information to a problem at hand), and task persistence (e.g., displays persistence, completes tasks, performs tasks efficiently). The second factor was associated with verbal intelligence and knowledge. It was loaded highly by behaviors indicative of communicative competence (e.g., converses well, communicates ideas well, converses easily on a variety of topics), verbal facility (e.g., is verbally fluent, displays a good vocabulary), and curiosity (e.g., displays curiosity, seeks explanations for things and causes for events, is intellectually curious). The third factor comprised behavioral qualities associated with practical intelligence and social competence. It was loaded highly by variables indicative of common sense (e.g., displays common sense, acts in a practical manner, has good habits with respect to personal health), acceptance of social conventions (e.g., accepts social norms, is on time for appointments), ethical judgment (e.g., has social conscience, makes fair judgments, is frank and honest with self and others), and interpersonal competence (e.g., deals effectively with people, is sensitive to other people's needs and desires, gets along well with others). The fourth factor represents facets of motivation. It was loaded highly by variables such as self-appraisal (e.g., knows his or her own capabilities, displays self-confidence, seeks appropriate help when needed), goal orientation (e.g., determines how to achieve goals, takes initiative for doing things that need to be done, displays dedication and motivation in chosen pursuits), and achievement (e.g., wants to make a good living, is well educated, studies hard). Factor scores for these dimensions were estimated using a regression method.

Results

Relations between Ability Performance and Self-Conceptions of Intelligence

The top part of Table 12.1 lists correlations between objective test performance and self-concept measures of intelligence. The first two columns indicate that objectively measured abilities are significantly related to both self-concept measures, but the correlations are consistently higher for academic than everyday intelligence. The only exception to this general pattern occurs for the Social Situations test, which shows a higher correlation with self-conceptions of everyday intelligence than it does with academic intelligence. One possible reason for these results is that the estimated reliability is somewhat higher for the measure of academic than of everyday intelligence. Therefore, correlations were corrected for attenuation in both performance and self-concept scores. With this correction, the pattern of results was maintained. Six of the seven ability tests had larger correlations with self-conceptions of academic than of everyday intelligence.

Table 12.1
Correlations Between Self-Conceptions of Intelligence, Ability Performance, and Demographic Characteristics

Variable	Self-Concept Variable					
	Academic Intelligence	Everyday Intelligence	Problem Solving	Verbal Intelligence	Practical Intelligence	Motivation
Ability Test Performance						
Letter Sets	.42**	.30**	.26**	.22*	-.08	-.03
Letter Series	.46**	.28**	.22*	.18	-.16	-.12
Matrices	.52**	.42**	.37**	.27**	-.07	.08
Verbal Analogies	.55**	.37**	.37**	.30**	-.15	-.06
Verbal Meaning	.49**	.41**	.39**	.36**	.01	-.10
Comprehension	.43**	.36**	.37**	.30**	.05	-.01
Social Situations	.18	.29**	.19*	.06	.01	-.04
Demographic Characteristics						
Education	.50**	.34**	.32**	.25*	-.04	.06
Age	-.24*	.06	-.08	-.04	.32**	-.02

** $p < .01$

* $p < .05$

These results may occur because test performance does not tap attributes that are important qualities of everyday intelligence. Correlations between prototypic measures and self-ratings on specific dimensions reveal that self-ratings of practical intelligence and social competence were positively related to self-conceptions of everyday intelligence ($r = .60$) and unrelated to self-conceptions of academic intelligence ($r = -.10$). Resemblance to the prototypes of both academic and everyday intelligence were positively related to self-ratings of problem solving ability (r's $= .64$ and $.54$), verbal intelligence and knowledge (r's $= .61$ and $.50$), and motivation (r's $= .21$ and $.38$). Thus, practical intelligence and social competence are important attributes of everyday intelligence but unrelated to academic intelligence.

In the third through sixth columns of Table 12.1, correlations between ability performance and self-ratings on specific ability dimensions are listed. As expected, self-rated problem solving ability was positively related to performance on each test. Likewise, self-rated verbal intelligence was significantly related to performance on five of the seven ability tests. Objectively measured performance, however, was not related to self-ratings of practical intelligence or motivation.

Educational and Age Differences in Self-Conceptions of Intelligence

The distinction between academic and everyday types of intelligence is also revealed in an examination of their relationship to demographic characteristics. In the bottom part of Table 12.1, correlations between education, age, and self-concept measures of intelligence are reported. Self-conceptions of academic intelligence are highly related to adults' level of educational attainment and decline with increasing age. Self-conceptions of everyday intelligence, on the other hand, show a smaller relation to adults' educational background and are unrelated to age. Comparisons of these correlations revealed that the self-conceptions of academic intelligence were more highly related to both education (t (102) = 1.97, $p < .05$) and age (t (102) = −3.43, $p < .01$) than was the measure of everyday intelligence.

Education and age also show different relationships with specific dimensions of people's intellectual self-concept. Educational background was positively correlated with self-assessed problem solving and verbal intelligence, but it was not related to self-assessed practical intelligence or motivation. Participants' age displayed negative but insignificant relations with self-concept measures of problem solving, verbal intelligence, and motivation. By contrast, there was an increase with age in self-assessments of practical intelligence. These findings indicate that individual differences in adults' educational background may be a more important determinant than age of their evaluations of their problem solving and verbal abilities. By contrast, age appears to be more important than educational background for self-assessments of practical intelligence and social competence.

Discussion

Results of this experiment replicate and extend findings of previous research on implicit theories of intelligence (e.g., McCrae & Costa 1985; Sternberg 1985b; Sternberg et al. 1981) in three respects. First, the findings highlight some differences and similarities between concepts of academic and everyday types of intelligence. The major difference between these concepts appears to be the greater emphasis placed on practical abilities and social competence in defining everyday intelligence. People's overall resemblance to the prototype of everyday intelligence was highly related to their self-assessed practical intelligence, but ratings on this dimension were not related to their resemblance to the prototype of academic intelligence. The findings also suggest that problem solving and verbal intelligence are important in implicit theories of both academic and everyday intelligence. Self-assessments on these dimensions of intellectual functioning showed similar positive relationships with self-conceptions of academic and everyday intelligence.

Second, results of Experiment 1 indicate that variations in adult's self-conceptions of intelligence can be partially accounted for by differences in demographic characteristics. Overall, the findings suggest that perceptions of intellectual functioning are more consistently and more highly related to educational background than they are to age. To the extent that age is associated with adults' self-concepts of intelligence, the present results indicate that resemblance to the prototype of academic intelligence declines with age, whereas self-rated practical intelligence increases with age. The larger relationship found between education and self-concept measures is similar to that reported for objective test performance. Most ability tests were designed for predicting successful academic performance, and educational attainment continues to show substantial relations to objectively measured ability performance during adulthood (e.g., Botwinick 1977). In the present study, education was more highly related to self-conceptions of academic than of everyday intelligence, and specifically to dimensions of problem solving and verbal intelligence. It was unrelated to adults' assessments of their practical intelligence or motivation, however.

Finally, results of Experiment 1 reveal that objectively measured intelligence shows a larger correspondence to adults' self-conception of academic than of everyday intelligence. This finding is generalizable across multiple indicators of intellectual functioning, with the exception of performance on the Social Situations test. The correlations between objective performance and self-conceptions of intelligence are comparable with those reported in other research (e.g., Cornelius & Caspi 1986; McCrae & Costa 1985; Lachman 1983; Lachman & Jelalian 1984; Sternberg 1985b; Sternberg et al. 1981).

Test performance was also associated with self-rated problem solving and verbal intelligence, but was not related to practical intelligence. Many of the ability tests included in the present study were not intended to assess practical abilities or social competence. However, it is surprising that neither the Comprehension nor the Social Situations test was related to ratings on the dimension of practical intelligence. Wechsler (1958) suggested that the Comprehension test is a measure of practical judgment, common sense, and the ability to evaluate past experience. Likewise, the Social Situations test has been described as an indicator of the ability "experiential evaluation," which is characterized by making good judgments and using social conventions in making decisions (e.g., Horn & Donaldson 1980).

If researchers' interpretations of these tests are correct, the negligible associations between performance and self-rated practical intelligence may result because adults do not accurately assess their practical intelligence. Perhaps feedback about one's performance in everyday situations is too ambiguous for adults to form accurate estimates of their practical abilities. It is also possible that these tests tap only some attributes identified with adults' conceptions of their practical intelligence. Therefore, a second experiment was conducted to investigate people's conceptions of ability tests and their relation to implicit theories of academic and everyday kinds of intelligence.

EXPERIMENT 2: CONCEPTIONS OF ABILITY TESTS

Neisser (1979) argued that omnibus scales of intelligence (e.g., Standard-Binet, WAIS) may be relatively successful in the assessment of intelligence because different tests included in the battery tap different facets of intelligence. A single ability test is unlikely to be a good indicator of intelligence because it will capture only some of the qualities associated with the construct. For example, the prototype of academic intelligence emphasizes both problem solving and verbal abilities. Tests of both kinds of abilities may show a moderate correspondence to this prototype but resemble it along different dimensions. In combination, performance on both kinds of tests may provide a reasonable approximation to academic intelligence. Indeed, in research on adult intelligence (Schaie 1979), a composite index of educational aptitude has been formed from performance on Letter Series and Verbal Meaning tests.

The primary aim of Experiment 2 was to investigate people's conceptions of ability tests designed from an explicit approach and to compare them with characteristics that experts attribute to prototypes of academic and everyday intelligence. College students were given the questionnaire used in Experiment 1 and asked to judge how characteristic they believed behaviors would be of a person displaying outstanding performance on one of nine ability tests. Based on the outcomes of Experiment 1 and Sternberg et al.'s (1981) study of IQ and self-conceptions of intelligence, it was expected that most ability tests would display greater correspondence to the prototype of academic than of everyday intelligence, because most ability tests emphasize problem solving or verbal abilities rather than practical intelligence or social competence. Therefore, in addition to the seven tests administered in Experiment 1, ratings were obtained for two tests designed by the present authors to assess everyday intellectual abilities in adulthood.

Procedure

The sample consisted of 90 young adults who were attending college in upstate New York. Participants were randomly assigned to rate one of nine ability tests. They were told to read the instructions for the test and were allowed to examine the practice and test problems included in it. Identifying information about the tests (e.g., the title) was removed. After examining the test, participants were given a deck of 105 cards with behaviors from the questionnaire used in Experiment 1 printed on them. They were told to sort the cards on a Likert scale into one of seven categories ranging from Very Uncharacteristic (category 1) to Very Characteristic (category 7) to characterize the qualities they believed would be displayed by a person performing extremely well on the test. Participants reviewed their placements of behaviors in the various categories after completing their sorting and could rearrange the placement of any behavior if they wished to do so.

Stimuli for the experiment included the seven ability tests administered in Experiment 1 and two recently developed tests.

1. Tests of fluid abilities included Letter Sets (Blieszner et al. 1981), Letter Series (Blieszner et al. 1981), and Figural Relations Matrices tests (Plemons et al. 1978). In the Letter Sets test, an examinee is shown five sets of alphabetic characters with four letters in each set. The task is to determine which set of letters does not belong in the class of the remaining four sets. In the Letter Series test, an examinee is asked to determine which one of five letters comes next in a sequence of alphabetic characters. The Figural Relations Matrices test involves logical classification. In it an examinee discovers the trends in rows and columns of a matrix of figures, and chooses one of five figures to go in an empty cell in the matrix.

2. Two tests involved verbal reasoning and knowledge. In the Verbal Analogies test (Guilford 1969), an examinee chooses a word that best completes an analogy. The Verbal Meaning test (Thurstone 1962) is a vocabulary measure in which an examinee selects one of five words that is synonymous with a target word.

3. Four tests included content relevant to practical intellectual abilties. In the Comprehension test (Wechsler 1955), an examinee is required to respond to a question (e.g., Why are child labor laws needed?), including in the response all information that is needed to answer it adequately. In the Social Situations test (Horn & Cattell 1966), an examinee is presented with an interpersonal dilemma and chooses from among four alternative responses the one that is considered best. Two tests developed by the present authors also involve practical problems. The Everyday Problem Solving Inventory (Cornelius & Caspi 1987) presents problems adults might encounter in several domains of everyday life (e.g., home management, shopping, interpersonal relationships). For each situation, an examinee is presented with four modes of responding, and rates the likelihood that he or she would act in each of the ways described. The Stressful Situations test (Cornelius & Rose 1987) describes hypothetical situations involving losses, threats, or challenges that

are likely to be stressful for the characters described. An examinee is asked to judge how effective different modes of coping would be in the situation.

Intraclass correlation coefficients were computed to examine the reliability among judges' ratings of these tests. Results indicated large coefficients for each test: Letter Sets = .88, Letter Series = .81, Matrices = .87, Verbal Analogies = .83, Verbal Meaning = .85, Comprehension = .79, Social Situations = .86, Everyday Problem Solving Inventory = .92, Stressful Situations = .86. These coefficients suggest that there was a high degree of consensus among judges about attributes characterizing performance on these tests.

Ratings of ability tests were factor-analyzed to identify a parsimonious set of dimensions underlying judges' evaluations of exceptional performance on the test stimuli. A principal-axis factor analysis with oblique rotation was performed using scores for the 28 variable clusters discussed in Experiment 1. Four factors were extracted with eigenvalues greater than 1. The factor solution is similar, though not identical, to that reported for the analysis of self-conceptions of intelligence in Experiment 1. Differences between the two factor solutions likely reflect differences in the type of ratings (i.e., conceptions of ability test performance versus self-conceptions) examined in these two analyses.

The first factor was associated with attributes indicative of practical problem solving ability. It included high loadings on items associated with decision making (e.g., makes good decisions, acts on decisions, stands by decisions), reasoning (e.g., thinks and behaves rationally, reasons logically and well), and quality of problem solving (e.g., solves problems well, poses problems in an optimal way, assesses well the relevance of information to a problem at hand). The second factor was indicative of verbal intelligence and knowledge. It was loaded highly by behaviors involving reading (e.g., reads widely, reads with a high comprehension, likes to read), verbal facility (e.g., is verbally fluent, displays a good vocabulary), and achievement (e.g., wants to make a good living, is well educated, studies hard). The third factor comprised behavioral qualities associated with social competence and practical intelligence. It was loaded highly by variables indicative of interpersonal competence (e.g., deals effectively with people, is sensitive to other people's needs and desires, gets along well with others), ethical judgment (e.g., has social conscience, makes fair judgments, is frank and honest with self and others), and giving advice (e.g., gives good advice, shares knowledge with others). The fourth factor represents several indicators of cognitive style. It was loaded positively by variables such as curiosity (e.g., displays curiosity, seeks explanations for things and causes for events, is intellectually curious), thoughtfulness (e.g., approaches problems thoughtfully, responds thoughtfully to others' ideas, thinks deeply), and style of problem solving (e.g., sees all aspects of a problem, deals with problems resourcefully, gets to the heart of problems). Scores were obtained for these four dimensions by averaging ratings for item clusters with large loadings on them.

Results

Characteristics Attributed to Ability Test Performance

In this section, we examine ratings of the tests on different dimensions of intellectual behavior to clarify differences among conceptions of these tests. A 9 (test) by 4 (dimension: practical problem solving, verbal intelligence, social competence, cognitive style) analysis of variance with repeated measures on the second factor was performed. Results indicated significant main effects for test (F [8, 81] = 2.66, $p < .01$) and dimension (F [3, 243] = 41.75, $p < .001$), and a significant interaction between these factors (F [24, 243] = 8.46, $p < .001$). Figure 12.1 shows the mean ratings of ability tests on these dimensions.

As expected, the interaction reveals that different characteristics of intellectual functioning are attributed to performance on different kinds of ability tests. Fluid ability tests (i.e., Letter Sets, Letter Series, Matrices) were judged highly on characteristics associated with practical problem solving ability; verbal ability tests (Verbal Analogies, Verbal Meaning) were rated highly on facets of vebal intelligence; and tests of practical abilities (Comprehension, Social Situations, Everyday Problem Solving Inventory, Stressful Situations) were evaluated highly on behaviors indicative of practical problem solving as well as social competence.

One-way repeated measures of analyses of variance were conducted, comparing ratings on these dimensions separately for each ability test. Differences among ratings on the four dimensions were significant for each test: Letter Sets, F (3, 27) = 17.75, p, $< .001$; Letter Series, F (3, 27) = 15.21, $p < .001$; Matrices, F (3, 27) = 16.37, $p < .001$; Verbal Analogies, F (3, 27) = 5.96, $p < .01$; Verbal Meaning, F (3, 27) = 23.05, $p < .001$; Comprehension, F (3, 27) = 3.12, $p < .05$; Social Situations, F (3, 27) = 12.48, $p < .001$; Everyday Problem Solving, F (3, 27) = 32.32, $p < .001$; Stressful Situations, F (3, 27) = 6.03, $p < .01$.

Ratings of the Letter Sets, Letter Series, and Matrices tests display a similar pattern. These tests were rated highest on characteristics of practical problem solving, followed by cognitive style, and lowest on behaviors indicative of verbal intelligence and social competence. The Verbal Analogies test received similar ratings on practical problem solving, verbal intelligence, and cognitive style, and ratings on these di-

Figure 12.1
Mean Ratings of Test Stimuli on Dimensions of Intelligence

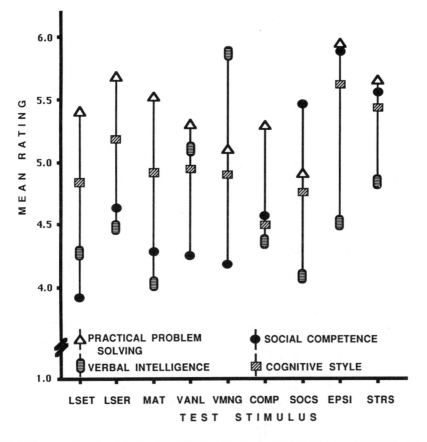

Test titles are abbreviated: Letter Sets (LSET), Letter Series (LSER), Matrices (MAT), Verbal Analogies (VANL), Verbal Meaning (VMNG), WAIS Comprehension (COMP), Social Situations (SOCS), Everyday Problem Solving Inventory (EPSI), and Stressful Situations (STRS).

mensions exceeded that on social competence. The Verbal Meaning test was rated highest on verbal intelligence, followed by practical problem solving and cognitive style, and was rated lowest on social competence. The highest rating of the Comprehension test occurred on practical problem solving, and this rating exceeded ratings on the other three dimensions. The Social Situations test was rated highest on social competence, followed by ratings on practical problem solving and cognitive style, and was rated lowest on verbal intelligence. Finally, the Everyday Problem Solving and Stressful Situations tests displayed similar patterns. Both tests were rated highly on practical problem solving, social competence, and cognitive style dimensions, and these ratings were higher than those on the dimension of verbal intelligence.

The results appear to coincide with researchers' interpretations of these tests and suggest that different tests tap different features of intellectual functioning. Exceptional performance on tests associated with fluid intelligence (i.e., Letter Sets, Letter Series, Matrices) was judged to be characteristic of problem solving ability. The Verbal Analogies test was characterized by high ratings on both problem solving and verbal intelligence dimensions, whereas the Verbal Meaning test was rated highest on indicators of verbal intelligence but lower on problem solving. The Comprehension and Social Situations tests were judged highest on practical problem solving and social competence, respectively. Tests designed by the present authors to assess everyday abilities (i.e., Everyday Problem Solving, Stressful Situations) were characterized by high ratings on both practical problem solving and social competence.

Resemblance between Ability Test Ratings and Prototypes of Academic and Everyday Intelligence

Prototypicality measures were computed to assess how similar ratings of the ability tests were to prototypes of academic and everyday intelligence. Following the procedure described in Experiment 1, prototypicality measures were obtained by correlating each participant's ratings of a test with the pattern of ratings characterizing experts' concepts of these two types of intelligence. A 9 (test) by 2 (type of intelligence: academic vs. everyday) analysis of variance with repeated measures on the second factor was conducted on these scores. The main effect of type of intelligence was significant: $F(1, 81) = 106.62$, $p < .0001$. This effect occurred because ratings averaged across ability tests showed a larger correspondence with the pattern of characteristics attributed to everyday ($M = .44$, $SD = .18$) than with academic intelligence ($M = .27$, $SD = .24$). This effect was modified by an interaction between test and type of intelligence: $F(8, 81) = 18.99$, $p < .0001$. Descriptive statistics for the prototypicality scores are presented for each test in Table 12.2.

Dependent t-tests comparing prototypicality scores for academic and everyday intelligence were computed separately for each test. Contrary to our expectations, these results showed that most tests displayed greater similarity to the prototype of everyday than of academic intelligence. Only one test (Verbal Meaning) showed a greater resemblance to academic intelligence, and one test (Verbal Analogies) showed no difference in its correspondence to the two prototypes.

Tests of simple effects were also performed, comparing the prototypicality scores for different ability tests. Results were significant for both academic—$F(8, 116) = 7.57$, $p < .001$—and everyday intelligence—F

Table 12.2
Resemblance Between Prototypes of Intelligence and Test Rating Profiles

Test Stimulus	Academic Intelligence		Everyday Intelligence	
	Mean	SD	Mean	SD
Letter Sets	.34	.16	.47	.12
Letter Series	.30	.22	.44	.22
Matrices	.32	.21	.45	.13
Verbal Analogies	.41	.18	.39	.15
Verbal Meaning	.50	.14	.26	.19
Comprehension	.24	.19	.44	.18
Social Situations	.00	.20	.39	.17
Everyday Problem Solving Inventory	.06	.23	.55	.16
Stressful Situations	.22	.16	.54	.19

$(8, 116) = 2.30$, $p < .05$. The prototype of academic intelligence showed its largest correspondence with ratings of verbal ability tests (i.e., Verbal Meaning, Verbal Analogies), followed by fluid ability tests (i.e., Matrices, Letter Sets, Letter Series). Ratings of tests of practical abilities (i.e., Comprehension, Social Situations, Stressful Situations, Everyday Problem Solving) displayed the least correspondence to the prototype of academic intelligence. By contrast, attributes associated with everyday intelligence showed the greatest resemblance to ratings of tests of practical abilities, followed by ratings of fluid ability tests, and the least resemblance to ratings of verbal tests.

To examine further the patterns of ratings, a profile was computed for each test by averaging ratings on each item in the questionnaire. Regression analyses were then conducted to determine which combination of tests would yield the best prediction of experts' prototypic concepts of academic and everyday types of intelligence. Dependent variables in these analyses were profiles of ratings for academic and everyday intelligence, and predictor variables were profiles of ratings for ability tests. Because the profiles for some of the ability tests were highly correlated with each other, a stepwise regression method was used. Academic intelligence was predicted best by ratings on the Verbal Meaning ($\beta = .67$, $F[1,102] = 103.63$, $p < .001$) and the Letter Series tests ($\beta = .25$, $F[1,102] = 14.44$, $p < .001$); together these tests accounted for 61 percent of the variance ($R = .78$, $F[2,102] = 78.48$, $p < .001$). The pattern of characteristics associated with everyday intelligence was predicted best by ratings on four tests: Everyday Problem Solving (β = .37, F [1,100] = 12.96, $p <$ .001), Stressful Situations (β = .25, F [1,100] = 5.48, $p <$ .01), Letter Series (β = .28, F [1,100] = 17.81, $p <$ .001), and Verbal Meaning (β = .24, F [1,100] = 14.36, $p <$ .001). Ratings on these four tests accounted for 73 percent of the variance (R = .85, F [4,100] = 68.27, $p <$ .001).

These results provide some evidence that different ability tests resemble prototypes of intelligence along different components or facets of intellectual behavior. In accordance with Neisser's (1979) argument, the findings suggest that a combination of ability tests may be required to assess adequately the multifaceted attributes characterizing concepts of intelligence. Academic intelligence was predicted best by ratings of tests involving verbal and problem solving abilities. In fact, the specific tests emerging as significant predictors in this analysis (i.e., Verbal Meaning, Letter Series) are identical to those used by Schaie (1979) as an index of educational aptitude in research based on an explicit approach. The best predictors of everyday intelligence included not only these two tests but also tests of practical abilities involved in solving everyday and stressful problems.

Discussion

Issues of ecological and external validity have assumed increasing prominence (e.g., Schaie 1978; Scheidt & Schaie 1978; Woodruff 1983), stemming in part from the perceived limitations of traditional ability tests for the assessment of adult intelligence (e.g., Dixon et al. 1985). To date, gerontological research on intelligence has been largely concerned with the investigation of verbal and abstract problem solving abilities. These abilities are certainly fundamental features of people's conceptions of intelligence (e.g., Berg & Sternberg 1985; Sternberg 1985b; Sternberg et al. 1981), and appear to correspond to performance on tests such as inductive reasoning, verbal analogies, and vocabulary. There is another side of intelligence, though, focusing on practical abilities and competence in social situations—dimensions of intellectual functioning that have been largely neglected in explicit theories of intelligence (see, however, Gardner 1983; Guilford & Hoepfner 1971; Sternberg & Wagner 1986). The lack of attention to these dimensions may have resulted from the focus on academic performance as the primary criterion for evaluating the validity of ability tests.

Academic and everyday kinds of intelligence are distinguishable because different facets of intellectual behavior are weighted differently in people's ideas about these concepts. Experts' conception of academic intelligence emphasizes both problem solving and verbal abilities, and people's conceptions of tests of these abilities provide good predictors of this prototype. These abilities are also significant in the prediction of experts' conception of everyday intelligence. However, independent of these, tests of everyday problem solving and coping with stressful situations also contribute to the prediction of the prototype of everyday intelligence. Thus, these findings suggest that problem solving and verbal abilities are important for both kinds of intelligence. They provide only a partial account of everyday intelligence, though, and need to be supplemented by measures that specifically tap features of social competence and practical intelligence.

Investigations of implicit theories of intelligence can be useful in scientific inquiry because they help highlight features of concepts that may have been neglected in explicit theories and suggest hypotheses for further research from an explicit approach (e.g., McCrae & Costa 1985; Sternberg 1985a, 1985b). For example, one result clearly emerging in Experiment 1 and other studies of adults' implicit theories of intelligence (e.g., Berg & Sternberg 1985; Birren 1969; Williams et al. 1983) is the belief that practical abilities improve with age. Findings from studies of practical knowledge (e.g., Demming & Pressey 1957; Gardner & Monge 1977) and more recently research on practical problem solving (e.g., Cornelius & Caspi 1987; Denney & Palmer 1981) are generally consistent with this result. The developmental profiles for practical abilities vary, depending on the specific domain of knowledge and type of everyday problem examined, but overall the findings suggest that practical knowledge and problem solving skills exhibit progressive changes at least from early adulthood through middle age. Although this pattern is similar to that reported for crystallized abilities, performance on tests of everyday problem solving and verbal meaning were only modestly correlated with each other (Cornelius & Caspi 1987; cf. Ford & Tisak 1983).

In conclusion, the scope of research on intelligence in adulthood and old age needs to be expanded to encompass investigations of abilities not typically considered in explicit theories. Results of the present research provide an intermediate step in the process of examining everyday abilities by linking implicit and explicit approaches. Findings of both experiments suggest that problem solving and verbal abilities are important qualities in everyday intellectual functioning, but they provide only a partial picture of abilities required for effective everyday functioning (cf. Block 1982). Further attention needs to be devoted to facets of everyday intelligence involving social competence, practical decision making, and coping with stressful situations in the study of adult intellectual development.

REFERENCES

Berg, C. A., & Sternberg, R. J. (1985). Implicit theories of intelligence across the adult life span. Manuscript submitted for publication. Available from Berg, University of Utah, Salt Lake City.

Birren, J. E. (1969). Age and decision strategies. In A. T. Welford & J. E. Birren (Eds.), *Decision making and age* (pp. 23–36). Basel: Karger.

Blieszner, R., Willis, S. L. & Baltes, P. B. (1981). Training research in aging on the fluid ability of inductive reasoning. *Journal of Applied Developmental Psychology, 2,* 247–265.

Block, J. (1982). Assimilation, accommodation, and the dynamics of personality development. *Child Development, 53,* 281–295.

Botwinick, J. (1977). Intellectual abilities. In J. E. Birren & K. W. Schaie (Eds.), *Handbook of the psychology of aging* (pp. 580–605). New York: Van Nostrand Reinhold.

Cattell, R. B. (1971). *Abilities: Their structure, growth, and action.* Boston: Houghton Mifflin.

Cornelius, S. W., & Caspi, A. (1986). Self-perceptions of intellectual control and aging. *Educational Gerontology, 12,* 345–357.

Cornelius, S. W., & Caspi, A. (1987). Everyday problem solving in adulthood and old age. *Psychology and Aging, 2,* 144–153.

Cornelius, S. W., & Rose, J. H. (1987, November). Concepts of effective coping: Theme and variations. Paper presented at the meeting of the Gerontological Society of America, Washington, D.C.

Demming, J. A., & Pressey, S. L. (1957). Tests "indigenous" to the adult and older years. *Journal of Counseling Psychology, 4,* 144–148.

Denney, N. W. (1982). Aging and cognitive changes. In B. B. Wolman (Ed.), *Handbook of developmental psychology* (pp. 807–827). Englewood Cliffs, N.J.: Prentice-Hall.

Denney, N. W., & Palmer, A. M. (1981). Adult age differences on traditional and practical problem-solving measures. *Journal of Gerontology, 36,* 323–328.

Dixon, R. A., Kramer, D., & Baltes, P. B. (1985). Intelligence: Its life-span development. In B. B. Wolman (Ed.), *Handbook of intelligence: Theories, measurements, and applications* (pp. 301–350). New York: Wiley.

Flavell, J. F. (1970). Cognitive change in adulthood. In L. R. Goulet & P. B. Baltes (Eds.), *Life-span developmental psychology: Research and theory* (pp. 247–253). New York: Academic Press.

Ford, M. E., & Tisak, M. S. (1983). A further search for social intelligence. *Journal of Educational Psychology, 75,* 196–206.

Gardner, E. F., & Monge, R. H. (1977). Adult age differences in cognitive abilities and educational background. *Experimental Aging Research, 3,* 337–383.

Gardner, H. (1983). *Frames of mind: The theory of multiple intelligences.* New York: Basic Books.

Guilford, J. P. (1969). *Verbal analogies test, 1.* Beverly Hills: Sheridan Psychological Services.

Guilford, J. P., & Hoepfner, R. (1971). *The analysis of intelligence.* New York: McGraw-Hill.

Horn, J. L. (1978). Human ability systems. In P. B. Baltes (Ed.), *Life-span development and behavior* (Vol. 1, pp. 211–256). New York: Academic Press.

Horn, J. L. (1982). The aging of human abilities. In B. B. Wolman (Ed.), *Handbook of developmental psychology* (pp. 847–870). Englewood Cliffs, N.J.: Prentice-Hall.

Horn, J. L., & Cattell, R. B. (1966). Age differences in primary mental ability factors. *Journal of Gerontology, 21*, 210–220.

Horn, J. L., & Donaldson, G. (1980). Cognitive development in adulthood. In O G. Brim, Jr., & J. Kagan (Eds.), *Constancy and change in human development* (pp. 445–529). Cambridge, Mass.: Harvard University Press.

Lachman, M. E. (1983). Perceptions of intellectual aging: Antecedent or consequence of intellectual functioning? *Developmental Psychology, 19*, 482–498.

Lachman, M. E., & Jelalian, E. (1984). Self-efficacy and attributions for intellectual performance in young and elderly adults. *Journal of Gerontology, 39*, 577–582.

McCrae, R. R., & Costa, P. T., Jr. (1985). Updating Norman's "Adequate Taxonomy": Intelligence and personality dimensions in natural language and in questionnaires. *Journal of Personality and Social Psychology, 49*, 710–721.

Neisser, U. (1979). The concept of intelligence. In R. J. Sternberg & D. K. Detterman (Eds.), *Human intelligence: Perspectives on its theory and measurement* (pp. 179–189). Norwood, N.J.: Ablex.

Plemons, J. K., Willis, S. L., & Baltes, P. B. (1978). Modifiability of fluid intelligence in aging: A short-term longitudinal training approach. *Journal of Gerontology, 33*, 224–231.

Schaie, K. W. (1978). External validity in the assessment of intellectual development in adulthood. *Journal of Gerontology, 33*, 695–701.

Schaie, K. W. (1979). The Primary Mental Abilities in adulthood: An exploration in the development of psychometric intelligence. In P. B. Baltes & O. G. Brim, Jr. (Eds.), *Life-span development and behavior* (Vol. 2, pp. 67–115). New York: Academic Press.

Scheidt, R. J., & Schaie, K. W. (1978). A taxonomy of situations for an elderly population. Generating situational criteria. *Journal of Gerontology, 33*, 848–857.

Sternberg, R. J. (1985a). *Beyond IQ: A triarchic theory of human intelligence.* New York: Cambridge University Press.

Sternberg, R. J. (1985b). Implicit theories of intelligence, creativity, and wisdom. *Journal of Personality and Social Psychology, 49*, 607–627.

Sternberg, R. J., Conway, B. E., Ketron, J. L., & Bernstein, M. (1981). People's conceptions of intelligence. *Journal of Personality and Social Psychology, 41*, 37–55.

Sternberg, R. J., & Wagner, R. K. (Eds.). (1986). *Practical intelligence: Origins of competence in the everyday world.* New York: Cambridge University Press.

Thurstone, T. G. (1962). *Primary mental abilities for Grades 9–12* (rev. ed.). Chicago: Science Research Associates.

Wechsler, D. (1955). *Manual for the Wechsler Adult Intelligence Scale.* New York: Psychological Corporation.

Wechsler, D. (1958). *The measurement and appraisal of adult intelligence* (4th ed.). Baltimore: Williams & Wilkins.

Williams, S. A., Denney, N. W., & Schadler, M. (1983). Elderly adults' perception of their own cognitive development during the adult years. *International Journal of Aging and Human Development, 16*, 147–158.

Willis, S. L., & Baltes, P. B. (1980). Intelligence in adulthood and aging: Contemporary issues. In L. W. Poon (Ed.), *Aging in the 1980s: Psychological issues* (pp. 260–272). Washington, D.C.: American Psychological Association.

Woodruff, D. S. (1983). A review of aging and cognitive processes. *Research on Aging, 5,* 139–153.

13

Practical Problem Solving in Adults: A Comparison of Problem Types and Scoring Methods

Cameron J. Camp
Kathleen Doherty
Sarah Moody-Thomas
Nancy W. Denney

Discussion of a recently conducted study of real-world problem solving is presented in this chapter. Specifically, measures of crystallized and fluid intelligence were related to measures of real-world problem solving in adults of different ages. Problem solving was measured by presenting vignettes of real-world problems and asking participants to provide solutions to these problems. In addition, participants were asked to describe problems from their own lives that they had solved. Thus, we were able to relate traditional measures of cognitive ability, responses to experimenter-provided problems, and responses to participant-generated problems. These three types of measures represent progressive levels of ecological validity in experimental stimuli.

Performance on most traditional problem solving tasks tends to decline after early adulthood (for reviews see Botwinick 1984; Denney 1979, 1982; Giambra & Arenberg 1980; Kausler 1982; Rabbitt 1977; Salthouse 1982). It has been suggested that this decline may occur because middle-aged and elderly individuals are not often called upon to perform abstract problem solving tasks such as those employed in traditional measures of problem solving (e.g., Denney in press; Denney & Palmer 1981; Denney, Pearce, & Palmer 1982). As a result, the skills required for abstract problem solving tasks are not well practiced in middle-aged and elderly adults. It has further been suggested that middle-aged and older adults may exhibit better performance on realistic, practical problems similar to the ones they might encounter in their everyday lives. In fact, one might speculate that older adults would actually outperform younger adults on practical problem solving tasks because of the cumulative experience they have had in similar situations.

Several studies of practical problem solving performance during the adult years have been conducted. Results usually indicate that, when age effects are found, middle-aged adults perform better than either younger or older adults (Denney & Palmer 1981; Denney in press; Denney, Pearce, & Palmer 1982). This sugests that the experience middle-aged adults have acquired during their lives does in fact facilitate practical problem solving performance. However, this research also suggests that there may be limits on the extent to which experience facilitates the practical problem solving performance of older adults. A review of this line of research and its implications for the study forming the basis of this chapter follows.

In an initial study dealing with practical problem solving ability in adulthood (Denney & Palmer, 1981), older adults performed less well than middle-aged adults. As a result of this finding, Denney and her colleagues made an attempt, (Denney in press; Denney, Pearce, & Palmer 1982), to bias practical problems in favor of elderly adults. That is, the practical problems that were developed were intended to be ones that older adults would be more likely to have experienced, either in their own lives or vicariously, than would either young or middle-aged adults. It was assumed that if experience alone determines problem solving performance, elderly adults would outperform younger age groups on such biased problems. However, older adults still performed less well than middle-aged and sometimes even young adults. Thus, experience may facilitate performance up to a point, but there also appear to be age-related limitations on performance during the later adult years.

Before concluding that there are limits on the performance of older adults with respect to all types of practical problem solving, it is important to determine whether those limits extend to practical problem solving in the social domain. Practical problem solving in the previously mentioned studies was measured by asking participants to provide solutions to problems presented in vignettes and reflecting a variety of problem domains (e.g., mechanical failures, coping with a chronic illness). Higher scores were given to solutions that reflected awareness of the many possible causes of a problem and the corresponding array of potential solutions, and the scores from all scenes were summed to create a single practical problem solving score for each participant.

Thus, while older adults showed declining scores for *general* practical problem solving ability, it has been suggested that they may perform better relative to young and middle-aged adults on *social* problems. For example, Denney (in press) hypothesized that since adults of all ages engage in social interaction with other people, social problem solving may be a domain in which adults of different ages have more or less common experience. Further, since older adults have had more cumulative experience with social problem solving as a result of having lived longer, one might expect that they would perform better than younger adults on such problems.

One purpose of the present study was to determine whether elderly adults are, in fact, better at solving social problems than other types of real-world problems. In order to address this question, we asked young, middle-aged, and elderly adults to report four problems that they had encountered in their own lives. For two of the problems we did not specify the content. For the other two we specified that we wanted them to be social/interpersonal problems. If elderly adults are better at solving social problems, we would expect to obtain an interaction between age and type of problem, with elderly performing better relative to the young and middle-aged subjects on the social problems than on nonsocial problems.

In addition to asking the subjects for problems that they had encountered in their own lives, we presented the subjects with four of the practical problems that had been used in Denney's previous research in order to determine whether a different developmental function would be obtained with subject-generated problems than has typically been obtained with the experimenter-generated problems employed in the past. Thus, a second purpose of the present study was to determine the age functions for the two types of problems: subject-generated and experimenter-generated.

A third purpose of the present study was to relate the performance on both the subject-generated and the experimenter-generated practical problems to standard measures of intellectual functioning. On the one hand, one might expect practical problem solving to be more highly related to measures of crystallized intelligence, since it involves acculturation, which is a defining characteristic of crystallized intelligence. On the other hand, one might expect practical problem solving to be more highly related to measures of fluid intelligence, since fluid intelligence is defined, in part, as the ability to solve problems. Thus, we wished to determine whether practical problem solving ability is related to fluid, crystallized, or both fluid and crystallized intelligence. To do so, performance on both the subject-generated and the experimenter-generated practical problems was related to a measure of crystallized intelligence, a measure of fluid intelligence, and a measure that contains elements of both. For this purpose, the Wechsler Adult Intelligence Scale-Revised (WAIS-R) Information subtest, the Raven's Progressive Matrices, and the WAIS-R Similarities subtest were used, respectively.

A fourth and final purpose of the study was to develop a new scoring scheme for measuring practical problem solving ability. Given that participants were generating half of the problem solving situations, we needed a "generic" set of criteria for scoring that would accommodate a variety of different problem types. A scoring scheme for practical problem solving based on the quality of a single (or primary) solution was developed. This scoring procedure could be applied uniformly to a wide variety of real-world problems, including solutions to experimenter-generated problems. This enabled us to compare scores generated by previous and current scoring schemes for the experimenter-generated problems. We wished to determine if the new scoring scheme might lead to different conclusions than those generated by the previously used scoring scheme.

The four main goals of the study were (1) to determine if older adults might outperform younger adults in solving social problems; (2) to determine how adults of different ages solve both experimenter- and participant-generated problems; (3) to relate practical problem solving to measures of crystallized and fluid intelligence; and (4) to develop a new, "generic" scoring scheme for measuring practical problem solving ability (and to compare it with previously used scoring schemes).

METHOD

Subjects

There were 119 adult participants in this research, representing three age groups: younger (25–35 years; 22 females, 24 males), middle-aged (45–55 years; 22 females, 16 males), and older (65–75 years; 18 females, 17 males). Participants were community-dwelling, nonstudent volunteers residing in the metropolitan New Orleans area. Ninty-eight percent of the participants were Caucasian.

Procedure

Two experimental sessions per participant were designed to resemble structured interviews. Attempts were made to ensure that each participant was interviewed on 2 consecutive days, with each interview lasting approximately 1.5 hours. The maximum amount of time permitted between experimental sessions was 72 hours.

Initially, the experimenter administered a demographic/medical history questionnaire and the Information and Similarities subtests of the WAIS-R. The participant was then asked to provide the experimenter with two problem situations. These first two of the initial problems were sought without qualifications about the problems' content. These problems will be referred to as "unconstrained" problems. After reporting the problem situation, the subject was asked to give his or her best solution to that problem and to rate the efficacy of that solution. Two more problems were then elicited. These problems also were produced by the participant, but were to be social/interpersonal problems. These two problems will be referred to as "constrained interpersonal" problems. As before, the subject reported and rated his or her solution to the situation. All problems were later classified into four major categories:

1. Social/interpersonal: interactions between the participant and an individual known on a personal basis (e.g., a marital problem or trouble with friends or neighbors).
2. Impersonal: environmental hazards such as mechanical failures or violence from unknown assailants.
3. Extrapersonal: problems in the environment of a more chronic nature and/or not covered by the first two categories (e.g., unemployment or a sick pet).
4. Self: problems whose focus was primarily internal, such as a health problem or making a decision about a vocation.

Four problems previously employed by Denney and her colleagues (Denney & Palmer 1981; Denney in press; Denney, Pearce, & Palmer 1982) were administered at the beginning of the second session. These problems dealt with "real-world" content and involved a broken refrigerator, a man who is requested by his physician to not perform heavy labor that is an integral part of his job, being a parent of a teenager late coming home from a date, and a newly widowed woman needing to maintain or increase social relationships. The participant was asked to give a solution to each problem. Finally, the participant was given Raven's Standard Progressive Matrices, then debriefed and thanked for participating.

In all, eight problems and solutions were used in the study. Responses to these real-world problems were independently rated as to the efficacy of the solutions. In addition, responses to the experimenter-generated problems were scored according to the criteria used in previous research by Denney and her colleagues, as described earlier.

RESULTS

Unless otherwise noted, group comparisons were conducted using analysis of variance. Tukey's HSD was utilized for post hoc comparisons. Occasional discrepancies in degrees of freedom used in different analyses are the result of missing data.

Demographics

Education

Education levels in the sample were high. Mean years of education (and standard deviations) for the younger, middle-aged, and older cohorts were M = 14.7 (S.D. = 2.2), 14.9 (3.2), and 12.8 (3.4), respectively. The difference in educational levels was statistically significant—F (2,116) = 6.06, $p < .01$—with older adults having less education on the average than younger and middle-aged individuals.

Health

Health was measured in two ways. The first measure was a self rating of health using a four-point scale; the second, the number of illnesses subjects reported having had in the past five years. For both measures, older adults were in poorer health than other groups (ratings, F (2,116) = 5.74, $p < .05$; illnesses, F (2,116) = 21.70, $p < .01$).

Intelligence Measures

The Information subtest, which generally measures real-world information available to an individual, (i.e., a primarily crystallized intelligence measure) showed no age-group differences. The Similarities subtest, which measures both available information and abstract reasoning (i.e., draws on both crystallized and fluid intelligence), showed a slight age effect, with the older group ($M = 17.9$, sd = 6.8) performing significantly worse than both the younger ($M = 21.2$, sd = 4.0) and the middle-aged groups ($M = 21.3$, sd = 4.7) (F (2,116) = 5.12, $p < .01$). The Raven's test, which is related to "performance" or nonverbal abilities, (i.e., a primarily fluid intelligence measure) showed a large age effect (F [2,116] = 21.70, $p < .01$), with older adults significantly worse than both the younger and the middle-aged groups in their performance in this task. This pattern is generally consistent with effects usually found in comparing age groups on intelligence measures. All intelligence measures were significantly correlated with each other and with years of education ($p < .01$).

Analyses of Problem Solving Abilities: Previously Used Scoring Criteria

Age Effects

An overall problem solving ability score was generated for each participant for the experimenter-generated problems, using the scoring criteria employed in previous research with these stimuli. Age group was a significant effect: F (2, 113) = 5.18, $p < .01$. Means (and standard deviations) for the younger, middle-aged, and older age groups were M = 11.1 (1.9), 10.8 (1.7), and 9.8 (1.8), respectively, with higher scores representing higher levels of problem solving ability. Younger adults were significantly different from older adults. No other comparisons were significant. Thus, older adults again were found to perform at lower levels of ability for these problems on these measures than younger adults.

Correlations with Intelligence Measures

Problem solving ability was significantly and positively correlated with all intelligence measures, as well as with years of education. Pearson product-moment correlation coefficients for the Information and Similarities subtests, the Raven's test, and education were $r = .34, .29, .40,$ and .39, respectively ($p < .01$ in all cases).

Multiple-Regression Analysis

A multiple-regression analysis was conducted to determine which factors uniquely predicted problem solving ability. Predictor variables included scores from the Information and Similarities subtests of the WAIS-R and from the Raven's Progressive Matrices. Chronological age was also used as an independent variable, and experimenter ratings of problem solving ability served as the dependent measure.

All four predictor variables were entered as a group, and significance tests for the full model as well as for individual b weights of predictors were conducted. The total model was significant: $F (4, 111) = 6.69, p < .01, R^2 = .19$. However, only the b weight for the Raven's score was significant: $p < .05$.

An examination of the correlational and regression analyses demonstrates that our initial scoring of problem solving ability found this measure to be related to measures of both crystallized and fluid intelligence. However, fluid intelligence accounted for the largest unique covariation between practical problem solving ability and intelligence.

Analyses of Problem Solving Abilities: Efficacy of Solutions

Self Ratings

The first analysis conducted on the ratings given by subjects to their own solutions was a comparison between ratings given for the two unconstrained problems versus the constrained/interpersonal problems across age groups. This analysis involved a (2 × 3) mixed-model analysis of variance, representing the within-S factor problem type (unconstrained versus constrained-social/interpersonal) and the between-S factor age level. There were no significant differences between ratings for these two types of problems. Age level was not a significant effect in this analysis, nor did age interact with problem type.

Next, we compared the average ratings for the participant-generated problems versus the experimenter-generated problems by age level, using a 2 × 3 mixed-model analysis of variance. This analysis represented the within-S factor problem type (participant- versus experimenter-generated problems) and the between-S factor age level. The problem type effect was statistically significant: $F(1, 115) = 17.02, p < .001$. Age level was not significant, though the problem type × age level interaction did reach significance: $F(2, 115) = 3.18, p < .05$.

Mean ratings for problem solutions were relatively low, indicating that individuals were often giving solutions they rated as the best possible. Since we had specifically asked for descriptions of problems that had been *solved* in the participant-generated problems, this is not a surprising finding. However, our older adults' ratings did not differ significantly across problem type. Ratings for the other age groups did. Older adults were more likely to have low (best possible) ratings for both types of problems, while other age groups rated their solutions as more efficacious for the experimenter-generated problems than for problems from their own lives.

Correlations between Self Ratings and Intelligence Measures

For experimenter-generated problems (but not participant-generated problems), self ratings of solution efficacy were significantly correlated with the Information ($r = -.19; p < .04$) and Similarities ($r = -.22; p < .02$) subtests, respectively (low self ratings = "best").

Correlation between Self Ratings of Solution Efficacy and Experimenter Ratings (Previously Used Scoring Criteria)

At this point we were interested in comparing the relationship between self ratings of solution efficacy and experimenter ratings (using scoring criteria employed in past research). The correlation between self ratings and these experimenter ratings was not significant: $r = -.10$. This may have been due, in part, to the fact that participants in general felt that their solutions were very good, which could have created a truncated range problem for the correlation analysis.

Correlations between Experimenter and Participant Ratings of Solution Efficacy

The correlations between solution efficacy ratings generated by participants and experimenters (new scoring criteria) were examined. These correlations were calculated for the total sample of participants as well as separately for each age group. No significant correlations were found for any of the experimenter-generated problems. As mentioned above, the experimenter ratings of solution efficacy for the experimenter-generated problems had a severely truncated range. Our participants were judged as generally able to find a direct, workable solution to these problems. These outcomes parallel the outcomes of analyses with problem solving ability scores using criteria from past research. Thus, for experimenter-generated problems, self ratings and ratings by experimenters for problem solving ability did not correlate.

A second pattern that emerged was that for self-generated problems, significant correlations were found for the second unconstrained and the second constrained interpersonal problems. Whether this pattern is artifactual or represents some type of "warm-up" effect, in which correlations between participant and experimenter ratings begin to rise with successive examples of different types of self-generated problems, remains to be seen.

A final pattern was that our oldest group had two significant correlations for the self-generated problems, compared with one each for the younger and middle-aged groups. Further research must determine whether this intriguing outcome represents some age-related increase in awareness of the quality of solutions to real-world problems of a personal nature. (The r's ranged from $-.27$ to $-.43$ for these sets of analyses, $p < .01$. A 5 meant an efficacious solution on one scale and a poor solution on the other scale, hence the negative correlations.)

Correlation between Old and New Experimenter Scoring Criteria

For experimenter-generated problems, measures of solution efficacy had been derived using both old and new experimenter scoring criteria. For these problems, it was possible to correlate ratings for the two methods of scoring solution efficacy. This correlation was significant; $r = .36$, $p < .01$.

Analyses of Problem Solving Abilities: Use of New Scoring Criteria

The ratings of solution efficacy generated by the experimenters using the new scoring criteria were analyzed in the same manner as the efficacy rating of the participants. The first analysis conducted was a comparison between ratings given for the two unconstrained problems versus the constrained/interpersonal problems across age groups. This analysis involved a (2 × 3) mixed-model analysis of variance representing the within-S factor problem type (unconstrained versus constrained-social/interpersonal) and the between-S factor age level. There was a significant difference between ratings for these two types of problems: F $(1,111) = 11.28$, $p < .001$. Means (and standard deviations) for the unconstrained and constrained-social/interpersonal problem solutions were 4.29 (1.05) and 3.82 (1.16), respectively. Thus, solutions to the constrained-social/interpersonal problems were rated as less efficacious by the experimenters than the solutions to the unconstrained problem type. Age level was not a significant effect in this analysis, nor did age interact with problem type.

Next, we compared the average ratings for the participant-generated problems versus the experimenter-generated problems by age level, using a 2 × 3 mixed-model analysis of variance representing the within-S factor problem type (participant- versus experimenter-generated problems) and the between-S factor age level. The problem type effect was statistically significant: $F (1, 109) = 49.91$, $p < .001$. Means (and standard deviations) for the participant- and experimenter-generated problems were 4.06 (.82) and 4.70 (.47). The experimenter ratings attributed higher levels of efficacy to the solutions given to experimenter-generated problems than to the solutions given to participant-generated problems. It should be noted that the solutions given to experimenter-generated problems were rated as being near ceiling level on a five-point scale, whereas ratings for solutions to the participant-generated problems deviated from ceiling levels. This was especially true for constrained-social/interpersonal problems, as demonstrated by the immediately preceding analysis. Neither age level nor the age level × problem type interaction was significant ($F < 1$).

Correlations between Experimenter Ratings and Intelligence Measures

Experimenter ratings of solution efficacy (new scoring criteria) for both participant- and experimenter-generated problems were correlated with intelligence measures and years of education. As was the case with self ratings of efficacy by participants, education was not correlated with solution efficacy measures, and intelligence measures did not correlate with solution efficacy for participant-generated problems. For experimenter-generated problems, however, efficacy ratings correlated significantly with both Similarities subtest scores ($r = .26$, $p < .01$) and Raven's scores ($r = .28$, $p < .01$), but not with Information subtest scores.

Multiple-Regression Analyses

Multiple regression analyses were conducted using scores from the Information and Similarities subtests of the WAIS-R and from the Raven's Progressive Matrices tests as independent variables. Chronological age was also used as an independent variable. Dependent variables included the average experimenter ratings for the first four (self-generated) and the last four (experimenter-generated) problems.

In each analysis, all four predictor variables were entered as a group, and significance tests for the full model as well as tests of individual b weights of predictors were conducted. Only one analysis produced significant results. For experimenter ratings for the experimenter-generated problems, the total model was significant: $F (4, 112) = 3.25, p < .01, R^2 = .10$. However, only the b weight for the Raven's score was significant: $p < .05$. Interestingly, this pattern of results for experimenter ratings of experimenter-generated problems exactly parallels the results from the multiple-regression analysis using the scoring criteria from past research reported above. Thus, for both ways of scoring experimenter-generated problems, a fluid intelligence measure was the best unique predictor of problem solving efficacy.

Frequency of Reports of Different Problem Classes

As described in the methods section, self-generated problems were classified into four general categories, each of which contained a variable number of subcategories. We wished to determine if age groups were different in the types of problems they reported. This was an especially important question for the constrained-social/interpersonal problems. A primary focus of the research was a comparison of social and nonsocial problems. It was assumed that statistical comparisons of the unconstrained versus constrained-social/interpersonal problems would yield such comparisons. However, if a majority of unconstrained problems were social/interpersonal in nature, and/or if a large number of constrained content items were not social/interpersonal (i.e., participants did not follow directions), our previous analyses would not deal with social/nonsocial comparisons.

For the unconstrained content problems, age level did not significantly influence use of any of the four problem categories, though older adults reported more impersonal and fewer social/interpersonal items than the younger and middle-aged groups. For the constrained-social/interpersonal content problems, age level was a significant effect for both social/interpersonal ($F [2,114] = 3.74, p < .03$) and impersonal ($F [2,114] = 3.26, p < .05$) problem categories.

Younger and middle-aged adults basically complied with our request. Perfect compliance would have produced mean scores of 2.0 social/interpersonal problems per group, and the means of these two younger age levels were very close to 2.0 (younger = 1.78; middle =

1.74). Our older adults, however, had a significantly lower number of reported social/interpersonal problems (1.50).

There are several reasons why we may have obtained these results. Older adults may have been less comfortable than other participants discussing interpersonal problems with young experimenters. Our older adults may have been less able than other age groups to distinguish between social/interpersonal and nonsocial problems. Our older adults may have encountered social/interpersonal problems less frequently in their daily lives than other age groups. Finally, our older adult sample may have viewed interpersonal situations as being less problematic than did younger cohorts.

Summary of Results

In summary, our older adults were less well educated and reported themselves as less healthy than our younger adults. Older adults were similar to younger cohorts on measures of crystallized intelligence, and worse on measures of fluid intelligence. These findings indicate that our sample was, in general, representative of naturally occurring cohort differences. Therefore, our results replicate general patterns of research findings in this area and are likely to have good external validity. In addition, our intelligence measures correlated with each other and with education.

For previous problem solving ability measures using stimuli from past research, older adults displayed poorer performance than younger cohorts. Problem solving ability measured in this way was correlated with all intelligence measures, though fluid intelligence was the most important predictor of performance.

For self ratings of solution efficacy, participants viewed their solutions to social and nonsocial problems as being equally efficacious. Younger and middle-aged adults rated solutions to problems from their own lives as less efficacious than solutions they generated for experimenter-derived problem. Older adults rated solutions to both types of problems as being equally efficacious.

Self ratings of solution efficacy were not significantly correlated with education. Efficacy ratings for problems from their own lives were not correlated with intelligence measures. Efficacy ratings for experimenter-derived problems showed only small correlations with crystallized intelligence measures, and were not correlated with experimenter ratings for these problems. Self ratings were correlated with experimenter efficacy ratings for some participant-generated problems. This was especially true for older adults and for the second example of both constrained and unconstrained content problems.

For experimenter ratings of solution efficacy, using scoring criteria created for this study, participants' solutions to problems from their own lives were rated less efficacious for social/interpersonal problems than for nonsocial problems. This conflicted with participants' data; they saw their solutions to both types of problems as equally good. Experimenter ratings showed higher efficacy for solutions to experimenter-derived problems compared with real-life problems of participants. This finding was in agreement with participants' self ratings. These experimenter ratings were not correlated with education. Experimenter efficacy ratings for real-life problems were not correlated with intelligence measures. For experimenter-derived problems, these experimenter efficacy ratings were most strongly related to fluid intelligence measures. Efficacy ratings using both old and new scoring criteria for experimenter-derived problems showed a small but significant correlation.

Older adults reported social/interpersonal problems from their own lives less often than younger cohorts. With creation of "social/interpersonal" and a "nonsocial" score for each participant, analyses demonstrated that the use of such scores led to the same conclusions as analyses comparing unconstrained and constrained problem content data.

DISCUSSION

One of the primary aims of the present study was to determine whether elderly adults might perform better, relative to younger adults, on social/interpersonal problems than on other types of problems. Since adults of all ages engage in social interaction, it has been hypothesized that older adults might perform better relative to younger and middle-aged adults on social problems because of their greater cumulative experience with social problems (e.g., Denney in press). However, the results of the present study provide a number of different types of evidence that indicate that older adults may *not* be more familiar with social problems than with nonsocial problems, and that elderly adults may *not* be better at providing solutions to social problems than to other types of problems.

Results indicate that older adults may not experience social problems relatively more often than nonsocial problems. When the subjects were asked to report problems they had experienced, the older adults reported fewer interpersonal problems than did the young and middle-aged adults. The young and middle-aged adults mentioned more social problems than nonsocial problems, while the older adults mentioned more nonsocial problems than social problems. Further, even when the subjects were told to make up social problems, the older subjects were less likely than younger and middle-aged subjects to comply with the instructions. When asked to report social problems that they had experienced, the young and middle-aged adults tended to report only social problems, while some of the older adults have nonsocial problems.

Since older adults are less likely than younger individuals to report social problems, both when asked for problems they have encountered and when asked to report social problems they have experienced, it seems reasonable to infer that older individuals may not experience more social problems in their everyday lives than do younger adults. In fact, one might conclude, on the basis on this evidence, that they may encounter fewer social problems than do younger adults. Cornelius and Caspi (1987) reported a similar finding in a study on practical problems solving in adulthood and old age. Older adults reported encountering problems dealing with family, friends, and work less often than did younger age groups, though no age effects were found for problems involving consumer, information, or home management situations. Older adults may, in general, be less likely to confront situations involving work or familial problems on a daily basis after retirement and after children have left home.

In addition to this evidence that older adults may not be relatively more likely to encounter social problems than other types of problems, there is evidence that older subjects are not relatively more efficacious when solving social as opposed to nonsocial problems. This evidence comes from two sources. First, the experimenters rated the subjects' responses to the social problems as less efficacious than the subjects' responses to the nonsocial problems, regardless of age. Further, the interaction between age and type of problem that would be expected if older adults performed relatively better on social problems was not significant.

Second, the participants' ratings of their own problem solving efficacy did not differ for the two types of problems; the participants apparently did not believe that they were more efficacious when dealing with social problems than when dealing with nonsocial problems. Again, the interaction that would be expected if elderly adults were relatively better at solving social problems was not significant.

On the other hand, we did not find evidence that, compared with younger cohorts, older adults were worse at solving problems from their own lives. This is at odds with the conclusions drawn from using previous scoring methods and stimuli. It may have been due to the different nature of stimuli (real-life versus experimenter-generated problems) or to the different ways of scoring problem solving efficacy used for participant- versus experimenter-generated problems.

A second purpose of the present study was to compare performance of different age groups on experimenter-generated problems versus problems from paticipants' lives. The use of previously employed stimuli and scoring criteria found older adults performing at lower levels than younger cohorts, a finding that replicated, in part, previous research outcomes with these stimuli. However, when solutions to actual problems from the lives of the participants were used and compared with problem solving ability for experimenter-derived problems, both experimenters and participants rated real-life problem solutions as less efficacious. This happened in spite of the fact that participants reported problems they had *solved* in their own lives, while experimenter-generated problems were presented to participants, who had to create solutions on the spot.

There were many possible reasons for these outcomes, for the two types of problems might have differed on a number of dimensions. One possibility worth exploring in future research is that of problem hypotheticality, or personal relevance/experience. Participants may have viewed the experimenter-generated problems as "hypothetical" situations. Adults may be more adept at solving the hypothetical problems or the problems of others than at solving problems in their own lives. Perhaps when problems are perceived as belonging to someone else, individuals are able to view them (especially social problems) in a more detached way. This might aid the effective integration of both emotional and logical components of real-world problems (see Labouvie-Vief 1986). Dealing with one's own problems may make it difficult to integrate both reason and feelings in arriving at solutions.

The lone exception to this finding was that older adults viewed their solutions to real-life problems as just as efficacious as their solutions to experimenter-derived problems. Williams, Denney, and Schadler (1983) studied elderly adults' perceptions of the relationship between age and their own problem solving ability. The elderly adults in their study reported that they thought that their problem solving ability had actually increased with age during the adult years. Thus, there is growing evidence suggesting that older adults do not believe that their problem solving abilities decrease with age, although it is not clear whether they believe that they remain the same or increase with age. In the Williams, Denney, and Schadler study, the subjects were asked how they thought their problem solving abilities had changed with age; in the present study the subjects were asked to rate how well they had solved the problems that they chose to report from their own lives. In any case, older adults do not seem to perceive themselves as declining in problem solving ability or producing less efficacious solutions to problems, compared with younger cohorts.

Another purpose of the present study was to explore the relationship between standard intelligence test measures and practical problem solving. On the one hand, one might expect practical problem solving performance to be related to crystallized intelligence, since practical problem solving involves learning about the culture, which is supposed to be a defining characteristic of crystallized intelligence. On the other hand, one might expect practical problem solving to be related to fluid intelligence, since fluid intelligence is defined, in part, as the ability to solve novel problems. Some of the processes involved in solving the novel, abstract problems that are used as measures of fluid intelligence might be similar to the processes involved in solving more practical, everyday problems.

The only practical problems that were significantly related to the intellectual measures included in the present study were the experimenter-generated problems, and they were related only when the experimenter scored the participants' solutions. The solution efficacy for experimenter-generated problems was significantly related to Raven's Progressive Matrices as predictor of unique covariation. Thus, the experimenter-generated problems appear to be related to fluid intelligence but not to crystallized intelligence. The participant-generated problems do not appear to be related to either fluid or crystallized intelligence. This could be due either to unreliability of measures for these stimuli or to qualitative differences in the types of problem solving skills and/or processes used to solve real-life versus experimental problems.

Another purpose of the current study was to create new, "generic" coding schemes of solution efficacy for both participants and experimenters, and to compare results of these coding schemes against results from the use of coding schemes and stimuli employed in past research. For experimenter-generated problems, efficacy ratings using old and new scoring criteria were significantly correlated, though the size of the correlation was modest. Participants' efficacy ratings were not correlated with experimenter ratings for experimenter-derived problems, though there were correlations between participants' ratings and those of the researchers for problems for participants' lives. The fact that the new coding schemes did not give weight to the generation of multiple solutions probably contributed both to a truncated range of variability for these ratings and to creation of qualitative differences in the two ways of scoring. It should be noted that when the new scoring scheme was used, differences were found between participant- and experimenter-generated problems.

Further refinement of these new scoring criteria and further comparisons with alternative forms of scoring practical problem solving ability (e.g., Cornelius & Caspi 1987) are clearly in order. At the moment, it appears that the conclusions drawn about the relationship between practical problem solving ability and aging depend on both the choice of stimuli and the scoring schemes utilized. Data from the current study suggest that declining performance with advancing age is not as readily found when using our new scoring scheme and stimuli. These conclusions, at the moment, must remain tentative until further research indicates that these new techniques have reasonable validity.

In real-world settings, individuals must deal with problems that are fraught with ambiguity and to which there may be no such thing as a perfect solution. Even if a "best possible solution" is found, individuals often display cognitive dissonance and likewise demonstrate an acknowledgement of the uncertainty inherent in real-world problems.

In our study, our younger and middle-aged samples seemed to follow the scenario described above. However, we also found evidence that while our older adults were as capable as other age groups of finding solutions to problems, they were more comfortable with the solutions to problems from their own lives than were other age groups. Given the correlations found in the older sample between efficacy ratings of both participants and experimenters (for participant-generated problems), the efficacy ratings generated by our older participants do not necessarily reflect inaccurate or overly optimistic assessments. Instead, older adults may feel that problems in life are less catastrophic and/or more "solvable" than do younger generations (after all, older adults have survived many problematic situations in their lifetimes). Further research would lend support to the idea that older adults view real-world problems as less catastrophic than younger generations (e.g., Erber 1986; Williams et al. 1983).

As the ecological validity of our research procedures increases, older adults have come to be viewed as more competent problem solvers. This shift in orientation has been accompanied (and often preceded) by corresponding shifts in our theoretical orientations toward adult cognitive development. In a search for measures of real-world problem solving, experimenters have begun to rediscover the unique qualities of mature thought. When the value of mature thinking is acknowledged by science and society, the place of the older adult within modern social systems may improve dramatically.

REFERENCES

Botwinick, J. (1984). Problem solving: Forming concepts. In J. Botwinick, *Aging and behavior*. New York: Springer-Verlag.

Cornelius, S. W., & Caspi, A. (1987). Everyday problem solving in adulthood and old age. *Psychology and Aging*, 2, 144–153.

Denney, N. W. (1979). Problem solving in later adulthood. In P. B. Baltes & O. G. Brim, Jr. (Eds.), *Life-span development and behavior* (Vol. 2, pp. 38–66). New York: Academic Press.

Denney, N. W. (1982). Aging and cognitive changes. In B. B. Wolman & G. Stricker (Eds.), *Handbook of developmental psychology* (pp. 807–827). Englewood Cliffs, N.J.: Prentice-Hall.

Denney, N. W. (in press). Everyday problem solving: Methodological issues, research findings, and a model. In L. W. Poon, D. C. Rubin, & B. A. Wilson (Eds.), *Everyday cognition in adulthood and late life*. New York: Cambridge University Press.

Denney, N. W., & Palmer, A. M. (1981). Adult age differences on traditional and practical problem-solving measures. *Journal of Gerontology, 36,* 323–328.

Denney, N. W., Pearce, K. A., & Palmer, A. M. (1982). A developmental study of adults' performance on traditional and practical problem-solving tasks. *Experimental Aging Research, 8,* 115–118.

Erber, J. T. (1985, November). Age differences in memory failure appraisal. Paper presented at the annual scientific meeting of the Gerontological Society of America, New Orleans.

Giambra, L. M, & Arenberg, D. (1980). Problem solving, concept learning, and aging. In L. W. Poon (Ed.), *Aging in the 1980s: Psychological issues* (pp. 253–259). Washington, D.C.: American Psychological Association.

Horn, J. L. (1982). The aging of human abilities. In B. B. Wolman & G. Stricker (Eds.), *Handbook of developmental psychology* (pp. 847–870). Englewood Cliffs, N.J.: Prentice-Hall.

Kausler, D. H. (1982). Thinking. In D. H. Kausler, *Experimental psychology and human aging*. New York: John Wiley and Sons.

Labouvie-Vief, G. (1986, November). Natural epistemologies and dimensions of development in adulthood. Paper presented at the annual scientific convention of the Gerontological Society of America, Chicago.

Rabbitt, P. (1977). Changes in problem solving ability in old age. In J. E. Birren & K. W. Schaie (Eds.), *Handbook of the psychology of aging* (2nd ed.). New York: Van Nostrand Reinhold.

Salthouse, T. A. (1982). Decision making and problem solving. In T. A. Salthouse, *Adult cognition*. New York: Springer-Verlag.

Williams, S. A., Denney, N. W., & Schadler, M. (1983). Elderly adults' perception of their own cognitive development during the adult years. *International Journal of Aging and Human Development, 16,* 147–158.

14

The Problem of the Problem

Patricia Kennedy Arlin

It is worthwhile to distinguish between contrived or formal problems and everyday problems, or to make the distinction between knowledge-restricted and knowledge-unrestricted problems (Bereiter & Scardamalia 1985). Numerous studies seem to suggest that the use of familiar or everyday materials in problem solving tasks facilitates performance, particularly in aging populations (Sinnott 1975; Sinnott & Guttmann 1978), though greater success with such materials has also been demonstrated among adolescent subjects (Kuhn, Ho, & Adams 1979; Linn, Pulos, & Gans 1981).

While a powerful argument can be made for these distinctions, particularly when the tasks sample the domain of "formal operations," other features of the presented problems may be even more powerful mediators than familiarity is.

It is time to take a closer look not only at the concept of everyday problems but at the problem of what constitutes a problem in the first place. A problem can represent "the partial transformation of a problematic situation into a determinate situation" (Dewey 1938). Or a problem is said to exist "when a response to a given situation is blocked" (Maier 1970, p. 203). Duncker (1945, p. 1) suggests that a "problem arises when a living creature has a goal but does not know how the goal is to be reached."

WHAT MAKES A PROBLEM?

Each of these views of what makes a problem a problem seems to imply that situations in and of themselves are not problems. Problems become problems when someone perceives them to be such. Problems become problems when there is a "felt need" or difficulty that propels one toward resolution. Problems become problems when discrepancies are noted, when contradictions are experienced so that at least a temporary state of disequilibrium is reached.

Disequilibrium may be an essential element of what makes a problem a problem. Piaget (1976, p. 17) asserts:

Cognitive equilibration never indicates a stopping point except provisionally, and this is not a situation to be deplored. . . . On the contrary, the fact that states of equilibrium are always transcended is due to something very positive. All knowledge consists in bringing up new problems at the same time that it resolves preceding ones.

The human being has been called a "problemizing being," a being who "feels the need for and a pleasure in posing problems in addition to those posed by the natural and social environment" (Getzels 1979, p. 9). Problems enhance rather than impede knowledge. Polyani (1958, p. 120) suggests that to "see a problem is a definite addition to knowledge . . . to recognize a problem which can be solved and is worth solving is in fact a discovery in its own right."

Problems are posed in the asking of questions of one's experience, in situations one encounters based on discrepancies one notes, or in perceived contradictions, whether apparent or real, or perceived similarities not previously noticed. The noting of a discrepancy or the recognition of a similarity or contradiction can be the first step in posing a question whose answer represents a solution to the problem the question defines.

Piaget, in his experiments in contradiction (1980), provides examples of contradictions that should provide problems for children but are not problems at all because the children do not perceive the contradiction. In his work on reflective abstraction (Piaget 1977), problems with similar structures or characteristics and similar methods of solution appear unrelated for some children because that which is similar goes undetected.

A problem, when perceived, typically gives rise to a question. The question so raised often dictates the direction that the solution will take. When a problem is posed for a subject, the problem is for the researcher a particular type of problem that he or she perceives to represent a "realistic" problem. The realistic problem is thought to have a structure similar to a more formal problem whose contents are thought to be foreign to the subject. The solution that the researcher has in mind requires particular mental operations. If the subject's solution matches the researcher's solution, the researcher infers that the subject has employed the set of required operations.

This poses a dilemma. The more familiar the problem may be to a subject, the less likely he or she may be to use higher-order operations in the search for a solution. Subjects develop "rules of thumb" and efficient solution methods that may be based on earlier trial-and-error strategies or on their familiarity with the problem's contents. This appears to be a "catch–22." Formal problems are not usually familiar problems, and their unfamiliarity may confound. If they are recast as everyday, realistic problems, they may no longer assess the individual's formal competence, for they may have been reduced to reflections on routines by the subjects.

A TAXONOMY WITH FOUR DIMENSIONS

This suggests the need for a taxonomy of problem types and solution forms if one is to claim the comparability of problems. At the very least, there is a need for a set of categorical descriptions of problem characteristics that are nontrivial in the design of contrived or formal versus everyday problems. A first step toward the development of a taxonomy is a search for appropriate categories to distinguish among and between the problems presented to adults for solution. The search for these categories includes the following sets of distinctions related to problem type that will be considered below: (1) presented versus discovered problems; (2) well-structured versus ill-structured problems; and (3) well-defined versus ill-defined problems. The characteristics that will be defined and considered in this chapter are (1) problem intensity, (2) problem temporality, and (3) problem familiarity.

Once the problem has been clearly defined in terms of type and characteristics, problem content needs to be specified. Does the problem require the manipulation of physical objects, of internal abstractions, of ego-invested materials, or of interpersonal or social contents? Finally, type, characteristic, and content need to be coupled with the type of operation or information processing required for solution if one is to assert that an everyday problem engages the subject mentally in the same way that the formal problem is said to engage him or her. These latter two dimensions of content and operations will not be addressed at length in this chapter.

Problem Type: Presented versus Discovered Problems

Presented versus discovered problems can be classified on the basis of what is known and what is unknown in the problem situation. Getzels (1964) identifies eight types of problems on the basis of this distinction. His categories can provide a first level of analysis in determining the comparability of everyday problems with their formal prototypes. Table 14.1 contains a modified version of these problem types. This continuum

Table 14.1

An Adaptation of Getzels' Presented and Discovered Problems Continuum

	Problem	Problem known by	Solution method	Method known to	Example
1.	given (known)	subject and other	standard method	subject and others	"Use the algorithm 2 raised to the nth power to find all possible combinations of 4 things."
2.	given	subject	standard method	others	Piaget's combinations of colorless liquid task.
3.	given	subject and other	no standard method	neither	Wason's 4-card problem.
4.	exists but remains to be discovered	others	standard method	others	Allegory interpretation problem.
5.	remains to be discovered	neither	standard method may or may not exist	subject and others	Development of an integrative review and the judgment of its adequacy.
6.	remains to be discovered	neither	standard method	subject and others	Choice and design of an experimental research problem.
7.	remains to be discovered	neither	standard method	others	Debugging a complex computer program.
8.	remains to be discovered	neither	no standard method	neither	Paradigmatic shifts.

provides a range for problems from presented to discovered (the former requiring little innovation or creativity for solution, the latter requiring greater invention and innovation).

Each type is defined in terms of whether the problem is presented at the outset or is to be discovered; who the problem is known by (the subject and/or others); whether a standard solution method exists for the problem; and whether and by whom the solution method is known. The final column contains examples of problems that are thought to represent each of the types.

Consider, for example, Inhelder and Piaget's (1958) combination of colorless liquids task. The problem is given by the researcher to the subject. Both know what the problem is: to find a mixture of the colorless liquids that will reproduce the color change. A standard method of solution exists and is known to the problem presenter. The subject may or may not know the standard solution method, and may discover the correct solution without ever consciously employing the standard method. Given these characteristics, the problem is a type 2 problem in Getzels' (1964) typology. Presentation of this problem in terms of colored chips or other more familiar materials may reduce the problem for the subject from a type 2 problem to a type 1 problem. In this case the change may not be a significant one. But if one begins with a type 5 or 6 problem and reduces it to a type 1 or 2 problem, there may be a serious issue of problem congruence.

Problem Type: Ill-Structured versus Well-Structured

Wood (1983) used classical decision theory to describe intellectual assessment tasks. He employed the language of inquiring systems to describe differences in the conditions under which a problem can be solved. His useful adaptation of the notions of well-structured versus ill-structured problems provides one means of making a nontrivial set of distinctions among and between problems.

Problems that are well-structured versus problem that are ill-structured are problems that vary both in terms of the completeness with which the problem can be specified and the certainty with which a solution can be recognized as being either correct or optimal. While Simon (1976) was one of the first to make this set of distinctions, it was Neisser (1976) who seemed to equate everyday or real-life problems with ill-defined problems.

Wood (1983) differs with Simon, "the processes used to solve ill-structured problems are the same as those used to solve well-structured problems," and makes a cogent argument for a difference. He proposes four distinct problem types in terms of the certainty associated with their solution: "(1) problems solved with certainty; (2) problems solved under risk; (3) problems solved under Bayeseian inference; and (4) ill-structured problems or "wicked problems" as Churchman 1971, would call them.

While Wood's emphasis on the certainty of the solution in relation to the structure of the problem is a useful one, it appears that, with certain important language differences, his four problem types are equatable with Getzels' (1964) types 1, 3, 6, and 8. Thus it seems that one can use Getzels' categories not only to describe presented versus discovered problem types but also to consider the solution method and to whom the method is known in order to map onto Wood's categories for inquiring systems and problem structure.

The usefulness of the consideration of the certainty of solution needs to be taken into account along with the nature of the problem when one begins to address the congruence of contrived versus everyday problem situations. Along with the familiarity of the problem presented to the subject, there is a need to assess the subject's perception of the certainty with which a solution can be obtained. If this is not taken into account, that which appears to the researcher to be a well-structured, presented problem may, in the eyes of the problem solver, be an ill-structured, "wicked" problem with no possibility of assessing the adequacy of the solution. Conversely, a problem that the researcher intends to be an ill-structured problem may be to the subject a well-structured problem that he or she solves with ease and certainty.

Problem Type: Well-Defined versus Ill-Defined

While little work exists to make a distinction between well-defined and ill-defined problem versus well-structured and ill-structured problems, it appears that the defining of the problem may require a different set of processes than is provided in a description of problem structure. Four possible combinations of problem structure and definition present themselves: (1) well-structured and well-defined problems; (2) well-structured and ill-defined problems; (3) ill-structured and ill-defined problems; and (4) ill-structured and well-defined problems. A determination of which combination applies seems important in determining the comparability of everyday versus contrived problems.

After one sorts out the type of problem being presented to the subject, other characteristics of a presented problem may affect the solution and the certainty with which one attains that solution. These characteristics include problem intensity, problem tempo, problem temporality, and problem familiarity.

Problem Characteristics: Problem Intensity

Intensity can refer to the motivational attraction or attractiveness of the problem to the problem solver that engages him or her sufficiently that it is worth his or her while to attempt to derive a solution. If a problem is perceived by a problem solver as trivial, then little effort will be expended in an attempt to derive a solution. Even if a problem solver can be described as a postformal thinker, such a characterization may indicate the maximal level of performance one can expect. It says little about the minimal performance that may be observed. The "attractiveness" of a problem or the intensity with which it engages the problem solver has received little notice in the literature. It may represent a crucial variable in assessing performance and in determining the comparability of problem types.

Problem Characteristics: Problem Temporality

Temporality refers to a historical continuum along which problem solvers interpret the problem as a problem they could encounter in their own historical present. If the problem is identified as one that the problem solver encountered as a younger person and is no longer of any relevance, little mental effort may be expended in any attempted solution. If the problem is considered one that could be faced in the present or the near future, it could more readily engage the problem solver to develop a type of general solution method, since he or she perceives that the effort so expended may save effort in the future.

Problem Characteristics: Problem Familiarity

Familiarity is implied in attempts to transform contrived, knowledge-restricted, or laboratory-based problems into everyday, real-life problems. One of the most common ways it is taken into account is to select materials that are thought to be the "stuff" of the problem solver's everyday life. Instead of presenting a "balance-beam" problem to assess proportional reasoning, one presents a problem involving recipes or car travel. In cross-cultural studies of cognitive development, the search for familiar materials can become an obsession. The assumption that accompanies all of these efforts is that if such familiar contents or materials can be identified, then the problems utilizing these materials are structurally comparable with their contrived counterparts. This may not be the case, however. A problem with familiar contents may be reduced from an abstract reasoning problem to one that is so familiar that it no longer is a problem. It is recognized as something one does quite often, and "rules of thumb" and previous successful solutions are accessed in deriving a solution to the presented problem. This leads to the question of whether this new problem with familiar content is a problem at all for the problem solver, since the solution becomes "obvious."

A second difficulty with the selection of familiar contents is that they may appear familiar to the researcher because the researcher associates them with the problem solver's everyday life. While the surface features of the problem may appear to be familiar, they may not be perceived as familiar by the problem solver. The use of fishing poles in place of Piaget's "bending rods" control-of-variables problem (Inhelder & Piaget, 1958) may be familiar to some adolescents, but to others it may be as foreign as the original bending rods. In the former case, the problem may become a nonproblem because the solution is immediately known through prior experience. In the latter case, the apparent familiarity may hinder solution because the problem solver senses that the materials are "real life" materials, and therefore he or she ought to be able to construct a solution easily but cannot.

How the problem is represented by both the researcher and the problem solver might be considered another problem characteristic. It can, however, be included in the discussion of familiarity, since "literal" or "naive" problem representations (Chi, Feltovich, & Glaser 1981; Larkin, McDermott, Simon, & Simon 1980) can be interpreted as "everyday" or "real life" problem representations.

CONCLUSION

The simple mapping of a contrived problem onto what is thought to be an equivalent everyday problem may not retain the comparability that is assumed in such mapping. Comparability requires the equivalence of problem type × characteristic × content × operation interactions for the contrived versus the everyday problem. Establishing the equivalence of two third-order interactions is not an easy task. Acknowledging the complexities may assist rather than hinder the development of equivalent problems. The results of these efforts could lead to greater comparability not only of problem types but also of results. Many of the conflicting findings in the study of adult cognitive development may be artifacts of the failure to assure that the problems under study are equivalent problems. These considerations pose a new set of questions and specify a new range of research problems for study. The raising of new questions and the discovery of new problems are stimuli to the researcher.

Piaget (1980) ended his study of contradictions with words that are an appropriate ending to this brief discussion of the "problem of the problem":

Clearly, though the modest facts assembled in this work may have permitted us to answer a few minor outstanding questions, they continue to pose a host of problems. This may well perturb even the most patient of readers, but does not daunt the research worker to whom new problems are often more important than the accepted solutions (p. 231).

REFERENCES

Bereiter, C., & Scardamalia, M. (1985). Cognitive coping strategies and the problem of inert knowledge. In J. W. Segal, S. F. Chipman, & R. Glaser (Eds.)., *Thinking and learning skills* (Vol. 2). Hillsdale, N.J.: Erlbaum.

Chi, M. T. H., Feltovich, P. J., & Glaser, R. (1981). Categorization and representation of physics problems by experts and novices. *Cognitive Science*, 5, 121–152.

Churchman, C. W. (1971). *The design of inquiring systems: Basic concepts and organization.* New York: Basic Books.

Dewey, J. (1938). *Logic: The theory of inquiry.* New York: Henry Holt.

Duncker, K. (1945). On problem solving. *Psychological Monographs, 58(5),* whole no. 270.

Getzels, J. W. (1964). Creative thinking, problem solving and instruction. In E. Hilgard (Ed.), *Theories of learning and instruction: The sixty-third yearbook of the National Society for the Study of Education.* Chicago: University of Chicago Press.

Getzels, J. W. (1979). Problem finding and research in educational administration. In G. L. Immegart & W. L. Boyd (Eds.), *Problem-finding in educational administration.* Lexington, Mass.: Lexington Books.

Inhelder, B., & Piaget, J. (1958). *The growth of logical thinking from childhood to adolescence.* New York: Basic Books.

Kuhn, D., Ho, V., & Adams, C. (1979). Formal reasoning among pre- and late adolescents. *Child Development, 50,* 1128–1135.

Larkin, J. H., McDermott, J., Simon, D. P., & Simon, H. A. (1980). Expert and novice performance in solving physics problems. *Science, 208,* 1335–1342.

Linn, M. C. (1983). Content, context and process in reasoning during adolescence: Selecting a model. *Journal of Early Adolescence, 3,* 63–82.

Linn, M. C., Pulos, S., & Gans, A. (1981). Correlates of formal reasoning: Content and problem effects. *Journal of Research in Science Teaching, 18,* 435–447.

Maier, N. R. F. (1970). *Problem solving and creativity.* Belmont, Cal.: Brooks/Cole.

Neisser, U. (1976). General, academic, and artificial intelligence. In L. Resnick (Ed.), *The nature of intelligence.* Hillsdale, N.J.: Erlbaum.

Piaget, J. (1976). *L'equilibration des structures cognitives.* Paris: Presses Universitaires de France.

Piaget, J. (1977). *L'abstraction réfléchissante.* Paris: Presses Universitaires de France.

Piaget, J. (1980). *Experiments in contradiction.* Chicago: University of Chicago Press.

Polyani, M. (1958). *Personal knowledge.* Chicago: University of Chicago Press.

Simon, H. A. (1976). Information processing theory of human problem solving. In H. Estes (Ed.), *Handbook of learning and cognitive processes* (Vol. 2). Hillsdale, N.J.: Erlbaum.

Sinnott, J. D. (1975). Everyday thinking and Piagetian operativity in adults. *Human Development, 18,* 430–443.

Sinnott, J. D., & Guttmann, D. (1978). Piagetian logical abilities and older adults' abilties to solve everyday problems. *Human Development, 21,* 327–333.

Wood, P. K. (1983). Inquiring systems and problem structure: Implications for cognitive development. *Human Development, 26,* 249–265.

15

Testing Cognitive Skills with Playing Cards

Iseli K. Krauss

The tests traditionally used in studies of intelligence and problem solving skills of elderly adults may not be appropriate for that population (Sinnott 1975). As Schaie (1978) noted, many traditional psychometric instruments were developed for individuals of a different cohort or for individuals with different sociocultural histories. Test-taking experiences may be limited in the current elderly population, although this will not be the case for later cohorts. Even the concepts underlying any given test may be unfamiliar to older adults.

For these and several additional reasons, traditional tests may lead to incorrect or biased assessment of cognitive skills in elderly adults. Since few norms are reported for older groups, the scores of elderly adults are generally compared with the norms of the younger groups for whom the tests were developed. While this practice provides information on how well an older individual is able to perform relative to a given young group, it does not allow us to compare a given individual with others of his or her own age group. In many instances, especially in clinical situations, that within-age-group comparison is precisely what is required.

On a very practical level, many aspects of traditional tests make it difficult for older adults to perform well even if they understand the concepts involved in the tests. The mechanics of test taking—which include reading fine print, managing a poorly designed answer sheet,

Support for this work was provided in part by NIMH Training Grant MH00070, and by NIA Grant AG04110.

Figure 15.1
Examples of Standard, Round, and Zigzag Cards in a Spatial Rotation or Memory Task Configuration

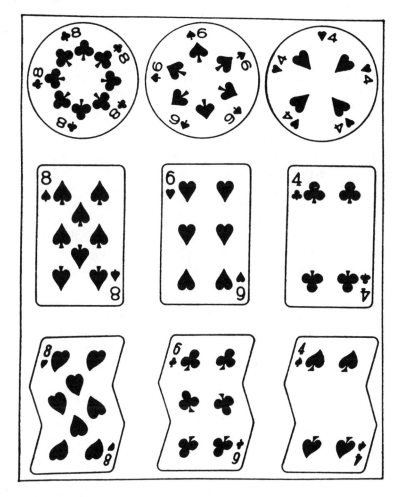

and writing in small spaces—put demands on older adults that are greater than those on younger adults.

To avoid the problems inherent in so many traditional tests of cognitive abilities, a set of tasks was designed for the older adult population. The tasks were designed to be nonthreatening to individuals not familiar or comfortable with traditional testing materials and methods. The tasks employ four styles of commercially available playing cards: standard poker cards, round cards, oversized cards, and zigzag-shaped cards. Three of the card styles are displayed in Figure 15.1. It was hoped that many people, especially elderly adults, who might find traditional tests intimidating would not be threatened by the tests but would be intrigued by the familiar and novel playing cards. Motivation to perform well would not be stymied by the materials themselves, so a realistic assessment of each of the several abilities of concern could be made. It was also hoped that the tasks would be of sufficient interest for those individuals accustomed to testing procedures.

By not imposing time limits, one barrier to effective performance for some individuals is avoided. Neither reading nor manipulation of answer sheets is involved, which avoids additional difficulties for those with reading, vision, or eye-hand coordination problems. Only large motions are needed, and these may be performed by either hand or both hands. Elbows have been used by some individuals who have difficulty controlling finger movements. By engaging the interest of those performing the tasks and by eliminating many factors thought to be detrimental to optimal performance in older individuals, a reasonably unbiased estimate of performance may be obtained.

The tasks are designed to assess the following cognitive skills: free and serial classification, multiple classification, spatial rotation, memory for spatial location, and cognitive flexibility. Although verbal abilities may be used in these problem solving processes, they are not the focus of the set of measures.

There is no overall model of intelligence assumed for these measures. That is, the tests were not designed to demonstrate or test for relationships among several abilities. They were intended, rather, to offer a means of testing a variety of abilities of interest to many researchers and practitioners with a coherent set of everyday materials.

TASK DESCRIPTION

Free and Serial Classification

The first card tasks, free and serial classification, are based on a Piagetian model and follow work reported by Denney (1974) and by Kogan (1973, 1974). The task is to group 32 playing cards of the four shapes (standard, round, large, and zigzag), all four suits, and two numerical values (queens and fives) into as many categories as one wishes. Such grouping continues until the individual reports being unable to think of any more ways to sort the cards.

The first sorting may be analyzed as a free classification task, using the number of groups into which cards are sorted and the number of attributes of the cards (size, shape, color, etc.) used as a basis for classification as performance measures. Because of low correlations with other measures, such as the subtests of the Primary Mental Abilities

(Thurstone & Thurstone 1949) and individual difference measures, this aspect of the tasks had not been fully exploited.

The number of attributes of the cards used as a basis for grouping on the consecutive sortings appears to correspond to Guilford's (1967) "spontaneous flexibility" criterion. The number of times the cards are sorted, regardless of the number of attributes used for regrouping purposes, corresponds to Guilford's "fluency" criterion.

Multiple Classification

For the multiple classification task, a matrix of three cards is presented along with five alternative cards, one of which completes the matrix. The problems are presented in an order determined by the number of attributes of the cards that must be considered for a correct response to be made. There are 12 problems. This task resembles the one used by Storck, Looft, and Hooper (1972), and draws from classification concepts of Piaget and Inhelder (1956).

Spatial Rotation

The spatial rotation task was designed to be useful in determining not only the level of spatial rotation skills but also the process being used to solve the problems and the sorts of errors that are committed (Coie, Costanzo, & Farnhill 1973; Piaget & Inhelder 1956). The task is to imagine rotating a fixed matrix of nine cards so that the side indicated by the test administrator is placed in front of the individual, then reproducing the mentally rotated matrix with a duplicate set of loose cards. Eight rotations are performed, four based on a matrix of nine standard cards and four based on a matrix of three standard, three round, and three zigzag cards. (See Figure 15.1). The first rotation for each of the two matrices is 180°, the second is 90°, the third is 270°, and the fourth is 160°. This last rotation, if successfully completed, results in a diagonally rotated matrix with one of the corners in front of the individual being tested.

Performance on this task may be assessed quantitatively by the number of correct rotations or qualitatively by the types of errors made (Coie, Costanzo, & Farnhill 1973). Previous work extending the Piagetian model of spatial development to the adult and elderly years (Bielby & Papalia 1975; Rubin, Attewell, Tierney, & Tumolo 1973; Rubin 1974) has shown a curvilinear relationship between age and performance on measures of spatial egocentrism. The very old and the very young have both performed at a lower level than young adults.

Memory

After years of domination of the use of verbal tasks in the assessment of memory, several investigators have become interested in nonverbal memory (e.g., Riege & Inman 1981). No memory task using playing cards as stimuli can be thought of as wholly nonverbal, since the cards may be verbally labeled in any of several ways. Nonetheless, a task requiring the respondent to remember not which cards had been seen but, rather, in which positions and in what relationship to each other several cards had been seen, may be presumed to have more spatial content than the typical verbal memory task.

The memory task is a variation of the spatial rotation task, in that the individual is again presented with a fixed matrix of nine cards, asked to memorize the arrangement, and then to reproduce the arrangement with a duplicate set of nine cards. In this task, however, once the individual indicates he or she has learned the arrangement, the matrix is removed before being reproduced. The scoring is such that points are gained for the number of aspects of the matrix that are used in the reconstruction of the arrangement. For instance, a matrix with a row of three cards having the same face value would earn a higher score than if the row contained cards of different values; if that same row were correctly placed with respect to the other rows, it would earn a higher score yet. There is a maximum score of 8 on this task.

Flexibility

The final task requires the respondent to learn a simple set of rules and to use those rules to determine whether the cards in each of 18 pairs are "the same suit," "the same number," or "different." In the first series the cards are all of the standard shape. In the second series the rules remain the same but all four card shapes are used. In the third or test series the cards are again of several shapes but the rules are changed. The respondent is now to indicate whether the cards in each pair are "the same shape," "the same number," or "different." The maximum score is 18. This task was included because loss of flexibility, or more frequently increase in rigidity, is frequently reported in the literature (Schaie 1987).

RELIABILITY

All the measures were administered twice to 24 men and 24 women ranging in age from 64 to 76 as part of a larger study (Krauss & Norris 1980; Krauss, Quayhagen, & Schaie 1980). The testing sessions were held two weeks apart, and each individual was tested by the same test administrator at both sessions. Test-retest reliabilities were determined by use of a repeated-measures analysis of variance followed by the use of the following formula (Schaie & Heiss 1964):

$$\frac{\text{I-MS error (repeated factor)}.}{\text{MS total}}$$

The resultant reliability is not confounded by the effects of the variables accounted for by the analysis of variance. If different levels of education account for a significant portion of the overall performance, there will be less error variance contributing to the test-retest factor and the additional factors with which it interacts. Furthermore, a significant interaction of those additional variables with the repeated factor would demonstrate that test-retest differences in scores across the tested population may be due to individual differences on variables included in this analysis. For instance, individuals with higher levels of education may have more reliable scores than individuals with lower education attainment.

The variables included in the analysis were age group (64–70, 71–76), education level (0–8 years, 9–12 years, some college or technical training, and college and above), and sex. Because of empty cells, only two of the three variables could be used in any single analysis. A summary of reliability coefficients and the variables interacting with test-retest performance may be found in Table 15.1. For comparison purpose, Pearson *r* estimates of reliability are also provided in Table 15.1

Task Reliability

Free and Serial Classification

The reliability analysis for free classification indicated that the second set of scores differed significantly from the first, with all groups using more aspects of the cards as variables by which to group the cards the second time they performed the tasks (F [1,40] = 4.09, *p* < .05). Gender was found to predict performance on this task only (F [1,40] = 5.01, *p* < .05), with men using more aspects of the cards for classification. However, the total number of separate groups produced did not differ among age groups, education levels, or between men and women. The reliability coefficient obtained in this analysis was .77.

Educational level significantly influenced the number of serial classifications produced (F [3,40] = 4.37, *p* < .01), but gender did not. There was a significant age-by-education interaction (F [3,40] = 2.88, *p* < .05), but these factors did not interact significantly with the test-retest factor. The reliability coefficient for the number of serial classifications produced was .72.

Table 15.1
Reliability Coefficients and Variables Affecting Reliability

Test	Pearson r Reliability Coefficient	ANOVA Method Reliability Coefficient	Significant Variables
Free Classification			
Number of groups	.65	.77	_____
Number of variables	.49	.59	Gender
Serial Classification	.59	.72	Education;
			Age by education
Multiple Classification	.70	.83	Test-retest;
			Test-retest by
			education
Spatial Rotation	.71	.76	Test-retest
Memory	.56	.73	Age by education
Flexibility	.57	.58	_____

Multiple Classification

The analysis of variance on the multiple classification reasoning scores showed a significant improvement in the number of correct responses on the second administration (F [1,40] = 5.67, $p < .05$). This retest factor also interacted with education level (F [3,40] = 3.40, $p < .05$). The reliability of this subtest was .83.

Spatial Rotation

An analysis of variance performed on the number of correctly rotated configurations demonstrated that performance increased significantly from the first trial to the second (F [1,40] = 4.37, $p < .05$). Reliability was .75.

Memory

Analysis of scores on memory for a spatial configuration yielded a significant age-by-education interaction (F [3.40] = 3.72, $p < .05$) and a reliability coefficient of .83.

Flexibility

The analysis of variance applied to the flexibility measure performance demonstrated no significant factors contributing to the variance. The reliability coefficent was .58.

Conclusions

Thorndike, as quoted in Cronbach (1949), listed several possible sources of differences in performance on a test, some of which could contribute to unreliability. These included general skills and techniques of taking tests, general ability to comprehend instruction, knowledge and skills specific to particular forms of test items, health, fatigue, and test wiseness. All of these factors have been suggested as reasons for poor test performance of older adults (Krauss & Schaie 1978). From the data reported here, we can see that these factors may be reflected differentially in men and women, in the more elderly of an older group and in the less well educated, especially in some skills.

The use of the Pearson *r* to determine test-retest reliability confounds all of these factors with the reliability of the test, since each of the factors considered contributes to the total variance and, perhaps, more to the first or second testing variance. Some individuals, by virtue of the level of education, for instance, are likely to show a greater improvement in performance on the second testing than other individuals with different education attainment.

It is evident that older adults may profit from practice on a specific test. The additional exposure to test materials may reduce anxiety, increase familiarity, increase "test wiseness," and lead to enhanced test scores. Finally, test-retest reliability, especially in older adults, may be more a characteristic of the population than of the tests in question.

RESEARCH FINDINGS

The card tasks have been used in several studies (Krauss & Schaie 1978; Krauss & Norris 1980; Stafford, Krauss, & Schaie 1981). The first study demonstrated that the tasks were acceptable to an elderly population and that education levels accounted for more of the variance in performance than did age for a group of community-dwelling California residents under the age of 71 (Krauss & Schaie 1978). A modification was introduced into one subtest (spatial rotation), simplifying the administration and scoring, before the set of tasks was administered to a second group, this one in New Jersey (Krauss & Schaie 1978). The third study was designed to test the reliability of the card tasks and was carried out as part of a larger study on spatial rotation (Krauss, Quayhagen, & Schaie 1980).

The card tasks were then administered to a group of participants in a major longitudinal study of intellectual changes with age (Schaie 1979). In this portion of that major study (Stafford, Krauss, & Schaie 1981) performance on the card task was compared with performance on the Primary Mental Abilities tests (Thurstone & Thurstone 1949). Fifty-eight individuals ranging in age from 30 to 79 were selected from those volunteering for additional testing. Seven men and 7 women from each 10-year age group between 40 and 89 and 3 women in their thirties were tested, with the exception that only 6 men in the 50–59 age group were tested. The mean number of years of education was 13.5 (SD = 3.0).

Free classification was not included as a variable in the analyses because the task itself is the first step of serial classification and because preliminary studies did not indicate that performance on the task was related to age or to education level. Since there were no numerical tasks in the card tasks, the PMA Number subtest was also omitted.

Task intercorrelations (Table 15.2) ranged from .03 to .78 (sign ignored), with the highest relationships demonstrated between the two sets of reasoning and spatial tests.

A factor analysis with promax oblique rotation (Ray 1982) was carried out to examine the relationship between the two sets of measures. Three factors were extracted. Correlations among the three factors were $-.11$, $-.14$, and $-.31$, indicating that they were almost orthogonal. The first factor accounts for a major portion of the variance in the PMA subtests; and while almost all of the card tasks load on the first factor, all three factors are necessary to account for the variance in those tests. These data are presented in Table 15.3.

The first factor may indicate a general reasoning skill that would account for performance on the verbal meaning, reasoning, and spatial relations tests of the PMA, and the multiple classification and spatial relation card tasks. The second factor is related strongly to spatial memory, the memory for the relationships among several objects. The third factor correlates highly with serial classification, a measure of productivity (Kogan 1973). This analysis indicates that the two sets of measures are related and may be considered to provide similar information on related, if not identical, abilities.

Observations made during all of the studies indicated that there was considerable interest in the test materials and the procedures. Most participants appeared eager to work with the materials, some asking where they could buy them for friends or relatives. Several participants spoke of the sessions with friends and suggested that they be part of the research. A few people were exhilarated by the testing session and spoke of going home to do some intellectually demanding task; a few

Table 15.2
Correlations Among Subtests of the Krauss Card Tasks of Adult Cognitive Abilities and Four Primary Mental Abilities Test (N = 58)

	Subtest								
	Multiple Classification	Spatial Rotation	Spatial Memory	Flexibility	Verbal Meaning	Reasoning	Spatial Relations	Word Fluency	Age
Krauss Card Tasks									
Serial Classification	.10	.27*	.22	.03	.13	.21	.09	.19	-.26*
Multiple Classification	—	.50***	.29*	-.32*	.69***	.77***	.57***	.37**	-.47***
Spatial Rotation		—	.16	-.36**	.54***	.59***	.40**	.36**	-.52***
Spatial Memory			—	-.18	.36**	.26	.29*	.12	-.41***
Flexibility (Errors)				—	-.39**	-.55***	-.40***	-.20	-.36**
Primary Mental Abilities									
Verbal Meaning					—	.78***	.62***	.54***	-.57***
Reasoning						—	.68***	.52***	-.67***
Spatial Relations							—	.39**	-.40**
Word Fluency								—	-.37**

***p < .001
**p < .01
*p < .05

Table 15.3
Correlations Between Factors and Subtests of the Krauss Card Tasks of Adult Cognitive Abilities and Four Subtests of the Primary Mental Abilities Test

	Factor		
Test	1	2	3
Krauss Card Tasks			
Serial Classification	.19	.19	.95
Multiple Classification	.77	.30	.09
Spatial Rotation	.63	.16	.28
Spatial Memory	.32	.96	.19
Flexibility (Errors)	-.50	-.17	-.03
Primary Mental Abilities			
Verbal Meaning	.86	.36	.13
Reasoning	.96	.26	.20
Spatial Relations	.72	.30	.07
Word Fluency	.54	.12	.20

asked to repeat the tasks to see if they could improve their performance. There was little evidence of a reluctance to begin or complete the tasks despite the considerable difficulty of some parts of the test.

CONCLUSIONS

The Krauss Card Tasks of Adult Cognitive Abilities have been found to be acceptable to a wide range of middle-aged and older adults. The reliability of the card tasks has been demonstrated to be within acceptable limits for these populations. Performance on the card tasks has been shown to be correlated to performance on traditional psychometric instruments and to be based on similar underlying dimensions. However, the card tasks also appear to provide information not available from the PMA, against which it has been compared.

The card tasks were intended to be used in situations where the individuals to be tested were unfamiliar with testing procedures or would have difficulty with those procedures because of vision or mobility limitations. They were also intended to be used in situations where test-taking motivation might be low. Although further testing with impaired groups should be carried out, the measures presented here represent an important step in the development of assessment measures that do not present unnecessary barriers to those whose abilities are being assessed.

REFERENCES

Bielby, D. D. V., & Papalia, D. E. (1975). Moral development and perceptual role-taking egocentrism: Their development and interrelationship across the life span. *International Journal of Aging and Human Development, 6,* 293–308.

Coie, J. D., Costanzo, P. R., & Farnhill, D. (1973). Specific transitions in the development of spatial perspective-taking ability. *Developmental Psychology, 9,* 167–177.

Cronbach, L. J. (1949). *Essentials of psychological testing.* New York: Harper & Brothers.

Denney, N. W. (1974). Classification abilities in the elderly. *Journal of Gerontology, 29,* 209–314.

Guilford, J. P. (1967). *The nature of human intelligence.* New York: McGraw-Hill.

Kogan, N. (1973). Creativity and cognitive style. In P. Baltes & K. W. Schaie (Eds.), *Lifespan developmental psychology: Personality and socialization* (pp. 146–178). New York: Academic Press.

Kogan, N. (1974). Categorizing and conceptualizing styles in younger and older adults. *Human Development, 17,* 218–230.

Krauss, I. K., & Norris, K. K. A. (1980, November). Individual difference contributions to test-retest reliability in tests of cognitive skills. Paper presented at the annual meetings of the Gerontological Society of America, San Diego.

Krauss, I. K., Quayhagen, M., & Schaie, K. W. (1980). Spatial rotation in the elderly: Performance factors. *Journal of Gerontology, 35,* 199–206.

Krauss, I. K., & Schaie, K. W. (1978, August). Five novel tasks for the assessment of cognitive abilities in the elderly. Paper presented at the triennial meetings of the International Gerontological Society, Tokyo.

Piaget, J., & Inhelder, B. (1956). *The child's conception of space.* London: Routledge & Kegan Paul.

Ray, A. A. (1982). *SAS users guide: Statistics.* Cary, N.C.: SAS Institute.

Riege, W. H., & Inman, U. (1981). Age differences in nonverbal memory tasks. *Journal of Gerontology, 36,* 51–58.

Rubin, K. H. (1974). The relationship between spatial and communicative egocentrism in children and young and old adults. *Journal of Genetic Psychology, 125,* 295–301.

Rubin, K. H. Attewell, P. W., Tierney, M. C., & Tumolo, P. (1973). Development of spatial egocentrism and conversation across the life span. *Developmental Psychology, 9,* 342.

Schaie, K. W. (1978). External validity in the assessment of intellectual development in adulthood. *Journal of Gerontology, 33,* 655–701.

Schaie, K. W. (1979). The Primary Mental Abilities in adulthood: An exploration in the development of psychometric intelligence. In P. B. Baltes & O. G. Brim, Jr. (Eds.), *Life-span development and behavior* (Vol. 2, pp. 67–115). New York: Academic Press.

Schaie, K. W. (1987). Rigidity. In G. L. Maddox (Ed.), *The encyclopedia of aging.* New York: Springer, p. 586.

Schaie, K. W., & Heiss, R. (1964). *Color and personality.* Bern, Switzerland: Hans Huber.

Sinnott, J. D. (1975). Everyday thinking and Piagetian operativity in adults. *Human Development, 18,* 430–443.

Stafford, J., Krauss, I. K., & Schaie, K. W. (1981). A modeling approach to the evaluation of card tasks assessing cognitive abilities in older adults. Paper presented at the annual meetings of the Gerontological Society of America, Toronto.

Storck, P. A., Looft, W. R., & Hooper, F. H. (1972). Interrelationships among Piagetian tasks and traditional measures of cognitive abilities. *Journal of Gerontology, 27,* 461–465.

Thurstone, L. L., & Thurstone, T. G. (1949). *SRA Primary Mental Abilities Test.* Chicago: Science Research Associates.

16

Everyday Problem Solving: Implications for Education

Diane Lee

Models of everyday problem solving classify problems along a continuum of structuredness, from well- to ill-structured. Well-structured problems are usefully thought of as "puzzles" resulting in a single correct answer reached through application of explicit rules within a closed system (Churchman 1971; Kitchener 1983). Ill-structured problems are known as "wicked" problems that are open to multiple solutions. The problem space is broad; parameters are unknown, in flux, and necessarily responsive to context. Teachers as decision makers cast into classroom activity are regularly confronted with wicked problems.

There has been a long-standing need for a model of adult reasoning that captures the complexities of problem solving involving life's wicked problems. Although many researchers have turned to Piaget's stages of cognitive development, his paradigm has proved inadequate. Formal operations "provides sufficient structure to describe scientific thought up to and including the operations of Newtonian physics. It is insufficient, however, for the description of Einsteinian physics," that is, to describe "relative judgments and to understand and deal with the complexities of interpersonal events" (Sinnott 1984, p. 302). Sinnott proposes a stage of postformal reasoning that does account for truth that is relativistic, the role of subjectivity within complex adult reasoning, and the presence of contradictory systems peculiar to wicked or ill-structured problems.

Professional teachers must make decisions and judgments about problems that engage life's ambiguities and uncertainties, and most often these decisions are made through subjective lenses. The purpose of this chapter is to explore teachers' everyday problem solving, using Sinnott's concept of relativistic operations.

THE CONCEPTUAL FRAMEWORK

Sinnott proposes the use of relativistic operations to provide one possible missing link between cognitive research and everyday problem solving, particularly of the ill-structured sort (Cavanaugh et al. 1985). Sinnott (1981, 1984) extends the work of Piaget and Riegel by describing a stage of cognitive development that is likely unique to adults, is sensitive to interpersonal relationships, and is able to accommodate contradictory systems. In fact, relativistic operations have been voiced most frequently in response to problems with a component involving interpersonal relational understanding (Sinnott 1984). This model may provide a new and useful way for us to think about teachers' everyday problem solving.

Teaching is necessarily intersubjective. For example, Scudder and Mickunas (1985) describe the life world of teachers and students in terms of a triadic dialogue. They note that a teacher-student relationship is constituted by being directed at the world, that is, a relationship concerned with the meaning of something. Akin to Buber's approach, they believe the relationship of teacher and student must be a personal one before educational dialogue can take place. In this interactive process, "attention goes beyond the rational and accounts for affective components as well" (Berman 1987, p. 203). It is within this conception of teaching and problem solving that the criteria for relativistic operations were employed.

THE METHODOLOGY

Three experienced or "expert" teachers, as they are often referred to (Berliner 1986), participated in this study. All of the practitioners were teaching at the university level in departments or colleges of education, and had taught at this level for a minimum of 12 years. All three were adult women.

These three teachers were a subsample from a larger ongoing study. They were selected for this study because they represented distinct problem situations: reflection-in-action, reflection-on-action, and the two combined (Schon 1983, 1987). One teacher reflects upon a problem that occurred during the class period and provides a glimpse of her thinking during teaching, what Schon calls reflection-in-action. A second teacher discusses her thinking about a problem after it had become a significant issue, although an immediate class situation brought it to the fore of her thinking. This represents Schon's concept of reflection-on-action.

The third participant shares her thinking as it related to the preplanned curriculum, as it related to her thinking during the class, and as she thought after teaching about the preplanned and enacted curriculum. This problem was not new to her. She had confronted the same problem many times in the past. Her thinking represents reflection-in-action and reflection-on-action, or what Carr & Kemmis (1986) call a self-reflective spiral, as it accounts for her thinking during preparation, during the act of teaching, and afterward.

The form of this inquiry was study of narrative and action through participant observation in classrooms and interviews with practitioners. Hence, multiple methods of data gathering were used. While observations were made, field notes were compiled and class proceedings were audiotaped. The audiotapes were transcribed, and the field notations were interjected as supplements to the transcripts.

Practitioners identified and discussed a problem of teaching during interviews. Specifically, the participants were asked, "Talk about the kind of problem solving you, as a practitioner, have been involved with: as you teach, the moment-to-moment decision making; before you teach, as you plan the curriculum; after class, as you reflect upon problems you experienced. What are some of the problems you've had to deal with?" To prevent external influences from structuring their responses, specific probes were not used; rather, statements such as "Tell me more about your thoughts in that situation" or "Just think aloud and say whatever comes to mind" were interjected as needed. In all but one instance entire interviews were audiotaped without interruption and then transcribed. The exception occurred during a classroom break when a teacher commented on decisions she made during the first half of the class. What was said during the break was reconstructed by the researcher immediately after the conversation. These thoughts were included with the interview, which was conducted immediately after the remaining class session. Thus, the data base for this inquiry is the personal knowledge of the practitioners as evidenced in their reflections on problems experienced in the day-to-day flow of their own lives.

By allowing teachers to articulate their own problems rather than imposing hypothetical situations, two purposes are served. First, it adds real, lived problems to the research on relativistic operations, which to date has focused more on contrived problems. Second, this procedure gives voice to teachers' "reflective grasping of what it is that renders this or that particular experience its special significance" (van Manen 1986, p. 4), and thus should carry a certain thoughtful awareness of the "details and seemingly trivial dimensions of our everyday educational lives" (p. ii). It was in this phenomenological spirit that relativistic operations were applied to teachers' reflections about their everyday problems.

DESCRIPTION OF THE MEASURE OF RELATIVISTIC OPERATIONS

Sinnott's criteria for relativistic operations can be invoked at multiple points and levels in problem solving activities. As such, their specification represents a sensitive tool for conceptualizing teachers' reflection-in-action and reflection-on-action. The eight criteria used in data analysis are summarized briefly below (Sinnott 1984, pp. 314–315).

Problem definition:	focusing on defining the problem in a certain, chosen way; a statement of the meaning and demands of the problem for the participant
Parameter setting:	naming key variables to be combined or made proportional in the problem other than those given in the demands of the problem
Metatheory shift:	producing abstract and practical (real-life) solutions as well as a shift between conflicting and abstract *a priories*
Process/product shift:	describing a process as one answer and an outcome as another, or describing two processes achieving the same outcome; stating that finding a solution is a never-ending process
Multiple causality:	stating that multiple causes exist for any event or that some solutions are more probable than others
Multiple solutions:	stating directly that there are many correct solutions intrinsic to a problem with several causes or that no problem has only one solution
Pragmatism:	choosing a best solution among several or choosing the best variant of a solution that has two processes; evaluating abstract and practical solutions separately for usefulness and difficulty
Paradox:	stating or questioning about perceived, inherently conflicting demands that are integral to the problem; being aware that a problem can be read in two or more conflicting ways

The working question was "Are criteria for determining the presence of relativistic operations useful for helping us think about teachers' everyday problem solving?" It was expected that these operations would provide a way of framing our understanding of how classroom teachers know, and come to know, their situation, and how this often tacit knowledge informs their action.

RESULTS

Findings are organized around the eight operations determining the presence of relativistic operations. Excerpts illustrating each operation are presented. Each practitioner's problem will be analyzed separately, using the framework of relativistic operations. Fictitious names were assigned.

Dr. Alcott

The problem that Dr. Alcott encountered in her language-arts methods class for student teachers was a conflict between the teachable moment and the preplanned curriculum. At the beginning of class, students were informed of the teacher's plans for their time together. Dr. Alcott had written references and key ideas on the board before class. She proceeded to lead a discussion about nonverbal communication and the impact of "silent language" on student behavior. As the discussion came to a close, students were asked to write examples of possible test questions based upon their discussion. The questions students created were written on the board. They ranged from the trivial to the unanswerable. Disliking what the students had written, the teacher experienced the immediate problem of "what ought to be taught?" Her thoughts were immediately converted to action as she switched from her preplanned activities and dealt with the problem of the moment.

Dr. Alcott articulated the problem definition this way:

I was caught in the midst of a typical problem of teachers. Do I continue with the planned curriculum or digress, knowing a detour will put us even further behind?

Conscious of the dilemma, she had to set limits to the problem that would direct her attention to the values at stake in the situation. She set the parameters as follows:

The situation is quite complicated for me because I am part of a team, and at the beginning of the semester we each agreed to cover certain material. It was obvious to me at that moment, however, that I needed to stop and attend to the art of questioning. Not only to help them to write "good" test questions but also to get them to think about themselves as teachers, about the kinds of questions they'll need to be asking themselves as practitioners.

Dr. Alcott realized she was caught between the immediate event and the context of the event. Metatheory shift was evident in the following passage:

I was really asking myself two things: "What should be taught in relation to the grand scheme of things?" and "What should be taught right now?" These are very different levels. I opted for teaching for the here and now.

The multiplicity of conflicting options posed a predicament for Dr. Alcott. She was forced to choose among multiple solutions:

There are several ways to view the problem. The thing for me to do, as far as my team is concerned, was to stick to the plans. The students would still be receiving important information. I could have lectured a bit longer, as I had planned, and referred to the importance of questioning briefly, but that would not reflect my true feelings about what was more important right then.

Multiple causes exist in relation to Dr. Alcott's dilemma; nevertheless one solution path was most probable:

There are many reasons for altering plans . . . how I feel, the silent messages I pick up from students. . . . Sometimes it's as simple as "I've run out of time and I have to choose what to include and what to omit." I changed midstream because I think teachers must know how to write good test questions . . . and because I want them to recognize the importance of good questions.

For Dr. Alcott the most efficient solution would likely have been to stay with the preplanned activities. She chose to digress, to entertain the problem as a pedagogical problem in the literal sense, as "leading the children," rather than as an instructional problem. "Had I thought about it in terms of the latter [an instructional problem], I would have proceeded with the preplanned activities." She chose what she considered the best solution among many. Pragmatism was represented in the following excerpt:

On the one hand, I could have remained with the agenda I set out at the beginning of class. The students, the undergraduates, are usually more comfortable when I stick to my plans. But, on the other hand, to dismiss the topic of questioning at that time would have relayed the implicit message that questioning was not important or at least not as important [as what had been scheduled].

Implementation was built into Dr. Alcott's problem. She did not detach thinking from doing; rather, her decision was immediately converted to action. Her deliberations exhibited all but two of the operations defined by Sinnott: process/product shift and paradox. This suggests a "rigor" and "relevance" underlying her "knowing-in-action" (Schon 1983, pp. 42, 49). Her thinking was not haphazard or irrelevant but, rather, was a thoughtful rendering of her decision making.

Dr. Baker

Dr. Baker is also involved with teacher preparation. Her responsibilities include placing student teachers in the schools and teaching methods courses. Every time she conceptualizes her methods course, she revisits the dilemma of how to integrate demands from the state, the field sites, and content objectives with her own values and beliefs. Her deliberations on this recurrent problem and resulting curricular decisions represent reflection-on-action.

Dr. Baker posed her problem this way:

Each semester I face anew the problem of determining what are reasonable content objectives for a three-credit course. . . . One of the hard parts in early childhood education right now is that there's not a really good fit between what is happening in a great many classrooms and the stuff we're talking about in class [at the university].

For determining appropriate content for a three-credit course in teacher preparation, Dr. Baker defined the parameters as follows:

Weighing . . . being sure that the content fits where the students are. Being sure that it's meaningful to them, to me. Being sure that it's something they won't simply have to learn in a rote way, that it's something they can use in a relevant context.

An example of metatheory shift exists in the following remarks:

Some of it is at a superficial level. Some of it is what the state says we've got to teach in order to have our students able to say that they're finishing an approved program. Some of it has got to be found someplace in the material, that is, it must be very practical. Translating texts and lectures into reality becomes a problem. Sometimes, to the extent possible, I try to resolve it not in theory but in favor of something that's not absolute, that's in some way tied to their experience. That means I do a lot of informal teaching.

Dr. Baker spoke of her problem as an ongoing process and highlighted the repetitive nature of its occurrence. Process/product shift was exhibited in the following passage:

Every semester I ask myself the same question, "What should I teach in this three-credit course?" Actually, I consider this throughout the course. I'm always asking, "Is this best?" . . . I don't like telling students the answers. I try to temper that with real-life examples so that it will be meaningful and not just feed them platitudes. . . . It's very easy to give lip service to the words and phrases without giving some real gut-level experiences as to what that means.

Dr. Baker realized that there were multiple solutions to the problem she posed. Her remarks highlight the importance of subjective knowledge in her decision making:

It isn't easy to decide. There are no real answers. . . . There are as many answers as there are students. . . . But you don't give up even though you sometimes get discouraged. If there's . . . any hope that you'll find a workable answer, you keep working on it.

In her search for appropriate content, Dr. Baker mentioned multiple causes underlying her dilemma and the factors that made some solutions more probable than others. She was caught between the state's dictates and the needs of her students:

There . . . are compromising situations because of our relation with the State Department of Education and the public schools that we can't change, up to a point. We can [say] and have said that we won't place our students in those classrooms. . . . One decision I've made is to go ahead and be open with my students. If they see me as either a wide-eyed idealist or as just another example of what teaching is all about, it's ok. We can [say] and have . . . occasionally said, "I know that state expects us to teach this . . . I'm going to put it on my course outline but I'm going to give it short shrift." Some of the things they want us to emphasize I think can be done in other ways. There are other ways to get at it, but they are hard to convey to the state. . . . I need to meet the student's needs. . . .

She was able to identify a best solution among several possibilities. Pragmatism was expressed as follows:

I guess there are really two questions, "What are reasonable objectives for a three-credit course?" and "What do I actually teach?" I teach what the state says I have to teach . . . and I teach what I believe I must teach . . . which is usually tied to experiences the students have.

Dr. Baker's problem centered on her desire to teach and model what she believed her students needed to know, and her obligation to teach what was prescribed by the state or what is practiced by cooperating teachers. Often she was confronted with incompatible demands, and the resulting tension led her to reflect on her previous actions. She wove a pattern of complex reasoning, and the warp and woof of her fabric included both intrasubjective and intersubjective knowledge. The recognition of relativism underlies her reflections on this problem situation. Dr. Baker exhibited all of the operations identified by Sinnott except paradox.

Dr. Catlin

Dr. Catlin is a professor of curriculum. Observations were made during a graduate course on curriculum theory. Master's and doctoral students were enrolled in the course, most of them experienced teachers preparing for administrative positions within school systems. The focus of Dr. Catlin's problem centered on a recurrent theme, "What ought to be taught?"

Dr. Catlin articulated her problem during class as the teacher and students engaged in dialogue about the topic the professor had planned. Questions unfolded during the dialogue, defining the problem:

What are the musts? What must we include in terms of public knowledge? What is the substance of codified knowledge? . . . This gets us into the what and how to teach. . . . I guess I would follow that question with another one. What opportunities exist for persons to gain knowledge throughout a lifetime?

In reference to "What are the musts?" Dr. Catlin defined parameters through questions. A sampling of those questions follows:

What is the cultural system? Does one system legitimate some kinds of knowledge and not others? Then whose system is legitimated? . . . How do we get at inner, phenomenological knowledge? We need to pose questions that will help individuals surface information they already know. . . . What curriculum design is appropriate for your school? What knowledge is central to the focus established there? What knowledge generated by the community becomes part of the curriculum without losing the focus? . . . Knowledge for whom? Knowledge for what purposes? . . . What obstacles may block a student's gaining a body of knowledge. . . . personally, systemically, or socially?

Dr. Catlin suggested abstract as well as practical solutions as she exhibited metatheory shift. She moved from the theoretical context to the life world of classrooms as she tackled the problem of "matteredness." Dr. Catlin began by invoking some of the prominent voices on this topic:

Let's look at what some of the curriculum writers say. . . . Barth says students make sense by talking. . . . Schwab has talked a lot about deliberation. . . . I think that the point I'm trying to make is that when you go back to most of these curriculum writers, the whole issue of dialogue, interaction, communication is very, very critical. But frequently, when it comes to the actual design problem, in schools we do not allow for the kind of dialogue and interaction that you hear of. . . . This keeps alerting us to the fact that what the theorists are saying and what is in reality aren't very much together. . . . What have you done in your schools? What factors entered into your deliberations? . . . I keep going back to the dialogic process. . . . I would suggest we take a look at what we're doing in classrooms. . . .

Dr. Catlin stated clearly that deciding what ought to be taught was indeed a problem for which there was no final answer. In confronting the problem she posed, she sought a dynamic solution. Process/product shift is observed in the following utterances:

To ask "What are you going to do?". . . . is closed. To ask "What ought to be taught for tomorrow?" is open. . . . There is a common body of knowledge, but there is no simple answer. If we think of [educational] opportunities over a lifetime, then we must continually ask the question [What are the musts?] over and over again . . . [outcomes included:] . . . to make options open . . . giving young people a lot of time to talk. . . .

Dr. Catlin recognized that several solutions were possible. The result is a "constructive turmoil" that fosters a search for possibilities (Lather 1986, p. 259).

Our thrust is to make options open. . . . So one of the options in the curriculum, when you're talking about substance in the curriculum, is giving young people a lot of time to talk . . . so that the faculty member can get at the perceptions of what the student is really learning, thinking, feeling, and can act accordingly. . . . But you get all these different ways that we can implement . . . we have not trained teachers frequently to be tuned in to students and to deal with the dialogic process. . . . And this is something I think we should do in teacher preparation. . . . You need to get into the culture of the child. . . . I can't give you one answer. I'll have to leave that unanswered. . . . I'm happy to work it through with you.

Dr. Catlin listed several reasons for examining the "musts" in curriculum development, realizing that there are several underlying causes making this problematic:

I think there are all kinds of reasons . . . we have not looked at . . . we have a disjuncture with our beliefs and our practices. . . . For example, folks on the firing lines have these tests that are imposed [from without]. And you have to give these test items whether or not you want to. . . . The test taking is one part of the curriculum. Personally, I see it as being a reality of life that we are being forced into these situations, and therefore one of the dilemmas is how do you put that part into the curriculum which has to do with test taking so that your youngsters can succeed in other kinds of situations without making that [tests] the total curriculum.

One of Dr. Catlin's students had commented that the easiest way to solve the problem related to future directions curriculum development might take is to let the "authorities" decide. "It's a great relief to me to be told by someone else what to do and not have to make that decision. . . . " At this point Dr. Catlin put her lecture notes aside and responded by suggesting alternative solutions while underscoring the most tenable. Thus pragmatism is represented by the following:

Many teachers today, when given prepackaged curricula, teach what is prescribed. . . . A more difficult way is to involve students, colleagues, ethicists, clergy, parents, so-called authorities, etc. . . . You can say we're going to teach to the test, which we see in many situations. Or we're going to develop a curriculum which has integrity to us. I think we can spend a little time and teach for the tests, and then get on with what really matters.

Dr. Catlin responded to her student's framing of the problem and decided at that moment to abandon her prepared text. During an observation the following semester, Dr. Catlin was discussing the same topic with another class. This time she included a discussion about the place of prepackaged curricula and standardized testing in her prepared remarks. As described by Carr & Kemmis (1986, p. 186), Dr. Catlin's situation reflects the "tension between retrospective explanation or understanding and prospective action" as she " 'looks back' to the previous moment for its justification, and 'looks forward' to the next moment for its realization." Dr. Catlin exhibited all of the operations except paradox.

None of these practitioners articulated all eight operations. Six of the operations were articulated by all three of the practitioners, and seven operations were articulated by two of them. This is consistent with Sinnott's previous findings (1984).

DISCUSSION

Sinnott's model of relativistic operations provided a useful framework for conceptualizing teachers' everyday problem solving. In the process of reflection these teachers displayed arts of inquiry akin to the ill-structured nature of the problems they confronted in their everyday practice. Their thinking did not fit into the analytic schemata of formal logic and mathematics; rather, their thinking could be described as divergent (Schon 1983). The teachers experienced their practical problems as ambiguous, convoluted, and spiraling, not as linear, sequential, or governed by specific procedures (Harris 1986). Theirs were not instrumental problems presented with "givens," fixed parameters, and single solutions. Indeed, the collective voices of these practitioners suggest a certain tension between knowledge as "the given" and the knowledge as personally constructed.

Movement from theory to practice, and from knowledge as given to knowledge as problematical, identifies contradictions between the objectivist conception of knowledge, that is, knowledge as "truth out there" and the subjectivist view of knowledge as that which is constructed from what is experienced through its relationship with the knower (Ginsburg 1986, p. 287; Polanyi 1958). Knowledge based upon "public principles that stand as impersonal standards" can be studied using "accumulated traditions" carrying a value-free neutrality (Berlak & Berlak 1981, p. 144). As such, knowledge is bounded by values external to the knower; and the stronger the boundaries, the more likely it is that knowledge will be viewed as "truth out there" and the less likely it is that students' and teachers' personal knowledge will fit the model of technical rationality.

The positivist epistemology of practice, however, fails to provide a relevant model for use in situations of uncertainty, instability, and uniqueness, and for those dimensions of everyday practice that are necessarily subjective. Sinnott's conceptualization of postformal reasoning adopts a view of knowledge that is dialectical, that allows for, yet goes beyond, "truth out there." Thus her framework is applicable to the study of the subjective understandings of teachers that inform their actions. These practitioners are able to extend their understandings by putting themselves as well as their experiences in question. This is intimately connected to Heidegger's notion of thinking, in which he maintains that thinking is putting oneself in the question (Heidegger 1968). By questioning this way, and hence reflecting-in-action and reflecting-on-action, these practitioners were participating in the informed, committed action of praxis (Carr & Kemmis 1986). Questioning values and commitments that underlie action is at the heart of the praxis.

The object to which these three voices were directed was the problem "What ought to be taught?" They did not pose this question in a way that limited their vision. Rather, as witnesses to possibility, these practitioners perceived multiple perspectives and sought tenable solutions, not final solutions. By posing problems in relative rather than absolute terms, their search was for "best fits" (Murphy & Gilligan 1980), for that student or that student group, that teacher, that subject matter, and that milieu (the four commonplaces of education as defined by Schwab, in Schubert 1986). By envisioning multiple solutions, each practitioner was able to reflect about what exists while remaining open to what could be. Berman (1987) writes that persons

.... having free will yet live in contexts that are simultaneously freeing and binding . . . [they] bring their total selves to the decision making process, they move back and forth between sustaining reflection and thoughtful action. They are aware of the need to deal with alternatives and their consequences, realizing that they never can have all the information available to make the "perfect" decision. (p. 203)

For these practitioners, everyday problem solving was a process, albeit with outcomes, but nevertheless a process to be structured and restructured, considered and reconsidered, preserved and altered. To be able to reflect, to see problem solving as a process that continues even after some solution has been enacted, is to be free. In this sense freedom is intentionally and reflectively chosen, and is pursued within the lived situation (Greene 1986). Thus oriented to freedom, these practitioners were open to possibilties for themselves, their students, and their profession.

Each practitioner expressed concern for persons and for her profession while attending to the complexities inherent in the problem she articulated. As noted by Greene (1986, p. 74), "To be concerned, after all, is to be conscious of a web of possibilities; to experience passion is to be invested in what might or might not be." These practitioners were so invested. Indeed, their thoughtful reflecting had the dialectic effect of making each more attuned to the meaning of her situation for herself and for those with whom she related. This personal engagement in their pedagogical worlds led not to final, single solutions derived from simple causes but, rather, to continued questioning, tenable solutions continually sought in the face of life's complexities. In displaying relativistic operations, these practitioners recognized multiple interpretive frameworks for experience, were able to compare multiple intellectual frames, and believed in the role of the subject in constructing knowledge and in determining truths (Benack 1984).

SUMMARY AND CONCLUSIONS

The purpose of this study was to examine teachers' everyday problem solving, using Sinnott's eight criteria for determining the presence of relativistic operations. Data support the applicability of this framework for the study of teachers' problem solving. Greatest utility was found in problem definition, the recognition of multiple interpretive frameworks, and the identification of the crucial role of self-reference as a regulatory agent in teachers' reasoning.

Results recall John Dewey's view (1934) that teachers must act mindfully, that is, in an active mode of paying heed, of caring, of futuring. Herein lies the relevance of the dialectic. Van Manen (1986) describes this dialectic, stating that on the one hand teachers must know and make decisions for students with caring; thus they must be fully engaged, interacting with maximum subjectivity. On the other hand, teachers must be sensitive to students' total field of limits and possibilities, and this indicates the need for reserve and distancing. Recognition of the inseparability of subject and object enabled these teachers to make relative judgments. Moreover, teachers were able to find a great diversity of meanings, meanings against which new learning experiences were projected and new questions posed. Within this process, problems were structured and restructured as teachers rejected the idea of fixed values, fixed goals, fixed knowledge, fixed truths. Teachers defined problems and asked "generative questions of themselves, their life's work, and of the phenomena that surround them" (Arlin 1984). For these teachers, education was infused with the reality of possibilities and ways of being. Through "reflective dialectic," the constant measurement of action against pedagogy, and "pedagogic praxis," action full of thought and thought full of action (van Manen 1986), these practitioners exhibited postformal reasoning displayed through relativistic operations.

REFERENCES

Arlin, P. K. (1984). Adolescent and adult thought: A structural interpretation. In M. L. Commons, F. A. Richards, & C. Armon (Eds.), *Beyond formal operations: Late adolescent and adult cognitive development* (pp. 258–271). New York: Praeger.

Benack, S. (1984). Postformal epistemologies and the growth of empathy. In M. L. Commons, F. A. Richards, & C. Armon (Eds.), *Beyond formal operations: Late adolescent and adult cognitive development*. New York: Praeger.

Berlak, A., & Berlak, H. (1981). *Dilemmas of schooling: Teaching and social change*. New York: Methuen.

Berliner, D. C. (1986). In pursuit of the expert pedagogue. *Educational Researcher*, 15(7), 5–13.

Berman, L. M. (1987). The teacher as decision maker. In F. S. Bolin and J. M. Falk (Eds.), *Teacher renewal: Professional issues, personal choices*. New York: Teachers College Press.

Carr, W., & Kemmis, S. (1986). *Becoming critical: Education, knowledge, and action research*. Philadelphia: Falmer Press.

Cavanaugh, J. C., Kramer, D. A., Sinnott, J. D., Camp, C. J., & Markley, R. P. (1985). On missing links and such: Interfaces between cognitive research and everyday problem-solving. *Human Development*, 28, 146–168.

Churchman, C. W. (1971). *The design of inquiring systems: Basic concepts of systems and organization*. New York: Basic Books.

Dewey, J. (1934). *Art as experience*. New York: Minton, Balch & Co.

Ginsburg, M. B. (1986). Reproduction, contradictions, and conceptions of curriculum in preservice teacher education. *Curriculum Inquiry*, 16(3), 283–309.

Greene, M. (1986). Perspectives and imperatives: Reflection and passion in teaching. *Journal of Curriculum and Supervision*, 2(1), 68–81.

Harris, I. B. (1986). Communicating the character of "deliberation." *Journal of Curriculum Studies*, 18(2), 115–132.

Heidegger, M. (1968). *What is called thinking?* New York: Harper & Row.

Kitchener, K. S. (1983). Cognition, metacognition, and epistemic cognition: A three-level model of cognitive processing. *Human Development, 26,* 222–232.

Lather, P. (1986). Research as praxis. *Harvard Educational Review, 56*(3), 257–277.

Murphy, J. M., & Gilligan, C. (1980). Moral development in late adolescence and adulthood: A critique and reconstruction of Kohlberg's theory. *Human Development, 23,* 77–104.

Polanyi, M. (1958). *Personal knowledge.* Chicago: University of Chicago Press.

Schon, D. A. (1983). *The reflective practitioner: How professionals think in action.* New York: Basic Books.

Schon, D. A. (1987). *Educating the reflective practitioner.* San Francisco: Jossey-Bass.

Schubert, W. H. (1986). *Curriculum: Perspective, paradigm, and possibility.* New York: Macmillan.

Scudder, J., & Mickunas, A. (1985). *Meaning, dialogue, and enculturation: Phenomenological philosophy of education.* Washington, D.C.: Center for Advanced Research in Phenomenology & University Press of America.

Sinnott, J. D. (1981). The theory of relativity: A metatheory for development? *Human Development, 24,* 293–311.

Sinnott, J. D. (1984). Postformal reasoning: The relativistic stage. In M. L. Commons, F. A. Richards, & C. Armon (Eds.), *Beyond formal operations: Late adolescent and adult cognitive development* (pp. 298–325). New York: Praeger.

van Manen, M. (1986). *The tone of teaching.* Portsmouth, N.H.: Heinemann Educational Books.

Wood, P. K. (1983). Inquiring systems and problem structure: Implications for cognitive development. *Human Development, 26,* 249–265.

17

A Self-Evaluation Framework for Understanding Everyday Memory Aging

John C. Cavanaugh
Kelly R. Morton
Connie S. Tilse

We would like to begin our chapter with a real-life anecdote. Imagine that you make your weekly pilgrimage to the supermarket, where you hand over a week's pay (or so it seems). Before leaving home, you are faced with a problem—figure out what items are needed and remember them. Upon arrival at the store, you push the cart around the maze of aisles and displays (which evokes a degree of empathy for those poor rats in learning experiments), and collect an assortment of goodies and necessities. After surviving the checkout line, loading the bags into the car, and the drive back home, you lug the weekly haul into the house. Just about the time you unpack the last sack, it hits—no bread.

This scenario is undoubtedly familiar to everyone—the problem of needing to remember but failing to do so is a universal human experience. But contained in this commonplace event are elements of a complex, dynamic, interactive process that involves making judgments about our abilities. In short, whenever we are faced with a situation involving memory, we evaluate ourselves as rememberers.

This chapter focuses on problems that involve memory. In particular, it is about the need for explicitly considering self-evaluations in memory theory, when self-evaluations about memory are made, and what implications memory self-evaluations have for performance. Along the way, we will briefly review some key aspects of self-efficacy attribution theory as well as the relationship between metamemory and performance. (We will argue that metamemorial knowledge is a factor that influences the self-evaluation process.) We will present a model of how we think self-evaluation processes fit into memory processing. Finally, we will speculate on the kinds of intervention and remediation problems that, based on our ideas, would be most efficacious.

First, let us return to our scenario in order to whet our appetites. Where would memory self-evaluations occur in grocery shopping? One place would be in the process of deciding how to go about remembering all of the items we need. Based on how good we think our memory is, we would most likely choose the strategy that represents the best trade-off between effort and effectiveness. We would also be able to explain why we forgot the bread. But what kinds of things influence these self-evaluations? Would we be likely to make different self-evaluations as a function of age? Does it matter what the outcomes of self-evaluations are? The answers to these (and other) questions must wait until we have provided the necessary background.

SELF-EVALUATIONS: A BRIEF PRIMER

Research and theory on self-evaluations constitute one of the largest literatures in social cognitive psychology. Consequently, we will not provide a comprehensive review of the field; rather, we will summarize the main ideas that we have found useful in thinking about the role of self-evlautions in memory. First, we will make the tie between meta-memory and self-evaluations by providing some insights into our own past. Second, previous work in social cognition has established that perceived control and certain types of self-evaluations have a significant effect on cognitive performance as well as on general well-being (e.g., Rodin 1980; Lachman & Jelalian 1984). This research has been based on several different theories; however, we have chosen to outline the con-tributions of two theorists, Bandura and Weiner, because their ideas have guided us the most.

From Metamemory to Self-Evaluation

Our interest in the role of self-evaluations in memory has its roots in our interest in metamemory. Metamemory can be defined as knowledge about one's own memory system and how it works (Cavanaugh & Perl-mutter 1982). The concept of metamemory has always had an evaluative component to it. What one knows about one's memory is certainly col-ored by one's evaluation of underlying ability, which in turn is influ-enced by how one judges ones' own performance. For example, a person thinks that he or she is terrible at remembering names, and always has been, and thus sees no point in trying. This kind of knowledge, espe-cially when we begin to cast it in terms of knowing how memory ability may have changed over the years and what reasons one has for this change, brings the concept of metamemory fairly close to the notion of self-evaluation. As we will see, self-evaluations involve examining a situation we find ourselves in and making several decisions about it, from how well we think we will do to why we did what we did. We think that memory self-evaluations are part of what is assessed in comprehensive metamemory measures.

Other researchers think so, too. Dixon and Hultsch (1983) have led the way empirically. They developed the Metamemory in Adulthood inventory, which consists of eight dimensions: Strategy (knowledge of memory strategies), Task (knowledge of memory processes), Capacity (predicted performancer ability), Change (perception of variability of memory abilities over time), Activity (degree to which one engages in activities that support cognitive performance), Anxiety (knowledge of the influence of emotions on memory), Achievement (perceived importance of having a good memory), and Locus (perceived personal control over memory ability). Hertzog (personal communication), using additional factor-analytic procedures, has identified distinct memory self-efficacy and memory knowledge dimensions. Dixon and Hultsch (1983) documented reliable age differences on the Locus subscale, indicating that younger adults were more internally oriented than were older people, who saw memory change as inevitable and uncontrollable. (They also found age differences on the Task, Capacity, and Change subscales). Moreover, for older adults, one of the best predictors of prose recall performance was Locus (Dixon & Hultsch 1983).

We think that, especially given the work by Dixon and Hultsch and by Hertzog, the time has come to make the ties among metamemory, self-evaluation, and memory processes explicit. To facilitate this integration, we will briefly review some of the central elements of self-efficacy theory and attribution theory that we have found most useful. Following this, we will present a framework that makes these connections clear.

Bandura's Self-Efficacy Theory

Bandura (1977) described self-efficacy as a cognitive evaluation of the fit between one's abilities and the task requirements in order to achieve a desired outcome. People see outcomes as contingent upon the adequacy of their performance. Thus, they rely on self-judged efficacy in deciding which activities to pursue and the amount of effort that will be expended (Bandura 1981, 1984).

Individuals appear to integrate task information concerning their capabilities and to regulate their behaviors and efforts accordingly. Bandura (1977, 1984) listed four major sources of efficacy information. The most influencial and generalizable source is that based on one's own performance accomplishments. Interpretation of performance accomplishments and the subsequent ascription of outcomes to effort or to ability seem to have different effects on self-efficacy. For example, linking failure to one's ability will lower self-efficacy, whereas linking failure to effort will not have such negative effects. The second most influential source of information is vicarious experience. Observing others performing activities successfully may give the viewer the expectation that he or she can also perform the activity. The third source of efficacy information, verbal persuasion, arises from an attempt to convince people verbally that they are capable of performing in ways they were incapable of in the past. The final source of efficacy information is emotional arousal. Circumstances that facilitate high physiological and emotional arousal may be viewed as stressful and lead to avoidance of these circumstances in the future.

Bandura (1978) summarized the self-regulation process as a continuous reciprocal interaction among behavior, cognition, and environmental influences. He also postulated a developmental progression in the awareness of one's behaviors (Bandura 1981). Individuals only gradually discover that they can control events, which leads them to become more attentive to their behaviors. A responsive environment enhances attentiveness and promotes positive self-efficacy. Reappraisals of self-efficacy are predicted to occur with advancing age in adulthood because of the many novel circumstances encountered as a result of environmental change. The internalization of negative stereotypes of aging, along with institutionalization (and its concomitant less responsive environment), may decrease self-efficacy considerably. For example, apparent cognitive deficits may be due to unfamiliar tasks rather than a result of inevitable (biologically based) changes. Attributing cognitive failures to declining abilities may lead to a loss of interest in cognitive activities, and subsequently to a loss of skill, since cognitive tasks become avoided or are viewed as too stressful. Older adults may also begin to dwell on their perceived inability, which makes them even more aware of cognitive failures (Bandura 1984). This line of thinking has been applied directly to memory aging by Cavanaugh (in press), who argues that a key to understanding memory aging lies in an increasing awareness of memory processing (via memory monitoring), which points out all too well the fallibility of the memory system.

Weiner's Attribution Theory

Weiner's (1983, 1985a) attribution theory specifies the types of causal analyses individuals employ when they try to explain or understand outcomes. Weiner believes that causal attributions are attempts to adapt to a situation by increasing understanding of oneself and one's environment. The manner in which people explain events affects self-esteem;

consequently, the kinds of attributions people make are important to know.

Weiner (1983) enumerated three dimensions along which people make causal judgments in their attempt to explain outcomes: locus of causality, stability, and controllability. These dimensions have both theoretical and empirical support (Weiner 1985a). Although the emphasis given a particular dimension may vary over time and situations, the underlying tripartite structure remains constant (Weiner 1985a).

The locus-of-causality dimension is similar to the internal-external division made originally by Rotter (1966) and developed by others (e.g., Levenson 1981). Locus of causality defines who or what force is perceived as responsible for outcomes. Internal attribution means that the individual himself or herself is believed to be responsible. External attributions include forces such as chance, fate, and powerful others. Locus-of-causality attributions are not necessarily stable over time; an individual may feel personally responsible for an outcome at one point in time in one set of circumstances, but may feel that luck was responsible at another time.

The stability dimension was added by Weiner to describe the degree of variability that is perceived in whatever cause is responsible for the outcome. Stability attributions are especially important in understanding a person's expectancy of success and for changes in expectancies over time. For example, if an older adult thinks that poor memory performance is caused by an inevitable erosion of underlying mental ability (neurophysiological decline), it is likely that this cause will be perceived as stable over time (i.e., it is unlikely that physiological decline is a transient phenomenon). This attribution of stability makes the person think that nothing can be done to remediate this process, so that the performance decrement must be accepted, which in turn may lead to feelings of helplessness and lowered self-esteem. However, if forgetting is attributed to insufficient effort, the situation for this older adult would be different. Effort level clearly varies from one memory situation to another, making this attribution low on the stability dimension. Effort, like physiological decline, is an internal process; however, an attribution to effort may result in feeling that remediation is possible, leaving self-esteem basically intact.

Weiner's controllability dimension is a unique addition to causality explanations. Controllability is defined as the degree to which the outcome can be influenced by either the self or another. If the person believes that someone can change the outcome, then the outcome is thought to be controllable. For example, if a person thinks that learning could improve performance, then the performance would be said to be controllable. To continue the earlier example of older adults, attributing the cause of memory problems to inevitable physiological decline would make memory problems uncontrollable, whereas an effort attribution would make the same problems controllable. Attributing problems to uncontrollable causes would appear to have potentially serious negative effects on self-esteem.

Weiner (1985b) has made explicit connections between specific combinations of attributions along the three dimensions and particular emotions. Specifically, Weiner assumes that the causal analysis process motivates behavior by creating an interaction between outcome expectancies and affective reactions. One well-established link is that between the locus-of-causality dimension and pride and self-esteem; outcomes thought due to internal causes are more likely to influence feelings about the self. Attributing negative outcomes to stable causes has been shown to be related to feelings of hopelessness, since the person believes that the future will not be different from the past.

Understanding the various combinations of causal attributions helps us interpret why people behave as they do. In addition, placing Weiner's ideas in a developmental framework helps sensitize us to the possibility that attributional patterns may change with age, in addition to varying across situations. For example, there is evidence that as adults grow older, they become increasingly aware of themselves as interpreters of events (Blanchard-Fields 1986), which may indicate that they are becoming more aware of the attributional process itself through their own monitoring of their thinking process. This research also shows that adults become increasingly capable of coordinating others' viewpoints and environmental contingencies with their own beliefs. As will be discussed later, this evidence is consistent with the hypothesized increase in awareness of cognitive monitoring processes with age (Cavanaugh in press).

Linking Self-Evaluations and Memory

The ideas expressed by Bandura and by Weiner are clearly applicable in many situations. For our purposes, we wish to focus on memory, and how self-evaluations fit with metamemory and memory processing. We would like to make three points in this regard. First, it is certainly the case that people make self-evaluations about memory performance; anecdotal examples range from students attributing memory failures on exams to powerful others (professors) who ask ridiculously picky questions to older adults attributing memory successes to their ingenious use of mnemonics.

Our belief that self-evaluations are a key component in memory also has an empirical basis. Lachman and Jelalian (1984) provided support for the notion that older adults may be more inclined to attribute their performance to internal factors. When asked to make self-evaluations about performance on two memory measures, older adults most often made internal stable attributions to ability, whereas younger adults most often made external stable attributions to task difficulty.

Expectations and beliefs may also be important for understanding the relationship between memory performance and memory complaints. In the Zarit, Cole, and Guider (1981) study, both memory training groups and discussion groups believed that participation would result in improved memory; both groups showed a decrease in complaints about memory. Research that documented higher levels of memory complaints among the older participants also documented beliefs in and expectations of continued memory decline with age (e.g., Niederehe, Nielsen-Collins, Volpendesta, & Woods 1981; Perlmutter 1978). Dixon and Hultsch (1983) found that older adults were more likely to believe in age-related memory decline than were their younger counterparts. And Williams, Denney, and Schadler (1983) found that almost all of the older adults they interviewed believed in memory decline with age. Interestingly, most interviewees thought memory decline occurs because one expects it to, and over half thought that some older adults use age as an excuse, since those individuals' memory abilities were really not as bad as they claimed!

The second point we wish to make is that it is equally clear that if self-evaluations about memory are made, they are based on some underlying knowledge base. We argue that the knowledge base that feeds self-evaluation is influenced by the results of previous self-evaluations. This knowledge base is metamemory.

The third point is that to describe the relationships among self-evaluations, metamemory, and memory processing adequately, that incorporates Bandura's and Weiner's ideas a working theoretical framework is needed. We will present a framework representing what we believe to be the central role that self-evaluations play in memory.

SELF-EVALUATIONS IN MEMORY PROCESSING: A MODEL

Now that we have briefly reviewed the key concepts in self-efficacy theory, attribution theory, and metamemory, we turn to self-evaluations as an intimate part of our everyday memory lives. The framework within which we operate is predicated on the assumption that every memory experience involves a self-evaluation of some sort. Furthermore, these self-evaluations are typically unconscious, but are available for introspection and, most important, modification. We want to emphasize that although many of the underlying elements of our ideas are not new (we will point these out along the way), the overall framework is a fresh approach.

Our framework, presented in Figure 17.1, was first described in Cavanaugh (in press). In this earlier work, the emphasis was on introducing the notion that awareness of memory processing is a key factor in understanding memory aging. Consequently, there was little in the way of explication of the various components of the model or specific recommendations concerning interventions. In the following sections, we will fill these gaps.

General Overview

In order to provide an overall feel for our model, we introduce it by providing a general overview. Its components represent a combination of internal and external factors that together influence personal decisions about memory ability. These personal decisions in turn influence performance and use of memory strategies. Several feedback loops provide updates on ongoing processing. Although it is depicted using some causal modeling conventions, it is *not* meant to represent a structural equation model. Each construct in the model represents a complex idea and could be the focus of a separate model.

We begin by assuming that four funadmental contexts influence memory processing, two internal (Biological Factors and Experience) and two external (Task Factors and Social Context). Captured here are the inner and outer contexts in which memory happens. Biological Factors provide the underlying neural substrate that defines the limits within which the person is capable of operating. Experience reflects the sum total of past interactions between the person and the environment that molds present interactions. Task Factors refer to the situation that presents itself to the individual, what the person is supposed to do, and any task-defined operational constraints. Social Context represents the larger social environment in which the person is embedded, and includes all of the prevailing sociocultural biases, stereotypes, and constraints that impinge on the individual.

These four building blocks shape the rest of the memory system. To be sure, the internal side of things is emphasized in our model, but only because we are more used to thinking in these terms vis-à-vis self-evaluations and memory. We are only beginning to understand the profound impact that external environmental factors have on memory performance in terms other than structural task components (e.g., types of to-be-remembered material, amount of material, etc.). We know even less about the influence of internal memory processes on the environment.

The two internal building blocks together influence the three constructs at the next level: Cognitive Level, Personality, and Executive Abilities. Cognitive Level is meant to reflect the current mode of thinking

Figure 17.1
Conceptual Model of How Self-Evaluations Fit into a General Scheme of Memory

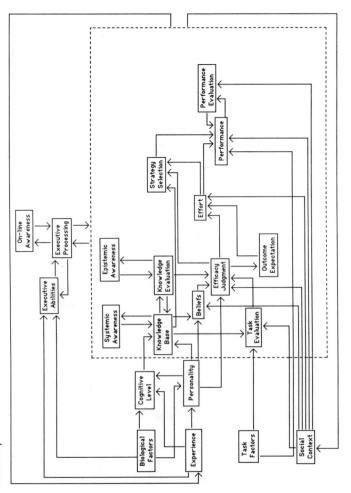

Note: All aspects inside the dotted box are influenced by Executive Processing, and all in turn influence Executive Processing, Experience, and Social Context.

in (quasi) structural terms. Cognitive Level is important to keep in mind because it provides the interpretive filter that imparts meaning to incoming information and is a major determinant of how we interact with the environment. Knowing a person's current Cognitive Level also has implications for intervention (a point that will be developed later). Personality represents the myriad traits, ego level, self-concept, temperament, moods, and all of the various topics that fall under the rubric of personality. We are not so much concerned with the individual connections between all of these pieces and memory as with connections between the styles that result from combining pieces and how these styles influence memory processes. The third construct, Executive Abilities, refers to all of the skills it takes to do the cognitive housekeeping. Executive Processing refers to those Executive Abilities that are currently being used. Executive Processing monitors, checks, updates, evaluates, and starts the process for revising all of the remaining aspects of the model. Our awareness of these processes is what is meant by On-line Awareness (see Cavanaugh in press).

The Knowledge Base contains all of the stored information that a person has. For our purposes, its most important part is metamemory, the accumulated knowledge one has about memory. It is this aspect of the Knowledge Base that was reviewed earlier, and was the initial impetus for the line of thinking that ultimately led to this model. The Knowledge Base is directly influenced by Cognitive Level and Personality; these latter two constructs shape what we know through their respective interpretive biases. Thus, what we know is certainly colored (and perhaps even driven) by how we think and how we feel.

When we become aware of what we know, we experience Systemic Awareness, which is what is typically measured in most metamemory questionnaires. At other times, we must make veridicality judgments on specific pieces of knowledge; taking exams is a common example of such situations. Such judgments constitute Knowledge Evaluation; becoming aware of them results in Epistemic Awareness. (More complete discussions of Systemic and Epistemic Awareness can be found in Cavanaugh in press.)

When we are faced with a memory situation (perhaps several items we need to remember to purchase at the supermarket), we need to figure out what it is we need to do. The construct Task Evaluation represents this step. What we decide about the task is a product of three direct influences: Task Factors, Social Context, and Knowledge Base. The impact of Task Factors is obvious; explicit instructions, for example, would have a clear influence on our interpretation of what we should do. Social Context provides a situational perspective. By this we mean that the interpretation of a task depends to some extent on the situation in which it is presented. For example, the need to buy milk may not have the same importance, depending on the urgency of the situation (perhaps there is a sufficient supply to last another day, as opposed to being completely out with a hungry baby at home). Finally, Knowledge Base factors come into play in terms of evaluating the familiarity of task; famliar tasks are stored in the Knowledge Base, while novel ones are not.

What we know, how we feel, and social contextual factors come together to influence Beliefs, the "truisms" we have about memory, aging, and "how the world works" in general. Our beliefs, with our evaluation of what we know and our personality, in a particular context, influence what we perceive our abilities to be (Efficacy Judgment). The Efficacy Judgment construct is used here not only in line with Bandura's original conceptualization but also as augmented by Weiner's idea that people's attributional judgments fall on three dimensions. (Exactly how this applies to everyday memory will be described later.)

How good is mnemonist we think we are has a direct bearing on how well we think we will do in the present memory situation (Outcome Expectation), how hard we will try (Effort), and how we will do it (Strategy Selection). This last construct is also influenced by what we know and the level of effort we have chosen. Performance and Performance Evaluation are both influenced by the Social Context, which may set constraints (e.g., demand characteristics); Performance is also influenced by explicit Task Factors (e.g., a specific mode of responding may be required) and by the memory strategy selected (i.e., good, efficient strategies usually result in better performance).

The feedback loops indicate that what we do at one point in time has a direct bearing on what we will do in the future. The importance of these feedback loops will become clearer when we describe the model in action. The point here is that what we do now affects not only our internal memory processing but also the social context in which we operate.

Self-Evaluations in Memory Processing

We now come to the heart of the matter—how self-evaluations fit in the scheme of things. Our consideration of this topic will be guided by two questions: At what points do people make the self-evaluations that affect memory? Why are these self-evaluations important for understanding everyday memory, especially in the developmental context of aging? Each of these questions will be discussed in turn.

In terms of the model depicted in Figure 17.1, we argue that self-evaluations occur at five points: Task Evaluation, Knowledge Evaluation, Efficacy Judgment, Outcome Expectation, and Performance Evaluation.

Because Task Evaluation and Knowledge Evaluation are discussed elsewhere (Cavanaugh in press), they will not be considered here.

The processes involved in Efficacy Judgment and Outcome Expectation are those described by Bandura (summarized earlier). In the context of the model, these two steps represent the point where the individual answers two very important questions: How good am I as a memory processor; should I do this task? How well am I likely to do in this situation? In memory situations, these self-efficacy judgments are influenced by a host of factors, as indicated in the model. Two that are especially important in the present context are Knowledge Evaluation and Beliefs.

The impact of Knowledge Evaluation reflects the influence of metamemorial knowledge judged to be relevant and valid to the memory situation the individual is in. What this connection implies is that only those aspects of metamemory that a person thinks are relevant to the situation have any possibility of influencing memory processing. The individual could have a vast storehouse of knowledge about memory, but if it is not activated and deemed relevant, it does not make any difference. Although this point has been emphasized in the metamemory literature for years (Cavanaugh & Perlmutter 1982), how this decision process occurs has still not been researched.

Beliefs also influence Efficacy Judgment. In this case, the influence represents the combination of metamemorial knowledge, personality characteristics, and social context. It is with this connection that we have the potential for the detrimental impact of internalized stereotypes about memory aging, for example. What we believe to be true about our memory abilities is only partly based on objective analysis; the rest derives from the interaction of this knowledge with personal style and social pressure. Clearly, internalized and verbalized stereotypes of inevitable memory decline could well drive the judgment that we are basically helpless concerning our memory ability. It also sets the stage for understanding how people could verbalize a belief in memory decline, yet at the same time admit that such a belief is probably a cover, since memory performance is not really that bad (Williams et al. 1983). What may be happening is that the individual reports the contents of the Belief component and reports his or her awareness (from On-line Awareness) of the fact that the Belief is a product of three ingredients that ultimately may not be that closely related to Performance.

To us, Efficacy Judgment is the key to the system; control this step, and you control subsequent processing. As depicted in the model, what happens at the Efficacy Judgment step profoundly influences everything else. We put so much emphasis on it because we believe that it is the intervention point of choice, for reasons that will become clearer later. For now, suffice it to say that we believe, along with theorists in the field of cognitive therapy (e.g., Beck & Emery 1985; Ellis & Harper 1975), that only by changing people's self-evaluations will you inculcate long-lasting and generalizable change.

In our model, the second self-efficacy component is Outcome Expectation. The judgment processes here are relatively straightforward. Based on what we decide in our Efficacy Judgment, we set our sights on a certain level of performance. Research that has examined the relationship between predicted and actual performance has focused on this step as the source of the prediction data. What is clear from the model, but has seemed to befuddle researchers, is why performance feedback does not typically have long-term effects. To us, the reason is obvious—Outcome Expectations are influenced directly only by Efficacy Judgments. Performance feedback must pass several interpretive steps before it has its indirect effect.

A third place where self-evaluations about memory occur is Performance Evaluation. At this point, an analysis like that described by Weiner takes place—the individual examines his or her performance and essentially explains why it was at a particular level. The person decides whether the performance was due to internal or external factors, if (all things being equal) that performance would remain stable over time, and if the performance could be modified. As noted in Figure 17.1, these self-evaluations in turn influence the system as a whole, primarily by incrementing Experience and affecting Social Context. The critical aspect of self-evaluations is that future memory performance (especially in a remediation or training context) depends in part on whether the individual sees performance as caused by something that is personally controllable (e.g., effort). These types of self-evaluations represent a central focus for intervention.

Why Are Self-Evaluations Important in Everyday Memory?

The best way to deal with the issue of why self-evaluations are important is to return to our opening anecdote about the forgotten bread. Based on the preceding discussion, an individual in this grocery buying situation will make an initial decision concerning adequacy at remembering. Clearly, a self-evaluation of good skills (high self-efficacy) will set up different expectations than a self-evaluation of poor memory skills. The point is that forgetting the bread would be evaluated differently in the two situations. Poor performance following a low self-efficacy judgment confirms poor skills, and is more likely to lead to an internal locus attribution. Poor performance after a high self-efficacy judgment, on the other hand, produces a conflict; an analysis must be done to come up with a reason for the failure. It is at this point that a key choice is made. If the decision points to an internal-stable attribution (e.g., maybe I'm not as good as I think I am—an ability problem), then the person may begin to monitor such failures more closely and move toward a lower level of confidence about his or her ability. If the decision results in an internal-variable attribution (e.g., I didn't try very hard—effort), then little damage is done to one's overall assessment of memory ability.

The point is this: In understanding how people come to know about their memory abilities and limitations, we must consider what the individual currently belives he or she is capable of doing, and how this compares with how well the person thinks he or she did. Modification of factors such as Beliefs, Efficacy Judgment, and so forth occurs only when mismatches occur between the judgments we make about our abilities and our evelution of our performance. Consistencies among these factors serve to reinforce what we already know, which has the important and interesting effect of making us more unlikely to change.

Thus we come to the paradox about memory self-evaluations. On the one hand, consistencies among Efficacy Judgment, Outcome Expectation, and Performance Evaluation serve to confirm and more strongly instantiate what we already know. This has the effect of making us more resistant to change. On the other hand, recurring inconsistencies among these factors are the grist for modifying future self-evaluations. How does this happen in everyday memory?

We think the process works like this. When confronted with a discrepancy, we search for an explanation that does not challenge our funadmental beliefs. This implies that we would be more likely to make some specific types of self-evaluations than others. For example, we would be more likely to make internal-variable-controllable self-evaluations involving effort than internal-stable-uncontrollable self-evaluations involving biological factors. This situation remains unchanged as long as we do not continue to be confronted with the same discrepancy over time, or—and this is key—to other people are not confronting us with an argument as to why our self-evaluations are wrong. Certainly, if time and time again we find ourselves forgetting the same kind of information, then we must face the facts and modify our self-evaluations. But what about this other, external source of input?

The input from Social Context becomes critical when other efforts at explaining discrepancies fail. For instance, if an attribution is made to effort, it is possible that increasing effort the next time will have no effect. In such instances the individual looks to other sources, and may turn to the environment. When this happens, the person may incorporate social stereotypes as the basis for an explanation. If the stereotype points to an internal, stable, unchangeable cause (such as inevitable memory decline), and if this attribution seems to work well, then the person will eventually come to use it routinely.

It is this latter scenario that we think happens when people begin to reinterpret their performance as indicating inevitable decline, manifested as increased complaints. It is our contention that the complaints arise not from poor performance but, rather, from self-evaluations. That complaints arise from our interpretation and evalution of our abilities and performances helps to explain the data indicating that complaints and performance are largely uncorrelated.

Let us recapitulate what we think is the connection between self-evaluations and memory aging. With increasing age across adulthood comes a reinterpretation of the causes of performance and evaluation of ability. This change is due to a failure of time-tested self-evaluations, which opens the individual to input from the social context. Incorporating the prevailing social stereotypes and converting them to self-evaluations result in a firmly based set of self-evaluations that tend to be unrelated to actual performance. In our view, the lack of relationship stems from the influence of social factors, and not from an inherent inability to make accurate self-evaluations. In fact, memory self-evaluations have no external objective standard by which their accuracy can be judged.

Remediation and Memory Training

One major application of memory research to people's everyday lives is remediating problems and training new skills. The literature mapping out the parameters defining good, efficacious training programs is extensive (see Poon, Rubin, &Wilson in press; Wilson & Moffat 1984). However, a consistent finding in the training literature is that, despite good maintenance on very similar tasks, most newly learned skills do not generalize to a wide variety of tasks (e.g., Poon 1985). The obvious question is why these skills, which are clearly well instantiated, do not generalize.

Although training programs could be improved, we believe that the chief reason generalization is so elusive is that most intervention is being directed at one of the points in the system least likely to have pervasive effects on behavior in many situations. In terms of our framework, this typical point of intervention is Strategy Selection.

But strategy training alone will not address the affective or self-evaluative processes that lie at the heart of memory. Our opening scenario is a case in point. Simply teaching the person a memory aid is effective only so long as it works. When it fails (which is inevitable), the attributional process may create a negative personal evaluation, leading to the abandonment of an otherwise good technique. Besides, most people do not complain that they remember too little, but that they perceive that they forget too much. This point is illustrated nicely in the dairy study conducted by Cavanaugh, Grady, and Perlmutter (1983). The older participants in their project reported being more upset about forgetting than younger participants, even when self-made importance ratings and type of information were taken into account. These differences were clearly based on fundamentally different types of interpretations about the episode of forgetting. This negative self-evaluation bias is what we firmly believe needs to be changed in order to achieve generalized improvements.

We contend that if broad-based effects are desirable, then intervention should be directed at the points where self-evaluations are made. We take our cue from the cognitive therapy literature (e.g., Beck & Emery 1985; Ellis & Harper 1975), which is predicated on the notion that changes in behavior come about through changes in how we interpret our inner and outer worlds. Teaching new coping skills alone will not lead to more effective behavior overall; to accomplish this latter goal, one must alter the self-evaluation process. Pursuant to our present focus, cognitive intervention for memory problems would be aimed at the self-evaluation components in our framework. As noted earlier, we postulate that the strategies used in a particular memory situation are driven by the self-evaluation process; consequently, changing strategies will have little long-term effect compared with changing the self-evaluations themselves.

What we are proposing is similar to the approach used in attribution retraining (Försterling 1985). Attribution retraining methods follow the theoretical models of Abramson, Seligman, and Teasdale (1978), Bandura (1982), and Weiner (1985a, 1985b). As documented by Försterling (1985), these techniques have been consistently successful in increasing task persistence and performance by getting individuals to reconceptualize the factors that "cause" their behavior. These theoretical underpinnings lead us to propose an intervention that trains older adults to attribute outcomes to causes that produce the least negative consequences for self-esteem and future performance. We think that older adults must first deveop the ability to analyze everyday memory situations and to better evaluate their own abilities in these situations before training them how to use new mnemonic techniques.

One essential ingredient in this approach is an understanding of personal controllability. If performance in a given situation can be personally controlled, then it is beneficial to recognize this fact and behave accordingly. But if performance is not controllable because of some constraint, it is important to know this and not waste time and effort attempting to exert personal control. Such realistic self-evaluations could be taught. Ultimately, people would become able to analyze everyday memory situations more appropriately, and become able to put them into an overall perspective that takes personal abilities, true age-related change, the normal fallability of memory, and external social factors into account.

In short, the goal would be to instill an acceptance of the fact that expecting perfect performance every time is unrealistic and unduly anxiety-provoking.

A closely related method has been used repeatedly (and very successful) by Langer and her colleagues. Rodin and Langer (1980) found that age-related deficits appearing to result from a faulty perception of control could be reversed with certain environmental interventions. In Langer's (1981) view, older people are continually at risk for exposure to uncontrollable events. This causes them to view themselves as old, and to evaluate themselves with the negative labels of old age. In general, Rodin and Langer (1980) believe that more successful aging results from feeling useful and purposeful, rather than feeling manipulated by one's environment. They argue that by enhancing a person's control through giving a sense of freedom or choice, positive behavioral change will result. Rodin (1980) reported several nursing home studies documenting that when people are given choices and are encouraged to take responsibility for their own lives, the results include increased alertness, sociability, and behavioral involvement, and better general health. We propose that these empirically supported principles of changes in self-evaluations, coupled with memory skills training when necessary, could have wide-ranging effects in everyday life.

Adopting a self-evaluation retraining approach has several distinct advantages over simply training memory skills. First, it deals directly with the focus of people's concerns—they believe that something is wrong with their memory even when confronted with objective evidence to the contrary. Cognitive therapeutic techniques deal effectively with this situation (e.g., Ellis & Harper 1975). Second, self-evaluation retraining is flexible; it can be directed at any of the points in our framework where self-evaluations occur. This allows intervention to be tailored to the needs of the individual, and to address only those aspects that need modification. In addition, self-evaluation retraining can be supplemented with skills training if required. Third, memory self-evaluation retraining could be made a component of a more general self-evaluation retraining concerning one's personal view of aging. Finally, since there is substantial evidence that cognitive approaches are effective with older adults in clinical settings, and seem to have relatively long-lasting effects (e.g., Fry 1986; Thompson, Davies, Gallagher, & Krantz 1986), it seems reasonable that the same results would be expected in the memory domain as well.

In sum, we believe that this marriage between more traditional memory strategy training and self-evaluation retraining will provide the optimal setting for addressing older adults' concerns about their memory. In this way, we can help individuals better understand the situations in which they can achieve maximum performance, and understand the fact that memory is an imperfect process that can fail at the most inopportune times. Being comfortable with ourselves as fallible rememberers may be the most important step of all.

REFERENCES

Abramson, L. Y., Seligman, M. E. P., & Teasdale, J. D. (1978). Learned help-lessness in humans: Critique and reformulation. *Journal of Abnormal Psychology, 87*, 49–74.

Bandura, A. (1977). Self-efficacy: Toward a unifying theory of behavioral change. *Psychological Review, 84*, 191–215.

Bandura, A. (1978). The self system in reciprocal determinism. *American Psychologist, 33*, 344–358.

Bandura, A. (1981). Self-referent thought: A developmental analysis of self-efficacy. In J. H. Flavell & L. Ross (Eds.), *Social cognitive development* (pp. 200–329). Cambridge: Cambridge University Press.

Bandura, A. (1982). Self-efficacy mechanism in human agency. *American Psychologist, 37*, 122–147.

Bandura, A. (1984). Recycling misconceptions of perceived self-efficacy. *Cognitive Therapy and Research, 8*, 231–255.

Beck, A. T., & Emery, G. (1985). *Anxiety disorder and phobias.* New York: Basic Books.

Blanchard-Fields, F. (1986). Reasoning on Social Dilemmas Varying in Emotional Saliency: An Adult Developmental Perspective. *Psychology and Aging, 1*, 325–333.

Cavanaugh, J. C. (in press). The importance of awareness in memory aging. In L. W.Poon, D. C. Rubin, & B. Wilson (Eds.), *Everyday cognition in adult and late life.* New York: Cambridge University Press.

Cavanaugh, J. C., Grady, J. G., & Perlmutter, M. (1983). Forgetting and use of memory aids in 20- to 70-year olds' everyday life. *International Journal of Aging and Human Development, 17*, 113–122.

Cavanaugh, J. C., & Perlmutter, M. (1982). Metamemory: A critical examination. *Child Development, 53*, 11–28.

Dixon, R. A., & Hultsch, D. F. (1983). Structure and development of metamemory in adulthood. *Journal of Gerontology, 38*, 682–688.

Ellis, A., & Harper, R. A. (1975). *A new guide to rational living.* North Hollywood, Cal.: Wilshire.

Försterling, F. (1985). Attributional retraining: A review. *Psychological Bulletin, 98*, 495–512.

Fry, P. S. (1986). *Depression, stress, and adaptations in the elderly.* Rockville, Md.: Aspen.

Klatzky, R. L. (1984). *Memory and awareness.* New York: Freeman.

Lachman, M. E., & Jelalian, E. (1984). Self-efficacy and attributions for intellectual performance in young and elderly adults. *Journal of Gerontology, 39*, 577–582.

Langer, E. J. (1981). Old Age: An Artifact? In J. L. McGaugh & S. B. Kiesler

(Eds.), *Aging: Biology and Behavior* (pp. 255–281). New York: Academic Press.

Levenson, H. (1981). Differentiating among internality, powerful others, and chance. In H. M. Lefcourt (Ed.), *Research with the locus of control construct* (Vol. 1). New York: Academic Press.

Niederehe, G., Nielsen-Collins, K. E., Volpendesta, D., & Woods, A. M. (1981, November). Metamemory processes and perceptions: Depression and age effects. Paper presented at the annual meeting of the Gerontological Society, Toronto.

Perlmutter, M. (1978). What is memory aging the aging of? *Developmental Psychology, 14*, 330–345.

Poon, L. W. (1985). Differences in human memory with aging: Nature, causes and clinical implications. In J. E. Birren & K. W. Schaie (Eds.), *Handbook of the psychology of aging* (2nd ed., pp. 427–462). New York: Van Nostrand Reinhold.

Poon, L. W., Rubin, D. C., & Wilson, B. A. (in press). *Everyday cognition in adult and late life*. New York: Cambridge University Press.

Rodin, J. (1980). Managing the stress of aging: The role of control and coping. In S. Levine & H. Ursin (Eds.), *Coping and health* (pp. 171–202). New York: Plenum.

Rodin, J., & Langer, E. (1980). Aging labels: The decline of control and the fall of reinforcement. *Psychological Monographs, 80*(1) (whole no. 609).

Rotter, J. B. (1966). Generalized expectancies for internal vs. external control of reinforcement. *Psychological Monographs, 80* (whole no. 609).

Thompson, L. W., Davies, R., Gallagher, D., & Krantz, S. E. (1986). Cognitive therapy with older adults. In T. L. Brink (Ed.), *Clinical gerontology* (pp. 245–279). New York: Haworth.

Weiner, B. (1983). Some methodological pitfalls in attributional research. *Journal of Educational Psychology, 75*, 530–543.

Weiner, B. (1985a). "Spontaneous" causal thinking. *Psychological Bulletin, 97*, 74–84.

Weiner, B. (1985b). An attributional theory of achievement motivation and emotion. *Psychological Review, 92*, 548–573.

Williams, S. A., Denney, N. W., & Schadler, M. (1983). Elderly adults' perception of their own cognitive development during the adult years. *International Journal of Aging and Human Development, 16*, 147–158.

Wilson, B. A., & Moffat, N. (Eds.), (1984). *Clinical management of memory problems*. London: Aspen.

Zarit, S. H., Cole, K. D., & Guider, R. L. (1981). Memory training strategies and subjective complaints of memory in the aged. *Gerontologist, 21*, 158–164.

18

Cognitive Intervention: A Review and Implications for Everyday Problem Solving

Deborah G. Ventis

Research has led to increasing recognition of the need for better understanding of the relationship between traditional cognitive research and everyday problem solving (e.g., Cavanaugh et al. 1985; Kenney 1985; Sinnott 1983).The purpose of the present chapter is to explore the implications of cognitive intervention for work on everyday problem solving. Because there are a number of reviews of research on cognitive intervention (Baltes & Barton 1977; Baltes & Willis 1982; Botwinick 1977; Denney 1979, 1982; Sterns & Sanders 1980; Tubbs & Ventis 1985; Willis in press; Willis & Schaie 1981), general issues rather than specific studies will be examined.

Problem solving has been defined as involving assessment of an initial state, definition of a desired state, and identification of ways of transforming the former into the latter (Reese & Rodeheaver 1985). Descriptive studies of age differences in problem solving between younger and older adults (for reviews see Giambra & Arenberg 1980; Rabbitt 1977; Reese & Rodeheaver 1985) have led to an increasing number of attempts to train specific cognitive abilities or to intervene in noncognitive ways to attempt to "improve" the performance of the elderly.

"Intervention" has a number of meanings in the study of developmental psychology. Reese and Overton (1980) emphasize that the aim of all intervention is to alter development for some specific purpose, namely, to acquire or strengthen something. The target of intervention may be either a deficit (an individual is defective because something everyone should have is weak or missing) or a difference (an individual is not deficient but lacks something that could be useful). Baltes and Danish (1980) argue that intervention with the elderly represents not just the application of a theory of aging but also a way of acquiring knowledge about the range of possibilities for aging. Cognitive intervention research not only has served as a means of exploring ways of altering cognitive development, but also has produced much of the evidence we have of the plasticity of adult cognitive processes.

One could make the generalization that problem solving abilities decline with age and that attempts to improve problem solving are somewhat successful. As is the case with most generalizations, however, this conclusion may need to be modified when other factors are considered. Age-related differences in cognitive functioning must always be examined in the context of a number of theoretical, methodological, and practical concerns. Each of these will be addressed in terms of its implications for everyday problem solving.

THEORETICAL ISSUES

Intervention Research and Reconceptualizing Adult Cognition

The struggle for new conceptualizations of adult cognition is central to understanding the relationship between traditional and everyday problem solving, and has been linked to outcomes of intervention research. From a theoretical perspective, intervention efforts have enhanced our understanding of the nature of developmental changes and the underlying reasons for these changes.

Cognitive intervention has provided a methodology for exploring the deficits experienced by adults as they grow older. Debate about the nature and extent of age-related decline in cognitive functioning (e.g., Baltes & Schaie 1976; Horn & Donaldson 1976) provided the impetus for many training studies. Much of the elderly work in this area focused on identifying specific cognitive skills that were no longer used spontaneously by older adults, or were used less efficiently. Intervention provided a means of assessing which of these abilities deteriorated (presumably as a result of biological decline), and which were maintained or could be influenced by environmental factors. The relative success of short-term interventions in improving problem solving performance has done much to bring about the rejection of the once prevalent view that aging brings about universal, irreversible, biological decrement. Hoyer (1987) emphasizes that successful cognitive interventions not only demonstrate the plasticity of adult intelligence but also represent a way of reconceptualizing adult cognition.

Despite changing views of adult cognition, Reese and Rodeheaver (1985) stress that research on problem solving in old age is still hampered by the absence of an integrative theoretical framework. As a result, general theories of adult cognition and conceptual issues in problem solving research will be discussed.

Applying Theories of Adult Cognition to Everyday Cognition

There is controversy concerning the utility of existing theories of adult cognitive functioning as explanations of everyday cognition. Willis and Schaie (1986a) discuss the psychometric, Piagetian, and information-processing paradigms as the major approaches used by cognitive psychologists in the study of intelligence. They argue that the psychometric perspective is most suitable for the study of practical intelligence in old age, where the focus is on intact abilities rather than emergent behaviors. Piagetian and information-processing approaches, they contend, are most useful in investigations of the acquisition of skills or of optimal levels of functioning, and thus are less appropriate for research on everyday cognition.

In contrast, in their discussion of the interrelationships between cognitive research and everyday problem solving, Cavanaugh et al. (1985) advocate a shift in attention to new structures that might characterize adult cognition. They explore the usefulness of relativistic operations using concepts from both Piagetian and information-processing theories as a way of conceptualizing adult thought. Information-processing approaches also are used by Hoyer (1985) and Charness (1985) in their attempts to explain the discrepancy between the apparent deficits found on traditional cognitive tasks and the comparatively better performance in everyday life. They both emphasize that performance in older adults varies with areas of expertise, and that individual differences as well as experiential factors may be important in determining which cognitive abilities are maintained, improved, or added during adulthood. Thus, reconceptualizations of adult cognition provide the theoretical framework for exploring the nature of everyday problem solving. Further direction comes from conceptual issues important to the study of problem solving.

Conceptual Issues in Problem Solving Research

In addressing the implications of intervention research for everyday problem solving, three issues seem of special significance: the competence-performance distinction, the issue of deficit versus difference, and the importance of individual differences and experiential factors. Each of these issues will be addressed individually.

Competence-Performance Distinction

The competence-performance distinction is perhaps the central issue involved in relating intervention research and everyday problem solving. The difference between competence and performance is the difference between what people are able to do under ideal conditions and what they do under ordinary conditions. Reese and Rodeheaver (1985), in their discussion of competence and performance in problem solving, attribute the difference to extraneous variables of memory, attention, motivation, and task familiarity.

Extraneous variables may be particularly important in linking cognitive intervention and everyday problem solving research. Memory processes, for example, have been of particular interest to researchers in both areas. Cavanaugh et al. (1985) emphasized the importance of memory and language comprehension as a missing link between everyday problem solving and cognitive research. Perlmutter (1986) speculates that much of cognitive development can be characterized as increasing environmental fitness mediated by memory. The speed and efficiency of elementary operations such as memory search are assumed to account, in part, for individual differences in complex information processes measured by problem solving tasks (Hoyer 1985).

Memory skills also are recognized as important to intervention; Robertson-Tchabo (1980) suggests that needs assessment for memory performance be a first step in cognitive skills training. Denney (1985) concludes that the study of memory holds more promise for enhancing our understanding of everyday cognition than the study of problem solving, because memory tasks are more easily designed to be familiar, and reflect ability differences more accurately. In contrast, Willis and Schaie (1986a) caution that the memory demands of most everyday tasks have not been investigated, and criterion tasks designed to measure everyday cognition may not accurately reflect the memory load of real-life problems.

Task familiarity is important in both intervention and everyday problem solving research. Denney (1985) notes that measures of problem solving have been made more relevant to everyday problems by using problems with familiar stimuli, familiar tasks, or both. She hypothesized (Denney 1982) that frequently used abilities (presumably those involved in familiar tasks) show less improvement with training because they are already close to optimal performance levels. Traditional problem solving tasks may require abilities that are unexercised and are more likely to improve with training. Although Denney may be correct in assuming that performance on traditional problem solving tasks declines as a result of disuse, it may be more interesting to consider why some abilities are used less.

The issue of optimal functioning is relevant to the study of new skills as well as of intact abilities. Baltes, Dittmann-Kohli, and Dixon (1984) view intellectual aging as selective optimization with compensation. Like Hoyer (1985), Charness (1985), and others, they see old age as a time when optimal performance may occur, but only within special skill areas. The role of environmental factors and individual differences is important in determining these areas of specialization. Fischer and Kenny (1986) state that environmental support is necessary for optimal functioning, regardless of developmental level, and is especially important when high levels of abstraction are required. Willis (in press) agrees that younger adults cannot be assumed to be performing at optimal levels. She cites evidence that peak performance may not be attained until well into adulthood, and that the number of trials in most training studies is too limited to test maximum levels of performance in adults of any age.

Intervention researchers encounter what Kuhn and Phelps (1982) call the "intervention study impasse." This is similar to the problem McCall (1977) observed of "can" versus "does." Showing that strategies can be trained in a laboratory situation tells us little or nothing about how strategy use changes developmentally. Demonstrating that older individuals can use problem solving strategies characteristic of younger people deals only partially with the competence-performance distinction. Kuhn and Phelps (1982) observed that developmental theories have focused on competence alone. They argue that a theory of the development of performance must focus not only on the development of new strategies but also on the abandonment of old ones. If, as they contend, abandoning old strategies is the more formidable task, older adults' performance may need to be represented by more complex theoretical formulations. Thus, in addition to determining which cognitive abilities remain intact, and exploring the nature of emerging abilities, those interested in problem solving might profitably consider whether strategies are abandoned rather than lost, and if they are abandoned, how and why.

Deficit versus Difference

Reese and Rodeheaver (1985) note the importance of determining whether age-related changes in problem solving reflect deficits or differences. Reese and Overton (1980) emphasize that both deficits and differences may be the focus of intervention. Cognitive intervention research has been directed exclusively at those age differences in problem solving assumed to represent deficits in cognitive functioning (Denny 1982). Labouvie-Vief (1982, 1985), however, has stressed that age differences in cognitive performance may mimic deficits but really represent adaptive reorganization and the acquisition of different, more desirable, qualities.

There is increasing interest in the discrepancy between the age-related cognitive losses documented by laboratory studies and evidence that everyday cognitive functioning within specific domains is maintained despite advancing age (Hoyer 1987). Cavanaugh et al. (1985) note that, depending on the standard chosen, age differences may represent deficits, neutral differences, or positive changes. The results of cognitive skills training provide one means of exploring such differences. If age changes in problem solving reflect differences rather than deficits, it would be more productive to shift the focus of intervention from restoring lost or abandoned strategies to fostering these differences.

Interindividual Differences

Increasing recognition of the multidimensional, multidirectional nature of aging and the importance of interindividual variability and intraindividual plasticity has led to an emerging view of aging as a differential process that, in turn, implies the need for differential intervention (Baltes & Danish 1980). Interindividual differences often increase with age during adulthood (Baltes & Willis 1977; Rabbitt 1982; Welford 1958). In addition, age-related performance changes occur in different individuals at different rates (Hofland, Willis, & Baltes 1981; Rabbitt 1982). Results of longitudinal research (Schaie & Willis 1986; Willis & Schaie 1985, 1986b) demonstrate that declines do not always occur in older subjects, even on abilities presumed to deteriorate with age.

Various reviews (Giambra & Arenberg 1980; Tubbs & Ventis 1985; Willis in press) have emphasized the importance of individual differences in explaining inconsistencies in training effectiveness. Earlier, Denney (1979) concluded that intervention studies that produce very rapid improvement in performance (e.g., Denney & Denney 1974) may be eliciting strategies already in the repertoire of elderly subjects, since the relative effectiveness of direct versus indirect training studies indicates that intervention may involve learning new responses.

Longitudinal research (Willis & Schaie 1985) has confirmed that training may produce different effects for different individuals. Willis (in press) discusses three possibilities: remediation, increment, and compensation. For example, Schaie and Willis (1986) found that training represented remediation for those exhibiting declines in spatial orientation, inductive reasoning, or both, but produced new performance levels for those showing no significant declines on either of the abilities.

Everyday problem solving researchers stress the need for greater attention to individual differences. The ways in which intervention techniques might aid in the study of such differences will be addressed in more detail in the discussion of methodological implications.

Successful Intervention Strategies

The nature of the specific targets of intervention and the effectiveness of specific intervention techniques can provide valuable information for those interested in everyday problem solving. If some abilities are more salient for everyday problem solving than others, those abilities involved in everyday problem solving may be less likely to show age differences, may be more easily changed by intervention, or both. Similarly, the types of interventions used in modifying these abilities may be identifiable as more or less suitable for use in the study of everyday problem solving.

Reese and Rodeheaver (1985) categorized the tasks used in problem solving research as real-life tasks, laboratory simulations of real-life tasks, and artificial tasks. Cognitive intervention research on problem solving has focused on artificial tasks. Everyday problem solving researchers usually have used laboratory simulations of real-life tasks.

Willis (1985) notes that the cognitive abilities targeted for training will, obviously, reflect the researcher's theoretical orientation. In keeping with the focus on intellectual decline, cognitive abilities selected by intervention researchers have been those on which older adults have been found to be deficient (Denney 1982). In contrast, everyday problem solving researchers have a greater interest in selecting tasks on which older adults demonstrate proficiency, although theoretical approaches to the study of everyday cognition may be directed at intact or emergent abilities.

Willis (in press) identifies Piagetian tasks, concept formation, set induction, and behavioral rigidity as the primary focus of intervention efforts directed at modifying problem solving skills. She also summarizes the work on psychometric abilities, concluding that figural relations, inductive reasoning, spatial orientation, and perceptual speed have received the most attention from intervention researchers. Although she notes that intervention efforts have been successful in modifying performance in each of these areas, sometimes with long-term results (e.g., Sanders & Sanders 1978), the processes by which these changes occur are not well understood.

Denney (1979) grouped intervention approaches into six categories: modeling, direct instruction, feedback, practice, changing response speed, and other noncognitive intervention techniques. She concluded that modeling, direct instruction, and feedback seem to be effective intervention strategies. As noted in the discussion of individual differences, indirect intervention methods, such as efforts to improve response speed and other noncognitive variables (e.g., motivation, self-confidence), were not effective in improving performance. Practice resulted in improved performance in some studies but not others.

Sterns and Sanders (1980) emphasize the distinction between training and practice, and cite experimenter input concerning processes or strategies to be used as an important component of training research. There has been much discussion of the finding that practice-only control groups show equal or greater improvement on performance compared with training groups in many intervention studies (Arenberg 1982; Hofland, Willis & Baltes 1981; Hoyer, Labouvie, & Baltes 1973; Labouvie-Vief & Gonda 1976; Plemons, Willis, & Baltes 1978; Rabbitt 1982; Roberts 1980; Schutlz & Hoyer 1976).

Analysis of errors may provide further information about the effectiveness of training versus practice. Willis (in press) states that error analyses of studies of inductive reasoning and figural relations reveal that retesting and cognitive training produce increases in correct responding, but only specific training reduces the number of commission errors and leads to more accurate performance. She also observes that error analyses of spatial orientation training, a skill on which few commission errors are observed, reveal that training produces increases in number of items attempted but little change in error rates, demonstrating the differential effects of different training procedures.

Work on expert cognition may provide a link between the role of practice in intervention research and everyday problem solving. Hoyer (1985) and Charness (1985) emphasize that performance in older adults varies with areas of expertise. According to Denney (1985), the study of expertise is the study of everyday problem solving within areas of individual specialization. Denney (1982, 1985) hypothesizes that abilities unexercised during later adulthood are lost through disuse, while those exercised in everyday problem solving are maintained. Denney (1985) has used a computer analogy for cognitive aging, likening age effects to hardware changes and skill effects to software changes. If cognitive training research concerns short-term change (Willis 1985), perhaps practice-only groups are an analogue for the way software changes occur with aging. Providing practice on specific skills increases the salience of those skills in problem solving sessions that follow, just as selective optimization in aging leads to better performance on tasks related to areas of expertise. If this is the case, manipulating the types of skills practiced may be more useful as an intervention technique than practice-only groups were as controls.

METHODOLOGICAL ISSUES

Methodological Problems in Cognitive Intervention

Intervention research has been hampered by inconsistent results, at least in part because of methodological weaknesses. Cross-sectional designs and the use of tasks designed for younger adults present serious problems for the interpretation of most intervention studies. Age differences, and their modification through intervention, are difficult to interpret because of the possibility of cohort effects (e.g., Baltes & Schaie 1976). Similarly, the use of a young adult standard of performance in training adults is often criticized (e.g., Sterns & Sanders 1980; Waugh & Barr 1982). Also, it is difficult to interpret the results of training programs developed for use with older adults because few researchers have attempted to train young adults.

In discussing the shortcomings of traditional problem solving tasks, Denney (1985) criticizes their predictive validity, face validity, and ecological validity. She cites concern about the external validity of artificial tasks as a major impetus for the study of everyday problem solving. Early attempts to study more "real-life" problem solving (e.g., Arenberg 1968; Sinnott 1975) found that older adults did show improved performance on the more realistic tasks, but the nature of the tasks did not eliminate age-related performance differences.

Questions about predictive validity have centered on the utility of traditional problem solving tasks in forecasting real-world performance beyond middle adulthood. Although there is substantial evidence that such tasks accurately predict performance in childhood and younger adulthood, there is much less information concerning older adults. Denney (1985), however, concludes that traditional problem solving tasks may have greater predictive validity than everyday problem solving tasks because they are more likely to reflect ability alone, rather than ability and experience.

With respect to face validity and ecological validity, Denney (1985) suggests that there is little evidence that traditional problem solving tasks are similar to situations encountered in everyday life. She recommends that face validity be improved as one way of increasing ecological validity of problem solving measures. Willis and Schaie (1986a) express similar concerns about the face validity of problems used to assess performance in real-life situations. Reese and Rodeheaver (1985) observe that performance on real-life tasks is often evaluated by using a restricted range of problem solving strategies rather than the broader range of alternatives that may be appropriate in everyday life. Thus, even problem solving tasks specifically designed to examine everyday problem solving may lack ecological validity.

Methodological Innovations

Intervention researchers have employed some methodological innovations to advantage, despite the methodological weaknesses inherent in many studies. Training programs developed for cognitive intervention research may be useful in furthering our understanding of everyday problem solving, despite concerns about the validity of traditional problem solving tasks used in intervention research. Willis and Schaie (1986a) suggest that psychometric abilities that have been the focus of successful cognitive interventions, such as figural relations, may be extremely important in everyday cognition. Thus, interventions intended to improve performance on everyday problem solving may profitably employ the same types of training programs used in cognitive intervention research aimed at more traditional types of tasks. For example, Sinnott (1983) found that modifying performance on ill-structured problems may not be so different from modifying performance on well-structured problems, given that processes used in solving well-structured problems (clarifying a goal, selecting a heuristic) may underlie ill-structured problems as well.

Experience with cognitive intervention research has led to increasing recognition of the value of breaking problem solving tasks into components. Sterns and Sanders (1980) emphasize the usefulness of task analysis in implementing specific intervention efforts, even individualized ones. This technique may be particularly helpful in view of the increasing emphasis on aging as a differential process. Cavanaugh et al. (1985), for example, state that neither Piagetian nor information-processing theories have provided the detailed task analysis needed for the evaluation of these theories. They cite the task analysis involved in thinking-aloud procedures (Giambra & Arenberg 1980) as one way of translating theoretical constructs into testable hypotheses. Sinnott (1983, 1987) has applied this approach successfully in the study of everyday problem solving.

Finally, statistical innovations used in cognitive intervention research also may be useful in the analysis of everyday problem solving. Willis (in press) notes that intervention researchers are interested in changes in the constructs underlying training tasks rather than in performance on the specific tasks employed. Therefore, what is important is change in the variance common to the underlying construct, rather than change in the variance unique to the measure used. Willis and Schaie (1986b) examined training effects through the use of factor analysis, with ability factor scores (which represent the variance common to the underlying construct) as the dependent variables. They interpreted significant training gains at the factorial level as evidence of training effects in the underlying construct. Willis (in press) observes that although factor analyses have been used primarily with psychometric approaches to the study of intelligence, they also can be used to examine latent constructs in research on memory and problem solving.

PRACTICAL ISSUES

One obvious assumption of intervention research is that it might be helpful in restoring or improving cognitive functioning in the elderly. One concern, however, is that age differences in problem solving may represent adaptive changes rather than deficits (e.g., Labouvie-Vief 1982, 1985). Although Lachman, Baltes, and Willis (1980) provide some reassurance that cognitive training does not adversely affect personality functioning, researchers designing interventions need to give greater attention to ethical questions, especially as they relate to everyday problem solving. For example, is the intervention going to foster, rather than interfere with, potentially adaptive changes? Do we know that the content of the intervention is likely to lead to improved problem solving ability, preferably over some extended period of time? What long-term plans have been made to monitor or continue to provide the intervention?

Successful cognitive interventions open up new possibilities for adult development. They demonstrate the potential for change in older adults and the value of continuing education, and provide methods for improving adult performance on specific tasks. Sterns and Sanders (1980) see the success of cognitive intervention research and the attendant development of specific methodological approaches for improving our understanding of cognitive behavior as the first step in educational intervention with older adults.

Tubbs and Ventis (1985) suggest that the evidence for interindividual differences in adult cognition, the ineffectiveness of many training procedures, and the apparent benefits of practice point to the utility of allowing older individuals to choose the types of abilities on which they feel the need for improvement. Presumably, the focus of these efforts would be skills important in everyday problem solving. It is assumed that interventions involving cognitive abilities identified as helpful in everyday problem solving would enhance our understanding of cognitive processes as well as provide skills that would be more clearly beneficial to the participants. Similarly, Willis (1985) notes that cognitive training research can contribute to the development of an educational psychology of the older adult by placing greater emphasis on individual differences in learner characteristics and the development of more individualized training procedures.

CONCLUSIONS

The connections between traditional research on problem solving and work on everyday problem solving are complex. Research on cognitive intervention may be helpful in refining theoretical constructs, devising methods, and applying the results of studies of everyday problem solving. Specifically, further examination of the role of extraneous variables, such as meory processes, may be of greater use in furthering our understanding of problem solving in everyday life. Greater attention to the role of individual differences, and refinement of methods to detect such differences, will be essential to the success of future research efforts.

REFERENCES

Arenberg, D. (1968). Concept problem solving in young and old adults. *Journal of Gerontology, 23,* 279–282.

Arenberg, D. (1982). Changes with age in problem solving. In F. I. M. Craik & S. Trehub (Eds.), *Aging and cognitive processes* (Vol. 8, pp. 221–235). New York: Plenum.

Baltes, P. B., & Barton, E. M. (1977). New approaches toward aging: A case for the operant model. *Educational Gerontology, 2,* 383–405.

Baltes, P. B., & Danish, S. J. (1980). Intervention in life-span development and aging: Issues and concepts. In R. R. Turner and H. W. Reese (Eds.), *Life-span developmental psychology: Intervention* (pp. 49–78). New York: Academic Press.

Baltes, P. B., Dittmann-Kohli, F., & Dixon, R. A. (1984). New perspectives on the development of intelligence in adulthood: Toward a dual-process conception and a model of selective optimization with compensation. In P. B. Baltes and O. G. Brim, Jr. (Eds.), *Life-span development and behavior* (Vol. 6, pp. 33–76). New York: Academic Press.

Baltes, P. B., & Schaie, K. W. (1976). On the plasticity of intelligence in adulthood and old age—Where Horn and Donaldson fail. *American Psychologist, 31,* 720–725.

Baltes, P. B., & Willis, S. L. (1977). Toward psychological theories of aging and development. In J. E. Birren & K. W. Schaie (Eds.), *Handbook of the psychology of aging* (pp. 128–154). New York: Van Nostrand Reinhold.

Baltes, P. B., & Willis, S. L. (1982). Enhancement (plasticity) of intellectual functioning in old age: Penn State's Adult Development and Enrichment Project (ADEPT). In F. I. M. Craik and S. E. Trehub (Eds.), *Aging and cognitive processes* (Vol. 8, pp. 353–389). New York: Plenum.

Botwinick, J. (1977). Intellectual abilities. In J. E. Birren and K. W. Schaie (Eds.), *Handbook of the psychology of aging* (pp. 580–605). New York: Van Nostrand Reinhold.

Cavanaugh, J. C., Kramer, D. A., Sinnott, J. D., Camp, C. J., & Markley, R. P. (1985). On missing links and such: Interfaces between cognitive research and everyday problem-solving. *Human Development, 28,* 146–168.

Charness, N. (1985). Aging and problem solving performance. In N. Charness

(Ed.), *Aging and human performance* (pp. 226–254). Chichester, U.K.: John Wiley & Sons.

Denney, D. R., & Denney, N. W. (1974). Modeling effects on the questioning strategies of the elderly. *Developmental Psychology, 10*, 458.

Denney, N. W. (1979). Problem solving in later adulthood: Intervention research. In P. B. Baltes & O. G. Brim, Jr. (Eds.), *Life-span development and behavior* (Vol. 2, pp. 38–66). New York: Academic Press.

Denney, N. W. (1982). Aging and cognitive changes. In B. B. Wolman (Ed.), *Handbook of developmental psychology* (pp. 807–827). Englewood Cliffs, N.J.: Prentice-Hall.

Denney, N. W. (1985, March). Everyday problem solving: How much potential? Paper presented at the Third Annual George A. Talland Conference on Memory and Aging, New Seabury, Mass.

Fischer, K. W., & Kenny, S. L. (1986). Environmental conditions for discontinuities in the development of abstractions. In R. A. Mines and K. S. Kitchener (Eds.), *Adult cognitive development: Methods and models* (pp. 57–75). New York: Praeger.

Giambra, L. M., & Arenberg, D. (1980). Problem solving, concept learning, and aging. In L. W. Poon (Ed.), *Aging in the 1980's* (pp. 253–259). Washington, D.C.: American Psychological Association.

Hofland, B. F., Willis, S. L., & Baltes, P. B. (1981). Fluid intelligence performance in the elderly: Retesting and conditions of assessment. *Journal of Educational Psychology, 73*, 573–586.

Horn, J. L., & Donaldson, G. (1976). On the myth of intellectual decline in adulthood. *American Psychologist, 31*, 701–719.

Hoyer, W. J. (1985). Aging and the development of expert cognition. In T. M. Schlechter and M. P. Toglia (Eds.), *New directions in cognitive science* (pp. 69–87). Norwood, N.J.: Ablex.

Hoyer, W. J. (1987). Acquisition of knowledge and the decentralization of *g* in adult intellectual development. In C. Schooler and K. W. Schaie (Eds.) *Cognitive functioning and social structures over the life course* (pp. 120–141). Norwood, N.J.: Ablex.

Hoyer, W. J., Labouvie, G. V., & Baltes, P. B. (1973). Modification of response speed and intellectual performance in the elderly. *Human Development, 16*, 233–242.

Kuhn, D., & Phelps, E. (1982). The development of problem-solving strategies. In H. W. Reese (Ed.), *Advances in child development and behavior* (Vol. 17, pp. 1–44). New York: Academic Press.

Labouvie-Vief, G. (1982). Dynamic development and mature autonomy: A theoretical prologue. *Human Development, 25*, 161–191.

Labouvie-Vief, G. (1985). Intelligence and cognition, In J. E. Birren and K. W. Schaie (Eds.), *Handbook of the psychology of aging* (2nd ed., pp. 500–530). New York: Van Nostrand Reinhold.

Labouvie-Vief, G., & Gonda, J. N. (1976). Cognitive strategy training and intellectual performance in the elderly. *Journal of Gerontology, 31*, 327–332.

Lachman, M. E., Baltes, P. B., & Willis, S. L. (1980, November). Ethical issues in cognitive training research with the elderly: Effects on personality.

Paper presented at the annual meeting of the Gerontological Society of America, San Diego.

McCall, R. (1977). Challenges to a science of developmental psychology. *Child Development, 48,* 333–344.

Perlmutter, M. (1986). A life-span view of memory. In P. B. Baltes, D. L. Featherman, and R. M. Lerner (Eds.), *Life-span development and behavior* (Vol. 7, pp. 271–313). New York: Academic Press.

Plemons, J. K., Willis, S. L., & Baltes, P. B. (1978). Modifiability of fluid intelligence in aging: A short-term longitudinal training approach. *Journal of Gerontology, 33,* 224–231.

Rabbitt, P. (1977). Problem solving and complex decision making. In J. E. Birren and K. W. Schaie (Eds.), *Handbook of the psychology of aging* (2nd ed., pp. 474–499). New York: Van Nostrand Reinhold.

Rabbitt, P. (1982). Breakdown of control processes in old age. In T. M. Field, A. Huston, H. C. Quay, L. Troll & G. E. Finley (Eds.), *Review of human development* (pp. 540–550). New York: Wiley.

Reese, H. W., & Overton, W. F. (1980). Models, methods, and ethics of intervention. In R. R. Turner and H. W. Reese (Eds.), *Life-span developmental psychology: Intervention* (pp. 30–47). New York: Academic Press.

Reese, H. W., & Rodeheaver, D. (1985). Changes in problem solving ability in old age. In J. E. Birren and K. W. Schaie (Eds.), *Handbook of the psychology of aging* (2nd ed., pp. 606–629). New York: Van Nostrand Reinhold.

Roberts, P. (1980, August). Cognitive training with the elderly: Variations on a frequent theme. Paper presented at the annual meeting of the American Psychological Association, Montreal.

Robertson-Tchabo, E. A. (1980). Cognitive-skill training for the elderly: Why should "old dogs" acquire new tricks? In L. W. Poon (Ed.), *New directions in memory and aging* (pp. 511–517). Hillsdale, N.J.: Erlbaum.

Sanders, R. E., & Sanders, J. C. (1978). Long-term durability and transfer of enhanced conceptual performance in the elderly. *Journal of Gerontology, 33,* 408–412.

Schaie, K. W., & Willis, S. (1986). Can decline in adult intellectual functioning be reversed? *Developmental Psychology, 22,* 223–232.

Schultz, N. R., & Hoyer, W. J. (1976). Feedback effects on spatial egocentrism in old age. *Journal of Gerontology, 31,* 72–75.

Sinnott, J. D. (1975). Everyday thinking and Piagetian operativity in adults. *Human Development, 18,* 430–443.

Sinnott, J. D. (1983, November). Individual strategies on Piagetian problems: Implications for theory and metatheory. Paper presented at the annual meeting of the Gerontological Society of America, San Francisco.

Sinnott, J. D. (1987, June). Experimental studies of relativistic, self-referential postformal thought: The roles of emotion, intention, attention, memory, and health in adaptive adult cognition. Paper present at the Third Harvard University Symposium on Postformal Operations, Cambridge, Mass.

Sterns, H. L., & Sanders, R. E. (1980). Training and education of the elderly. In R. R. Turner and H. W. Reese (Eds.) *Life-span developmental psychology: Intervention* (pp. 307–330). New York: Academic Press.

Tubbs, L., & Ventis, D. G. (1985, November). Cognitive intervention: A review and meta-analysis. Paper presented at the annual meeting of the Gerontological Society of America, New Orleans.

Waugh, N. C., & Barr, R. A. (1982). Encoding deficits in aging. In F. I. M. Craik and S. Trehub (Eds.), *Advances in the study of communication and affect* (Vol. 8, pp. 183–190). New York: Plenum Press.

Welford, A. T. (1985). *Aging and human skill*. Oxford: Oxford University Press.

Willis, S. L. (1985). Towards an educational psychology of the older learner. In J. E. Birren and K. W. Schaie (Eds.), *Handbook of the psychology of aging* (2nd ed., pp. 818–847). New York: Van Nostrand Reinhold.

Willis, S. L. (in press). Cognitive training in later adulthood: Remediation versus new learning. In L. Poon, D. Rubin, & B. Wilson (Eds.), *Everyday cognition in adult and late life*. New York: Cambridge University Press.

Willis, S. L., & Schaie, K. W. (1981). Maintenance and decline of adult mental abilities: II. Susceptibility to experimental manipulation. In F. Grote and R. Feringer (Eds.), *Adult learning and development* (pp. 40–57). Bellingham: Western Washington University.

Willis, S. L., & Schaie, K. W. (1985, November). Cognitive training in a longitudinal sample. Paper presented at the annual meeting of the Gerontological Society of America, New Orleans.

Willis, S. L., & Schaie, K. W. (1986a). Practical intelligence in later adulthood. In R. J. Sternberg and R. K. Wagner (Eds.), *Practical intelligence: Origins of competence in the everyday world* (pp. 236–270). New York: Cambridge University Press.

Willis, S. L., & Schaie, K. W. (1986b). Training in the elderly on the ability factors of spatial orientation and inductive reasoning. *Psychology and Aging, 1,* 239–247.

19

Summary: Issues and Directions for Everyday Problem Solving Research

Jan D. Sinnott

Authors of the chapters in this volume have demonstrated that what has been rather loosely called "everyday problem solving research" is a rich and varied collection of ideas, processes, methods, and interests. The "field," if it can truly be called one field, has become so diverse that it is time for this chaotic complexity to be ordered in a newer, more structured way. The aim of this new ordering need not be to give the mantle of orthodoxy to only one set of ideas and reject the rest; the aim can be to provide translations and clues to any investigator so that he or she can come from an entry point and still make use of any of the ideas. This means that although I may enter the field with an interest only in aging and Piaget's theory, I still can make use of attributional models (for example) because I now can see their connection with problem solving. The net effect could be to enlarge my options and to make my own research better.

The issues raised and addressed by researchers so far suggest that three major themes will be the focus of future work: (1) tasks, theories, scoring systems, paradigms—in other words, everything that we're currently doing—will be refined and analyzed, and made better; (2) we will try to understand and parameterize the comparative utility, strengths, and weaknesses of each of the various approaches used so far; (3) each investigator will be moving from a focus on one particular "first approach" or special interest to a more expanded, multifaceted way of seeing the issue or the process. In other words, we'll find ourselves moving from the first stages of scientific inquiry, in which some fragment of a process is described in a general way or some theory in hand is arbitrarily imposed on new material, to a later stage of scientific inquiry in which macromodels and sophisticated hypothesis testing are appropriate. We might say that the field will be "coming of age" in the near future.

ISSUES

Eight general issues have been addressed by researchers in everyday problem solving and stand out as important right now:

—The nature of tasks and scoring systems

—Selection of models and theories

—Choice of macro- or microlevel analyses

—The importance of context

—Fitting strategies specifically to the chosen purpose of the research

—Relations between problem solving and other cognitive processes

—Value of nomothetic and ideographic approaches

—Interpersonal aspects of problem solving

We will now address each one in turn, further describing the issue, predicting the direction research will take, and making recommendations.

Tasks and Scoring Systems

As we noticed in Chapter 5, quite a variety of tasks have been labeled "everyday problems" because no one has defined exactly what an "everyday problem" is. Yet very different processes might be found in solutions of probability problems using familiar items in unfamiliar ways compared with those in (for example) solutions of philosophical "everyday" problems about the nature of a good life. How these tasks can be scored is another element of the dilemma. Can scoring systems be used across several kinds of problems? Do they tap into the same underlying process? Camp et al. in Chapter 13 have taken some steps in the direction of common interpretations and scoring systems, and many other investigators have created tasks and scoring systems of their own. But development in this area has been haphazard. In the future we can expect greater refinement and more precise definitions of measures and scoring systems, and even more varieties of both as new contexts are studied.

Recommendation: Systematically create problems and scoring systems based on theories, representative of many contexts, and (as much as possible) scorable using some common scoring systems.

Models and Theories

We have barely scratched the surface in tapping specific theory bases for problem solving studies. What, for example, would an everyday cognitive problem inspired by Eric Erikson's theory be like? What are the strengths and weaknesses of Piagetian approaches compared with artificial intelligence approaches? Which theory best fits everyday problem solving questions arising from a clinical context as opposed to an organizational-decision-making-over-time context? In the future, problem solving reserach will address these questions, and create more theories and more refined theories and models.

Recommendation: Explore as many theoretical models as possible and clearly contrast them to show their specific utility in certain domains. To fill whatever gap still exists, if any, create new theories and models.

Macro- vs Microlevel Analyses

Some of our authors have chosen to address problem solving questions mainly at a very general philosophical/paradigmatic/theoretical level, while others have looked mainly at the specifics of methods. Both are certainly important, but they are difficult to compare. Perhaps because it seems rather obvious, the distinction between macroconcerns and microconcerns is seldom discussed. But unless it is present in awareness, we will never have a comprehensive theory of everyday problem solving that will tap into the larger knowledge bases in psychology and allied sciences. In the future we can expect to see progress on both a macrolevel and a microlevel of conceptualization and analysis.

Recommendation: Be aware of the level at which you are describing phenomena. As far as possible, analyze what a microlevel function might be for a macrolevel process you propose, or what a macrolevel process would look like for the microlevel system you are using.

Importance of Context

Psychology as a whole recently has discovered context and deemed it important to the understanding of process. Our authors are probably more aware of this issue than are most psychological researchers. They tend to be aware of context issues and often use context as a variable. Context can be of many types. A logical problem, for example, can be posed in the context of human characteristics or the context of shopping decisions. Responses to one problem when subjects are in their own home contexts may differ from their responses to the same problem when they are in a lab context. The developmental state of respondents is a changing context for their answers; indeed, examination of *change* and examinations of one certain *period* in time are different contexts of inquiry. The respondents' motivation forms an intrapersonal context that differs from time to time, from person to person, and from problem to problem. In the future, more studies will vary contexts systematically, especially by testing middle-aged and older respondents, by shifting problem settings or demand characteristics, by controlling or manipulating salience, and by analyzing change.

Recommendation: Use as many contexts as possible; control for context.

Purpose of the Research

As mentioned in Chapter 1, this book has not been focused equally on all areas of psychological problem solving. No doubt the reader also has noticed that some of the work reported here was meant to be exploratory, while other work made use of a more sophisticated level of experimentation and hypothesis testing. Research in everyday problem solving might be performed for many reasons, including controlling and predicting behavior, exploring, modeling phenomena, and supporting results of other basic and applied studies. Research in everyday problem solving might be performed to resolve clinical questions, look for patterns of information processing, model the steps in experts' performance, or examine developmental changes in adaptive functioning. There seem to be very useful and less useful ways to approach each of these purposes. Rather than trying to make general statements about everyday problem solving, in the future we may be much more clear about our purposes, and then target the kinds of problems, the levels of analyses, the context variables and models more specifically to those purposes. Again, the comparative utility of various approaches for various purposes needs to be assessed, and empirical studies will address this question.

Recommendation: The purpose of an everyday problem solving study—its place in the hierarchy of scientific activities that ranges from casual observation to experimentation, and in the subarea of psychology (e.g., clinical, cognitive) it is meant to serve—should be made explicit. Tailor the research approach to that purpose.

Role of Other Cognitive Processes

Some of our authors—for example, Cavanaugh et al. and Sinnott—have begun to examine how everyday problem solving fits within the overall cognitive system that includes other processes, such as memory. Certainly none of our authors would say that problem solving is a totally separate cognitive process with no links to other cognitive processes. How cognitive processes interface with one another, how they perhaps allow an organism to be more adaptive, remains a relatively unexplored area of investigation but a potentially rich one. Future investigators may feel more comfortable about looking at problem solving, memory, day-dreaming, vocabulary, and such in a more complex, interconnected way. In the process some greater order may be imposed on the broad problem solving literature, as well as on the developmental literature. This requires both analytical and synthetic approaches on the part of investigators, as well as a willingness to see respondents as whole, functioning persons.

Recommendation: Examine several cognitive processes in problem solving studies, and look at their overall—perhaps compensatory—effects for the respondent.

Nomothetic versus Ideographic Approaches

Most of the studies of everyday problem solving have examined the behavior of groups of persons on some task for which there is a "right" and a "wrong" answer. Few have tested a single individual on many tasks to look at individual variability across tasks; few have used think-aloud procedures to see what individuals seem to be doing, as they process everyday material, that is unexpected from the point of view of the investigator. Although these latter studies sound at first like descriptive "fishing trips," they can be useful in testing hypotheses (see Sinnott, "Model" chapter, this volume) and in studying context and intervention and training effects. Future studies will no doubt make greater use of these ideographic approaches suggested by Giambra and Arenberg (1980) for questions that fit such approaches.

Recommendation: Whenever possible and appropriate, use intensive studies of a single individual's performance and collect think-aloud data.

Interpersonal Aspects of Problem Solving

As Meacham and Emont argue in Chapter 2, and as thinking-aloud data show, individuals don't seem to solve problems "alone," but with an actual or internalized social group influencing their performance and helping them along. Yet most of our studies virtually ignore the social and interpersonal influences on everyday problem solving. But if problem solvers act so as to survive in what they view as a social context and a social world, we need to examine the interface between the social and the personal for these problem solving processes, or run the risk of misinterpreting what respondents are doing. Future studies will add the social/interpersonal dimension in order to better address the process and development of everyday problem skills, as well as the motivation behind such skills.

Recommendation: Address in every way possible the social and interpersonal elements of everyday problem solving.

An Overall Perspective: Problem Solvers as Adaptive Living Systems

As we look toward future progress in everyday problem solving research, we perhaps begin to see that the uncertain starts and the fragmentation that are always, of necessity, part of any concept-forming process are gradually being transformed. They are being changed into a clearer overall understanding of the logic that rules the adaptive performance of the individual thinker, living in a world of other thinkers. Our study of everyday problem solving gradually has less of a "hit or miss" quality as we grasp the pattern, as we "have the concept" of how things fit together. We are getting to be better concept learners on this ill-structured everyday problem.

For some thinkers (e.g., Miller 1978; Sinnott in press) the best way to describe what we suppose is happening, and the best way to describe which studies and which analyses are most important to do right now, is to mount information in a general systems theory framework. The human thinker is then seen as a "system," interacting with many other living systems (in effect, within a society). Thinking—in this case, solving problems—is one subsystem within that person that helps ensure that he or she does what living systems always try to do, that is, continues to live, even in a changing, challenging environment.

This cognitive subsystem helps the thinker process information in the right amount to permit adaptive growth and to prevent overload at each step in the development of the order within. If one part of the system becomes weak, the others may change to let the whole continue to grow; if the other systems in the environment send information, our adaptive thinker adds it to the framework or structure there already, or ignores it to save the current framework. So our problem solver, as an adpative system, could perform many different cognitive acts to achieve the same end, or could perform a single cognitive behavior to achieve many system purposes. He or she may "enlarge" problem space, or "reduce" memory, to resolve a vexing family problem; he or she may "enlarge" problem space both to resolve the family problem *and* to better organize the larger and larger information store that comes with middle age.

If we begin to look at problem solving processes in the framework of ways to enhance *system* survival, we might predict some very complex cognitive responses: For example, individuals with too little information *or* individuals with lots of information but too little energy for a search would give simple, "small problem space" solutions to everyday problems to maximize their resources. Without knowing the state of the system, it would be hard to say if small or large space is "better" for problem solving. These parameters of this ill-structured problem become very important because so often, when creating a systems hypothesis, we start our prediction with "It depends . . . on the other variables in the whole system. . . . "

As we look toward the future, we might expect more everyday problem solving research, more refinements and comparisons, and more consideration of the role of this skill in the functioning of the whole person-in-society. This research area has not been one for the faint of heart, or for those who like to know in advance, with certainty, whether their hypotheses will be supported. But it has offered (and still offers) the rich rewards and intellectual adventures that come to those pioneers who ask new and difficult questions.

REFERENCES

Giambra, L. M., & Arenberg, D. (1980). Problem solving, concept learning, and aging. In L. W. Poon (Ed.), *Aging in the 1980's: Psychological issues* (pp. 253–259). Washington, D.C.: American Psychological Association.

Miller, J. G. (1978). *Living systems*. New York: McGraw-Hill.

Sinnott, J. D. (in press). General systems theory: A rationale for the study of everyday memory. In L. W. Poon, D. Rubin, & B. Wilson (Eds)., *Everyday cognition in adulthood and late life*. New Rochelle, N.Y.: Cambridge University Press.

Index

Contributors

Patricia Kennedy Arlin, University of British Columbia

Cameron J. Camp, University of New Orleans

Noel Capon, Columbia University

Mario Carretero, University of Madrid

Avshalom Caspi, Harvard University

John C. Cavanaugh, Bowling Green State University

Jennifer Cook, Towson State University

Steven W. Cornelius, Cornell University

Nancy W. Denney, University of Wisconsin

Kathleen Doherty, University of New Orleans

Nancy Cooney Emont, State University of New York at Buffalo

Fredda Blanchard-Fields, Louisiana State University

Sheryl Kenny, Cornell University

Deirdre A. Kramer, Rutgers University, Livingston Campus

Iseli K. Krauss, All University Gerontology Center, Syracuse University

Deanna Kuhn, Columbia University

Bonnie Leadbeater, Teachers College, Columbia University

Diane Lee, University of Maryland, Baltimore County

Mary A. Luszcz, Flinders University of South Australia

John A. Meacham, State University of New York at Buffalo

Kelly R. Morton, Bowling Green State University

Dennis R. Papini, University of Arkansas
George W. Rebok, State University of New York at Geneseo
Rickard A. Sebby, Southeast Missouri State University
Jan D. Sinnott, Towson State University, Baltimore
Sarah Moody-Thomas, University of New Orleans
Connie S. Tilse, Bowling Green State University
Deborah G. Ventis, College of William and Mary

About the Editor

JAN D. SINNOTT, Ph.D., associate professor of psychology at Towson State University at Baltimore, has been doing cognitive aging research in cooperation with the National Institute on Aging (National Institutes of Health) since 1980, and is a practicing clinician. She is the author of some 70 publications, most in the area of problem solving and cognition. She has been conducting research in this field since 1972, and was one of the first to extend Piaget's theory to everyday problem solving. She is currently doing experimental cognitive research integrating information-processing and artificial intelligence approaches with general systems theory and Piagetian theory, and is coeditor of the *Beyond Formal Operations* volumes soon to be published by Praeger.